"I love this book! I highly recommend it for people interested in the afterlife because it is so easy to read & understand. If each of us were to seriously consider the afterlife enough to explore & gain experience of it, as Patricia has described in her book, then our personal fears about death & dying would be significantly diminished. "
Elisabeth Kubler-Ross, M.D. *On Death & Dying, The Circle of Life*

"What Patricia is writing about is one of the most exciting things you can do! You don't need NASA, it's inside of you & you can learn to control it!"
Art Bell, Talk show host of *Dreamland* and *Coast to Coast AM* radio programs

"It is vital for us to know how to achieve expanded states of consciousness to prepare us for conscious evolution. Patricia Leva performs a great service for us all by writing this book.   **Barbara Marx Hubbard**, *The Book of Co-Creation, Conscious Evolution*

"An in-depth & comprehensive look at out-of-body experiences. I especially enjoyed the comparisons & viewpoints of various experts that are quoted throughout the book. This book is overflowing with useful information that the novice or experienced out-of-body explorer will find helpful – a truly valuable addition to OBE literature."
William Buhlman, *Adventures Beyond the Body*

"A lot of information is packed between these covers, but it's all in a conversational & readable style. Prepare for a road trip of a lifetime. "
NAPRA *ReView* magazine, May-June, 1998

"Ingenious 'how to' instructional manual for those interested in learning how to use non-ordinary states of consciousness in everyday life. Not only does Leva discuss where Bob Monroe went in his classic *Journeys Out of the Body*, but she describes *where she went* when using Monroe's Hemi-Sync® training wheels for accessing normally-subconscious levels of awareness in everyday reality. This *personal* approach is critical. Without personal experience in these states, you really don't know what you are talking about. Highly recommended."   **Elmer Green**, Ph.D., Director Emeritus,
Voluntary Controls Program, Menninger Clinic, *Beyond Biofeedback*

"I think the use of the "traveling/city/interstate" metaphor is very ingenuous & that it's a great way for those beginning to explore these systems to get an overview!"
Lee Stone, Hillsborough, North Carolina

"It appears that you have brought consciousness education to the lay person's (me) level. Congratulations! What an accomplishment!"
Mary Ellen Dahlkemper, Erie, Pennsylvania

"I've spent the better part of a lifetime exploring consciousness. It's taken years to learn how to separate the actual knowledge that I've been seeking from the dogma that often wraps around it. Patricia's modern metaphor of the body & mind as a vehicle for seeking wisdom very successfully sidesteps religious & philosophical discussion & provides workable methods for expanding one's search for truth."
Doug Hughen, Denver, Colorado

Traveling the Interstate of Consciousness: A Driver's Instruction Manual: Using Hemi-Sync® to Access States of Non-Ordinary Reality. Copyright © 1998 by Patricia Leva, MA, RN. Printed and bound in the United States of America. All rights reserved. No part of this book may be reproduced in any form or by any electronic or mechanical means including information storage and retrieval systems without permission in writing from the publisher, except by a reviewer, who may quote brief passages in a review. Published by Q Central Publishing, Longmont, CO. USA.

To contact the author: Email -- QCentral@aol.com
Website -- http://www.qcentral.com
•

First Edition, First Printing -- January, 1998
Second Printing -- June, 1999
•

Cover & Interior Design
Ann Alexander Leggett - Louisville, Colorado
Char Campbell - Boulder, Colorado
•

Copy Editor
Barbara Teel - Loveland, Colorado
•

Illustrations
Patricia Leva, Q Central Publishing, Longmont, Colorado
•

Library of Congress Catalog Card Number — 97-92502
•

ISBN 0-9658963-8-2

TRAVELING THE INTERSTATE
OF
CONSCIOUSNESS

A DRIVER'S INSTRUCTION MANUAL

USING HEMI-SYNC TO ACCESS
STATES OF NON-ORDINARY REALITY

PATRICIA LEVA, MA, RN
INTERSTATE TOUR GUIDE

Q CENTRAL PUBLISHING
LONGMONT, COLORADO

THE INTERSTATE OF CONSCIOUSNESS

"A play on a familiar term in the American road system. Here it is used to indicate a route to follow from one stage of consciousness to another, both within time-space and along the seemingly endless spectrum of the (M) field."

Robert Monroe, *Ultimate Journey*

With humble and immense gratitude,
this book is dedicated to

MOTHER GAIA

who so beautifully supports us on our travels
exploring the far and near reaches of consciousness
while we experience her mountains, air, waters, and heat
discovering who we truly are.

INTERSTATE KEY POINTS OF INTEREST

✦✦✦

ROUTE 4
LEARNING HOW TO EXIT, SUSTAIN & CONTROL TRAVEL

ROUTE 5
DOWNSHIFTING TRAVEL EXPERIENCES
INTO THE GEAR FOR EVERYDAY LIVING

ROUTE 6
EVOLVING CONSCIOUSNESS: ON-LINE CONVERSATIONS

ROUTE 7
TRANSPORTATION VEHICLES

ROUTE 8
MAP MAKERS & TRAVEL AGENTS

ROUTE 9
THE CONSCIOUSNESS FORCE: WHAT IS IT?

ROUTE 10
DISCOVERING THE BEAUTY OF OURSELVES & OUR COSMOS

APPENDIX A

APPENDIX B

APPENDIX C

OVERLOOK & TRAILHEAD ILLUSTRATIONS

...

ROUTE 7

ROUTE 8

ROUTE 9

ROUTE 10

THE TRAVEL PLAN

You are about to embark upon a journey onto the Interstate of Consciousness into unexplored country, the frontier of non-ordinary states of awareness. The travel plan is to explore the states, cities, and neighborhoods in the near and far reaches of consciousness and to investigate the adventuring skills necessary to experience this expedition to its fullest potential. This journey will be achieved, in part, by reading the real life stories of courageous travelers to these realms and the thoughts of others very interested in this region of the Interstate.

You will meet the pioneers and cartographers who have blazed the trail. They possess a fervent desire to expand beyond the mundane, ho-hum, areas of day-to-day awareness conditioned by the five human senses. With this desire in hand, they have ventured into the space beyond physical reality, the non-physical locale that taps into realms containing big picture experiences with spiritual and mystical elements. As a tourist on the Interstate, you will see how these explorers have been discovering answers to life's important questions, how they have been able to enrich their everyday abilities and gain a larger world view of themselves and the universe. After taking this voyage, you may want to join these courageous pathfinders for a longer, more personal excursion.

THE PURPOSE OF THE TRIP

This manual will show you how to drive onto what Bob Monroe, well-known author of *Journeys Out of the Body*, described as the Interstate of Consciousness. This territory encompasses the entire continuum of waking and non-waking states of awareness. Since much is known about the physical, ordinary side of life, this manual will be concentrated on the non-ordinary locale on the Interstate and the skills that help you, the driver, to enter, sustain, and control experiences into these territories. The main goal of this journey is to gain an understanding of full consciousness by living a powerful and full life on all planes of existence. This will be achieved by exploring the possibility of becoming significantly more conscious about one's ability to drive through life, by examining methods to cross back and forth between physical and non-physical reality, and by exploring techniques that show how to apply non-reality accomplishments in practical, everyday situations.

Larger life meaning achieved in this territory comes from developing two kinds of abilities; one being physical talents known as *superhuman skills* and the other, non-physical powers. Some would call these *supernatural skills*, yet experienced Interstate travelers would suggest these are natural skills which have been temporarily shelved.

LEARNING HOW TO BUY, DRIVE & MAINTAIN YOUR INTERSTATE VEHICLE

This book is a driver's instruction manual showing you how to efficiently and effectively operate your car in this new territory. You will find such useful tips as choosing an Interstate car, caring for the battery under the hood, obtaining the right grade of high-octane gas for the trip, how to magnify the horsepower in the engine, learning to shift paradigm gears, learning to use the cruise control for the long stretches between cities, and how to shift into warp overdrive for the cities in the far reaches of consciousness.

The necessity of acquiring good driving habits will be emphasized especially those actions that will expedite getting onto the right entrance ramp of the Interstate leading to the cities of consciousness beyond physical reality. Examples of how to safely navigate around high curves and large fear barricades, and how to locate and adeptly move — at will — into cities of no-time, no-space and beyond will be explored.

THE CARE & MAINTENANCE PLAN FOR LONG TERM TRAVEL

With the path of consciousness evolution being relatively new, people tend to select the most appealing and snazzy Consciousness Expansion Vehicle (CEV) without considering its construction, fuel economy, reliability record, or long term maintenance requirements. For this reason there is a section in the manual on how to choose the right CEV from the many natural and neurotechnologies now available at many dealerships across the globe. This will show how to match the features of a particular vehicle to the natural inclination of you, the driver, and will discuss the reasons for selecting a CEV in this manner. Included in a later chapter as an extra bonus is a maintenance plan to support long term vehicle use. This general, all-purpose plan has three service packages: the 5,000 mile

Mind-Body Tune-Up, the 50,000 mile Mind-Body Tune-Up and the MegaMajor Overhaul.

CONSCIOUSNESS: THE SPIRIT OF THE DRIVER BEHIND THE WHEEL

In taking this journey through these pages, you will most likely become more conscious about your consciousness. Consciousness has an alias; it is better known as *the highly creative and spirited Force behind the wheel*, a personal guidance system squarely rigged under the hood. Some have called consciousness "instinct," others merely call it "the Force." During this trip, you will have many opportunities to become acquainted with how your consciousness can teach you how to fully grip the wheel of your life and drive, at will, into and out of <u>all</u> the cities on the Interstate.

THE ITINERARY

This travelogue adventure begins with a description of a few important on-ramping skills to expedite your ability to drive easily onto this part of the Interstate. It quickly moves onto the highway using a step-by-step description of the basic TMI traveling process and along the way, provides detailed descriptions of various non-physical states of consciousness located through the use of the educational neurotechnology called Hemi-Sync, a sturdy set of CEV training wheels to keep you firmly on the road. I add my own personal odysseys on the Interstate and reports of clients participating in my practice as a TMI Gateway Outreach Trainer. These real life stories are intended to give some concrete form and order to non-physical realities, but are not to suggest any firm "how to" structure nor are they to be construed as dogma in any way. Personal experiences tend to have highly relative characteristics; however, when they occur again and again, the resulting commonalities can be used as basic anchoring guides. While the vehicle of Hemi-Sync is used here to describe what experiences in the non-physical territory can be like, this is not to suggest limiting the choice of vehicles to the use of Hemi-Sync. Modern consciousness research suggests that our psyches have no real or concrete boundaries. Accordingly, experiences described here can be accessed in a multitude of ways using many tools and several natural elements together.

USING TRAINING WHEELS
TO KEEP THE VEHICLE ON THE ROAD

Today there are a procession of down-to-earth educational technologies promoting human consciousness expansion. As individuals look for a larger context in which to live life's moments, these particular tools are becoming more and more popular. They could be viewed as the hot wires under the hood of the car, the reality translators that help the Interstate explorer decode the jumble of incoming life data into deeper, fuller life meaning.

Of the many technologies utilizing the modality of sound, Hemi-Sync has a special feature. Just like training wheels, its precise tonal patterns provide an enriched, balanced learning environment due to its ability to produce various degrees of symmetry in the hemispheres of the brain and in the energy field. Using an extra set of wheels on the Interstate, these help you stay on the road. For this reason, Hemi-Sync has been chosen as the main means of transportation in this manual. Clients who have been able to develop deep meditative abilities say that they are amazed at the ease and quickness with which non-ordinary states of consciousness can be accessed at will and sustained through use of Hemi-Sync. The technology of Hemi-Sync creates the ability to locate a particular road and sustain balanced, even travel on that road. This stabilizing effect will be discussed at length and in detail in the manual.

There are many implications about this balancing process as it relates to the theory of quantum physics; in particular, how energy and matter are related. Quantum physics helps to explain how an individual can physically experience something abstract, know it has a physical counterpart, and be able to apply this physical counterpart in everyday circumstances. Because there is a need to bridge the gap between science and practice in this realm, some exploration into this question of transferring learning from non-physical to physical reality will be considered using quantum physics and holographic models of thought.

BACKUP NECESSITIES FOR THE TRIP

A few preliminary trip essentials will explain the context for this trip. In the average person's conversation the topic of consciousness is usually tiptoed around or it hangs precariously "out there" in abstract, vague word tones. However, the adventuresome pathfinder takes another approach.

They want less fluff and more concrete understanding about this element of life. They yearn to know more about what it is to be fully conscious saying, "There is far more to me than what I have been taught." Typically this search is kick-started within the grassroots of personal experiences.

Down in the trenches of real life, several sharp realizations have recently been made by many. They are: we are *more* than what meets the eye; in our growing world, the scientific model is unable to account for unusual experiences; and there are limits to the human sensory system and its ability to explain extraordinary experiences. These establish the motivation for this manual.

WE ARE MORE THAN WE THOUGHT WE WERE

To help us realize the tremendous impact of this silent but powerful belief rearranging itself under the hood, Barbara Marx Hubbard, well-known Futurist, has talked about the transformation of humanity. She says, as a culture, we are transitioning from the awareness of being Homo Sapiens to Homo Universalis, or shifting from being ordinary, everyday humans to the awareness of being *powerful, universal, galactic beings*. Essential to this change is the growing understanding that we are more than Darwin, Freud, and Einstein thought we were.

Many questions takes flight while this transformation begins. What does it mean to be a fully conscious human? When does consciousness begin? Is there a beginning? An ending? What is consciousness? How did we come to qualify and quantify consciousness as we do? What motivated us to acquire those definitions? Do they still hold? What did we use to acquire our present knowledge about consciousness? How are consciousness and life connected? What are the signs that sentient or conscious life exists? Does the definition of sentience contain the meaning of consciousness or is there more? Does consciousness continue after death? If we broaden our understanding and abilities about being conscious, what does that mean for us in the future? What do we gain and lose if we travel down this path? In this search, do we lose ourselves, our humanity as we now know it? Or is it possible to gain something greater when all is said and done?

ADDING NON-PHYSICAL EXPERIENCES TO
THEORETICAL IDEAS ABOUT CONSCIOUSNESS

The answers to these questions are beginning to appear in the documentation of personal experiences. This information is starting to illuminate the broader reaches of consciousness. Having attended presentations at professional conferences offering various theories on this topic, I have come to the conclusion that an important factor has been left out of the equation. This is the concrete, experiential input of people who have been conducting their own personal research. Rather than inserting anecdotal accounts into the scientific model as a sidebar, more concerted research could actively involve the hands-on *experiences* of these pioneers.

Generally, when the scientific model is applied, postulates and hypotheses of consciousness research are placed directly over the experience as if to prove the experience fits the questioned form in some manner. The experimenter becomes intimately entangled in the experiment and thus influences the outcome to a greater degree. Theories simply describe a point of view about a specific detail, but not necessarily the true scope of the experience. Many people accept theory as providing magnified, explicit, and useful information, yet theory is not the same as reality. Theory, by virtue of its purpose, exists to study a factor or several factors, but is not able to include the anomalous elements that invariably enter into the realm of consciousness. The experiential approach incorporates these factors and helps to address the larger pattern behind the existence of various realities.

Michael Talbot has commented that strict objectivity is impossible to achieve. In *The Holographic Universe,* he suggested some changes to the scientific model and qualified his remarks about the necessity for these changes. Talbot highlighted the need for scientists to experience first-hand what they are studying. Regarding role changes for the scientist he says, "A shift from objectivity to participation will also most assuredly affect the role of the scientist. As it becomes increasingly apparent that it is the *experience of observing* that is important, and not just the act of observation, it is logical to assume that scientists in turn will see themselves less and less as observers and more and more as experiencers." (1)

THE LIMITS OF THE FIVE HUMAN SENSES
AS A MEASUREMENT SYSTEM FOR REALITY

When a scientific project is carried out, the five human senses are the primary means of obtaining information. All conclusions using this measurement system affect the outcome and all subsequent decisions and actions. Unfortunately, the application of this method accesses a minor sliver of information about the breadth and depth of the electromagnetic spectrum we call reality. (2) As you read the stories of the travelers, you will notice the near and far reaches of consciousness do not necessarily involve the use of human senses; in fact they require a broader, eclectic mixture of senses and alternative information-gathering methods. Using the scientific model as a stand-alone system for understanding both physical and non-physical domains of the Interstate of Consciousness is like instructing a dog to cook a meal. The means to the end will provide a limited feast.

In the following pages we'll journey into a specific locale of consciousness and one by one, explore various New Lands through the eyes of voyagers who have embarked on their own personal research projects. This experiential approach will provide intriguing elements forming the answers to the question on the tips of many tongues which is "What is consciousness?"

THE EXPEDITION STAFF

Four separate groups of people have helped to create this educational travelogue. Over 70 personal stories of people whom I call the travelers share their non-ordinary experiences with gusto. These people have been learning how to journey into this locale with great proficiency. Their intriguing narratives will give substantial credibility to the idea that we are much more than a thinking brain encased in skin and bones. Their stories will also provide material to consider the pros and cons of various methods for entering this part of the Interstate. These accounts come from clients and from members of the Voyager Mailing List (VML), an online cyberspace service sponsored by TMI which has, on the average, between 450-500 members all over the world. Not only do the travelers share their innovative methods and unique experiences, but also their learnings, insights, and how their lives have changed as a result of these experiences.

KEY INTERSTATE TRAVEL AGENTS & PATHFINDERS

In addition to the traveler stories, the work of six early explorers who laid out the foundation for touring this part of the Interstate will be described. Included are **Georges Gurdjieff** and his student, **Peter Ouspensky,** who mapped out critical roadway areas of the Interstate; **Robert Monroe**, who has identified specific cities on the Interstate map and provided easy and simple methods to access these places; **don Juan** and his student, **Carlos Castaneda**, who have supplied the driving skills necessary to maintain travel at a safe but useful speed; and **Gene Roddenberry**, who has educated us about what travel in these locales might be like. There are more key individuals who have contributed to this venture; however, these particular people are outstanding in their devotion to the advancement of consciousness education and training.

Included are the viewpoints of a few of the growing legion of theorists and philosophers who have become very visible recently in their efforts to describe consciousness. Woven throughout the manual are the contributions of researchers who have studied the effects of certain elements of consciousness. These are incorporated where appropriate in order to add a compelling element to this travel expedition.

TOUR GUIDE EXPERIENCES

Concurrent with the traveler experiential input are my own ideas, models, and experiences of non-physical realities. These began in 1986 when a colleague introduced me to educational opportunities offered by The Monroe Institute (TMI) in Faber, Virginia. Its purpose at that time was to offer "inquiry, information, and innovation" in the field of human consciousness. Before starting into TMI training, I remember wanting to find my soul as if there were some kind of physical element involved, and wanting to know what senses and skills I would be taking with me when I died. In other words, I wanted to find out if there was more to me which determined my experience than just my body. What tremendously motivated me were unexplainable and surprising bedside nursing experiences of people in numerous hospitals from all walks of life. My unanswered question marks about life and death grew over the years and eventually forced me into wider horizons.

Having read Robert Monroe's books and used some of the educational audiotapes of TMI, I decided to enter the TMI Gateway Outreach (GO) Trainer Program in 1987 in order to take the Monroe Institute programs out into the world, closer to the everyday person. What follows is a description of my journey into experiences with consciousness. This written journey has been gathered from ten years of personal adventure as a TMI GO Trainer in the United States and Canada facilitating Hemi-Sync workshops and working with individual clients and groups in settings from the corporate boardroom to behind prison walls.

Prior to my TMI GO Training, I had been an educator and trainer since the early 1970s. In particular, my days as a brain training specialist (the role of an educator who helps individuals understand how specific areas of the brain are used to determine thinking styles) inspired me to ask questions about the connections between the brain and consciousness. These experiences led me directly into the regions of the Interstate of Consciousness where humankind is warily looking around.

THE SPINNING VEHICLE:
BREAKING THROUGH THE TIME-SPACE CONTINUUM

Throughout this book I was inspired to share a pivotal learning tool for me. This was an evolving experience with the act of spinning. I found myself threading it throughout the chapters to underscore and tie main thoughts together. Frankly, I couldn't get around the constant nudges to include snippets of my spinning fun. I thoroughly enjoyed its insistence for I realize now it was a vital clue in my life which helped me untangle hazy memory fragments of non-ordinary experiences I had as a child and later, as a nurse. After completing the first chapter, I noticed there was a writing form that looked back at me, an actual experience of spinning in and out of ideas. It still remains. The driver behind the wheel, my consciousness, has guided me to maintain this approach as it will lead you easily onto this section of the Interstate.

WHAT TO BRING FOR THE TRIP

While taking the grand tour through these pages, please try to keep an open mind while suspending personal beliefs and values. Traveling into the unknown, the non-ordinary states will, at times, trigger hesitation and fear. At other times, feelings of exhilaration and a few bell-ringing insights might occur. Should there be resistance at some point, temporarily postpone these thoughts and feelings. Later on, attempt to read that section again to reflect if anything has changed in any way. On any highway there are usually a few potholes (a foreign word or phrase). Please refer to the glossary which will interpret these words or phrases.

One final piece of advice. As you journey onto the Interstate of Consciousness, know that the Force of consciousness is always with you.

THE JOURNEY BEGINS

Onward we say,
Revving the engine boldly, then timidly,
Oh, just take the leap!
Into the near and far reaches
To explore What is Consciousness
Or whatever that means.

CROSSING THE CONTINENTAL DIVIDE
OF CONSCIOUSNESS

*"One does not become enlightened by imagining figures of light,
but by making the darkness conscious."*

Carl Jung

ROUTE 1

THE CONTINENTAL DIVIDE OF CONSCIOUSNESS

My carefree childhood days of sneaking out to the next door neighbor's driveway to get in a few stolen spins were absolutely great! I'd strap on my beat-up, old rollerskates whose loose wheels rattled back and forth, and begin to skate my circles. At first, I'd start with big, swirling shapes, then slowly my swirls became smaller and smaller. I'd swing myself out against the whirling kinetic push until I sensed I'd fall over the silent edge of air, then yank myself back into the comfort of the circle as I spun round and round. I can remember brief, hazy half-pictures of these moments, of spinning as fast as I could while trying to keep my precarious balance. I wanted to stay contained in that spin as long as I could, for it seemed to put me beyond myself, beyond the bounds, limits, and pressures of being a child.

SPINNING MYSELF WHOLE

This spinning memory, for over half a century, was to become a pivotal teaching tool, a step-by-step experience that stretched my awareness and gave me knowledge about the larger reality of myself and the world. As if it had a life of its own, my spinning adventure took on various forms. It popped up at the most unsuspecting times, and projected me into realms I had not imagined. Spinning around and around helped break the veil of my constructed pictures of reality, that "believed" identity I had assumed over the years, and threw me, as someone is thrown overboard, into unknown, foreign territory. Over the years, the end result of my spinning ventures soon opened up new frontiers of awareness within me, bringing with it a certain core confidence. This quiet revolution gradually magnified the joy and trust I had in myself and in my relationships with others, and it enabled me to feel more solidly connected to my purpose for being on this planet at this time. When my spinning adventures started, I began to discover what it means to become aware — beyond the physical, mundane things of life — and how this larger perspective enriched my everyday living. Its mysterious lessons throughout the years necessitated that I throw my notions about who I thought I was out the window. And to think it all began with a little child's game!

WHAT IS LIGHTHEADEDNESS ALL ABOUT?

My first lesson about consciousness came in the form of questions I asked myself after taking a turn on my wheels in the neighbor's driveway. These questions were on the order of "Where was I when I was dizzy?" for I certainly wasn't "here." After the dizziness wore off, I wondered why the aftermath felt so good to me. And why was I doing this crazy stuff in the first place? What urge was I unconsciously expressing? What was this state of lightheadedness all about? Why do we get jumbled in the dizziness? Why do we attempt to lose ourselves in other similar spinning situations, whether it be rollercoaster rides, driving hilly roadsides, drinking parties or any event involving whirling?

Everyone knows spinning eventually produces sparkling crystals of light in the head and a feeling of confusing dizziness, an edgy, momentary sense of nothingness, the go-between here and there, the edge of passing out. Out where? Doing what? Am I still conscious when I am dizzy? Each and every time I went to that edge while spinning I was beginning to ask myself, "What is this thing I call me?"

THE THREE MAIN THEORIES ABOUT CONSCIOUSNESS

People searching for answers to these questions find theorists in the field of consciousness research divided into three distinct groups. There are some who say that nothing is occurring in the person who has passed out. These are the **Dualists**. (1) Their thinking is based on the "either/or" belief that the body and the mind function separately, and that the body's brain produces accurate pictures of how things are. If, as this thinking goes, the body with the brain attached passes out or falls unconscious, then the mind will be out to lunch too. Therefore, being unconscious is equivalent to being dead or without brainpower. The first Dualist was the famous French philosopher, Descartes, who created one of history's most momentous sound bites, *"Cogito, ergo sum."* (I think, therefore I am.) Dualists of today tend to use rational-biological models to explain how consciousness works. The idea that mind is located in the brain was the subject of a *Time* magazine cover story in a July 1995 issue (2) titled "In Search of the Mind: Scientists Peer Into the Brain Looking for That Evanescent Thing Called Consciousness." Believing that the seat of consciousness is located inside the brain, Dualists look for a physical location for consciousness within the brain. Likewise, this perspective assumes that only sentient beings having the ability to reason possess consciousness.

Still another side of the question about the mind/brain/ body/consciousness playground is being developed by a firmly entrenched group of neuroscientists and philosophers known as the **Materialists**. (3) They say the mind and brain are one entity and that consciousness resides somewhere within that combination. A Materialist sees the brain with the mind attached merely as a meat machine, a mechanical information factory. Just as steam is produced by a steam engine, consciousness is produced by the brain say the Materialists. This approach is represented by Daniel Dennett, Director of Tufts University's Center for Cognitive Studies, who has been working and writing on consciousness since the 1960s. He believes that artificial intelligence machines will soon demonstrate that we're all machines. No doubt the Materialists are having a field day with the ongoing chess matches between IBM's Big Blue supercomputer and Garry Kasparov. Dennett goes on to say that materialism in one form or another has gained an edge over the Dualists, but others aren't so sure. Richard Restak, author of three books about the brain says, "I still find it difficult to believe that this three-pound mass of protoplasm with the consistency of an overripe avocado is the seat of who I am." (4)

A new group of thinkers centered between the Dualists and the Materialists has recently emerged to offer yet a another approach which resurrects some of Descartes' ideas. Called the **New Mysterians**, they believe consciousness has an illusive scientific component which hasn't been discovered yet. They think consciousness is an immaterial force that guides the body through life. Descartes called this force the soul, one connected with the subjective side of human experience. The New Mysterians say consciousness is more of a soft science than the Materialists would have us believe. Their approach addresses the flip side of Descartes' statement by asking the question, *"When I am not thinking, who am I?"* (5) This is what I was toying with when I was busy being dizzy and spinning myself beyond the edge of my physical reality landmarks. For when I was spinning my thinking slowed to a snail's pace.

Not known to be associated with any of these camps, nonetheless Fritjof Capra has substantially contributed to this subject. He makes an important distinction between mind and brain in his book, *The Web of Life*. Referencing the research findings of Gregory Bateson, Humerto Maturana, and

Francisco Varela, Capra suggests that the mind is not a thing, but a process; in order for the mind to exist, the brain is not a necessary prerequisite. "A bacterium, or a plant, has no brain but has a mind. The simplest organisms are capable of perception and thus of cognition. They do not see, but they nevertheless perceive changes in their environment — differences between light and shadow, hot and cold, higher and lower concentrations of some chemical and the like." (6) Capra equates cognition with the process of knowing. Generally speaking, cognition is thought to be the process of making thought-related computations in the brain. However, Capra suggests a higher process is involved, that of knowing. He distinguishes this further by saying that knowing is merely a higher form of intuition, a level of mind. (7) His ideas, indeed, broaden the definition of cognition beyond current machine-like cognitive functionality and have significant potential to expand the possibilities about consciousness.

THREE PEAKS OF THE CONTINENTAL DIVIDE OF CONSCIOUSNESS

We now have lightly examined various belief systems in relation to consciousness developed by three theoretical groups. Each of these seem to be separate and different perspectives, or is there more about consciousness than what theory can offer? These theories are similar to seeing three treacherous peaks on a lofty elevation. When grouped together the peaks form a mountainous ridge, a pattern leading somewhere. The terrain of consciousness looks perplexing, even threatening, if seen as a bunch of separate ideas; however, if we add the subjective component, the actual hands-on experiences of travelers into this equation, then the mountainous ridges threaded together become a path. Uniting the three differing theoretical belief systems with the stories of the travelers creates what I propose to call the Continental Divide of Consciousness, a ridge where various thoughts, beliefs and Knowns about consciousness exist. This continental divide may appear too lofty and rocky for some, yet it is becoming increasingly accessible by others. If a more comprehensive understanding of consciousness is undertaken, then we will broaden the foundation supporting life experiences. If a comfortable place of understanding could be established on top of this mountainous ridge, the resulting overlook could smooth out disparate points of view. What happens when one achieves balance while walking on narrow ledges? A new road often appears, one that leads to expanded awareness, and new vistas open up to broader, more meaningful lifestyles. That balanced road is the one less traveled. It affords the ability to travel the full length of Interstate of Consciousness.

LOCATING THE DIVIDE ON THE MAP

Consciousness has its own mysterious way of attracting our attention so that, when we are ready, we will be led to explore its territory. Urges, longings, and desires are the leading cues. For many, it is an internal prompting, a primal urge to "Be still an instant and go home," (8) home being a known place inside where we feel safe, totally accepted and loved. For others it is an internal yearning to achieve as much as possible in order to feel very satisfied at the end of life's journey. Still for others, it is searching for the answer to "Is this all there is to my life?" As I reflect back on my early spinning memories, I remember having a thirsty appetite, a desire that felt like the pulling memory remnants of a home.

Each of my periods of spinning dominated my attention and made me ask questions. At times these generated still more questions than answers, and they triggered more and more explorations. A rolling ball. My first-hand experiences left me clues to what and how full consciousness is achieved, the sense of being totally in the here and now, yet solidly connected to a broad, universal source.

SPINNING ON THE EDGE OF SOMETHING

My spinning path has been a lifelong vision quest, a focused search for the power within my consciousness so I could identify with it in a concrete way, then learn to use it. It wasn't enough to steal away a few moments during the warm days on our neighbor's driveway. As a budding teenager I walked miles in winter to the ice rink, tied on my stiff, oversized ice skates and traced figure eights, large snakes, and extravagant rings into the frozen water. Again and again I would search for the sensation of pushing the edge, feeling how far could I go, out where the force kept me safe — home — before falling back into the coarse reality of losing my balance in my spinning frenzy. The crispness of the air, the shouts and shrieks of all the other girls and boys my age trying the spins and turns added a different dimension to this experience. As I noticed myself revolving at ease in my own world, out on the peripheral edge, I caught sight of my friends as if they were etheric visions made of colorful, wispy vaporous fumes. Then I'd go way beyond the edge, lose my balance, jerk and fumble about, trying to figure out where I was, ruminating on my thoughts like a cow chewing her cud, then find myself popping back into reality, abruptly back, skating straight lines for a while. Other times in between the seasons I'd try to repeat that same spinning search by twirling into faster and faster airy rings during ballet class, but the painful act of doing this on my crushed, bleeding toes prevented me from getting into the comfort of that freeing, non-ordinary sensation.

Whether seeing people skating at super speeds on their roller blades or becoming utterly fascinated while watching televised ice skating competitions, I have wondered if skaters are aware of the urges and yearnings of what their skating represents on a deeper level. Now years later, I know some of the reasons why I spun myself so close to the edge of losing myself those many times, and what I was looking for.

BEYOND THE EDGE: THE FORCE OF CONSCIOUSNESS

Variations upon the theme of spinning continue to be a favorite pastime of children. Kids know it's about being "in the zone." In their uninhibited manner, they know this is about experiencing "the Force," another word for consciousness. During dizziness, they are closer to their true self memories of freedom, lightness, and easiness which are characteristics of the Force. As adults we are just beginning to recognize being "in the zone," a state where everything works in harmony, inside and out, is a peak performance state. Distance runners speak of the runners' high and artists talk of "being at one" with the medium and subject, that subjective experience of being in partnership with one's own intuitive knowing. All these are examples of urges to experience non-ordinary or exceptional places within ourselves, those heightened emotional, mental, and mystical states of consciousness not found in ordinary reality.

DO CHILDREN KNOW THE FORCE?

Do these non-ordinary states of consciousness, the unusual powers of consciousness, stay with us throughout life or do they come and go?

Joseph Chilton Pearce talks about children being aware of these states for most of their youth. (9) Before the age of seven, he thinks kids demonstrate primitive psychic skills and are capable of 'primary perceptions' such as ESP or telepathy, and after the age of seven, they often have psychokinetic abilities. James Peterson adds more understanding to what children know about non-physical realities. In his book *The Secret Life of Kids*, he discusses the differences between psychic and spiritual elements concerning unusual experiences that young children often have. He defines a psychic experience as one where there is a distinct awareness of an object and a subject separate from each other. In sharp contrast, the spiritual experience is a highly "subjective feeling that tends to unite one to the environment in a wave of expansiveness...and profoundly affects or changes one's character long after the experience itself has faded away. Childhood spiritual experiences are more rare than psychic experiences which are extremely common in a child under the age of seven." (10)

Using the work of Rudolph Steiner, Peterson says the etheric energy body (see glossary) of a child is fully functional at the age of seven, the astral energy body matures between 12-13 years of age, and adult psychic ability appears between ages 18-21. In most children, overt psychic skills seem to diminish rapidly throughout their young life, perhaps because children are taught to focus on physical reality. In doing so, they put aside their non-ordinary abilities. Sometimes teenagers and young adults, in times of crisis or intense peer pressure, search for heightened states of awareness by abusing chemicals instead of reaching back into their early psychic and spiritual abilities for solace and problem-solving. For all of us, capturing the Force, that larger part of ourselves, and being able to use these energies concretely is becoming more and more a necessity in these turbulent times of change.

A FAILED RESEARCH STUDY CREATES A NEW OVERLOOK

We cannot agree yet on the Force because we simply don't have enough tangible, conscious experience with this element in our lives. However, we are getting close. One of the first steps was taken over a hundred years ago. In 1887, an experiment with an unexplainable ending brought humankind's thinking about consciousness to the forefront. At that time, classical physicists thought they knew the interrelationships of light and matter, space and time. Scientists thought that light consisted of waves, and these waves moved through a curious medium called luminiferous (light-carrying) *ether*. Since the early 1800s studying the nature of the ether had been a continuing preoccupation. It was thought that since it couldn't be seen or measured with instruments of the day, ether must be an ultra-fine gas.

With the goal of studying the nature of the ether, two professors, Albert A. Michelson and Edward M. Morley, of what is now known as Case Western Reserve University in Cleveland, Ohio, became interested in calculating the degree to which the earth's motion affected the speed of light. During their experiment, despite repeated attempts, they couldn't detect any variation in the velocity of light under any circumstances. Yet observations on the properties of light at that time had indicated that the waves moved in a manner that could be accommodated only by a very dense solid ether. The scientific community was completely baffled by the results of this experiment. While this failure led physicists to abandon the ether theory, they didn't fully grasp the implications of their failed experiment at that time. Later on Albert Einstein, who learned from the mistakes of these two scientists, said this about Michelson, "It was you who led physicists in new paths and through your marvelous experimental work paved the way for the theory of relativity." His acknowledgement of their supposed failure led him to study energy in a most basic, but more creative manner. He zeroed in on the the relationship between energy and matter.

In 1987 while attending several lectures and exhibits in Cleveland during a seven month centennial celebration of the Michelson-Morley experiment, (11) I became aware of the connection between what was formerly called the ether and my experience of the Force while I was spinning myself into lightheadedness. During a presentation describing the experiment and its results, I had an insight that the ether and the Force were one and the same. When I get these insights, my physical body shivers, making me pay attention. (See Glossary for Body Wisdom.) I did not know how I came to this conclusion, but I tucked this insight away for future use. As a result of my impressive case of the shivers, I knew this awareness contained considerable potential. Little did I know that, for the next decade, I would be in the midst of many hands-on experiences that would give me conscious, practical experiences with the Force.

SPLITTING UP WHILE SPINNING:
TOO MANY QUESTIONS FOR A LITTLE KID TO THINK ABOUT

When I was spinning, I knew I felt split. A part of me was thinking and controlling my body while another part of me was energetically feeling a push, a Force. I wavered between staying physical and wanting to lose myself through spinning. But I thought I would lose consciousness and much worse, lose me if I went too far into my spinning. At that time I did not know that my experiences would be leading me into discovering some of the connections between body, mind, and consciousness. First of all, this lightheadedness and the Force, what was it all about? Losing consciousness, why did I think I was going to lose me in the process? Others had told me this was true. As a child of nine, I had already absorbed the belief of my elders which said, "It's an *either/or* life out there. If the body-brain is not controlling me, then I'm not me." But this still didn't explain the memories of the Force I had tucked in the recesses of my mind, nor did it give me a clue why I would think about a part of me losing consciousness or losing me all together.

> Robert Monroe says, "Well, this happens all the time with you. Don't you 'lose' consciousness every night when you fall (go to, drop off, sink into) asleep? When you get hit on the head, the same thing happens. You 'faint', and there you 'go' again. A doctor puts a needle in your arm and pushes the plunger. Bam! You're 'out' again (out where?), and they can start the cutting up process. You drink too much booze and you 'pass out'. Out to where? Overdose on drugs and you've lost it. There's a big difference, you say, and you're right. That's the second part. On one end of the spectrum, there's a catnap and when you wake up (come back?, 'regain' consciousness), your physical body is still functioning albeit somewhat sluggishly. On the other end, you don't wake up and your physical body is not operating. What we tend to overlook are all the stages in between." (12)

PURPOSE OF THE TMI EDUCATION & TRAINING PROGRAMS

The Monroe Institute (TMI) introductory education and training programs which focus on personal consciousness development are called

Gateway Voyage programs. These programs introduce the learner to states of consciousness beyond physical reality. Training events sanctioned by TMI in the field are delivered by certified TMI Outreach Trainers. Other TMI Residential Programs at Faber, Virginia are led by TMI staff trainers. The training makes use of Hemi-Sync, a sound-assisted learning technology which acts as a guiding vehicle enabling one to enter and ride the entire Interstate of Consciousness. This Interstate is comparable to a highway leading to a number of different places, some being ordinary reality, others non-ordinary reality. These places are unique aspects of awarenesses each containing a different, but special focus.

Early non-ordinary Interstate experiences generally involve meditation or other methods of quieting the mind before entering this reality, these unknown areas. For the purpose of this traveling manual, please assume that the word "travel" implies journeying into non-ordinary states of consciousness, still foreign countries for most of us. Later on, as meditative practice becomes easier and more familiar, travel includes bringing non-physical realities and skills into ordinary reality. For example, using dream content to make decisions in everyday situations. Consequently, the goal of all the Gateway Voyage Residential Programs at TMI is to gently guide individuals into the experience of their non-physical energy in such a way as to be generative and transformational. Training at TMI and with associated TMI trainers empowers individuals with the capacity to generate their own questions and answers about the Interstate of Consciousness and enables them to use this process to eventually develop the means to express full consciousness in their lives. Other consciousness educators describe the concept of full consciousness as, "exceptional, positive well-being."

GETTING ON THE ENTRANCE RAMP TO THE INTERSTATE: TWO KEY SKILLS

As a result of their many detailed journeys, Bob Monroe and don Juan, famous for their non-ordinary adventures, gave us several clues about how to approach the Interstate. Just as most of us have learned that one wouldn't enter today's interstate at a snail's pace on a moped while talking on a cell phone to Great Aunt Grace, there is a way to easily navigate the entrance. Traveling the ramp requires a combination of two abilities. One is to acquire a belief-free mind set which Monroe calls a Different Overview

(D/O). This is comparable to having a 360 degree wrap-around car sunroof/windshield, and the other is having the right kind of fuel for traveling as Victor Sanchez, a student of don Juan, recommends. (13) First, we will consider how to develop a D/O.

THE DIFFERENCE BETWEEN A BELIEF & A KNOWN

Many of us make assumptions about traveling into the unknown which come from hand-me-down stories from well-meaning folks. Often, these stories are based on ideas which have been passed on by still others with more ideas. Many of these ideas have been developed through assumptions rather than real, hands-on life experience. Monroe talks about adjusting or changing parts of a belief system to develop a D/O after verifying a new idea at least three times. He says, "A belief is nothing more than stuff to fill a vacuum caused by a lack of knowledge. Believing is not the same as knowing. However, a belief system can become so ingrained and widespread as to engender the illusion of knowledge. Developing a D/O will require reconsideration of any belief that is not 100% knowledge." (14) It was once believed that the Earth was flat, until that belief could be challenged as a result of the direct experiences of early explorers. It was also believed that under anesthesia, patients did not know what was going on during surgery, until someone without this belief thought to ask them to describe what went on during surgery. Various belief systems have changed as a result of continual exploration and personal verification which provides expanded data.

Joe McMoneagle, long-time TMI staff consultant, explains this further by saying, "Learning that is accomplished without experiential input goes straight into an I BELIEVE place and not into the I KNOW place." (15) Figure 1 illustrates the on-ramping process which is simply a *letting go* approach. This provides an opening so that a D/O will be created. At the beginning of meditative practice, it is becomes very beneficial to eliminate or neutralize any beliefs that will directly create an expectation about non-physical reality. When one goes into the place of I DON'T KNOW, which often feels like being at the bottom of a well, it becomes necessary to drop any I BELIEVES and get very comfortable with not knowing. Initially, in meditation the I DON'T KNOW place literally looks dark and seems like it is full of absolute nothingness. However, by temporarily suspending beliefs and expectations it becomes possible for this dark "nothing" place to literally become a bridge or the means to move up and out into spacious, wider perceptual horizons. Exploration on the Interstate without the Left Brain persistently saying, "I believe this…and I believe that…" will help to eventually develop I KNOWs. (See Known in glossary.) During the traveling experience, the "I" component usually is realized first and then, later on, the "KNOW" component follows. During Gateway Excursion Weekends, I describe the place of I DON'T KNOW as the place of the unknown or the void; the silent, blackened place of the mind, the no-thought place. In eastern meditative practice this place is called satori. Most of us stubbornly resist the I DON'T KNOW place, tooth and nail, yet if we patiently sit in the void with no expectations or beliefs attached, gradually a certain comfort will settle in. After a while, experiences in non-physical reality will soon emerge.

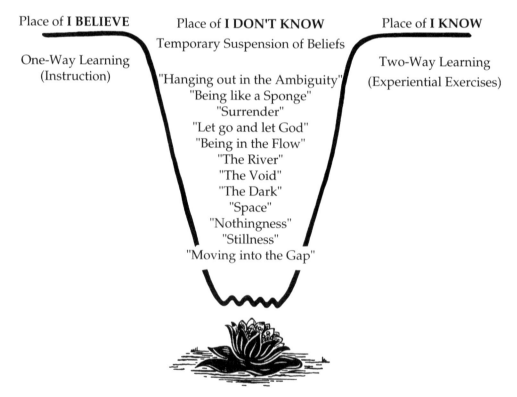

Place of **I BELIEVE**   Place of **I DON'T KNOW**   Place of **I KNOW**

One-Way Learning   Temporary Suspension of Beliefs   Two-Way Learning
(Instruction)   (Experiential Exercises)

"Hanging out in the Ambiguity"
"Being like a Sponge"
"Surrender"
"Let go and let God"
"Being in the Flow"
"The River"
"The Void"
"The Dark"
"Space"
"Nothingness"
"Stillness"
"Moving into the Gap"

Figure 1 Going From I Believe to I Know (16)

VOIDS, GAPS, HOLES, CAVES, & WORMHOLES

In several different ways, many well-known meditation trainers have emphasized the importance of getting acquainted with this interior place of I DON'T KNOW by using various analogies. In his televised PBS classes, Deepak Chopra refers to the void as the "gap" and frequently advises moving or slipping into the gap to gain Higher Self wisdom. In Chapter 8 of this manual, Bob Monroe describes his first encounter with the void as a nine-year-old when he falls into a cave. Later, he used his cave experience to develop the concept of Different Overview. In the popular TV program *The X-Files*, during an episode called "Leonard Betts" which explores regeneration of physical body parts, a highly-charged conversation occurs between the two main characters, Mulder played by David Duchovny and Scully (Gillian Anderson). In her role of a forensic physician-antagonist, Scully finds it impossible to figure out how a decapitated body can regenerate its head. Mulder stares at her, then says, in an elegant, but laser-like manner, "Scully, the unimaginable happens in the gap!"

In the past, voids were thought of as places of no-things, but now, interestingly enough, voids in space exploration, better known as black holes, are talked about as intriguing objects, places to be researched and defined. Mental attitudes have shifted about the dark elements of life. In the past many of us were afraid of dark things, now we are curious enough to study them! Note the hole in the middle of Figure 1. This area is the **key** to understanding how to enter the states of non-physicality. The place of I DON'T KNOW is where consciousness can engage the gears to shift phase back and forth between realities. Please refer to Figure 1a. The center between two worlds, or states of consciousness, is the eye of the soul, better known in sacred geometry terms as the vesica pisces.

The "eye" represents a location where a neutral, but propelling Force resides similar to what is known as a wormhole in *Star Trek* terminology. In the early plots of the popular *Star Trek Deep Space Nine* (*DS9*) series, a Bajoran wormhole was the center of attraction. In their exploration, *DS9* characters discovered the wormhole contained unstable energy. In the more recent *Voyager* series, the characters are now developing the ability to stabilize the wormhole so travel within its environment can be more predictable. How coincidental! A wormhole in *Star Trek* terms is defined as a "subspace bridge (or tunnel) in the structure of space." (17) Another term for wormhole is a space warp containing negative space, space enfolded on itself. Inasmuch as a black hole is gravity enfolded on itself, becoming so dense that it is fathomless, this suggests the wormhole, the "eye" place, and the I DON'T KNOW place are one and the same. I suggest these are inner and outer manifestations of the same locale. Back in 1784 John Mitchell suggested that the most massive bodies in the universe might not be visible because of their incredible gravity. (18)   Holding the equivalent of millions of suns condensed into the space occupied by our solar system, the black hole's intense gravitational pull "eats" the evidence of its existence, thus creating the awareness of nothingness or the feature we know as a void.

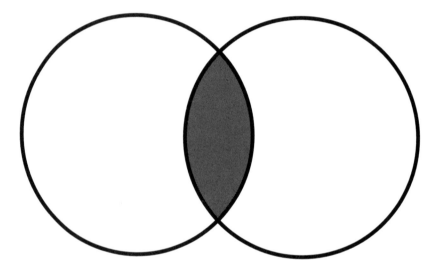

Figure 1a   The Vesica Pisces

THE VOID AS THE BRIDGE BETWEEN TWO STATES OF CONSCIOUSNESS

In 1935 Albert Einstein and Nathan Rosen presented their theory related to the purpose of black holes as being bridges (19) connecting one universe to another. The Einstein-Rosen Bridge concept provides a means to explore two sides of an experience, a physical dimension connected with its non-physical counterpart. This gives some explanation for what many travelers have described as a conduit between two different states of consciousness. William Buhlman refers to this as an energy tunnel or a "highly organized temporary opening or rift in the non-physical energy membrane and that appears to open automatically to allow life-forms to pass through. After the life-form (consciousness) passes within the higher-frequency energy dimension, the tunnel opening immediately returns to its original shape and form." (20) I propose this rift is caused by a state of I DON'T KNOW, the act of perceiving nothingness or the void. The act of perceiving nothing is one of two key skills to get on the entrance ramp leading to the near and far reaches of consciousness.

For personal growth, try to intentionally play with this bridge analogy for this will provide numerous experiences on how to consciously move into the I KNOW place. The first step leading toward the I KNOW place in meditation is to develop the desire to experience this totally blank state, wormhole-like place long enough until it becomes a comfortable KNOWN. This surrendering process jump-starts the engine of the driver to move easily into the place of I KNOW.

In the void phase, early meditative experiences will frequently have swirling colors, fleeting faces, and figures. After a while one becomes accustomed to them and with familiarity, they disappear only to reappear later as meditative practice becomes commonplace. Oftentimes, at first, the void appears now and then as if there is a pulsebeat coming and going. This is an indication there is a current of energy of the ether or the Force *pulsating*. Consciousness, indeed, pulsates as a waveform. The actual pulsating current of energy is the current of the soul's energy enlivening the physical vehicle. This pulsation is different from the pulsation of blood through the human body. It has a different rhythm and varies like the human pulse. When one's comfort level with the void rises, adventuresome travel begins. Then the higher mind, or what Bob Monroe calls the Total Self, actively takes command. Thereafter, experiences which mirror parts of full consciousness then play themselves out.

To make Interstate entry easy, there are a series of energetic techniques used in TMI training programs called the Preparatory Process. These are taught before Interstate travel in the non-ordinary states begins. (Please refer to Chapter 4 for a description of the Preparatory Process.)

To move into the I KNOW place, it is important to jettison any "I believe this… & I believe that…" thoughts and temporarily suspend any ideas, concepts or other techniques that have formed those belief systems. Traditionally in the past, the place of I BELIEVE was developed by people using "Believe me, I know…" one-way instructive, judgmental methods. This often created a competitive learning environment because the natural inclinations and instincts of the learner weren't incorporated. When the deeper yearnings and knowings are utilized or are stimulated, this produces two-way experiential, cooperative learning. Two-way learning is a highly creative act between the person and his/her higher consciousness, the teacher, the Total Self. I KNOWs are the end-products between the partnership developed with Total Self (I AM) and the Physical Personality Self (Me). Monroe always encouraged an individual to acquire his or her own KNOWNS and KNOW-HOW formulas especially when entering the states of non-ordinary consciousness along the Interstate. He strongly discouraged any teachings that would create a belief system that wasn't of the participant's own creation. For this reason, he did not support an education and training process that included religious or organizational beliefs.

During the early stages of meditative practice, it is beneficial to take a position of being an observer and a sponge, acting as if there aren't any Knowns or beliefs; then after training ends, one's own truth detector, better known as discernment, can be used to determine what is right and not right. *Discernment is the active use of intuition, trusting an inner voice, whereas judgment is the active use of Left Brain logic or rational thinking.*

A LESSON WITH THE OLD MAN IN THE CONSCIOUSNESS

As I reflect back on my initial "on-ramping" efforts in my own traveling process, I was surprised to discover that my consciousness possessed a natural, creative, intelligent quality that I associated with the image of a very mature, all-knowing grandfather or sage. Stan Grof, M.D., calls this ability, the radar function of consciousness. "In non-ordinary states there is an automatic selection of the most relevant and emotionally charged material from the person's consciousness. It is as if an 'inner radar' system scans the psyche and the body for the most important issues and makes them available to our conscious minds." (21) This sage-like quality of my Total Self automatically came out whenever necessary. For instance, one of my first challenges came in the form of having to let go of my resistance to the structured approach taught at TMI for entering various states of consciousness. The steps of "first do this, now do this" became increasingly maddening to me. Today I can laugh at my resistances, but back then I remember fighting this in many devious ways because I believed this…and I believed that. I came up with all kinds of excuses to go around, dilute, avoid, misunderstand, defy, and rebel against the TMI five-step Preparatory *letting go* Process. In other words I was resisting moving into the void, the unknown part of myself. This became very evident to me during a Gateway Excursion Weekend in Cincinnati. Again I attempted the Preparatory Process throughout the weekend, creating a major struggle. I ended up with a painful migraine due to my internal head trip of literally questioning everything that was done. Thank goodness, my Trainer, Connie Stafford, was very perceptive and patient with me as my consciousness let me hit some major highway barriers. Gradually I took baby steps to turn those barriers into opportunities to eliminate my self-importance. By giving in here and there, I found myself gradually sliding comfortably into the void, the place of I DON'T KNOW. Until then I had led a life acquiring a ton of beliefs as if they were ribbons won during a swimming competition. After letting go enough, I came to the conclusion there was a clever, higher mind inside of me I could tap into if I let go even further. There ensued a tug-of-war phase, a push-pulling effort on my part. But by taking more baby steps I gradually learned to trust the fact that I had to give up my self-importance and simply let go…into the Preparatory Process and into the void.

After repeated experiences of learning to let go, eventually I discovered the sage characteristic was an actual quality of my consciousness, a black and white, concrete quality, meaning "its" intelligence seemed to have a cosmic, all-knowing nature. My Total Self has its own built-in drive train, the moving Force. It was much later on that I came across Grof's writings about the radar function of consciousness. I learned to pay more and more attention to my instinctual nudges aided by my body wisdom symptoms as a helpful guidance system. As I acquired more trust, this wise part of me seemed to have its own highly creative ability to guide me into easier and more productive life situations. This may sound as if this kind of intelligence were outside of me and, at times, I chose to perceive it as outside of me. But as I gradually eased into the void of myself, this guidance system felt as familiar and comfortable as if it were a long lost, wise relative who had been abandoned long ago.

Looking back over this path I created, I was amazed! In particular, I couldn't have planned a more perfect lesson in Cincinnati at the beginning of my Interstate travel than to have designed an experience in which I had to learn, on my own terms, to cooperate with my own authority figure swooping around in the form of an unknown, mysterious, lost relative. I came to this insight ten years ago, not knowing how crucial this letting go lesson was going to be in the future. Interestingly enough, many participants on the Gateway Excursion Weekends have talked about and demonstrated the very same issues about learning how to surrender to the void during the entrance phase of the Interstate while maintaining personal integrity. In addition, participants say that they recognize the same sage-like qualities associated with their own consciousness as well when they embrace their Total Self in the void.

MAGNIFYING THE HORSEPOWER OF THE ENGINE

Besides developing a different overview (D/O), another key element which significantly helps to create a smooth entry onto the Interstate of Consciousness is having the sufficient amount and the right kind of gas in the tank before starting out on the trip. Newer engines in many cars today are perfect metaphors for what's advantageous to drive into these regions of the Interstate. Many of today's engines are now designed to be high-performance and high compression-oriented. Thus, different gasoline is required to fuel the trip. Since there are various types of gasoline sold at gas stations these days, it is important to read the label on the pump to see what octanes are available. For this kind of traveling into non-ordinary realities, the higher the octane, the better. Having high octane gas in the tank makes the trip easy, sustainable, and fun. On the other hand, the engine will not operate efficiently on low octane gas. In fact, in a few cases, the use of an emergency towing service will be needed.

BUYING HIGH OCTANE GAS FOR THE TRIP

What does it require to create high octane fuel in the tank? Victor Sanchez explains this well when he describes the "stalking" techniques of Carlos Castaneda (22) as taught by the sorcerer, don Juan Matus. Stalking is Carlos' term for learning to save, redirect, and increase energies in order to build up an energy reservoir for traveling. Based on the premise that *individuals are fields of energy rather than solid bodies*, don Juan taught Castaneda to become impeccably careful about choices regarding the use of energy. He suggested that any act be an act of impeccability, which implies that each act should be carried out with careful awareness of either fortifying or weakening the field of energy. Unfortunately, the average person's energy is consumed by doing routine acts determined entirely by past memory. This ritual drains what little energy is available and leaves low octane gasoline in the tank. Sanchez says,

"A large part of our time is spent remembering the past (while we do tasks). Only we don't realize what we are remembering is not reality but rather images fabricated by our internal dialogue concerning what happened to us. We don't remember facts but interpretation of facts. We are unaware of our real past because we are too involved in repeating to ourselves a mythical history that our ego has developed to justify its existence." (23)

Thus, don Juan advanced on a training mission to show Castaneda how to stalk his use of energy, that is to pay special attention to how he made choices to do things in his life. From the very obvious drains such as undoing habits, routines, and rituals to the covert, sneaky leakages such as undoing the ego, erasing personal history and self-importance, don Juan made Castaneda pay attention and stop those actions based on past beliefs. Sanchez has excellently discussed Castaneda's ideas about the insidious places where we stash our energies, thereby leaving the gas tank of our vehicles nearly empty. Consider reading his book, *The Teachings of Don Carlos*, for excellent exercises on how to stop gas leakage and how to buy and use higher octane fuel. Refer to the section called Practices for the Right Side of the Energy Body, in particular, the exercises on stalking.

Interstate travel requires a well-maintained energy engine in the car, one that is tuned, lubricated, and able to use high octane gas. Most of us have left the care and upkeep of our innerspace vehicle to the mythical car gods in the sky. This is as good as leaving the drain plug out of the oil pan after a lube and oil change. The car can be driven onto the Interstate ramp but most likely, the engine will start knocking, seize up, and become a draining junk heap. (See Chapter 7 for a description of a car maintenance plan supporting easy traveling for the long term.) From my trainer and coaching experience, I have noticed that many people have difficulty accessing and/or sustaining altered states of consciousness because they spend their day at jobs or in lifestyles which weaken the energy field, leaving very little fuel to sustain travel into non-ordinary places. The fire or the spirit of the energy has been drained from the consciousness; thus, the total horsepower of the engine is not tapped. Subtle problems in traveling ability develop, such as not being able to visit a desired locale on the Interstate, getting off track easily, not being able to enjoy the ride, having constant preoccupations rattling around inside, feeling frequently discouraged ("have we got there yet?"), or being unable to let the body deeply relax. All these are symptoms that the energy field does not have enough high octane gas to fuel the trip.

THE 'PINGING, SPUTTERING, KNOCKING IT SELF OUT' ENGINE

Take a look at the waking moments of an average individual who starts a regular day. Typically, this person is awakened by loud voices coming from a radio rudely interrupting the end of already fleeting dreams. Turning to the sleeping body lying next to him, he vigorously shakes her best chimeral impressions away, then slowly forces his legs upright pushing the still sleeping feet to the floor, thinking…"What day is this?…I have that meeting at 9 o'clock…I'm not ready for this…time to let the dog up from the basement before…wonder when the kid will start the (*!#) loud music…should I make some eggs or take a shower first…I bet the paper is ripped again…gotta have some coffee to get the mind moving…maybe my boss…" and the automatic routine reactions go on and on throughout the day. Instead of acting from the body's wisdom, and using the Total Self promptings, the practice-pretend lifestyle of this individual continues its circling, dying, draining habits based on past conditioning. In that same day if this person tries to meditate or to access a non-ordinary state, gaining entry and/or sustaining an altered state of consciousness is going to be difficult. For in Sanchez's words, there won't be enough available "free" energy unattached to the past memories to support this individual's efforts to have an enjoyable journey on the Interstate. Since *anything* on the path of the Interstate of Consciousness will necessarily involve energy, it will be very beneficial to have a sufficient amount of high octane fuel in the tank to carry one through all the adventures whether they be the ordinary or non-ordinary varieties.

CONSCIOUSNESS: THE SPIRIT OF THE DRIVER BEHIND THE WHEEL

It will be helpful to have a general reference point to start this journey, so let's talk about what consciousness is when applied to Interstate journeys, its nature and qualities. Consciousness includes various attentional states in both physical and non-physical reality. When some talk of being conscious, they are referring to a higher consciousness known by many names: Creative Intelligence, Cosmic Consciousness, The Power Within, The Force, Universal Intelligence, Cosmic Mind, Higher Self, Total Self, Core Self, the Primary Source, and God. When I talk of consciousness I am including all of these names.

A BRIEF BUT INTENSE DEFINITION OF CONSCIOUSNESS FOR STARTERS

What is the nature of the Force or consciousness? Here are some possibilities to ponder. They have sprung from my Knowns. To me, consciousness is an energetic Force of constant movement. It's a creative, intelligent energy which aspires toward wholeness. It makes use of a group of Knowns that provide it the means for its own movement or growth. These Knowns represent the developmental growth process of consciousness accumulated as consciousness learns to express itself.

Let's break that down into simpler terms. The Force, known as consciousness, contains a resource bank of Knowns with potential energies attached. We could call these Knowings. The act of Knowing brings to the surface that which one already knows unconsciously underneath. Knowing goes beyond reasoning, as it is the maturing, seasoned version of intuition having potential energy attached. Knowing means using an ability to sense truth both intuitively and intelligently. I have discovered the Force is not deterministic, static, nor hierarchical in nature but, if the Force is overshadowing the energy within which is static, temporarily it may appear to have these non-moving qualities. This is the case where nothing seems to be happening, where an individual has stagnant energies. Likewise, this stagnation may be present in some form in one's lifestyle for a time. However, the Force of consciousness is generally a dynamic energy possessing innate creative intelligence.

I have experienced the Force as having a highly creative component which makes use of synchronistic moments in life. Sometimes we call these *deja vu* moments or coincidences. Woven throughout *The Celestine Prophecy*, James Redfield (24) describes how the energetic Force (or consciousness) makes itself known in this manner. Redfield specifically explains this idea in his Insight #1, the principle of coincidence or synchronicity present in all of nature. Unfortunately, our attention has shifted away from recognizing, honoring and using Mother Nature's gifts. Instead, the majority of us have centered on the concerns of daily living such as downsizing, annuities, fast food, and Disney World. Yet Mother Nature continues to present messages of the Force despite our priorities and attentions being elsewhere. Many have found there are powerful lessons to be learned by reading the creative messages presented in nature. If we were to get to know Her better, such as through Her weathery moods, we would learn about balance, focus, and coherency, all so evident in her designs, omens, cycles, and immensely creative moments. Synchronicity isn't just a quirk of Mother Nature. She's not an egocentric neighbor with an unpredictable bad temper. Rather, Her coincidental patterns demonstrate Her Total Self in action. When synchronicity occurs, this is the I KNOW momentarily showing us options. In the synchronistic moment, Knowing arrives.

This is the beginning of a partnership with the Force, between the I AM and the Me, the conscious cooperation with synchronistic omens either in ordinary life or non-physical realities There are provocative results due to this partnership. For instance, I have learned that when I cooperate with the Force, meaning when I let go into it with my integrity intact, I have found an essential part of myself, my creative intelligence. My creative intelligence has very little to do with my IQ so highly valued in physical reality, nor my EQ (emotional quotient). Finding this essential part of me began to give me answers to the other part of the sticky question, "If I let go into the spinning, will I lose me?" As things progressed, I discovered that my consciousness has other qualities. It is highly reliable, dependable, and trustworthy, unlike my IQ and EQ. Over and over I tested this both in non-physical and physical reality and found these qualities to persist. Of course, in truth, I was testing myself at a much deeper level.

TWO KINDS OF CONSCIOUSNESS

There are two kinds of consciousness. Many I BELIEVEs in today's environment focus on improving or expanding **Human Consciousness** or the awareness of physical reality. This involves using the five human senses coupled with the lower nature (physical, emotional, mental desires). It is often where the Interstate journey into the near and far reaches of consciousness begins. If expansion of human consciousness is the goal, then the mind, the ego, and the personality are all targets for change in the early stages of travel. Traveler beware. Physical, emotional and mental issues are tackled here. When the focus shifts to the bigger picture, then another component of consciousness is being embraced, that of **Spiritual Consciousness**. This involves the combined awareness of both physical and non-physical reality while using the Total Self's promptings, better known as the soul's senses which are different than the human senses. (In Chapters 8 and 9 the senses of the soul are described using the work of Castaneda and Dennis Holtje.) Spiritual consciousness requires higher octane fuel to travel the entire Interstate. So it makes sense to acquire and keep this grade of fuel stored in the tank for easy traveling.

The next stop on our journey will be to explore the cities and neighborhoods of non-ordinary reality which exist on the Interstate of Consciousness and investigate the two driving skills that support a pleasurable and growth-filled excursion into these locales.

INTO THE UNKNOWN I GO

With an eye on all those 'states in between'
I jump inside from I Believe to I Know,
and back and forth in between until
I let go into my own comfort of knowing.

TRAVELING THE INTERSTATE OF CONSCIOUSNESS

"If he is indeed wise, he does not bid you enter the house of his wisdom, but rather leads you to the threshold of your own mind."

Kahlil Gibran, *The Prophet*

ROUTE 2

LEAVING THE STRAIGHT & NARROW DRIVING TO MISS DAISY !

In his last book, *Ultimate Journey*, Bob Monroe (1) described the Interstate of Consciousness as a "route to follow from one state of consciousness to another, both within time-space and along the seemingly endless energy spectrum of the (M) field." Monroe's internationally known books documenting his extensive 40 year journey in these regions of the Interstate established credibility for his now famous declaration:

"You are more than your physical body. Because you are
more than physical matter, you can perceive that which is
greater than the physical world."(2)

During the TMI Gateway Voyage program, participants are shown how to explore the possibility of being more than a physical body. On my first Gateway Voyage, I went to get answers to several childhood questions. "What happens when I lose consciousness? What is this Force that takes over when I am spinning? Where did it come from and what is it good for?" Over the years in my own learning process, two concepts became very important to me. One originated from Monroe who said, "We are all waveforms of energy." The other came from Joe McMoneagle, who expanded on this idea by emphasizing the process of participating with the Force in order learn about it and take on its intelligence or its power.

When teaching some middle school children a few Hemi-Sync meditative techniques, I played the lyrics of the Billy Joel hit song, "River of Dreams," to show them that we are all waveforms. I began to move to its wonderful, undulating rhythm. As I lightly swayed around, I drew a sine waveform on a blackboard to illustrate the waveform. My dancing movements triggered something inside of me. Afterwards I played that tune over and over, dancing to its rhythm, until it dawned on me that I could dive into the waveform to experience its energy by *becoming* it rather than letting it lead. My dancing movements brought the realization that I hadn't actually played with the possibility of moving with the Force *in the lead*. While Monroe explained the overt aspects of energy flow, McMoneagle elaborated on this idea by describing its subtle aspects. (3) Both emphasize a dynamic rather than static characteristic of energy. This implies that a new driving method must be learned, one that doesn't anticipate going down a straight and narrow path. However, many do aim for the middle road, as I did during the early years of my Interstate journey!

That particular TMI training helped me to realize that there were two parts of me, one being physical reality and the other, non-physical reality. The body/brain was the obvious physical matter of me and my mind/spirit were the non-physical energy components of me. I could say I am composed of both *matter* and *antimatter* elements. I noticed that I put more attention and value on the physical part of me than my non-physical aspects. This meant that I came to know more about my physical reality than my non-physical reality. To demonstrate this to the middle school students, I used the sine wave diagram in Figure 2a. The horizontal line drawn through the middle indicates where physical and non-physical reality separate, or so we think. I described how the waveform changes above and below the line; it merely changes form. I told the kids my physical reality awareness, the "Me" resides above the line and my non-physical reality, the "I AM" or Total Self resides below the line. Up until 1986 I knew a lot of what was above the line and very little about what was below. In fact I had almost totally forgotten what I had known as a child concerning what was below the line. Somehow this part of my memory had shelved itself until I began dancing to the lyrics of the River of Dreams song. An aha! hit me and I felt shivers. I put two and two together in some peculiar sort of way and came up with the insight about becoming a waveform of energy. Hmm-m. Bob Monroe was saying more than a bunch of words!

Physical Reality

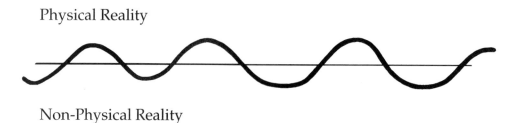

Non-Physical Reality

Figure 2a The Learning Cycle of Consciousness: Energy as a Waveform

The horizontal line in Figure 2a represents the Continental Divide of Consciousness described in Chapter 1. Crossing that line, moving in and out is the waveform energy of an individual in its constantly changing form. Each sine wave is a snapshot view of both "Me" and the "I AM" personifications. The "Me" encompasses physical reality above the line, which includes my body and my brain. In early travel experiences, the "I AM" Total or Cosmic Mind is more easily accessed in non-physical reality. Later on, this gradually becomes accessible in physical reality as well. Some would say my brain contains my mind, others would say my mind expands to fill the container at my command. That's where the Divide becomes debatable and obvious. Presently two consciousness factions favor a perspective that "mind is what the brain does" (4) and agree that there isn't a physical place in the brain that houses the mind. (5) A new idea is emerging which is the mind, a vehicle of consciousness, is the source of transportation (a car) between physical and non-physical realities.

THE MIND: THE BRIDGE TO FULL CONSCIOUSNESS

During a 1987 Gateway Outreach Train the Trainer workshop, Bob Monroe commented that the mind was a bridge to the consciousness. In the years that followed, over and over I drew this sine wave out in diagram form during presentations before vice presidents, CEOs, nursing administrators, engineering managers, wellness directors etc., until I deeply internalized this concept! This is similar to the metaphor that the mind is like a wormhole, a bridge between points in space. Wormholes, according to (Star)Trekkies, are subspace shortcuts. They thought in the early episodes of *Deep Space Nine* that the wormhole contained extremely unstable energy with the endpoints fluctuating widely across time and space. Back here on this journey, my traveling experiences have shown me repeatedly that the mind can be directed as a Force to become a vehicle for linking physical and non-physical realities and a conduit to experience its own Force or consciousness. (See Figure 2b.)

Non-physical consciousness is located below the line. Below is a metaphoric word to name a particular approach or a method used to locate this region. Consciousness isn't a locale, it's relative to the perceptual intention of the beholder. Diving beneath in this sense means getting serious by using a personal goal (intention) to make non-physical realities into Knowns. Diving below means getting focused. When the unknown or darkness is made conscious, we become aware of the grand beauty of ourselves, the totality of the Self which includes discovering other parts of ourselves. Going beneath also means riding the waveform as if becoming the waveform and surrendering to its unique rhythm and order. This exploration can take place in both physical and non-physical realities. For example, if I spend too much time in my garden communing with the plants, my physical reality eventually will assert itself with obviously dusty floors and dirty sinks phoning messages to me. The reverse is also true. If my days are spent in furious superwoman pursuits, then I will find my non-physical daydreaming on the increase during the daytime and my dreaming intensifying during the night as if something were trying to rebalance the waveform. When I became intimately aware of my waveform, I became fascinated with my own rhythms, unique forms, and peculiarities, something similar to acquiring "street smarts" during the driving approach to the Interstate of Consciousness.

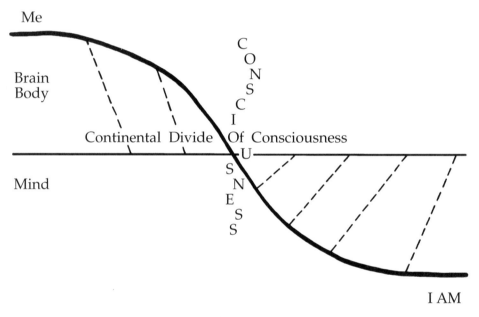

Figure 2b The Learning Cycle of Consciousness: Multidimensionality

ROADWAY SKILL 101: DRIVING ONTO THE ENTRANCE RAMP

My early excursions onto the Interstate were studies in letting go of the parent's hand. You ask what parent? This was my invented (outside authority) Me that said it was wrong to go into dark, unknown places. Virtually hundreds of my clients have described this belief and its associated fears to me in countless forms. For me, this hanging on was soon to change.

THE USE OF DREAMING TO PARTNER WITH THE I AM

My letting go lessons began with a series of recurring dreams I had about falling into a bottomless well. Once in the well, I felt a shriveling cold and a dread of being alone. I fell non-stop, down into a limitless space. At one point after having a number of these scary dreams, I decided to change the plot. I made the decision before I went to sleep to stop my pointless but terrorized falling. I did this by resolving to use my newly developed willing skills to stop this boundless free falling. I also decided to accept the consequences without knowing what they were. The skill of using the will is a simple use of firmly-willed intention without any logic attached. (See Chapter 8 in Castaneda section for more on the skill of will.) I had no idea what using this new skill would do, but I knew in the past this had stopped my endless, circling, end-over-end motion while at a TMI Gateway Voyage Residential Program. Later that night I went into a free fall down the well once more, but this time I willed myself to stop. I didn't tell myself to stop (a thinking process), I willed it using energy from my solar plexus (a perceiving process), then suddenly I heard a WHOOM and felt a sensation similar to a parachute opening to stop my falling and anchor me in place. What's more, the dreaded cold, dank atmosphere now had changed into a dark, enfolding comfortable place with tiny sparkling lights. I spent a little time getting comfortable in this new place. Through a series of other innocent moves, again using my newly found Focus state skills, I was able to climb out of the now more comfortable well of darkness and move myself into friendlier territory.

Afterwards, I knew those dreaming experiences were metaphoric lessons from my expanded "I AM" self, telling me how to handle Me in my physical reality. This was one of the first times when I (the non-physical part of me) consciously became the waveform below the line and learned how to take the ramp to higher ground. This also indicates I was becoming more lucid in my dreams which calls for partnering with the Total Self. I discovered this learning came about when, instead of manipulating or fighting the falling sensation, I *allowed* my falling (went into the void and got comfortable), then while falling, I called upon my will center to stop the movement. My higher "I AM" intelligence responded as if "Me" and "I AM" acted together.

Still thickheaded, I didn't realize the full implications of *being* a waveform. I continued to treat myself as if I could go straight into various states of consciousness and collect $200 as I passed "Go." I thought it was just a matter of going around and around the board doing the techniques taught to me at TMI until something outside of me clicked, or better yet, hit me on the head and showed me the "right way." Not so. More letting go lessons were obviously required.

DANCING WITH THE WAVEFORM

The rhythm and order of the waveform began to fascinate me. I began giving up my beliefs about achieving certain things in meditation, expecting great visions and insights, experiencing wondrous, mystical events, and wrapping myself in numerous meditative rituals methodically carried out at the crack of dawn. I gave up wearing cotton, using crystals, chanting certain mantras, and keeping my legs uncrossed (to keep the energy circuit open). I gave into being who I was and made my meditation process simple. As a TMI GO Trainer, my Gateway Excursion Weekends also became easier, co-creative, fun events. No longer did I have to be the teacher. I turned myself into the student as well and dropped my need for producing glorious results, whatever that was! During that process I became a waveform in my own way. In everyday life, I started trying consciously to make my life simple and easy, taking out the drama, the extra physical effort and the need for struggle and duplication. Instead I looked for the fun, the light and surprising events sprinkled throughout my days. This tremendously impacted my family, my co-workers, and my close friends. As I retrained myself for a simpler life, I also had to retrain others to the fact that I was changing. As a consequence, I had to make more and more (what others thought were) radical changes down the road. In my mind's eye, I wrote two words, *easy and simple*, one on each hand, in capitals across my palms and kept reminding myself where I wanted to be — in an easy and simple waveform because I wanted to learn the basics. Since then, quite literally, I have gradually learned to ride my waveform in spite of my fear of rollercoasters!

On my Interstate journeys, I have acquired Knowns about the multidimensional layers of myself by exploring the non-physical realities of the Interstate which could be likened to finding subselves. This is still a fascinating realm. Soon I found home base, my core firmly rooted and unfailingly present for this human form and all the time, it was right under my nose! I, the essential core or the truth of me, gradually became obvious and concrete. To friends and family, I began to refer to it as my golden unending core, my reserve bank. Experiences that formerly had been potentially harmful, I tackled because I had that golden core established. I knew I was more than my physical body because I had discovered some basic understanding of what and who I was in non-physical reality. This balanced out my understanding of who I am. So these physical reality experiences were just a piece of the pie, not the whole thing. It was a fascinating process. Finding myself in the dark helped me become real and known to myself. A crazy dichotomy. My remodeling process and the discovery of specific Knowns about myself began to answer my childhood question, "Will I lose myself if I go beyond lightheadedness?" As you might expect, my surrendering process has continued as I travel more and more miles on the Interstate.

ROADWAY SKILL 201: BECOMING THE WAVEFORM

Further on-ramping lessons involve the realization of the unique nature of the waveform. This is *movement*, not static, feeble attempts at movement, but actual flowing movement — not straight and narrow line movement, but up and down, in and out flowing, vibrant movement. Within this waveform lesson on movement, there are components that are aware and not so aware, coherent and incoherent, straight and not so straight, sane and crazy, a melting pot of diversity and creativity. An unstable wormhole effect the Trekkies would call it. McMoneagle has said, "Think of the mind and how it would work. It would act as part of that waveform stream cycling in and out of different levels of power. It's not operating power that we're talking about. We're talking about how long and how deep we have dipped into the information stream." (6) The dipping process of the waveform is not a difficult idea to grasp. It is much like a polar bear swimming about looking for its next meal. The head is up and the head is down; metaphorically speaking, the polar bear is catching life with both physical and non-physical energy. Flowing with the waveform is not a tentative "grabbing-for-the-survival" feast; likewise, this life is not a practice life. It's not enough just to live above the water line. The idea is to combine the best of the two worlds using the physical while in the non-physical state and to use the non-physical while in the physical state. Perhaps the polar bear goes beyond water movements and the smell and sound cues and uses some kind of non-ordinary sensing device that leads the bear to his dinner. The bear has to literally flow with the rhythms of the water and energy in order to synchronize its movements to hone in on dinner. Usually we keep these two elements separate, never the twain shall meet. We either swim or we eat. For me this translates into checking out my own radar, my conscious and unconscious intention, before I attempt traveling the Interstate. The old saying works well here, "garbage in, garbage out" or what is intended on the front end will be manifested on the Interstate. Hence, if I am thinking I am merely pretending to be my waveform, then I am going to have a lot of fantasy experiences which will drain my energies and leave me clueless in the process.

Solara, author of *How to Live Large on a Small Planet*, talks about the dipping process in detail using the art of surfing to explain various kinds of waveform energy rhythms. She suggests lying down, trying to sense the pulsating currents of energy inside the body, becoming aware of the currents outside the body, then letting them flow together. This will couple you with the waveform rhythm. She identifies nine pulsating energy forms within the wave: calm, wild, battering, choppy, splashing, still, riptide, swooning, and quantum surf wave forms. (7) Mastering the art of surfing different kinds of waveform energies brings about balanced movement with the rhythms of life.

RULES FOR RIDING THE WAVEFORM

McMoneagle encourages us to forget the rules we learned about physical life when we are entering the Interstate. These are the same rules I learned about being afraid of the dark and letting outside authority be my guide; consequently, I had to suspend them in order to move into the place of I KNOW. I have emphasized Joe's rules with my clients and Gateway Excursion participants as we begin a consciousness training workshop. I encourage them to be very observant of their approach because what is put out in intent is manifested right back into existence whether it be physical or non-physical reality. McMoneagle wrote rules for the training of remote viewers (people who are able to view the past, the present and the future as an aspect of themselves projected to a location different from where they are located), but I find these rules apply equally as well within this larger context.

Rule One: You will probably sense at different strengths with each dip into the cycle. In other words, you gather different and varying amounts of data at the individual learning levels with each dip.

Rule Two: At times you are generating additional information that has no relevancy to the target information you're attempting to collect. In other words, your brain is generating chatter which has nothing to do with Universal Intelligence.

Rule Three: You are also dealing with natural human instincts and habits that inhibit you from doing the right thing. These instincts or habits corrupt the information you're trying to process. Some of these are:

- You feel you must absolutely reach a conclusion. This is the last thing you should be trying to do.

- You may be setting yourself up by thinking things must work the way you envision them as working, when they may actually work in an entirely different fashion.

- Everything you are thinking must make sense. But in the stream, each part or piece of information is nothing more than that, a piece of a large puzzle. As in a jigsaw puzzle, different parts do not necessarily have to go together.

- You feel you must be right the first time around; you must succeed or you will be a failure. This generates fear of failure or an unnecessary requirement to perform.

Rule Four: There are major philosophic questions cropping up, and they directly affect your belief and concepts of reality. Not addressing them, or rejecting a change in a belief or concept, will impact on the results of your efforts. (8)

GETTING ON THE INTERSTATE OF CONSCIOUSNESS

There was a part of me as a child that knew how to move to the edge of the Force, then she would fall out of that spinning and wouldn't go further. As a child, do you remember your own freedom-searching movements? Do you remember when you would move to the edge of getting what you wanted, to the very edge, then at the last moment, you ran back? Do you still do that in areas of your life?

Bob Monroe has provided the opportunity to take consistent, self-validating, concrete steps in a safe and gentle manner onto the Interstate of Consciousness by means of TMI Gateway programs which help conquer the fear about the dark, unknown side of ourselves. This self-exploration process is like taking a new car for a test drive onto a newly opened highway.

In the first miles of the TMI training, individuals are taught five mechanical skills which help to clear and "rev" up the energy field. Then they are shown how to exit into a "city" (called a Focus state) which is located by using highly precise, sound frequencies. This is done using specially mixed Hemi-Sync tonal patterns unique to each city. (See Chapter 7 for a theoretical description of Hemi-Sync technology.) Along with the learning exercises, an encoding process is used (the act of memorizing a symbol or a set of words as an anchoring key) to help reenter that state of consciousness without the use of Hemi-Sync sounds after the training ends. Hemi-Sync technology merely acts as training wheels to rebalance the electrical energy in the brain and the energy field, so that traveling can be achieved. Just as training wheels are a steadying device to stay balanced and focused, so does Hemi-Sync sound technology literally provide balance so that the act of driving the car (your consciousness) down the road to new cities readily becomes manageable.

While in a city, participants are guided to recognize general characteristics of that city. Inasmuch as each city is a place of focused consciousness, the name "Focus state" was given to each city and assigned a number to distinguish between cities but not to quantify them. Presently, the educational programs at TMI offer the opportunity to progressively shift consciousness into 13 different non-physical "cities" going from Focus 3 through 35 and beyond using experiential Hemi-Sync learning activities narrated by Bob Monroe and Darlene Miller, Director of Programs at TMI and other staff members. The trainers act as travel guides who facilitate an individual's own learning process. The training proceeds through the Focus States, city by city, depending on which program is being conducted. During the journey what becomes apparent is how much we don't know about ourselves, our abilities, and capacities and the way we are connected to other energetic forms. Because the consciousness is being guided into realms having non-ordinary energies, non-ordinary events and entities are going to be experienced. These are reflections of an aspect of person who is driving the consciousness to experience a particular Focus State event.

TOURING THE CITIES ALONG THE INTERSTATE (THE FOCUS STATES)

A map having many places and dimensions begins to appear as one travels this surprising, but reassuring Interstate. The waveform that I thought was Me enlarges to reveal various layers of my Self as the consciousness. Each layer seems to be another full person. By using simple Hemi-Sync sounds as triggering devices, this tool opens up a magnificent rainbow of layers within Self to be experienced as individual aspects and also as a totality. (See Figure 2c.) The layers permeate each other, yet there is a definite awareness of the key characteristic of a "city" within each layer, even "cities within cities" after one gets to be an accomplished traveler. We shall now begin touring the cities along the Interstate and look for their distinctive features and attractions.

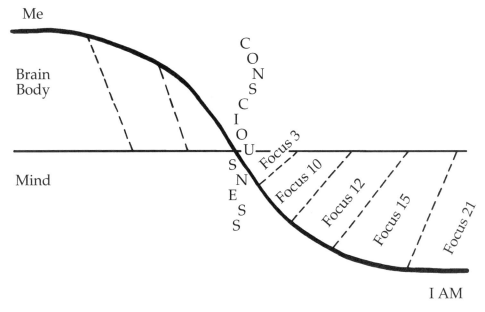

Figure 2c The Learning Cycle of Consciousness: Focus States in the Non-Physical Consciousness Layers

THE CITY WITH AN EASY ATTITUDE

Focus 3 has a simple, but sweet city atmosphere coming from its relaxed but clear-minded environment. While in this town, the mind chatter is tuned down to a mumble or is nonexistent, and the body behaves like a smoothly running engine, a purring pussycat. There is a sense of restfulness and mellowness. Clear, crystalline thinking is the key feature of this environment. In this city breathing begins to slow and muscle twitches and itches are noticed as the body releases into deeper relaxation.

FOCUS 10: THE CITY WITH UPTOWN & DOWNTOWN ATTRACTIONS

The metropolis environs of **Focus 10** has a distinct "split" flavor in the air. This comes from body memory being tuned down to nothing, so that the physical body symptoms normally associated with physical reality are operating at minimal input. At times the body seems numb or in a pseudo-paralyzed state with fingers, toes, and the area around the mouth tingling due to decreasing circulation. This relaxing/numbing feeling is present more than Focus 3's body awareness. A coolness is sometimes experienced as the body temperature drops, and the mind becomes more focused and attentive. The coolness is not necessarily felt as outside temperature changes, but as inside tissue coolness or relaxation signals. Inhaled air takes on a cooling feeling as if it were cleaner and clearer. A noticeable perceptual distinction can be experienced which is the mind perceiving in an electric, crisp manner, while the body feels increasingly heavy or non-existent. This is why this state is often called the *split state* of *mind awake and body asleep*, a key feature of Focus 10.

Sometimes, at intervals, the acute awareness of bodily functions called *hypersentience* occurs in this city. This can be experienced as the seeing of electrical flashes of dendrites communicating back and forth in the brain, hearing the swish of arterial blood flow, feeling the pores of the skin open, etc. The five human senses continue to provide accessing cues so that visual, auditory, kinesthetic experiences are common. Visual experiences tend to be very colorful in nature because the cone muscles in the retina of the eye are being stimulated in the alpha phase (See Chapter 6 for explanation of the alpha brain state) of Focus 10. These visions, similar to those experienced in dreams, have an acute clarity about them at times.

The cities of Focus 3 and 10 have interrelated characteristics.

Experiences in these cities tend to be earth-like in nature, reflecting back physical reality because they are closest to the electromagnetic wavelength of earth frequencies. This is the main attraction of both these cities, their earth-like familiarity. When using these cities for practical applications such as problem-solving, decision-making, goal-setting etc., it is beneficial to take questions or issues that are of a "here and now," everyday theme and apply them in these cities. For example, if a problem-solving approach is used for Focus 10, then questions which have to do with the nuts and bolts aspects of living are applicable for this state of consciousness. It can be said that Focus 3 and 10 are cities of a third dimensional nature; that is, they represent a perceptual experience that deals with going beyond physical matter which, in this case, is the body and physical reality. Progressively turning the body messages and memory down, then off, relieves the mind of the physicality which has a personality and a past record attached. The personality has an ego that likes to chatter thoughts about resisting the BIG adventure into the unknown. The ego of Me likes known situations. For example, mind chatter messages such as "afraid of the dark, scaredy cat" "you can't do this, silly!" "this is crazy, this is weird stuff" and "if only your Mother could see you now!" keeps the mind preoccupied with staying in physical reality. Letting go into the Hemi-Sync sounds as well as doing the Preparatory Process before phasing into Focus 3 or Focus 10 will turn off this mind chatter.

THE 'PILLSBURY DOUGH BOY' EFFECT IN THE CITY OF FOCUS 12

Using different Hemi-Sync tonal patterns, one can tune the brain and the energy field into more coherent vibration. This creates the ability to exit into the megalopolis habitat of **Focus 12**. In this city the mind becomes an intuiter, perceiving through a non-verbal, sometimes precognitive filtering system. Symbols more often than everyday images tend to be present. All-at-once knowings or intuitive flashes can occur. Grey or black and white symbolic patterns tend to predominate due to the stimulation of the rod muscles of the retina of the eye in the theta phase (see Chapter 4) of Focus 12. The human sensory system is now operating around the 20% level, meaning accessing information through the five human senses is diminished by approximately 80%. Minimal sensory flavored experiences that do appear come in compressed form. This is called *synesthesia*, a fusion of senses in which one sense evokes another. For instance, a color may talk or emit a life-like hearing ability ("colored hearing") or sounds may have associated color flashes. In other words, the senses seem crowded together rather than being discrete separate entities as in physical reality. This ability is the result of a partnership between the cortex and the limbic portion of the brain or the middle brain which is responsible for general feeling states. Neurologist Richard Cytowic in a unpublished study observed that blood flow decreases in the cortex of synesthetes and increases in the limbic area. (9) In some rare cases there are people who have synesthesia experiences in physical reality on a routine basis. Some children are inclined to report this ability, but stash it away during their growing years. In Focus 12 unusual colors beyond the spectrum of human perception are sometimes perceived. Observing the passage of time changes significantly while in this city. Whereas there was an inner thought that time was clicking away in Focus 10, time seems to fly in Focus 12. Participants vary immensely in their estimation of the passage of time during Focus 12 activities, but they come very close to approximating the passage of time in Focus 10 experiences. Humorous experiences, comedic satire, or just plain playful experiences in Focus 12 often contain metaphoric material that applies to physical reality

Overall, the best word for describing Focus 12 is "expansive" because the mind (consciousness) in this city can reach out or literally expand relative to where it wishes to be. Expanding perceptual ability is the key feature of this city. According to the intention of the perceiver, the perceptual field is often described as big and blown out. I call this the "Pillsbury Doughboy Effect" in Focus 12. It becomes especially apparent when phasing from Focus 12 to Focus 10, where there is a narrowing, condensing sensation when shifting phase to Focus 10, whereas there is a widening, expanding sensation as one phases into Focus 12. It takes a few seconds to perceive the anchoring characteristic of a particular Focus state, then it becomes apparent the field of perception has shifted. One does not go "up" or "down" when shifting consciousness, but the perceptual window and the means to perceive that window changes. In 1995-6, I conducted a Group Mind study to investigate key characteristics of Focus 12 as it is described in groups. Gateway Excursion participants were asked to define Focus 12 characteristics immediately after experiencing Focus 12 for the first time. Results from this study in Appendix A shows consistent reporting of Focus 12 characteristics by four different Gateway Excursion training classes.

Keeping in mind the key characteristic of "expansion" about Focus 12,

Monroe pointed out that a different communication system based on intuition would have to be learned in order to work with the majority of data stream input in this city and in other Focus States. For this purpose, there are two Hemi-Sync tapes, called NVC I & II, (Non-Verbal Communication) in the Wave series of the TMI "Adventure" album that center on this skill of intuiting. NVC, short for non-verbal communication, is not to be confused with physical responses without words, but rather is mind-to-mind communication. These two tapes, similar to spelling tests and word drills used in the traditional school setting, build the ability to instantaneously intuit meaning from a symbol. Deciphering language presented in dreams is similar to NVC, the meaning of which is unique to the intention of an individual.

Aligned with Monroe's effort to support the development of the meaning-making process of NVC, Ronald K. Siegel, an experimental psychologist with the Neuropsychiatric Institute at the University of California, Los Angeles, (10) has devoted a great deal of his talent to the study of hallucinations, especially among the Huichol Indians in Mexico. His research at UCLA has included studying the effect of taking mild depressants, amphetamines, psychedelics drugs, and placebos. His findings are helping to create a map of images and movement occurring during hallucinogenic events that may be clues to brain function and consciousness. Siegel has discovered there are a few basic geometric patterns that occur repeatedly in the early stages of hallucination. Some of the most common are cobwebs, lattices, spirals, tunnels, gratings and cones. Siegel described the visual effects of the psychedelic voyage as being dominated by symbols in his research subjects.

> "First, organized geometric patterns appeared. Slowly they took on blue tints and began pulsating. Thirty minutes into the voyage, lattice and tunnel forms increased significantly, along with some kaleidoscopes. When nearly two hours had passed, colors shifted to red, orange and yellow. Explosive, rotating lattice tunnels predominated, overlaid by complex images drawn from the subject's life." (11)

Siegel has found that the specific images of hallucinations can vary between persons depending on each person's store of memories and fantasies and the chemical neurotransmitters present in the brain of the individual; some may be glorious mystical visions that evoke ecstasy, while others may be frightening patterns and movements. As a general rule

Focus 12 experiences do not seem to contain a heavy overlay of emotional content coloring the input of NVC, but involve the highly symbolic representation identified in Siegel's work. Perhaps this curtailment of high emotional overlay is the result of hemispheric synchronization occurring in Focus 12, which supports a balanced, easy flow of electricity in the brain. Whereas, in drug-induced hallucinations, hemispheric synchronization is not prolonged nor evenly produced.

LEARNING TO DECIPHER NVC SYMBOLS IN FOCUS 12

To give further understanding of the symbols that appear in Focus 12, Angeles Arrien in *Signs of Life* (12) has offered a way to decipher the NVC symbols which commonly appear in Focus 12 experiences. I have adapted her approach for the Gateway Excursion so that participants can learn to recognize the meaning of symbols and the NVC events that occur in Focus 12 and other Focus states. The Arrien model is not used at TMI, but is my addition. By studying fairy tales which contain symbols across cultural lines and in various historical times, Arrien has determined that five symbols repeat themselves over and over, as if to suggest a form of language. She discovered that five universal symbols (circle, square, triangle, equidistant cross and spiral) have persisted throughout cross-cultural linguististic studies. These are also known as the Platonic Solids (the tetrahedron, the hexahedron [cube], the octahedron, the dodecahedron, and the icosahedron) in sacred geometry terms. All patterns in creation result from one or some combination of these five forms. (13)

During the Gateway Excursion I ask participants to take the Arrien Preferential Shapes Test to determine the order of the five symbols, thus identifying the current importance and meaning the symbols may have in their present life circumstances. Then they apply this source of information to their Focus 12 experiences during the Excursion. Arrien says, "The meanings attributed to the shapes describe universal aspirations, needs, and fears; each shape symbolizes a specific inner and outer experience relevant to humankind." (14) To better demonstrate how practical this information is relevant to understanding symbolic communication, the symbols each contain energetic potentials. To identify current symbol preference, Arrien suggests drawing the shapes listed in order of preference and labeling the order, one through five — one being the most preferred and five being the least preferred. She gives directions in her book for determining the meaning of the symbols relative to their order of importance and how to specifically apply them to aspirations, resources, needs, and fears evident in everyday life. Her book is an excellent educational tool in itself as it is illustrated to teach the impact of symbols through various pictures of commonly known environments, architectural sites, and artifacts. For the purpose of applying this information to Focus 12 experiences, the following explanation of the five universal symbols is offered. (See Figure 3.) However, it is highly recommended that Arrien's book be used to gain an in-depth understanding of the symbols and their pervasive impact on our lives both in physical and non-physical realities.

Figure 3 Energy Language System: The Five Universal Symbols

The **CIRCLE** represents *wholeness* and the experience of unity, the pulling together of a multitude of experiences, the gestaltic totality. When people are engaged in a search for wholeness they strive for independence, internal cohesion and personal integration. They seek space or room to find and establish themselves in order to develop their own unique identity; thus, they don't want to be captured or trapped in a situation that will limit their growth. People who have reappearing circles such as bubbles or wheels in physical and non-physical reality may have fears related to the opposite of wholeness which is the fear of being broken into segments or losing parts.

The **SPIRAL** is the symbol for *growth and evolution*, of returning over and over to the same point, but at a different level of awareness and skill. Those finding the spiral meaningful in their lives have a strong need for novelty and newness. Consequently, they often resist routines and rituals. While they are capable of doing many projects, they might have some difficulty following through or completing them due to their inevitable need for change.

The **SQUARE** represents *security, solidity, and stabilization*. Drawing out a square signifies the process of constructing a base or a grounding foundation. Persons drawn to the square are builders and implementers, for they like to achieve concrete results. Having a strong need for accountability, responsibility and closure, they desire results and consistency. Their overriding fear that stops or inhibits partnership with this energetic form is that the project or relationship they are involved in will not achieve results, and their efforts will be a waste of time and talent.

The **TRIANGLE** is known to be related to pyramids, arrowheads, and sacred mountains and represents *discovery and revelation, goals, dreams, and visions*. People who are attracted to triangles are focused on developing and achieving goals and objectives and are inspired by triangular forms. These people are usually known as visionaries, whose greatest asset is the ability to follow their dreams. This could become their downfall for when taken to the extreme, they could become so involved in their dreams that they accomplish nothing day-to-day.

The **EQUIDISTANT CROSS** or the plus sign symbolizes *relationship and integration* which involves the skills of coupling, conceptualizing, synthesizing, integrating and balancing. These people need a connection to a group, another person or to themselves. People who are attracted to the equidistant cross will prefer quality over quantity in relationships and/or projects. They love collaborative work as opposed to competitive work environments. Their underlying fear is the fear of abandonment, isolation or the loss of connectedness which is sometimes experienced as two "arms" of the cross shorter than the other two.

Not only do these symbols frequently appear as NVC in Focus 12 and other expanded Focus state experiences, but also in physical reality. Over and over, people tend to doodle certain shapes. They repeat this attraction by being drawn to the same symbol on tee-shirts or other clothing. They choose particular houses incorporating their favorite symbols, buy products or services based on certain company logos, or they design business cards, company stationery, or commercials all reinforcing a particular meaning-making symbolic process.

In 1988 a friend of mine sat next to a little old lady on an airplane. In the middle of their conversation, hours after takeoff, she opened her purse and took out three index cards and handed them to my friend with these instructions. "These are for you. You are to meditate once a day on these symbols keeping your mind free of other things." On the cards was drawn the equidistant cross, the triangle, and the circle with a small circle within. My friend thought this was an interesting challenge so she tried this for a short time and found she was unable to stay with the process of using the cards. One day she showed me the cards and as she did this, I felt my now familiar body shivers breaking out all over. This signified to me that I was to use the symbols, which I did on a daily basis. When I meditated while looking at them, I found the symbol soon began to recede, then pulsate and spin. I sat in silence for weeks working with them allowing whatever intelligent tidbits to come to me. Eventually I was inspired to use Focus 12 while meditating with each symbol and began to receive specific information. Later on I had a dream about being in Egypt and received information through the use of an instrument. This device, resembling a key, was placed against my third eye while several people toned and overtoned sounds. The key looked like the combination of two symbols put together — or the circle and the cross. Later on, I discovered this was the ankh (the crux ansata) which represents regeneration of life on the physical level, or eternal life through the immortality of the soul.

THE SYMBOL OF THE SNAIL AS A PHYSICAL REALITY MESSENGER

Another event involving a living, breathing symbol happened during a turning point in my life. I took a walk in the Cleveland Metroparks with my partner, Brad. It had rained so the trail was still wet and slippery. Not really paying attention, I almost crushed a brown snail squiggling on the trail with my right foot. The snail was moving toward a busy road winding through the parks. Brad picked up the snail and put it on the other side of the road so it could continue on its way into the woods. My curiosity antennae went up. We talked about what information this messenger was bringing. The snail was moving toward the right of me, which is toward the future. (See Figure 22, Chapter 9, Window of Opportunity exercise.) I noticed it was my right foot that almost killed the little critter. The right side also has to do with physical, masculine acts. That was all we could make of this encounter so we continued our walk. Just minutes later the exact same thing coincidentally happened again, but with a different snail on a different place on the trail. This time I picked up the snail, walked it across the road and placed it deep in the forest. Needless to say, this really got my attention. Brad began quizzing me again, "So what does the snail mean to you?" The first thing that came out of my mouth was that the snail carries its home on its back. When I said that out loud I heard an internal, inaudible "click" and felt shivers again. This was the message of the snail, symbol of the spiral representing growth and change. I had been dealing with a lot of sadness about selling the family home, a symbol of my traditional child-raising years ending. A year on the market and the home wasn't selling. I didn't know it then but I was still hanging onto the home, not wishing to leave all that it represented, stopping any change that might occur with the sale of the house. Consciously I wanted to sell the house, but unconsciously there was unfinished business that kept me hanging onto the house. Thanks to the snail, I decided at that moment to work on my willingness to become my Home, to be at home wherever my 24th relocation landed me next and not to look back. The home sold within a month!

Thus, it is important to become mindful of symbolic communication in both waking and non-waking life, for these are pieces of NVC information able to be translated by the older part of the brain, the mammalian, rather than the language-related function which provides a more fundamental way of viewing the world. Once this meaning-making process of using symbols starts, there is something quite beautiful and centering about trusting the NVC symbols as a key component in the communication process. This is part of the sage characteristic of the Force or consciousness.

SOUND GENERATED SYMBOLS

The work of Dr. Hans Jenny (15) adds further understanding to the importance of symbols as means of communication when they appear in

Focus 12, and other non-physical states of consciousness. He studied the use of the human voice as it transmits energy in the form of symbols. Using a one-sided frame drum having a thin upper membrane covered with sand, he asked a person to tone a vowel such as an "A." Within seconds the sand moved into a mandala form, repeatedly showing the same mandala symbol on successive sessions with the intoned "A." If the vowel changed, the mandala-like form changed. Specific sounds or combinations of sounds always produced specific patterns or combinations of patterns. This pattern-making process using sound as a stimulus was predictable and could be repeated with the same results. It seems apparent that the human voice is a messenger for symbols which are transmissions of energetic forms. As we begin to understand energy transmissions enfolded in sound, we will give more importance to a larger communicative process taking place. Our primitive Morse code manner of talking and making sense of what we are saying to each other will significantly change because we will become more conscious of what we are transmitting and receiving.

THE DAISY AS A PERSONAL ROTE

For years, during long conversations on the phone, in long lectures at school or at conferences, or waiting for the doctor, I'd find myself drawing, of all things — daisies! At times I couldn't stop myself. As if magnetically conditioned, my fingers would habitually trace the daisy over and over. In 1979, while in the Adirondacks, I found a clue concerning the reason I was unconsciously drawing this particular symbol. During a week long workshop on group facilitation, the trainer asked us to make an Indian shield to identify what gifts we had as facilitators. This shield was to be made of materials that were laid out on a long table. Piles of posterboard paper, scissors, crepe paper, glitter, foil paper, yarn, glue, cellophane, and magazines beckoned to be conquered and pasted onto our shields. In silence, each of us meditated on what was to be portrayed on our shields, then we spent the better portion of the day in silence assembling works of art. After meditating, I looked at the table filled with artistic possibilities and found, much to my surprise, noisy agitation growing inside in the area of my solar plexus. Walking over to my log cabin, I sat on the bed and noticed my tumultuous feelings were disappearing. Then, for some odd reason, I reached under my bed for a cache of dried flowers I had been storing away and brought them back to the workshop. My eyes checked out the glitzy Hollywood-looking shields that were being made. Guilt gleamed back at me as I played with the shriveled, wild plants in my hands.

Normally I would develop a Grand Plan to sort out my ideas. Then I would put them in order, think through the color scheme, analyze the effects and so on, but here I was, looking at a mess of dried weeds in my hands with my head saying absolutely nothing! What in the heck was I doing with a bunch of dried weeds while everyone else was spraying, gluing, and nailing together virtual masterpieces? I just sat there mystified. Then, for the first time I can remember, I let go of my analytical way of being creative and let something else take over. The shield and I went back and forth, guiding each other into an abstract rendering of something I still don't fully understand to this day. I found myself cutting out an undulating flower form and weaving the wild, pesky weeds, dried flowers, and pressed grasses together. It turned into what looked like a kite with a woven tail that made the form very alive. The design on the outer rim of my shield looked like successive petals unfolding. What gravitated to the center was one simple, brilliant, but pristine daisy. Later on, I discovered the daisy to be the central part or the seed component of the Flower of Life symbol. (See Figure 4.) Why was this so important that I would remind myself again and again of its silent meaning?

Figure 4 Flower of Life Symbol

According to sacred geometry studies, the Flower of Life symbol, being a series of tetrahedrons (four-sided triangles) conjoined at strategic points, signifies the essential field of energy of an individual. Bob Monroe would call this particular complex signature that I was doodling a ROTE. (16) His definition of a ROTE is a "Related Organized Thought Energy, transmitted from one mind to another, a mental book or recording, complete with emotional and sensory patterns." All along it seems I was receiving a nudge from my Total Self to learn about my energy field and how to use it in a dynamic manner. Since then the daisy symbol has stimulated my investigation into what the tetrahedrons stand for as a grouping of energy configurations and how these patterns within my energy field can be used. My understanding of how the light body, being a geometric field of energy, has grown considerably. This simple little symbol embodied in real life flowers has helped me gain insights into how each of us in our energetic cocoons link and communicate with all other fields of energy.

Let's take this a few steps further than Monroe's initial statement. Essentially, we are fields of energy, one of which is the denser physical body field, yet we have been acting as if we are only one of those layers which possesses a single life that begins and ends on this planet. In the Adirondack woods, I began to remember the essence of me, who I was, the core essence, and those insights, in part, were revealed through the process of making and gradually learning to see the larger meaning of my Indian shield. This symbolic receiving and transmitting process propelled me to search for more answers about who I was. Growing up I had been told I was of Italian-Irish heritage, intelligent, creative, and people-oriented, but this didn't seem to get to the bottom of the questions I uncovered in my childhood spinning days.

Symbols are part of a communication process which transmits imagery and information using the brain and the body's ability to process that imagery. Where Siegel identified the main symbols used by the brain to process experience in some non-physical realities, Joseph Chilton Pearce in *Magical Child Matures* described the general areas of the brain where activation occurs that determine the representation of the imagery received. The waking state activates the old reptilian brain which sits on top of the spinal column; the dreaming state uses the limbic or old mammalian brain located in the middle of the brain; and the deep sleep state activates the neocortex or new brain area. He says that explicate (explainable, unfolded, outside) order regarding imagery comes from physical reality. Implicate (implied, enfolded) order comes from the dream state and potential order comes from the causal or deep sleep state. Pearce goes on to say:

"Yogic psychology considered the state of deep sleep the causal process, which relates to the new brain. They referred to our dream state as our subtle system, which relates to our midbrain, and our waking state as our physical process, which we have found translates through the old brain. The new brain uses geometric patterns such as cone, grid, snowflake, cobweb, and so on, infinitely variable within their sets and capable of endless syntheses between classes of pattern. These are precursors to all other types of imagery. The images of movement and light or dark contrasts of our old brain, and the fluid, colorful images of our dreaming brain, are composed out of those geometric families of the new brain." (17)

THE CITY OF NO-TIME

The place called **Focus 15** could easily be called a suburb of heaven for it is a city of mellow peace and exquisite unconditional love. For some this is experienced as enfolding nothingness. The characteristic feature is that it is a timeless place containing quantum or large groups of information rather than detailed bits. Information about other places, people, elements in different times other than the present can be accessed in Focus 15 and sometimes will be transmitted in quantum, gestaltic forms. Movement in Focus 15 becomes instantaneous and is achieved by learning how to *will* oneself to move about this city. Sometimes, this is accomplished by feeling an intention centered in the solar plexus and willing that intention to outpicture or manifest itself. At other times, the throat center or the third eye can be used as a place of activation. Just as one learns to drive a car as a teenager, it takes practice to use will as a steering wheel or transporting tool. This was demonstrated in the popular movie *Ghost* by the lead character played by Patrick Swayze who, in a subway scene, learned how to move a soda pop can using the energy produced by his will center. He later used this skill to tell his fiance, played by Demi Moore, that she was being pursued by a killer. Isn't it interesting that the concept of will is being taught vicariously to the viewing public? There are many other examples of will skill-building being amply described for the general public. (See Chapter 8 on Steven Spielberg, Gene Roddenberry, and Carlos Castaneda.)

While the city of Focus 12 is a place of early timelessness where things flow easily and effortlessly in peaks and valleys, Focus 15 is a pure, smooth state of timelessness having very little ebbs and flows, where time does not exist as a measurement of experience. During Focus 12 and 15, body temperature fluctuations occur. This is evidence of the pulsating, changing nature of the waveform. The alternate cooling and warmth is not necessarily annoying although sometimes it is helpful to keep a blanket handy. In Focus 12, a beginning experience of intuitional information processing appears where one begins to learn how to intuit from feeling-based data, from a sensing of how things are and could be in a larger universe. During the experience of Focus 12 or 15, if one taps into logical, analytical Left Brain activity, most likely a down phasing to Focus 10 will occur. This will be evident because the unique characteristics of Focus 10 usually reappear. Therefore, it is better to use the Right Brain to access material in the cities of Focus 12 and 15, and to use the Left Brain after travel is finished to analyze and sort out the material. In Focus 15, intuitional experiences become very strong and usually contain very little emotional charge. In fact, people have loudly complained about the "nothingness" aspect of this state of consciousness. This could be their projection returning to them concerning what it is like to experience that degree of energetic balance or coherency. In Focus 12 and 15, the experience of the fourth dimension of Self is a perceptual backdrop with intuition being a key process for experiences. One of the main attractions in these two cities is learning how to use the will to manifest experiences.

THE SPACIOUS CITY OF FOCUS 21

The inner city of **Focus 21** lies at the edge of this universe; it's the stepping stone into the cosmos. Monroe called it the "Edge of Here & Now" to emphasize its unique qualities. Here the mind is crystal-clear and the body is detached, meaning totally compliant with what the mind is perceiving. Hardly a twitch or itch will be felt. If present, these are perceived deeply beneath the focus of the mind. The mind is the consciousness following the cosmic mind's knowledge of what is right to experience at that time. There is an overriding feeling of selflessness and connectedness here called" non-locality," perhaps because the constraints of space in the form of gravitational pressures have fallen away. Often an enfolding whiteness dominates perception while knowings flow. Whereas in Focus 15 there is a sensation of individual self having a beginning and ending, in Focus 21, this awareness is beginning to disappear because Focus 21 is the end of the time-space continuum as we know it. The day before his death, physicist David Bohm emphasized that the principle of non-locality is a more important than he formerly thought. "Space is merely an idea we have abstracted from a wavelike whole," Bohm said. "It is the brain that creates the illusion of location." (18)

ON EASY STREET: ESTABLISHING KNOWNS IN FOCUS 21

In the city of Focus 21, using the will through intention becomes a necessary skill as a mode of transportation. The illusion of location is gone in Focus 21, the place of no space as well as no time. Think about it. I, in a non-local universe, have no home address and no time. Space and time in this city are inseparable. Therefore, travel is instantaneous; space is relative. Thus, the intention of the traveler will be acutely projected into what is experienced according to what the will wills. Wide open questions, the "big Kahuna" questions, can be asked in this state, such as questions about creation, about the universe, the cosmos, the soul extension, the soul, the oversoul (the soul group), and the source of all. What becomes intriguing is to ask questions in Focus 21 about personal origins, essence qualities, life purpose, and methods for achieving that purpose. When experiencing this city of no-space, no-time, keep in mind that beliefs and personal philosophy will be most certainly challenged.

Personally speaking, in Focus 21, intuitions have become vivid Knowings. These are pure all-at-once insights, having no reason, logic or method behind them. An indicator that a Known has been created is that they carry no emotional charge in their message. A Known will pop in, seem very simple, and perfect for the experience at hand. One can miss a Known in its pristine clothing, for we have long learned to search for entertaining, stand-out, dramatic answers to our most mystifying questions. If it is too easy or appears too simple, then we automatically reject the experience. When a Focus 21 answer comes, it most often arrives through pure awareness or quantum wholes. So be prepared to ingest these, to consume them in their totality. If looking for form, *the form of knowing is often formless* in the city of Focus 21. One could miss the all-at-once simple signature of a Known or an experience in Focus 21 because it is stripped of its matter, space and time constraints.

LIVING LIFE BETWEEN LIVES IN FOCUS 22-26

The cities of **Focus 22-26** are places of transformational energies, habitats that help process the changes that occur during crisis or momentous life events. Focus 22 is a place of awareness where individuals who are in comatose or partially separated physical reality (catatonia, delirium, dementia, toxic alcoholism etc.) exist. As a psychiatric nurse in an acute healthcare setting, I experienced very curious events with patients diagnosed as "split from reality." I used my Focus state abilities to communicate with them by entering Focus 22 offering them a grounding means to reconnect with physical reality. Clearly, I knew their thoughts in this state. Some chose to accept help, some stayed disconnected. Focus 23 is the residence of those who through traumatic or other circumstances, be it suicide, sudden death, or man-made disasters, are existing in a in-between realm. They haven't been able to move on from this planet. Soul retrieval or the experience of assisting those in this locale to move on is accomplished in this city with the help of a guide. Travelers who access Focus 23 and become a part of the soul retrieval process also experience a similar transformation, a retrieval of lost parts of themselves. Monroe calls the cities of Focus 24-26, "Belief System Territories," — places where non-physical lifeforms reside who are existing within encultured philosophies and religious ideas. Included in this area are individuals from all regions, histories and cultures.

PARK PLACE: THE CITY OF FOCUS 27

The city of **Focus 27** has an earth-like resemblance, taking the form of a resting place designed for those lifeforms who have just experienced physical death. It is a consensus reality created by groups of lifeforms to provide a comforting place for synthesis, integration, and life reassignment. Known as "The Park," its environment is generally composed of beings who are counselors and advisors as well as close friends and relatives of the one being received. These friendly ones support and give comfort to the newcomer. Two to three days before death of the physical body occurs, the dying person may periodically show signs of being in Focus 27 when they describe seeing and/or talking with deceased friends and relatives who are part of their transitioning process. Their conversations may contain a sense of peaceful resignation, a sign of knowing what's beyond in Focus 27. Generally, this city has characteristics similar to a place of rest and recuperation, but the specific features of Focus 27 are highly representative of the unique desires of the traveler.

THE CITIES FOR GROUP REUNIONS: THE GATHERING PLACES

The cities of **Focus 34 & 35** are mentioned in Monroe's book, *Far Journeys*, as the place of "The Gathering," where very intelligent beings reside in parallel universes. People who have experienced this state of consciousness remark about the unpolarized quality of interactions, i.e., the lack of negative or positive value being present. In these states of consciousness, the beings communicate in a manner indicating a strong unconditional but firm radiance. Frequently these cities are known to be meeting places to rejoin the soul group with whom an individual has had long term association. From my perspective, a soul group is defined as a group of 12 soul extensions combining to reconfigure and actualize the essence of a soul. A soul extension is one who experiences a lifetime occupied by a soul aspect expressing itself as a unique, extended essence of God. This gives validation to the view that a person often operates from a limited soul perspective within one lifetime. Using a fictitious plot, James Redfield incorporates the non-physical soul group in his second book, *The Tenth Insight*, with physical people. He introduces the notion of reconnecting with and using the talents of the soul group while in physical reality. The last scene in the movie *Ghost* portrays the soul group helping the main character, played by Patrick Swayze, to rejoin them. Having seen this movie several times, I have noticed that the audience's reaction during this scene is quite remarkable. There is a deep, gasping silence punctuated by soft crying, perhaps indicating a collective memory being triggered in the audience about these states of consciousness and their comforting qualities.

TOURING THE NEIGHBORHOODS IN THE CITIES: DIMENSIONAL COMPONENTS OF SELF

A road map pattern begins to emerge after touring the cities along the Interstate of Consciousness. (See Figure 5.) While each of the Focus cities helps locate a specific field of energy, the dimensions within each Focus state produce local color similar to what neighborhoods accomplish for cities. Just as each of the boroughs of New York City create a distinctive flavor in their own right, so do they contribute to New York City's flamboyant, energetic signature known as the "Big Apple." Joshua David Stone, Ph.D. says there are nine different dimensions or neighborhoods associated with our cosmic physical universe. (19) The tenth dimension and beyond reflect back consciousness beyond physicality. He goes on to say there are 24 dimensions associated with all reality and that the Planet Earth utilizes seven of those dimensions on this planet. Presently we recognize and use three of the nine earth-related dimensions. In our third dimensional mentality, according to Dr. Stone, "We have identified with form rather than with essence. We have identified ourselves with temporal time rather than with eternity. We have identified ourselves with the visible rather than with the invisible. We have been living in a negative hypnosis." (20)

Focus States	Dimension	Key Process
Focus 27 & Beyond	7	Being
Focus 22-27 Transcending Death (Change)	6	Transformation
Focus 21 Transcending Space	5	Knowing
Focus 12 & 15 Transcending Time	4	Intuition
Focus 3 & 10 Transcending Matter	3	Reasoning

Figure 5 The M Field Road Map: Focus 3 to 27 & Beyond

Keeping this bigger picture of the 24 dimensions in mind, it is possible to discern a consciousness pattern incorporating these dimensions as components within each Focus city. I propose that each Focus city has an overriding dimension, but that it also has other dimensional aspects within it. To illustrate, if one strikes the "A" note on a piano, this note is made of various tones resonating to create the sound of "A." The resonating tones are the various dimensions of the A note. The following road map describes the main dimensional themes of the Focus cities. Every journey through the

Focus States into non-physical reality decreases the perception of time, space, and physical matter defining characteristics we know as physical reality. Gradually, a step-by-step transcendence occurs. Physical reality is replaced by another separate reality.

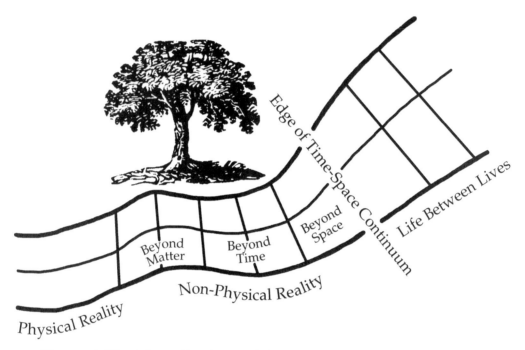

Figure 6 The Three Regions of the Interstate of Consciousness

THE THREE REGIONS OF THE INTERSTATE

As my own travel progressed along the Interstate of Consciousness, I discovered there was a widening ladder of perception that became evident as I journeyed through the Focus states. (See Figure 6.) In hindsight, when looking at my experiences and those of my clients, it was fairly easy to see this process as an unfolding roadway revealing multidimensional and expanded components of a Self. Three distinctly different regions made themselves apparent once I consciously experienced the bigger picture. These are *physical reality*, *non-physical reality*, and a period which many call *life between lives*. Inasmuch as the continuum of life to travelers may seem to separate itself into three different kinds of life experiences, this could be due to our preference for using linear explanations. Admittedly, I am illustrating these regions in the same manner to offer a possible way to conceive of the unfolding layers of multidimensionality according to familiar understanding, but I intuitively know this isn't as linear as it looks. Given this caveat, let's explore the various stages of dimensionality within these regions.

Each region has several learning approaches which seem to be more beneficial than others. In the waking state, the process of reasoning is the main approach to experiencing life. In the non-waking states, the processes of intuition and higher knowing prevail, and in the period of life between lives, the processes of transformation and beingness are commonly used. (See Figure 7.)

Within each region are various states of consciousness representing the progression of consciousness to experience itself. Monroe originally called these areas of focused perception "locales" because the consciousness literally dials to a certain frequency domain associated with each state of consciousness. To experience an array of locales is to experience one's own multidimensionality. Within each Focus State various dimensional experiences can be possible. These contribute to a somewhat predictable cycle of spiritual development for an individual.

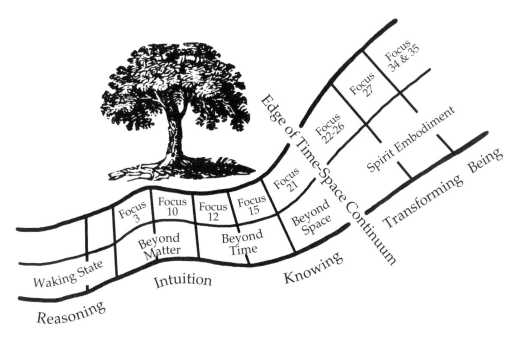

Figure 7 The Key Learning Processes in the Regions of the Interstate

VISITING DIFFERENT NEIGHBORHOODS IN A FOCUS CITY

To explain what I have experienced as different dimensional stages of spiritual development on the Interstate, I will use the element of time as a teacher. I'll describe how time is commonly perceived through these stages. The process is similar to the hands of time changing the face of the watch. It literally looks different as time passes or as travel proceeds through the Focus States. Please remember that this is just a proposed way of understanding how the dimensions in the various Focus States reflect or mirror back spiritual development. This not meant to be an upward journey, rather it is cyclic in nature as I have experienced it as well as clients and participants in workshops. The map is meant to be a temporary model, one to use as a transitional guidepost which could well evolve into another temporary model as we explore the Interstate.

Imagine a person listening to a radio program. If she moves the knob of the radio dial, the reception will change. That changing perception is what is possible in a Focus state city. By using the Hemi-Sync tonal patterns as a tuning device, the reception of different dimensional levels can result. A *dimension* is a means by which perception can be examined and measured for the magnitude or degree of its energetic density. Thoughts are things. As we develop intention (inner, purposeful thought), our thoughts merge with the subtle energies of the non-physical environment and restructure it according to fundamental rules. William Buhlman has described four principles which illustrate the nature of the interaction between thought and energy. This is explained in detail in his excellent book, *Adventures Beyond the Body*. These basic principles lay a foundation for understanding how energy works — the energy of you and the energy of the object of your interaction.

1. Thought is a form of energy.
2. Focused thought possesses the innate ability to influence, restructure, and ultimately mold energy.
3. The less dense the energy structure or environment, the faster the restructuring may occur.
4. The effectiveness and speed with which thought-energy restructures an energy environment are determined by the intensity of the thought and the density of the energy upon which it is acting. (21)

Thought-energy interaction produces various kinds of energy environments or dimensions within an experience. The dimensional variations can be described as neighborhoods within cities. (See Figure 8.)

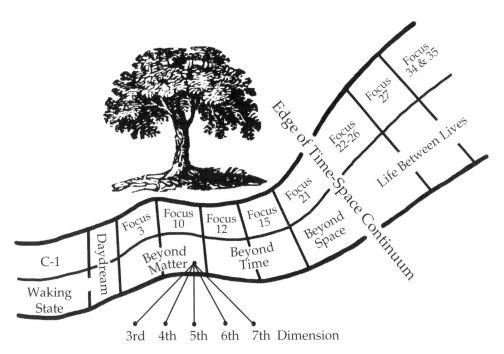

**Figure 8 Dimensional Locales of the Interstate:
Neighborhoods in the Cities**

Every Focus city has numerous neighborhoods, each possessing a different density or degree of coherence which defines the connections between homeowners. Picture an urban neighborhood in everyday reality. It might be one where there is a neighborhood watch association, planned social events, and community covenants to follow. This would be a densely compacted, very physically connected, three dimensional neighborhood. Visualize another neighborhood, one located on a sprawling, arid mountainside. Each family group lives on several areas. Each prefers to be a community unto itself. There are no overt rules, parties, nor neighborhood associations; in fact, there are no formal group connections in evidence. For examples sake, this rural neighborhood would be similar to a fifth dimensional neighborhood environment. Being a rural or an urban neighborhood would be similar to being connected with a particular Focus city.

I lived in Cleveland, Ohio for many years. One day while reading a two-page newspaper ad in the *Cleveland Plain Dealer,* I was amazed to find out that Cleveland was home to over 100 suburbs. Each of these suburbs has developed unique characteristics, little cities within the larger city. Going from one suburb to another was not difficult to distinguish as the homes, businesses, and people within one suburb made it their business to proudly advertise a unique environment and lifestyle separate from neighboring suburbs. For instance, the experience of buying things in the suburb of Parma, strictly a blue-collar factory environment that birthed the setting for the popular TV sitcom, *The Drew Carey Show*, was very different from shopping in Solon a few miles down the road, a community full of transient, hi-tech career professionals. Parma's roads have a boxy, tight scale layout whereas Solon's streets are wider and less crowded featuring large storefronts. These suburbs/neighborhoods define the distinctive features of Cleveland and represent its dimensional aspects. So too, the neighborhoods within a Focus State portray various degrees of energetic density being expressed in a particular Focus State.

In order to explain how this would apply in the abstract world of consciousness, I am going to single out third, fourth and fifth dimensional pictures of reality and use these dimensions coupled with the element of **time** so that the concept of dimensionality will become clear. Examples will be given to show how time displays various degrees of mass (density) from the most solid to the most unsubstantial. While reading these descriptions, notice how a particular "thought" in a city restructures the environment to mirror back what is being thought about relative to different dimensions of time in the Focus States. Various neighborhoods will emerge distinctly different in each Focus State city. Each city has the potential to contain nine dimensional environments. For the sake of simplicity, only third, fourth, and fifth dimensional characteristics will be described. For learning purposes, the general characteristics of three dimensions making the most impact on present time will be discussed, then specific neighborhood descriptions as the density factor changes will follow.

The **third dimensional (3D) neighborhood perspective** is an I/It relationship. I and time are separate and dependent on each other. This is similar to the relationship portrayed between Archie and Edith Bunker, plants and water, and the sky and clouds.

The neighborhood that takes a **fourth dimensional (4D) neighborhood perspective** is one where there is a you/I independent relationship demonstrated by Prince Charles and Princess Di, the Republican and Democratic parties, and oil and water.

The **fifth dimensional (5D) neighborhood perspective** is an I/thou relationship or an interdependent relationship such as Jimmy and Rosalyn Carter, the community of Findhorn, Scotland, and an employee-owned company. Now let's look at the cycles of spiritual development with time as viewed by human consciousness. This will show when consciousness focuses on a particular dimension of the invention we call "time." It then demonstrates specific dynamic changes in density which projects out into a picture of reality.

VISITING 3D, 4D & 5D NEIGHBORHOODS

In the early 3D stage of spiritual development, our neighbor, Mr. Time, seems to be against us; he picks fights, controls us, seems separate and outside our domain, ticking aimlessly away. When he gets rowdy and out of control, we call the police and admit he is greatly affecting our lives. In this neighborhood where fences separate the yards, time seems like an outside element that twists days into months and moments into hours. This happens because we choose to see time as a physical entity controlling and pulling us forward. The saying "There's not enough time in the day!" would be a 3D picture of reality with outside elements appearing to control individuals. People adjust their pictures of reality according to what the ticking hands say on their watch — it's time to get up, it's time to eat, to have a meeting, to get a raise, to run a marathon, to make love. This tight, dense perspective has to do with perceived rigid connections to outside authority in all forms whether it be governmental, religious, or family influences. Fear and survival are the basis for actions in this state. As for that fencing between the houses, while it keeps things orderly, this advertises a need to project an artificial outside authority in order to limit and predict the passage of energy.

In mid-to-late 3D states of spiritual development, partnering with dense energy is attempted. This is typified by the change many of us made when we switched from analog to digital watches. This is where individuals begin to take responsibility for their internal thoughts, so they monitor their behaviors, not necessarily watching the minutes tick by but what *makes* the minutes go by. This takes the form of furious time management actions such as tracking everything they do in daily planners, making computerized reminders for sales calls, car pooling, annuity purchases etc., and plotting the most efficient and effective way, time, and place to have children. Perceived with pressure, or less dense mass, the energy of time here is experienced as a valuable resource, a commodity to be weighed, spent or lost. People living in this kind of neighborhood would have invisible sonic fences, to be less physically intrusive and more internally sensitive.

Signs of early 4D would be to attempt a more active and fluid partnership with time, such as becoming aware and making effective use of body circadian rhythms; i.e., identifying 'owl' or 'lark' behavior or sensing the right time to do a project or to ask for a raise. Fourth dimensional behavior takes the form of developing more trust in one's own intuitional urges from the gut, by sensing the willingness and/or readiness of people, resources, environments, and by tracking trends and patterns as if there is an inner clock ticking inside. This comes from the perspective that time as a neighbor is intriguing, maybe somewhat eccentric, but still interesting. A later 4D stage perspective makes use of feelings as an important and valued source of data by accessing this source first, then checking with common sense and logic regarding the timing of things to be said, done, or known. Mr. Time is now considered a neighborhood ally who will come as needed. Generally Mr. Time seems to fly in this stage. A guiding belief here is a trust that time will make itself known when it is proper and right.

Early 5D stage experience relative to time involves an inner sensing, a knowing having no emotional charge. In this neighborhood, Mr. Time is treated like an old, time honored and cherished friend. There is a flowing of the knowing — when, where, what, and how to proceed. That's the key. Time seems to be non-existent — absolutely no clicking, ticking reminders. In this stage, there is enough multileveled experience of all of the I/I (3D), you/I (4D), I/thou (5D) neighborhoods to know that time is a many splendored element depending on the density perspective of the beholder. Experiencing these various communities of time along the Interstate gave me the understanding that as an individual, I was no longer a creature of earth but of a much larger place contained within myself.

Because Focus 15 and 21 are states of timelessness, there is great potential for acquiring a new D/O about time as one experiences this element in the various neighborhoods of these cities. In these states various past time periods could be investigated from this present-day time period. For instance, a particular historical event could be researched in Focus 15 to gain more information and understanding.

At the beginning of the Gateway Voyage Residential Program at TMI, participants are asked to remove their watches and put them into a basket for safe-keeping until the program is completed. This, in part, symbolizes the temporary removal of physical reality and its heavy dense dimensional characteristics. Needless to say, this has become a TMI signature learning event for many people who attend a Residential Program there.

THE CYCLES OF SPIRITUAL DEVELOPMENT:
INTERDIMENSIONAL STAGES

Now that Mr. Time has given us his point of view as one aspect of our universe, we can now consider the general picture of the possibilities of consciousness by exploring the concept of being multidimensional beings. Multidimensionality is the idea that we, with our different subselves — brain states, Focus cities, and dimensional neighborhoods — live in and with our different dimensional aspects much as a chameleon can change colors on a moment's notice. Our multihued abilities stem from each of us carrying, as Barbara Marx Hubbard says, "a synthesis of elements that make up the Earth and our bodies. From hydrogen and helium atoms, collapsing in the crucible of burning stars, the minerals and metals in our bodies were formed four billion years ago. We are the living products of that design innovation." (22) The following is an explanation of the various stages of interdimensional development from a broad dimensional perspective having a spiritual consciousness theme.

This model is the background for the previous discussion on dimensions as it relates to the element of time and is meant to be seen as cyclic and generative in nature. Some of the content is channeled information gathered by ZaviRah and Zavirah, (23) to whom I am grateful. (See Figure 9.)

ACQUIRING FULL CONSCIOUSNESS THROUGH THE
CYCLE OF INTERDIMENSIONALITY

First and second dimensional humans lived on this planet eons ago. We humans evolved in a neutral manner as 1D beings having cellular lifeform in a civilization known as Pangea. As we matured we acquired second dimensional aspects, purely feminine ways of living as gatherers, not hunters, receiving the earth's nourishment to grow the physical body and mature its basic instinctual drives housed in the reptilian brain sitting atop the spinal column. At that time, the mind had intuitive skills as evidenced by a large pineal gland linked to the pituitary gland thus creating a very evident bulge in the third eye area and a protruding forehead. Humans, known as Lemurians during the reptilian age, were generally blind. They used their third eye to perceive and communicate telepathically and their forebrain to project their consciousness forward, rather than being preoccupied with past actions as we now are. In our present day 3D state, we are mastering the use of reason, having developed physically quite well from our Lemurian and later Atlantean ancestors. To do this, we unwired the third eye capabilities and learned to see using the optic nerve. The 3D human can be said to have originated with the discovery of Lucy (the remains of a female hominid) in Ethiopia, when the brain cavity enlarged to incorporate the newly emerging cortex containing the rudiments of reasoning ability.

	Third	Fourth	Fifth
Belief	You, The Enemy	I, The Creator	I/Thou, Co-Creator
Locus of Control	Outer Directed	Inner Directed	Inner & Outer Directed
Decisions	Reactive Facts	Proactive Sensed Data	Creative No Emotional Charge
	Competition Judgement	Cooperation Intuiting, Knowns	Collaboration Discernment
Relationships	A-Shaped Dependent	H-Shaped Independent	M-Shaped Interdependent
Dreamwork	Minimal Recall Vague Dreaming Vivid Dreaming	Lucid Dreams Conscious Control of Assemblage Point	OBEs Remote Viewing Bilocation
Time	Controls Me Separate Resource	Peaks & Valleys Partnership	Smooth, No-Time Time Skips
Space	Out There Not In Body Voice Disownership	Personal Space Space Management	Fluid, No-Space Will-to-Good
Matter	Solitary Body Attachment	Solitary Mind Detachment	Oneness Unattachment

Figure 9 Differentiating 3rd, 4th & 5th Dimensions

THE DEVELOPMENT OF THE 3D HUMAN

The 3D human advanced through the Middle Ages, the Industrial Revolution, and now exists in the Age of Information, still mastering the use of the cortex. Today, at the peak of logical left brain skill development, we are beginning to explore the nature of our overall mental capabilities. To this end, Congress dedicated the '90s as the "Decade of the Brain" in order to provide more resources to achieve this goal. The mental mind is now considered of equal value when compared to the wheel, fire, metal, gold, and money — the driving symbols of our 3D lives. Enchanted by the glorification of brain power skills, we now have become gods unto ourselves with the result that life is viewed as having an enemy in some form, where there are victims and victimizers, top dogs and underdogs, haves and have-nots. We have come to believe that we have to exert an immense amount of physical effort and struggle in order to achieve success. Success is usually enjoyed after accumulating many material things, the modern day red badges of courage. Consumerism, our reality sound bite, is the main menu of the workplace, the family, the marriage, and recreational activities. Relationships centered in a 3D stage tend to be dependent, tightly bonded, symbiotically entwined situations where if conflict presents itself, the couple will have identity crises and competitive, confrontational strategies will be used. Generally, minimal recall of dreams or no dreaming is often reported in the early 3D stage.

In the middle of the 3D stage, we begin to see thoughts as powerful tools; thus, we explore our belief systems and try to manipulate them to control reality. At this point people start to pay more attention to their dreams. Dream recall increases and with that reports of vague, fragmented dreaming episodes are usually common. Time from a 3D perspective controls us because we see it as a separate entity, another enemy. Space is experienced in a rudimentary form, having pseudo-dimensional qualities. In fact, many of us have a hard time living inside our bodies, even accepting our own voices or faces on driver's licenses and in family photos and video tapes. Space is felt to be a gravitational force infringing upon us, keeping things in place — again another outside entity. Only matter that lives, moves, breathes, and above all, thinks, is considered real life-containing matter, and it rates mattering about. This provides clues as to reason the abortion issue has kept our attention for so long. Only recently did the notion of our planet, Gaia, come to be considered as life-containing matter. In 3D, God has been destroyed because God, not being of matter, can't matter.

THE DEVELOPMENT OF THE 4D HUMAN

In our 4D Self now emerging in the human collective, we begin to learn about the non-physical parts of ourselves so the dreaming self, the inspirational/creative self, the out-of-body self begins to look attractive. This "less dense" approach to life frees one to give consideration to other forms of matter — the non-physical components. Could this explain why the 30 year-old *Star Trek* programs which celebrate other forms of life continue to gain in popularity?

In 4D a tweaking of intuitional awareness begins to become helpful and stimulating. For instance, intuitional gut feelings are used to help make decisions, and dreaming plots that offer solutions to life's challenges are valued. The power of being vulnerable, more open, becomes more apparent and usable. Puritan work ethics cease, and less struggle, more simplicity begins to be valued. The notion of responsibility for self, family, and country changes from dependent, duty-bound roles to independent and accountable approaches. Two strong individuals vie for the prize during conflicts in independent relationships, and the outcome involves considering the good of both. No longer is the world viewed as created by a lifeless power, but is seen as something created from within. Dreamwork involves lucid dreaming where there is beginning to be a blending of physical into non-physical reality. Conscious control of the assemblage point (See Chapter 8 under Carlos Castaneda) is attempted and learned in the later phase of this dimensional stage. Time is viewed as a helpful resource, sensed in peaks and valleys. The mind is used to find the times and places to be most productive. Space is experienced as a useful commodity such as the development of mini-vans, space management in workspace and the preservation of Open Spaces.

Intuition grows by leaps and bounds, into a cognitive form having emotional value. It begins to have a transcending time/space quality. Discernment (or discrimination) is the standard of measurement in this dimension as opposed to judgment in 3D. Matter is now a matter of gradual detachment to form through metaphoric meaningful experiences. Learning is often centered on how things work and growing in a hierarchical manner by being good and reborn spiritually according to a known higher purpose for living.

THE DEVELOPMENT OF THE 5D HUMAN

In our 5D Self, interconnectedness becomes a theme, wherein all matter is believed to contain life; therefore every creature and element counts. Intermeshing diverse parts becomes a way of living. Conflict and controversy are used as opportunities to develop innovative results. Striving for balance is the key in a 5D environment. An interdependent relationship respects the individuality of all concerned and is able to blend together to create a mutual win-win solution to conflicts. The ability to observe self from the big picture perspective aids in the maturation of the emotional body, for it is used in a fluid manner instead of becoming stuck in blocked, repressed emotional patterns. Being part of a co-creative approach to life rather than treating and massaging the effects of a situation begins to take center stage. This changes the concept of death, illness, age, and love. Knowing is the standard of measurement for what is reality. Dreamwork can involve planned and spontaneous out-of-body journeys, and/or remote viewing, or bilocation experiences. In 5D, knowing is literally perceiving without emotion. One develops the ability to merge the spiritual with the mental, emotional, and physical selves to freely follow one's true inclination. Time is seen as a sensing device to know when there's a sense of no time; then peak performance and success pop in. Space allows and becomes a creative resource. Matter is now a component not a necessity nor a ruling element. Discernment skills are well-developed as a result of knowing the true self and becoming a creature of the Universe.

The idea of dimensionality can be recorded as an effort made by the logical, reasoning side of ourselves to understand how energy appears to fit itself into separate, discrete ranges of experience. However, my overall experience has taught me there is no separation, but rather a phasing or a gradual gradation between my energetic experiences. This is especially apparent as one "comes back from" the more expanded Focus states of consciousness. While I know a part of me has chosen to perceive boundaries between one state of consciousness or another in order to satisfy my questioning mind, another part of me knows all forms of consciousness are connected. It is said, "Look thee above, or look thee below, the same shall ye find, for all is but part of the Oneness that is at the Source of the law. The consciousness below thee is part thine own, as we are a part of thine." (24) As multidimensional beings of the universe, as dimensional human beings of Earth and as people at home, work and with friends, we have endless possibilities on the Interstate of Consciousness.

It looks like there is a fork in the road ahead on our journey. How to distinguish between the High Road and the Low Road on the Interstate of Consciousness is the next item on our itinerary.

EASY RIDER

Becoming me and I AM
While traveling the Interstate of Consciousness
Through the cities and the uptown and downtown neighborhoods
Using the M-field road map to go Home.

THE ROAD TO EVERYWORLD:
BALANCED CONSCIOUSNESS

Not to have eyes that catch, but to remain untangled,
unblinded, unconfused is to find balance and he who
holds balance beyond sway of love or hate, beyond
reach of profit or loss, beyond care of praise or blame,
has attained the highest post in the world.

Lao Tzu, *The Way of Life*

ROUTE 3

THE HIGH ROAD TO UNLIMITED KNOWLEDGE & FAME

"Been there, done that" has become a favorite piece of jargon to use these days. Many times I wanted to circumvent my mysterious spinning memories or forget all about them, but they kept coming back to mind highlighted by neon red question marks. It was difficult to sift through my childhood reminiscences looking for a quick fix puzzle piece that would give me a clue as to why I couldn't fully enjoy my spinning. Yet come to think of it, this obscure piece was buried beneath the pressures of 21 years of Catholic upbringing, raising three very free-spirited children, working my way through four careers and relocating 24 times to various cities. It's no wonder that I nicely avoided answering the spinning question for years. For the majority of my life, I had been riding on top of the wave, making physical reality experiences a high priority. This bias kept me on the High Road to Unlimited Knowledge and Fame all the while maintaining a "been there, done that" attitude.

One day I was in my graduate advisor's office determining my plan of action for my next block of classes. I remember feeling overwhelmed with the possibility of what classes to choose next because I thought I wanted to know it all, right then! In the middle of an intense discussion about the pros and cons of each class, I looked up and saw a sign above my advisor's head reading, "The more I know, the less I understand." Suddenly my mind stopped dead. That statement seemed to make our conversation moot. Feeling the disarming dichotomy of the situation, I remember saying to myself, "Well, this is the pits. Here I am, thoroughly obsessing about learning everything I can when I know I'm understanding less and less as I discover more and more!"

THE END OF THE HIGH ROAD

That was my point of no-return, of ending the "been there, done that" crazy race race on the Interstate. What followed was a testy period of realizing the limits of my acquired knowledge about how life, people, and the world worked. I began to be influenced by Jean Houston who frequently emphasized learning the *process* of life, people, and the world along with with its substance. In a 1983 keynote presentation (1) for the American Society for Training and Development National Conference (ASTD), she described how one of her mentors, Margaret Mead, had pointed out that we are taught beginnings and endings of the process of things, but we skip over the middles. For instance,when we ask the chicken or the egg question (Which came first, the chicken or the egg?), we look at the beginning of each and try to determine which creates the most important result. While we know how they are both eaten in the end, we minimize their unique growth and how we are connected to that process. As a result of our culture over emphasizing the front and back end of things, major entertainment industries have sprung up around money-making games of knowing the right answers or letters to unidentified questions, popular words, and names. The phenomenal popularity of *Jeopardy, Wheel of Fortune,* and *Trivial Pursuit*, is society's way of reflecting back the "been there, done that" mentality and, at the same time, avoiding the process of tackling life's big questions. A lot of money has been won by knowing titles, names, dates and products while denying concepts and processes indicates there are gaps in our experience banks. It is possible that recent civilization has neatly avoided all those stages in between waking and sleeping. Nonetheless, life's mysteries keep beaming back at us because we have taught ourselves to have pinhole perceptions.

ADVANTAGES OF EXPANDING CONSCIOUSNESS

There are some advantages to broadening our consciousness; in fact, there are a great many. If we were to end the avoidance, we would be able to adjust to the growing world economy beyond our continental boundaries without periodically wanting to impeach our presidents for signing bills that do just that regarding world trade agreements. If we would adjust to the growing possibility that there is worth in combining resources with Third World countries and ancient tribes, we might experience a majestic plan for humankind, such as joint partnerships between shamans and traditional physicians. The avoidance ends with ourselves, one day at a time. The larger Road to Everywhere, to larger group consciousness, starts inside on a personal level. I suggest it begins with creating balance in our own personal lives. Honoring the Decade of the Brain, we could begin expanding our own awareness with the grey matter we own. There is an interesting historical fact about our brain's anatomy and physiology whose majestic plan is unfolding right under our noses. Stuart Litvak and A. Wayne Senzee in *Toward a New Brain* point out:

"Consider the accompanying graph which charts the change in human brain size over the past ten million years. A pattern is certainly apparent here. The gradual enlargement of the brain (in proportion to body weight) over epochs rules out any randomly inclined influence and establishes a definite continuity of growth...An increase in brainpower must inevitably accompany this physical growth of the organ...However, our graph (based on comparative skull size) also shows us that human brain enlargement has generally leveled off the last 100,000 years. We believe, nonetheless, that mental evolution has not likewise abated during this period, and that the internal organization of the brain has continued to evolve, or has at least rearranged its infrastructure in correspondence with the increasing sophistication of human intelligence." (2) (See Figure 10.)

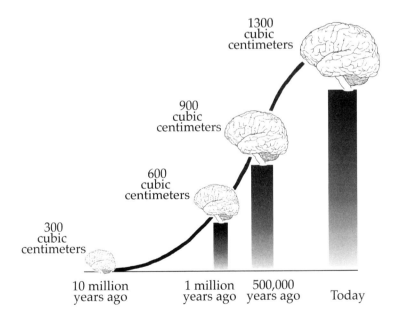

Figure 10 The Growth of the Human Brain

If the genetic grand plan embedded in our brain calls for continual rearranging of the grey matter to meet the demand, why are we so unconscious and rigid about doing this in our personal lives? In this same vein, interesting changes in the mental networks are taking place in the way we work, meaning the turbulent, rearrangements of priorities and value systems. In the 1980s the way we worked involved a hierarchical system with a boss or CEO at the top, managers and supervisors just below, followed by the majority of people — the workers at the bottom distanced from any business decision-making or business planning. (See Figure 11.) This model incorporates the work of Richard Carkhuff, Ph.D, known for his human resource development expertise (3) as well as my own human resource development consultancy experiences.

Figure 11 The Way We Work

CHANGING THE ENERGETIC CONNECTIONS IN THE WAY WE WORK

During the '80s the business of work was accomplished in one of three ways; 50% was spent in meetings, another 25% in personal processing, and the remaining 25% in communicating. Up until the 1980s the working hierarchy had evolved according to a pyramid-shaped working flow. At the top sat the boss. In the middle were the managers and supervisors who acted as conduits carrying the boss's decisions to the workers who would implement them. Below, a shadow triangle, representing a second organization of how work really got done, stood stiffly entrenched.

A shift occurred in the mid 1980s whereby the top of the pyramid became fluid due to mergers and buyouts. CEO after CEO used golden parachutes to fly off into the sunset for greener pastures. This state of flux forced the burden of responsibility further down the pyramid. Without a chief, the worker bees jumped in to save the day. Armed with MBA degrees, middle managers, on the move, powered up downsizing and rightsizing game plays to exercise their decision-making abilities. Inside the organization, they brought the novel idea to the workplace that true ownership comes from within an individual. This resulted in changing the pyramid-shaped working flow pattern.

THE ENERGY OF THE CIRCLE AT WORK IN GROUPS

In the '90s the triangle has now flattened to a circle with the advent of matrix management, project groups, employee-owned companies, ESOP plans, quality improvement circles and world markets ventures. All these workgroup formations have demonstrated that consciousness was no longer obsessed with what things looked like but how the work got done. Various exchanges are now taking place. The shadow organization gave the best of its reality-based learnings to the overt workplace players and the middle managers sat down and began training the workers to develop more effective and caring human relationship skills.

This change to a circular working pattern has resulted in a change in the way we work these days. The individual now spends the majority of his or her time in personal processing (50%) instead of in groups, while devoting 25% in higher-order processing activity due to high-tech innovations, and 25% in interpersonal processing. Decision-making and strategic business planning activities are often passed down the line so that the majority of employees feel a concrete sense of ownership in the company, and their talents are more effectively used. But something is still missing, a link which would lead us into even more natural working-living lifestyles. It has lain fallow for a long time.

Throughout these changes, the brain stands ready for this surge in demand on its infrastructure as Litvak and Senzee have pointed out. It isn't as if we are telling our brains to shape up and the structure responds.

On the contrary, the structure has been preparing for this demand for centuries! Here is a big question, one that begs for an answer. What is it in our makeup that knows the necessity for this structural change in our brains? Is it some element in our collective consciousness?

If our brain infrastructure is so poised, why do most of us live in the doorway of that tremendous palatial infrastructure? One person relished living in more rooms of the mansion of his brain than most. That person was Albert Einstein. When, at 76 years of age, he died, his brain's glial cells were counted during an autopsy in 1955. The glia are known to increase in number proportionate to enriched, learning experiences. The autopsy found that Einstein had 73% more glial cells in a specific portion of his left hemisphere than 11 other men age 47 to 80. Since the left hemisphere represents only one-quarter of the brain, he left an inspiring legacy for those to follow. (4)

If our brain stands ready with infrastructure primed, and if we are using very little of its capacity, isn't it time to increase the use of the internal perceptual gears? Is the road to unlimited knowledge and fame paved with limited consciousness, leaking gas tanks, and illusionary bricks made of a hard-earned puritan work ethic? Isn't it obvious we are spinning our wheels? If we pulled off this road for a while, long enough to get a broader view of where we were going, we could discover another avenue around the bend — the road to full consciousness or the Road to Everywhere.

LOCATING THE ROAD TO EVERYWHERE

The Road to Everywhere lays within and without. In sharp contrast to the Road to Unlimited Knowledge and Fame, it has more lanes, bridges, and no speed control devices. It involves learning how to ride the Continental Divide of Consciousness with a car that has perfect wheel alignment so that balance can be achieved between physical and non-physical reality. I know if I had spent less time and energy in physical reality activities; then I would have more understanding of the non-physical reality experiences I've had and been able to apply them in a practical manner in my everyday life. At the very least, by now the utilization rate of my glial cells could be higher if that would have happened!

I have wondered why autistic savant patients, many of whom I have cared for, are so capable and brilliant. I've thought about why their brains seem to demonstrate genius abilities in specific realms, but they cannot function as ordinary people do. In the movie, *Rainman*, Dustin Hoffman portrays Raymond, an autistic savant. Raymond demonstrates that he can memorize whole portions of a phone directory, have instant recall of hundreds of names, or figure out betting combinations and win at the racetrack for his brother, played by Tom Cruise, but he can't speak using appropriate emotion or remember how to tie his shoes. Perhaps some collective consciousness element is again providing us a glimpse of the bigger universe within by demonstrating the power of chaos or the interval (See Chapter 8, Law of 7) through so-called unusual people: autistic individuals, schizophrenics, people with Down's Syndrome and people with elephantitis among others. If we were to open to fuller consciousness, we would be able to see the worth of the unusual as an equalizer and diversity as building strength in our culture.

HAVING GOOD WHEEL ALIGNMENT FOR A SMOOTH RIDE ON THE ROAD

Balance on the Road to Everywhere can be achieved by becoming adept in non-physical realities. During the process of traveling the Interstate of Consciousness, this part of the Force, the Total Self, becomes evident to the point of being predictable and reassuring. This is demonstrated by the degree of balance or evenness perceived in the Focus States as opposed to physical reality. Here is an example. Because the perception of clarity in some of the Focus states is even more pristine than in dreams, the act of coming back to physical reality, at times, feels like physical reality is the place of illusion, of heaviness, of bumbling, and a lot of effort. After being in a place of clear thinking and quick emoting (Focus 10), it is sometimes difficult to return to dull, dippy reasoning and slow, painful emoting. As a consequence, I've learned how important it is to combine non-physical with physical reality to make everyday life less of a chore and more of a perfect, moment-by-moment event. (See Chapter 5) For instance, I've continued working with my dream state characters and plots during my waking state to sharpen my problem-solving skills in everyday life. I find that I am more quick-witted, energetic, and calm if I blend the two states. If I do compartmentalize my dreamtime work as if it didn't exist, then often I will redream the theme several times in various ways. Using the Focus states while in everyday situations can be as energizing as driving onto the highly negative-ionized atmosphere of Niagara Falls or across the immense Royal Gorge in Colorado. The expansiveness of human skills learned in the non-physical Focus states is immense!

THE LOWER ROAD TO EVERYWHERE: NO SPEEDING TICKETS ALLOWED

In the 1940s, Bing Crosby became well known for his Road movies. As a war baby, I can fondly recall how these films inspired many people, especially my parents, poverty-stricken immigrants from Europe, to wholeheartily believe in the Road to Unlimited Knowledge and Fame. With their picture of reality firmly in place, they were startled when I made a sharp turn off this High Road and turned into the Adirondack woods during the summer and early fall of 1979. I lived on the grounds of a converted Vanderbilt estate 30 miles from the nearest town, in a rustic log cabin away from televisions, phones, newspapers, and shopping malls. I purposefully exited from the High Road under the guise of doing my graduate internship at the innovative National Humanistic Education Center (NHEC) near Old Forge, New York, run by Howard Kirschenbaum and Barbara Glaser. At the time I was feeling a growing sense of pressure in my lifestyle and wanted to bolt because I felt life was so unnatural.

NHEC, later known as Sagamore Institute, was the perfect place to recenter myself under Howard and Barbara's guidance. While earning 18 credit hours toward my master's degree with the brown bears and loons watching, I began to look earnestly at what I now call the Road to Everywhere. During those five months, I found myself falling into the simple rhythms and easy patterns that Mother Nature provided me. I was given the nickname of "city girl" by other staff members in the early days while I was there. It didn't take long for some unusual things to start occurring. Midway through the summer, my eyes seemed to see beyond physical forms and into colors not existing before, my hands could sense my way on pitch black nights on the mountain paths, my taste buds were enlivened tremendously, and my hearing seemed to extend into frequencies and distances well beyond my usual range. This told me that the city girl had really forgotten a lot.

LEARNING TO SLOW DOWN & GET CONSCIOUS

Feeling adventuresome, I attempted my spinning again in a special place in the woods near a crystalline creek that emptied into Sagamore Lake. While wavering at the edge of the Force and feeling its kinetic force pushing and pulling me, I let go into its comforting power and suddenly found myself flying high above the trees, flying with a sense of incredible lightness, agility and freedom. It was only a brief moment before I returned within my spinning and sank peacefully onto the soft ground, saying over and over to myself in utter amazement — I remembered!

Many friends and close relatives have told me that ever since that sabbatical, I was not the same person. That summer in the woods was life-changing for me. After the experience of living with Mother Nature's rhythms and woodsy perfumes, it took me months to acclimate back into the regular world when I returned. There seemed to be a wall of plastic between me, everyone, and everything. Everything seemed to move incredibly slow and with such heaviness, as if my movie of life had shrunk. I acutely sensed the superficiality of it all such as people who were going through fake motions, with false faces, and bogus reasons.

As I write this, I am aware of this same slam dunk of energy, at times, when I come "back" from a particularly deep experience of the Focus states. This quick change of energy shifting from deep non-physical to physical, triggers something in my body's mind about knowing I am returning in a rude manner and so it resists this change by shuddering and stiffening. It must be similar to when the astronauts experience reentry from outer space. So too, for five months I experienced the balanced, open space of the Adirondacks and when I came back, the shocking unbalance of city life, when cast sharply against the evenness I felt in the Adirondacks, threw me off center for some time.

In the back of our minds, we all have memory traces of something larger than ourselves living in our human modes. I think I knew this every time I went for a spin as a child. At the 1992 International Society for the Study of Energy and Energetic Medicine (ISSSEEM) Second Annual Conference in Boulder, Colorado, I heard Gerald Jampolsky, M.D. tell these two stories. (5) He was preparing to deliver a presentation at a West Coast conference when a young child came up to him and asked, "Mister, what were you like when you were new?" It is safe to say that the child obviously knew about a self of Jampolsky that was different than the self standing before him!

Here is another story that Jerry tells with the same theme. A couple brought their newborn baby home and introduced the new child to his three year old sister. Later on, the daughter asked if she could be alone with the new baby. At first the parents were hesitant, but they relented since there was a monitor in the nursery. The three year old went into the bedroom, shut the door and could be heard asking, "Baby, can you tell me about God because I'm beginning to forget?" In the service of remembering how to be physical, we have forgotten how to be non-physical.

On the Road to Everywhere I wanted to know how consciousness evolves. In meditation using the various Focus states I asked many questions about the flow of life and how consciousness works within that flow. I discovered a larger picture than previously presented in history books which I would like to share here. For some of you, the following information is going to seem unfamiliar and perhaps unsettling. On the other hand, for some of you, this model will help you put labels on what you already know. Toward the goal of exploring this bigger picture, I ask that you try to suspend your beliefs in this realm to consider the following information which I acquired using the Focus state energies.

THE JOURNEY OF A SOUL ON THE ROAD TO EVERYWHERE

The journey that a soul takes through lifetimes is a cyclic process of remembering and forgetting. This is similar to the opening and closing process of the petals of a lotus flower. One blooming and dying cycle will be described which is known as a cosmic day. During the Gateway Excursion Weekends, I describe this process as similar to sands flowing through an hourglass depicting the flow of energy as a soul manifests through various lifetimes. There is a foreign-made film out in video format called *Orlando* which shows this same movement of consciousness throughout 300 years of an individual's consciousness. The film won a nomination at the Cannes Film Festival in the early '90s.

HOURGLASS MODEL

The hourglass symbol represents a cosmic day in the life of a soul. I call the top of the hourglass midnight. The location of midnight is the godhead, the point of pure Source. Some know this as heaven or Home. Because the process is cyclic, the bottom of the hourglass is midnight just as the sands return to flow from the top of the hourglass. I discovered the beginnings of this information in a Focus 21 experience. The ebb and flow or the alpha and omega (figure eight symbol) is superimposed over this model which has to do with knowing and non-knowing. In the center of the narrowing energies of what I call twelve o'clock noon is where we, as a collective earthly group consciousness, are residing presently. (See Figure 12.)

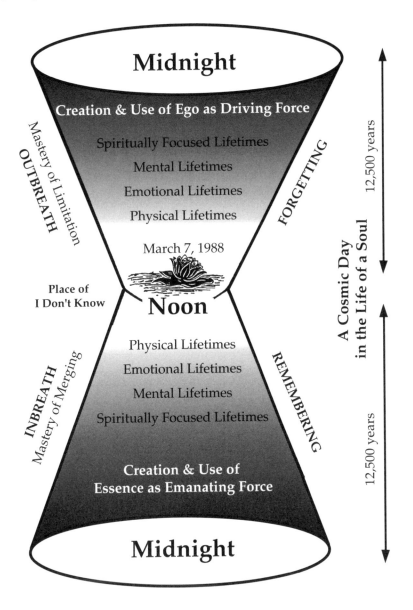

**Figure 12 The Road to Everywhere:
A Model on the Development of Consciousness**

This model can be closely patterned after the the biblical parable of the prodigal son who left his father, struggled through a life of debauchery, then packed up and went back home taking with him his new-found identity and the lessons he learned about separation. Humankind is now completing 12,500 years of forgetting our spiritual consciousness in order to develop human consciousness. (6) During that time we progressively went further and further away from our heavenly home and in the process, became like Gods unto ourselves. It was in the grand plan to do this in order to create an individual identity separate from God so that the beauty of not only the individual but of God would be fully experienced. During the last several decades we have all but eliminated the symbol and practice of having a Primary Force in our life. Instead, as a collective race we now worship goods, gold, and ourselves, which produces mastery of limitation through the creation and use of the ego, the false Self.

THE CYCLE OF FORGETTING & REMEMBERING

In the "fall" or forgetting, ebb phase, in order to become physical, the energy of the soul steps down in frequency or contracts to manifest itself in various forms. In order to become dense in this part of this universe, the energy forgets (puts aside) the memory of Home. As it becomes less and less light, form is created. The loss of lightness accounts for the forgetting. During the midnight to noon phase, the soul has hundreds, even thousands of incarnations. To experience a unique identity separate from the Source, a soul experiences various sets of lessons during four types of incarnations having either spiritual, mental, emotional or physical themes. The spiritual incarnations are on a different, more expanded frequency than mental incarnations, which are more expanded than emotional incarnations and so on. The phase of forgetting ended for the soul in physical form on this planet on March 7, 1988. There are some souls who are delayed and some that have expanded beyond in this process, but the majority of souls have stopped forgetting the memory of lightness and have begun to awaken to both physical and non-physical realities. Twilight of the forgetting was around 1902, and full dawning of noon will be around 2118. During the forgetting phase, the goal was mastery of limitation through the use of the pseudo-god identity called ego. During the coming remembering phase of another 12,500 years, the goal will be mastery of merging through beingness (essence) and learning to go Home. (For more description of essence refer to the ten basic Knowns of traveling in Chapter 10 and also Chapter 8 on Gurdjieff.) The journey back Home will go through the same pattern, but now it will be light expansion lessons having themes of increasing light frequency. The next 12,500 years begins with a period of 2,000 years of photon energy radiance which will enable us to change the environment we live in. This energy will provide the background for the development of advanced technologies to make our lives easier and more harmonious. This band of radiance, looking like the Milky Way, made itself known in 1961 by means of satellite pictures. (See Chapter 7 in the Maintenance Plan section for further photon belt description.) The photon particle is assisting in the acceleration of time and the remembering and retrieving of innate mechanisms supporting the return to wholeness. Perhaps this is what historians have referred to as the Golden Age in the past and some individuals have prophesied as the upcoming Golden Age.

Noontime (the wake-up call) of Mother Earth's remembering was August 16-17, 1987 or the Harmonic Convergence. The crack of the new Aquarian Dawn for Mother Earth will be March 21, 2010; however it's already manifesting here in spiritual form. Our dear planet achieved sacred status in 1987, meaning under her own volition, she began to turn to Light. On December 21, 2012, there will be a glorious cosmic event for the soul extensions still in incarnation on earth. This is when the Mayan calendar ends, bringing full consciousness availability for all those on Earth. On the larger macro level, the hourglass contraction and expansion energy cycle depicts the inhale and exhale process in the life of the Prime Creator (God), which is a brief cosmic day in the life of Mother Earth or 4.4 billion years long. (7) According to our perception of time, that's a long day's night, but to God that passes in an instant. Obviously, we have a lot of speeding up to do to understand this concept.

This information is not part of the TMI training process; however I feel it is broad-based enough to provide a background in order to understand the general movement of consciousness throughout the ages. I offer this model as a way to center oneself into the milieu of exploration we find ourselves in today.

BITS OF REMEMBERING

During my childhood spinning, when I became lightheaded, I began to remember fragments of Home which contained incredible lightness. My early remembering was fearful because this amount of light was difficult to perceive and hold in my life at that time. Likewise, I felt fearful because I remembered that I also had dark aspects and I wasn't comfortable in the dark. As I became accustomed to this and let myself go more often, it became a Known in this physical reality, and I could remember more and hold more of my lightness. What prompted this along were vivid, repetitive dreams; first about front doors of homes with plots about going over the threshold, then about very inviting cozy homes almost life like in nature, and finally a dream that portrayed a half-moon window atop a white front door with a magnificent, shimmering, lighted, gold chandelier beckoning. I had seen that same energetic beam in a Focus 15 experience. In my everyday life, I began to do workshops called *Coming Home: Discovering My Divine Purpose* which brought the most marvelous people on the same search. One day in a gift shop on Sanibel Island, Florida, a card fell into my hands. The front of the card pictured the exact same scene of the chandelier dream long after I had dreamed it.

The Road to Everywhere pictured in Figure 12 is just a model. Models encourage me to learn for myself what is true and not true. The way I approach them is that they temporarily hold an idea until actual experience and discernment can take place. When a Known takes up permanent residence, the model no longer is important. Due to the nature of drawings, this model has its limitations. Please keep in mind that different lifetimes are experienced through dualistic, linear eyes; thus, instead of separate lifetimes, this could be happening all at once.

As you can imagine, the Road to Everywhere turns into the Road to Everyworld. It enlarges to fit the explorer's intention to travel. As coincidence would have it, this humorous reminder (remembering) appeared on an America Online mail list. On some level we already know about the Road to Everywhere because we are telling each other the rules of the road.

RULES FOR BEING HUMAN

1. You will receive a body.
> You may like it, you may hate it. It will be yours for the entire period this time around.

2. **Lessons will be presented.**
   You will be enrolled in a full-time informal school called life. Each day in this school you will have the opportunity to learn lessons. You may learn the lessons or not, or you may think them irrelevant and stupid.

3. **There are no mistakes, only lessons.**
   Growth is a process of trial and error and experimentation. The "failed" experiments are as much a part of the process as the experiment that ultimately "works."

4. **A lesson is repeated until learned.**
   A lesson will be presented to you in various forms and with more and more energy until you have learned it. When you have learned it, you can then go on to the next lesson.

5. **Learning lessons does not end.**
   There is no part of life that does not contain its lessons. If you are alive, there are lessons to be learned.

6. **"There" is not better than "here."**
   When your "there" has become a "here," you will simply obtain another "there" that will, again, look better than "here."

7. **Others are merely mirrors of you.**
   You cannot love or hate something about another person unless it reflects to you something you love or hate about yourself.

8. **What you make of your life is up to you.**
   You have all the tools and resources you need. What you do with them is up to you. All the choices are yours.

9. **Your answers lie inside of you.**
   The answers to life's questions lie inside of you. All you need to do is look inside, listen, and trust.

10. **You will forget all of this.**

11. **You can remember this when you choose to do so.**

   -Author Unknown-

The next place we are touring is the Educational Station along the Interstate where we can progressively move through several rooms to gain a comprehensive understanding of the TMI educational methods used to create productive consciousness expansion voyages. In the first room there will be an explanation of how the training programs of TMI started. In the adjoining room guidelines for traveling into this locale will be offered followed by a technical description of Hemi-Sync, brief and general in nature. Moving into the next classroom, there will be a step-by-step explanation of the TMI traveling process offered, followed by suggestions for a productive traveling environment. Scheduled in the last classroom is a discussion on learning how to understand the results of traveling and being able to apply these experiences in everyday situations.

RULES FOR THE LOWER ROAD

Poised brain infrastructure hanging in the void.
Soul remembering and forgetting like it was a long way home.
Spinning, lightheaded, dizzy, allowing,
Turns onto the Lower Road to Everywhere.

Becoming a waveform, dipping and bobbing
Through physical and non-physical reality
Soul remembering more Light and Sound
Cruising down the Road.

LEARNING HOW TO EXIT, SUSTAIN & CONTROL TRAVEL

"If you realized that the nurtured spiritual part of yourself would accompany you on your eternal journey and that everything else you have labored so hard to accumulate would vanish the instant you depart this world, would it alter your daily agenda?"

Walter Cooper, *Restoring the Shattered Spirit*

ROUTE 4

EARLY DAYS OF TMI TRAINING PROGRAMS

Most of us have been nomads on our meditative journeys. We don't know where we went, how we got there, what "there" versus "here" was, and what to do when we got there. When Monroe had his first few out-of-body trips, they caused him concern. Being very self-directed and curious, he assembled a team of friends and set out to determine what it was causing his out-of-body experiences (OBEs). During this time he experienced progressive skill improvements directly related to OBEs such as increased memory, attention, and comprehension abilities. Unable to track down physical, physiological problems or traumatizing events causing his OBEs, he directed his efforts toward researching this phenomenon scientifically. Bob founded the Whistlefield Research Laboratories in the early 1950s for this purpose. His first project was to study the use of sound to accelerate learning during the sleep state. By 1958 research had identified specific means to keep the mind awake and at the same time to induce sleep. This method was used because accelerated learning cycles were detected in light to deeper states of sleep. After investigating how to develop precise applications of sound, he discovered that certain tonal patterns elicit non-ordinary states of mind. The outcomes of peak performance learning in blended states of sleep, coupled with being able to access non-ordinary states of consciousness on a predictable basis, formed the early "body of knowledge" supporting consciousness expansion training at TMI.

The first training program called the M-5000 was presented at Esalen Institute in California in 1973 by Bob Monroe and an engineer associate, Bill Yost. This hugely successful event included hour-long taped Hemi-Sync exercises in Focus 10 and 12 interspersed with breaks, meals, and short rest periods using a weekend format round the clock. (1) Nancy (Scooter) McMoneagle, Monroe's stepdaughter, became the first Director of Training at TMI. She was very instrumental in developing the early Residential Programs as well as coordinating and conducting international and local community programs for nearly 20 years at TMI. Her leadership provided the groundwork for what was to become an extensive international teaching-learning network. From that first M-5000 weekend in 1973 to March 1995, over 8,000 people have attended the Institute's training programs at TMI. It is estimated that over two million people world-wide had purchased the Hemi-Sync tapes and CDs for their own traveling use up to that time.

The M-5000 developed into the Gateway Programs which included the Excursion (one day in Focus 10); the Weekend (2 1/2 days in Focus 10 and 12); The Advanced 15 Weekend (2 1/2 days in Focus 10, 12, and 15); and the ten day Explorations which later became the Gateway Voyage Residential Program. Today there are numerous Residential Programs which are all six day training events including the Gateway Voyage (a prerequisite for all other TMI Residential Programs), Guidelines, Lifeline, Exploration 27 and Heartlines. (Refer to *Ultimate Journey* for these workshop descriptions or contact TMI for Residential Program information.) (2) In addition, TMI sponsors other training events conducted by accredited Gateway Outreach Trainers in various cities throughout the world.

TRAVELING GUIDELINES FOR THE LOWER ROAD TO EVERYWHERE

Educational traveling on the Interstate can take place in one of three ways; using the Gateway Experience (Home Study) series of Hemi-Sync tapes or CDs, by attending a Gateway Voyage Program, or by using a combination of both approaches.

THE CONDUCIVE ENVIRONMENT

If traveling is occurring in the privacy of a home using the Gateway Experience Wave series, the learning environment should consist of a stereo system placed so that the traveler is comfortably sitting or lying between the two speakers. In place of a stereo speaker system, headphones can be used. On the stereo system, the dolby and equalizer options should be turned off and the speaker reception balanced, if this is an option. Before settling in to listen to a Gateway Experience tape or CD, it is advisable to be fairly well-rested and in between meals as these two factors may tend to interfere with learning. In addition, the excessive ingestion of caffeine, nicotine, chocolate, or other stimulants will not be conducive for non-physical learning to occur. It is not necessary to use headphones during the use of Hemi-Sync technology; however, headphones help the listener screen out any incoming stimulus other than the Hemi-Sync sounds. If headphones are desired, use larger ones covering the ears, and place the left headphone on the left ear etc. In cases of subtle hearing loss, try reversing the headphones by putting the right headphone on the left ear. If there is a history of hearing loss or surgical repair with subsequent hearing loss, Hemi-Sync can still be heard as many of its sounds are in the inaudible range. Individuals with impaired hearing often report a kinesthetic response which takes over as a leading cue in the early stages of learning; however learning will still occur without the ability to observe any physical response. Hearing loss is not a liability as one of the TMI staff trainers is known to have a hearing loss in one ear. Working with a totally blind client during an 18 month period, I was amazed at her comfort level and perceptibility in the Focus states. (3) In sight-impaired individuals, the feeling of fear stemming from being in a dark or unknown environment is usually pretty well conquered. Acceptance of the dark tends to be a distinct asset in this training setting.

CHILDREN & THE USE OF HEMI-SYNC

It is absolutely delightful to work with children who wish to travel the Interstate. Between the age of 11 and 13, children typically begin to approach the idea of consciousness training on their own; although, as our generation matures, the age factor will most likely decrease as the cortical functionality of the child increases. Being more receptive and less habituated, children will often do quite well, while their parents tend to be surprised at their child's achievements on the Interstate. When parents accompany and/or monitor their child's progress, I've noticed a new bond forms — one that is more free, respectful, and easygoing. I think this is prompted, in part, to a change that occurs between parent and child which lessens any top dog/underdog agendas and provides fresh space for individuality in the relationship.

THE IMPACT OF HEMI-SYNC ON COUPLE RELATIONSHIPS

Exploring and discovering the unknown together can smooth out any relationship, providing a breath of fresh air. This applies to couples who travel the Interstate as well. Couples who live together and attend the

Gateway Voyage programs or who are doing the Gateway Experience Wave series together might consider a separate learning arrangement, since there is a tendency for their thoughtforms to become entangled at intervals. This will become apparent when they report having similar experiences more often than not. To help them do their own individual work, I recommend that couples separate (position themselves across the room) during the training phase and then process together afterwards. Once the training phase is over, they can choose to travel together or individually. Then there are times when couples wish to increase the energy that is available between them so it is advantageous to work together at this point. To personally be a part of the creation of a new, refreshing bond between couples as a result of traveling on the Interstate has been a very satisfying and uplifting experience.

GROWING CONSCIOUS TOGETHER

In Canada this situation developed during two Gateway Excursion Weekends nearly a year apart. On the first Excursion, the husband enjoyed a very satisfying experience, developed many insights and continued working to attain more skills with the help of my coaching over the phone throughout the following year. He was so happy with his progress that he decided to encourage his wife to come with him when he attended a second time. Thinking he was now the man "in the know" during the second Gateway Excursion, he carefully watched his wife learn the process, without giving her much assistance. Much to his surprise, she easily learned the steps and accomplished many significant things. She told her husband she had had similar experiences throughout her life, but didn't know what they were or how to control them. Later they phoned me to say the Excursion opened up a new avenue of exploration for them as a couple, which I hear frequently from many couples.

Another stateside couple has unlocked new spiritual ground in their relationship. He took the Gateway Excursion first and very seriously proceeded to practice the process on a regular basis. He began to notice synchronistic omens appearing in his life which appeared to carry important information regarding his job and family. His wife approached me saying she wanted to join her husband in his search because he had become more centered and peaceful. Sandy told me she wanted to have what he was developing. She attended the Gateway Excursion later on in the year and marveled at what she experienced. In particular, she said it gave her unique confidence to have this kind of growth; whereas, before, she thought this kind of experience should have been her husband's forte. They describe this in their own words.

"When Sandy and I talked about our Hemi-Sync experiences over the last year, we both agreed that the most significant gain as a result of going to the workshops and monthly support meetings was that this monthly, mutual participation gave us two factors which help both our communication process and its content. These two factors are consistent form and common subject matter. Both factors help us relate better to one another. We have had some very interesting and enlightening discussions about our spiritual values and lives as a result of conversations related to our Hemi-Sync experiences. Without this stimulus, we might have kept the doors of shared spirituality shut.

"Sandy and I have been and are concerned with learning from our personal history so we can get on with our lives instead of being stuck in our own ego-defenses where we attempt to remain in denial and self-pity about some of the negative aspects of our lives. However, prior to attending Hemi-Sync workshops and the follow-up training afterwards, we had no consistent material, time structure, and very little common spiritual understanding between us. Sandy follows a path of a feeling, religious orientation, and she is still dealing with aging parents who are deeply involved in their dramas, their denials, and their expectations of their old ways. I follow a path that led me to read all of Castaneda's works and take a left-brained, often over-intellectualized approach to my personal development. Unfortunately, without detailed study of Castaneda and Monroe's original works much of the knowledge that is in these books was beyond my intellectualizations. Now, having participated in the Gateway program and continuing with the Explorer Support Group, we have gained a timetable, have mutually understandable subject materials to use, and opened the door to shared spiritual values in a hands-on way. We now have a common basis for talking about the processes, and we have behavioral models and information that we get from the support group's work.

"One significant advantage is that Sandy and I are both moving toward a middle ground in our communications with each other. I am more in touch with the 'feeling' aspects of our experiences and Sandy has a better understanding of the cognitive and intellectual components of our experiences. Hence, our understanding about each other's approach, left-brain versus right-brain, has helped improve our communication with each other. Sandy is getting the Castaneda and Monroe material through Patricia's presentations, and I am listening and relating more to what Sandy is experiencing and feeling when we talk about what happens. We both talk more during the time between meetings as we continue to study and use the processes, the encodings, and materials. As a result of these experiences we have rebalanced our married life and brought ourselves into an area that has been very enriching and stimulating."

S and B.C. from Loveland, Colorado

This couple has described themselves as "babes in the woods when it comes to spirituality." They are supporting each other in their meditative work and have expressed in the Explorer Support Group how their relationship has taken on a fresh new perspective, especially regarding understanding each other and being able to communicate that understanding.

PRECAUTIONARY MEASURES

On the flip side of the coin, there are a few precautions about the use of Hemi-Sync technology that should be taken into account by individuals who are experiencing serious situations. In some cases, some of the blended tones adversely affect individuals with a chronic history of severe psychiatric problems. Before Hemi-Sync training is determined to be appropriate, those persons having acute reality boundary factors, such as those with schizophrenia and borderline personality, should individually be assessed beforehand by TMI trainers who are working in collaboration with professionals in the psychotherapeutic community. Furthermore, those individuals experiencing chronic depression, post-traumatic stress disorder, and manic-depressive episodes and who are determined to be appropriate training candidates, should be closely monitored throughout the traveling experience. Psychotropic medications, in some instances, depending on the pharmacological category, may affect the perceptual abilities of the participant. Persons with a seizure disorder should not use the Hemi-Sync tapes. Individuals with class I and II type diabetes who are not closely monitoring their nutritional and/or insulin requirements, should also be assessed for their capacity to hold attention, process abstract information, and keep focused. The trainer will be able to detect these effects and develop one-to-one strategies and supportive mechanisms so that training will be effective for these individuals on these medications. A disclaimer needs to be inserted here. All of these factors can affect consciousness training in a positive manner. Sometimes these barriers to perception, such as psychotropic medications, high blood sugars, and schizophrenia can be therapeutic for an individual or facilitate events, so it is wise to keep a balanced view in this regard. What appears to be a problem for a person may also be an opportunity for change and growth.

HEMI-SYNC AS AN ALL-TERRAIN VEHICLE

In the 1995 TMI product catalog, Hemi-Sync is described as "a patented, state-of-the-art, auditory guidance technology which provides access to specific states of consciousness. Carefully researched blends and sequences of sound patterns evoke 'whole brain' functioning through the synchronization of the two hemispheres of your brain." On an introductory sampler tape called *The Way of Hemi-Sync*," Bob Monroe demonstrates the auditory guidance process. He guides the listener to hear a tone in one ear, then Monroe shifts the tone to the other ear so that the listener hears the same tone in the other ear. Monroe then changes the sound so that initial sound is heard in one ear and a different sound is heard by the other ear. The listener notices a wobbling, vibrato sound called the binaural beat.

F. Holmes (Skip) Atwater, Director of Research at TMI explains the resulting vibrato sound, "The sensation of 'hearing' binaural beats occurs when two coherent sounds, one to each ear, of nearly similar frequencies are presented. The brain then detects phase differences between these sounds. This phase difference normally provides directional information to the listener, but when presented with stereo headphones or speakers, the brain integrates the two signals, producing a sensation of a third sound called the binaural beat. Perceived as a fluctuating rhythm at the frequency of the difference between the two (stereo left and right) auditory inputs, binaural beats appear to originate in the brainstem's superior olivary nucleus, the site of contralateral integration of auditory input. This auditory sensation is neurologically routed to the reticular activating system (RAS) and simultaneously, its volume is conducted to the cortex where it can be objectively measured as a frequency-following response (FFR)." (4)

Atwater further states, "This perceptual phenomenon of binaural beating and the objective measurement of the FFR response suggest conditions which facilitate alternation of brain waves and states of consciousness. There have been numerous anecdotal reports and a growing number of research efforts reporting changes in consciousness associated with binaural beats....Binaural beats in the delta (1 to 4 Hz) and theta (4 to 8 Hz) ranges have been associated with reports of relaxed, meditative, and creative states, sensory integration, and used as an aide to falling asleep. Binaural beats in the alpha frequencies (8 to 12 Hz) have increased alpha brain waves and binaural beats in the beta frequencies (typically 16 to 24 Hz) have been associated with reports of increased concentration or alertness, improved memory, and increases in focused attention in mentally retarded adults." (4)

Atwater discusses the factors effecting the Hemi-Sync process. "Passively listening to binaural beats may not automatically engender an altered state of consciousness. The Hemi-Sync process includes a number of procedures; binaural beats are only one element. We all maintain a psychophysiological momentum, a homeostasis which may resist the influence of the binaural beats. These homeostatic states are generally controlled by life situations as well as by acts of will, both conscious and unconscious. One's subjective experience in response to binaural-beat stimulation may also be influenced by a number of other mediating factors. For example, the willingness and ability of the listener to relax and focus attention may contribute to the binaural-beating effectiveness in inducing state changes. Naturally occurring neurological ultradian rhythms, characterized by periodic changes in arousal and states of consciousness, may underlie the anecdotal reports of fluctuations in the effectiveness of binaural beats. External factors also thought to play roles in mediating the effects of binaural beats. The perception of a binaural beat is, for example, said to be heightened by the addition of pink noise to the carrier signal, so pink noise is often used as background. Music, relaxation, exercises, guided images, and verbal suggestion have all been used to enhance the state-changing effects of the binaural beat." (4)

Much of the work by The Monroe Institute involves states of consciousness not normally accessed by the average person. These states of consciousness are those "other states in between" to which Monroe has referred. As he discovered, they are located in various stages of sleep. Each Focus state has a particular blend of Hemi-Sync tonal patterns that locates the state in non-physical reality. (In order to understand more about this technological process, information in Chapter 7 the section called "The Vehicle of Hemi-Sync" should be referenced.)

OVERVIEW OF THE FREQUENCY RANGE FOR BRAIN STATES

The brain state containing mostly **Gamma** frequencies (20-60Hz) involves momentary experiences of high creativity and also mystical or transcendent experiences where a sense of ego boundary has vanished. The **Beta** brain state (13-20 Hz) evokes the waking state, **Alpha** (8-13Hz) provides light relaxation, **Theta** (4-8Hz) stimulates light sleep, and **Delta** (4-0Hz) summons deep sleep. Generally speaking, Hemi-Sync tonal patterns center primarily in the alpha, theta, and delta range and also include gamma and beta tones in certain Hemi-Sync patterns, depending on the purpose of the tape or CD application. (See Figure 13.)

The 90 Minute Energy Cycle

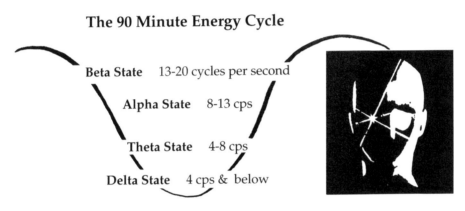

Beta State   13-20 cycles per second

Alpha State   8-13 cps

Theta State   4-8 cps

Delta State   4 cps & below

Figure 13 The Cycle of Energy Flow Through the Brain States

HOW ENERGY CYCLES THROUGH THE BODY

Normally, in one day's time, there are rhythmic 90 minute cycles of moving from beta down through alpha, theta, and delta and back up on a regular basis. Periodic disruptions of that rhythm occur because of such things as training a baby to eat at four hour intervals by giving four hour feedings, or working eight to nine hours straight with high caffeine intake doing Type A behaviors, or eating a heavy protein-loaded meal spiked with a cocktail beforehand, then going to sleep shortly thereafter for seven to eight hours. These conditioners, be it food, artificial sleeping or work habits, force the 90 minute cycles into shorter cycles where theta and delta activity is not used or minimally used. For example, during the detoxification process, recovering alcoholics say they don't feel rested after eight hours of sleep because they have conditioned their brain to stay primarily in alpha. This is evidenced in EEG readings. An EEG is an electroencephalogram or a graph produced by a machine that tracks the electrical movement of the brain. (5) Feelings of decreased stress, lessened anxiety and increased relaxation are the result of prolonged alpha brain state stimulation which the alcoholic is looking for when she or he drinks.

By coincidence, this spiraling 90 minute cycle of energy through beta to delta and back to beta flow looks suspiciously like the waveform of "Me" and "I AM" as it travels on the Interstate of Consciousness. Day and night, this pattern repeats itself; although we artifically lengthen and shorten the various states within the cycle so the sine wave form representing consciousness becomes distorted or out of shape. This literally produces narrow pictures of reality.

Despite this abuse to the natural brain cycle, the energy field and subsequently the brain can be retrained to locate and cycle naturally to its own unique cadence by means of Hemi-Sync consciousness education and other brain balancing approaches. Each individual is synchronized to his or her own waveform rhythm. This rhythm demonstrates a unique signature sound pattern in the family unit as evidenced by the maternal bonding research of Drs. Kennell and Klaus. (6) In the early moments of birth, the cry of the newborn when tracked on an oscilloscope matches the voice oscillations of both the mother and father. How fascinating! Synchronicity even appears *in utero* and provides a lifeline during the birth process.

It is important to learn about the general characteristics of the flow of energy through the brain so that one can observe general shifts in consciousness and the subsequent shifts in thinking and perceiving powers. Let's look at this from a brain balancing point of view. The beta state in the brain consists of random, incoherent electrical energy. This can be seen using EEG readings. In contrast, when the brain is in the delta state, an EEG will show very coherent, consistent electrical activity. In beta the sympathetic component of the CNS (central nervous system) is stimulated which is responsible for the voluntary functions of the human body. When the brain is in alpha through delta, the other half of the CNS (the parasympathetic system) is stimulated which is responsible for the involuntary functions. This is an important distinction to make because in light to deep sleep states (deeper alpha through delta), what functions were formerly considered uncontrollable or involuntary become controllable due to the increasing coherency level of the electrical activity. A paradox exists. *As we relax into the sleep states, we become coherent, intelligent beings!*

Interestingly we're discovering that the seat of consciousness resides in the states of coherency. Carl Jung was right. The dark or unknown can be made conscious or at least be known in deeper states of consciousness.

There are other implications for learning how to consciously use the sleep states to balance the brain's activity. When only the beta state is used in waking reality while sacrificing the "juice" of the other states, then information is perceived from "messy beta" which provides unbalanced, limited and narrow pictures of reality. For instance, if you lose your car keys and want to recall where you last saw them, typically your memory of losing them is going to be filed in the haphazardly functional state of beta where minimal parts of the brain are barely working together. But, if the act of recalling the keys involved healthy doses of alpha through delta as well as beta, you most assuredly would be able to remember where the keys were because the various parts of the brain were in synchrony or in partnership. Since traditional Westernized educational systems customarily emphasize the use of beta brain state teaching methods, it's no wonder that much of the learning content and process in our schools doesn't stick.

Richard Gerber, M.D. (7) talks at length about the importance of recognizing the difference between coherent and incoherent consciousness and the potentials of the latter.

> "Coherent and focused consciousness of the type achieved in successful remote viewing may have qualities similar to coherent reference laser beams used to display and decode more conventional holograms. Ordinary light from incandescent light bulbs is known as incoherent light. Incoherent light moves randomly, with light waves traveling chaotically in all directions. One might think of average human thought as random and incoherent. Conversely, laser or coherent light is highly focused, with all light waves traveling in step, similar to soldiers marching in a parade. If the energy produced by an incandescent bulb were to be made coherent, the resulting focused laser beam could probably burn a hole through a steel plate. One can extend the analogy to the productions of coherent thought activity (as reflected by increased brain wave coherence). In addition to being highly focused and ordered, coherent light can also decode holograms. There is also some evidence to suggest that increased coherence of brain wave activity may be associated with other psychic events such as

psychokinesis and remote viewing. Scientific studies of transcendental meditators tend to confirm this "coherence" hypothesis. Long-term meditators attempting certain psychic feats (also known as siddhis) were found to have brain wave patterns of increased energetic coherence during psychic events. (8) Other researchers have also found a definite shift in brain wave frequencies toward the delta/theta range (1-8 cycles/second) along with increased hemispheric synchronization during human psychic functioning. (9) (10) The key principle here is that coherent consciousness may display properties which go beyond ordinary waking consciousness. Going from incoherent random thought to coherent consciousness may be as powerful a transition as going from incandescent light to the brilliant energy of a laser beam. By achieving this highly focused level of awareness, we may be able to tap into normally unconscious or latent human abilities…Achieving such specialized states of consciousness may allow an individual to gain access to hierarchical levels of information enfolded within the structure of matter/energy fields and space itself. Expanded human awareness may be the most important tool for exploring the holographic universe and the multidimensional human being."

Likewise, the Hemi-Sync educational process helps the traveler, using a step-by-step approach, to expand his or her human awareness, so that the information enfolded within the holographic universe can be accessed, sustained, and controlled. As human consciousness evolves toward developing these inherent talents, individuals will be able to create their own conscious evolution.

OVERVIEW OF THE BASIC TMI TRAVELING PROCESS: DRIVING INTO & OUT OF THE CITIES ON THE INTERSTATE

Ocean surf with swirling Hemi-Sync tones mimicking the ebb and flow of the tide begin each training tape. Monroe calls the first miles out onto the Interstate the **Preparatory Process**. This is an introductory approach designed to acquaint the traveler with techniques which will help create smooth entry onto the Interstate and introduce the traveler to the hands-on experience of a balanced perceptual energy field. For some who are accustomed to a frenzied, chaotic lifestyle, this will be a decidedly, welcomed change! The Preparatory Process, a basic, mechanical skill-building process, is done in the city of Focus 3, a kindergarten level of brain balance. This is equivalent to tuning the brain to the higher end of the radio dial and locating, for example, the station around 107.1 FM on the dial. Then as one turns the dial into the lower brain state radio stations, one is able to access higher frequencies due to the brain balancing factor. Until recently these higher frequencies have not been accessible nor sustainable in physical reality due to the overriding incoherent state of consciousness we've trained ourselves to live and breathe in. Yet with the precise locating and balancing characteristics of Hemi-Sync sounds, we are able to enter and control our consciousness vehicle, the mind, while traveling deeper and deeper into non-physical realities.

While in the enriched learning-balanced environment of Focus 3, three skills of the Preparatory Process are taught: relaxing to ocean surf music, constructing and using an Energy Conversion Box, and learning how to do Resonant Tuning.

The **Energy Conversion Box** (ECB) is a metaphoric, but also a hands-on tool symbolizing the traveler's ability to put incoherent beta pictures of reality aside while helping the traveler to put his or her electrical field of energy into a basic state of balance. At any time during the entire traveling process, the ECB can be used to suspend current body aches and pains, job concerns, relationship issues or specific thoughts and feelings about attempting or sustaining this travel process, by putting these issues, one-by-one, in symbolic form into the ECB. Since the energy conversion process is being done in the enriched brain-balancing environment of Hemi-Sync, this significantly decreases the amount of mind chatter that typically preoccupies meditation. While helping people learn the Preparatory Process, I've heard hundreds of descriptions of ECBoxes which have been quite intriguing and clever. They vary from tiny jeweled baskets made of delicate material such as shells or glass having perfumed drawers or sections (the womanly variation) to dumpster-size (men are very big on this!), electronically equipped, monster-eating metal crunchers. As you can imagine, the most creative and clever ECBs have been constructed by kids. What's important is to let this ECB be created in the mind's eye by imagination. Over time, the form of the ECB will change and different devices will be added representing newer problem-neutralizing abilities. The majority of workshop participants usually forget to use the ECB throughout the Focus state learning exercise they are doing. It's there, use it to your heart's desire to clear your mind of messy beta meanderings.

The next Preparatory Process skill is called **Resonant Tuning** by TMI. Resonant Tuning is also known as vowel chanting in other meditation approaches. Learning to tone an OM is considered so beneficial that there is a separate 30 minute TMI Resonant Tuning tape offered as a single learning tool to be used by itself. Resonant Tuning prepares the energy field to phase shift by setting up resonance in the energy field surrounding the physical body. By causing increased coherency in the energy field, this resonance locates or "dials" the field to a particular frequency. This resonance opens a gateway to various cities and neighborhoods of non-reality. Just as Alice in her Wonderland Dreamtime fell down the rabbit hole into other realms, meditators often fall unconsciously into this portal and become unable to recognize where they are. To locate this gateway, let's explore the simple act of Resonant Tuning and its specific energetic symptoms that accompany the opening of the gateway.

TMI suggests the use of the universal sound, the OM as do many Eastern meditative methods or any vowel sound that feels comfortable. Resonant Tuning can be done in two ways; by sounding a singular "OM" sound, or by slowly saying a threefold "Ah-Oh-Um" sound. One's own cadence, pitch, and rate is encouraged. On the inhale, white, sparkling energy is imagined coming into the body through the solar plexus. This fresh energy is swirled up to and around in the head. On the exhale, it is continues down through the middle of the body. It is suggested to keep the fresh energy in the energy field while moving the denser old, stale energy out through the balls of the feet. During the toning process, it is possible to feel a warm, electric sensation moving throughout the body; however, if this isn't happening, there is nothing wrong. Oftentimes, a resonance will be felt in the back of the jawbones and sometimes this vibration will travel down the spine. As time passes, breathing begins to slow down and at times, seems to stop. When sufficient relaxation and awareness occurs, it will become apparent that breathing has stopped. In its own time breathing will start on its own again, but with more attention beginning to linger in the moment after the exhale and before returning to the inhale. At this point it becomes very important to stay consciously awake and alert during the changing of consciousness, while allowing the body to move gently into deep relaxation as if sleeping.

THE BREATHWORK CYCLE OF RESONANT TUNING

Breathwork has three phases. The first two, the in-breath and out-breath phases, represent feminine and masculine energies, respectively. They are also known as receiving-yin and giving-yang energies. What often is skipped over or totally ignored is the third phase, the still, nothingness period that appears after the exhale. As Resonant Tuning continues, this third phase becomes more noticeable. Eventually it will last longer than the in-breath and out-breath combined. As self-mindfulness moves more and more into this third place, what is known in scientific terms as the powerful Einstein-Rosen bridge opens, making way for the meditator to easily move into his or her intended non-physical state of consciousness. An energetic way of explaining this process is when the energies of the female (inhale) combine or merge with male energy (exhale), this creates a state of no-mind. The third phase of breathwork is where a powerful force of the Universe resides, a unifying force, a bridge to all the layers of what Bob Monroe called the Total Self (full consciousness) or what many say is the Divine Cosmic Mind. Some call this bridge the "Tao," the "state of grace," the "River," or the "eternal moment" in breathwork. In sacred geometry terms, this third place is also known as the vesica pisces which is the symbol of two circles merging horizontally. The "eye" section, where two circles partially merge, is location of the vesica pisces energies. This looks like the infinity symbol known to contain both alpha (the beginning) and omega (the ending) of all things. The *fused* area is where the most potent, creative space within the circles is found. (See Figure 14.)

William Buhlman (11) calls this portal an energy tunnel and proposes its energies are very similar to that of a black hole. He refers to the work of Albert Einstein and Nathan Rosen in 1935 who discussed the function of black holes as bridges to any where and any time. The Einstein-Rosen bridge was the first proposed explanation for the existence of parallel universes and dimensions. Many equivalent terms exist and are used by well known personalities, TV programs, and popular films. *Star Trek* fans know the bridge as a wormhole, a concept which is increasingly explored in *Deep Space Nine* and *Voyager* programs. The film, *Contact*, has a long scene where an astronaut experiences the Einstein-Rosen bridge while traveling from earth to the planet, Vega in a spaceship looking exactly like the vesica pisces. Deepak Chopra refers to the bridge as the gap, Gregg Braden refers to this locale as the Zero Point, and don Juan describes this as the Assemblage Point. I refer to this locale as the void. The void becomes increasingly more evident when transiting to states of highly expanded consciousness. All these terms are specifically described in later chapters.

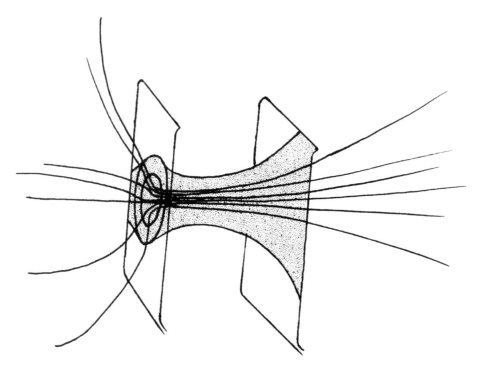

Figure 14 The Bridge Between Two States of Consciousness

This connecting link, the bridge between two states of consciousness, is found in the place of I DON'T KNOW, a locale having no light, at least at first glance. At the maximum peak point wherein matter (physical reality elements) and antimatter (non-physical reality elements) forces combine, an implosion occurs. In our polarized way of perceiving, this feels like being drawn into nothingness. Perhaps a black hole? In early bridge experiences, the traveler often describes a pulling forward or an "expanding outward" effect while in the I DON'T KNOW place. This is an awareness of the imploding energy, but from a polarized point of view. Outward is also all at once inward. Riding or staying with this sensation will automatically link the traveler, as if on a cable, to the other side or another state of consciousness. This is the radar-like or sage quality of consciousness Stan Grof described. While within the energy tunnel, the potential for all-knowing exists. For instance, those who report having had near-death experiences review their life as if they have all-knowingness. They describe an energy tunnel sculpted of brilliant, white light. Having moved onto the bridge, the traveler will report that the picture of reality experienced before the bridge is now gone. Monroe would suggest a phase shift in consciousness has occurred. During early non-physical journeys on the Interstate, this shifting happens fairly fast, as one goes from one state of consciousness to another. Travelers don't usually notice the bridge in Focus States nearest to earth-like frequencies. Later on, the traveler may become fascinated with the propelling or revving sensation, so they describe how they have stopped to consciously explore the bridge as a locale having its own unique characteristics.

THE ENERGY TUNNEL EXPERIENCE

An exercise to explore the bridge is developed on a TMI tape called *The Portal*. This provides the experience of learning to consciously move at will into the void, explore its environment, then move through and out the other side. Here is how the narrator describes the bridge on this tape: "In the vast and unlimited universe, there is an opening many light years from the earth, an opening that is cloaked only by a void. It has been called a black hole and is thought by many to be a place of antimatter where time and physical space are swallowed and cease to exist. Since time and space are irrelevant beyond the celestial door, a traveler or explorer may easily visit this place."

A facsimile of the energy tunnel is shown in the TV show called *Sliders*. Characters in this series use a device called "the timer" to open a temporal rift into space, then they each jump into the momentary energy tunnel and slide into another reality. Long before this show was produced, many Interstate travelers discovered its non-physical equivalent during their journeys and used this energy tunnel to enter other cities of non-physical reality. Over the past forty years, TMI has been developing educational exercises using Hemi-Sync sound technology to help incur, at will, various phase shifts in consciousness. Each shift necessitates learning to enter the bridge and transport oneself into various states of non-ordinary reality.

Consequently, Resonant Tuning contains tremendous potential, a virtual high speed elevator to more expanded territories. It can be done easily for short periods in everyday situations to clean any accumulated garbage rattling around in the nooks and crannies of the mind, or simply to re-energize and/or refocus the mind. Sounding the OM in the shower is especially beneficial, as the purpose of Resonant Tuning is to clean and charge the energy field with a universal, all-purpose frequency. This opens the bridge; its span stretches out to another state of consciousness, and presto! A lighter, larger way of viewing the world emerges.

COMPLETING THE PHASE SHIFT SKILLS

Tuning the brain and the energy field to around 106.1 FM, metaphorically speaking, accesses the *mind awake/body asleep* radio station of Focus 10. More mechanical skill-building is required to exit into this city off the Interstate and enjoy its full benefits. The step-by-step Preparatory Process continues by repeating the first three steps (Ocean Surf Relaxation, ECB, RT) and adding three more skills which are the Gateway Affirmation, the Resonant Energy Balloon (REBAL), and five Function Commands. These complete the Preparatory Process steps which are beneficial to support phasing into the city of Focus 10 and sustaining presence there. When the **Gateway Affirmation** is said, this simply means there is an *intention* to direct oneself on a specific path signified by what the Gateway Affirmation says. A dictionary (12) definition of intention is, "the determination to act in a specified way; anything intended, a purpose." Firmly said affirmations turn off the messages of the chattering ego invested in staying in physical reality, and help turn the ignition on to travel into non-physical countries. To assist that purpose, Bob Monroe wrote:

THE GATEWAY AFFIRMATION:

I am more than my physical body. Because I am more than physical matter, I can perceive that which is greater than the physical world. Therefore, I deeply desire to expand, to experience; to know, to understand; to control, to use such greater energies and energy systems as may be beneficial and constructive to me and to those who follow me. Also, I deeply desire the help and cooperation, the assistance, the understanding of those individuals whose wisdom, development, and experience are equal to or greater than my own. I ask their guidance and protection from any influence or any source that might provide me with less than my stated desires. (13)

Years later, this original version has been rewritten into a somewhat different format:

> I am more than my physical body. I am part of the Creative Miracle of Life. Therefore I deeply desire to feel my connection to the Creative Source — to feel the power and intelligence, the inspiration and creativity, the peace and love, the confidence and strength that are all part of who I truly am. Also I deeply desire the help and cooperation, the assistance, the understanding of the Creative Source. I feel deeply grateful for the perfect guidance and protection and love that surround me and support me. (14)

As travel progresses, it will be helpful to devise a personal affirmation similar to the Gateway Affirmation and to include any other intentions that form the purpose for that particular experience. When saying an affirmation, stay clearly focused on the intention and put any other thoughts that might arise into the ECB. *Clarity, desire, intensity and an attitude of gratitude* are key factors in developing an intention that will be manifested in the city of Focus 10. To reinforce previous comments, as intention is put forth, results will be actualized more quickly in these states of consciousness because the Hemi-Sync environment is a coherent learning environment. As the coherency increases, the density of the thoughtform decreases. As the density of any Focus State lessens, the energy thoughtform gains in its ability to restructure and manifest itself accordingly. Movement onto the Einstein-Rosen wormhole bridge begins with intention as expressed in the Gateway Affirmation.

REVVING UP THE ENGINE

Next, the **Resonant Energy Balloon (REBAL)** is constructed. This activates the energy field surrounding and permeating the physical body. The purpose of the REBAL is to save, concentrate, secure and protect the now coherent field of energy. This construction process can make the Light Body apparent to the traveler in some manner, whether it be an increasing sense of warmth, a gradual awareness of the light quotient in the field, or of movement of energy in the field. Construction is done in two steps. The first step is to expand the energy field by imagining straight lines of energy coming out the top of the head, flowing down the middle of the body, down through the legs and out the balls of the feet, then back up to the top of the head, creating a moving fountain of energy. This looks much like the old-fashioned slinky toy. After moving the energy in this fashion for 15-20 times or until sufficient movement is generated to feel the expansion of the energy field, the second phase of the REBAL is begun at the feet by spiraling this energy up through the middle of the body, out through the crown of the head, then spiraling it around the body to form a tight cocoon. At this point the energy field contracts in and becomes discernible by the gradual increasing or building up of vibrations. This sometimes produces a feeling of a "revving up" motion. Directions given by the TMI staff trainers and in the Gateway Experience series say it doesn't matter whether the energy is coiled clockwise or counterclockwise at this point. I would like to suggest that it does matter. I have discovered that the REBAL is significantly intensified if a third spiraling phase is added. Here is an explanation for this additional third spiral.

ADDING AN ADDITIONAL TURN TO THE REBAL

Soon we are going to be able to "see" sound because light is an artifact of sound, the Sound Current that animates all life. Seeing in this manner of speaking refers to the soul's ability to see, a non-ordinary way of seeing. (See Chapter 8 on Castaneda's description of seeing and Chapter 9 on Sound Current.) Light is another way of saying to be enlightened (illuminated). The day is now here for us to look at light through using sacred geometrical forms. These are specific energy forms containing universal energy potentials. Our physical body is a dense field of energy. It is visually apparent because its energy is slow moving and contracted. The body is surrounded by less dense, more expanded fields of energy, not yet apparent to the naked eye in most people. These less densified fields are in the form of a series of pyramids or tetrahedrons. (A tetrahedron is a solid figure with four equal triangular faces.) Several tetrahedrons put together look like a daisy or an opened lotus flower. What is important at this time is to focus in on the energy field with the physical body contained within it, picturing two pyramids joined together, one with its top pointing up, the other with its top pointing down, each pyramid halfway encased in the other. (See Figure 15.)

Two Directions of the Electron Spiral of Light

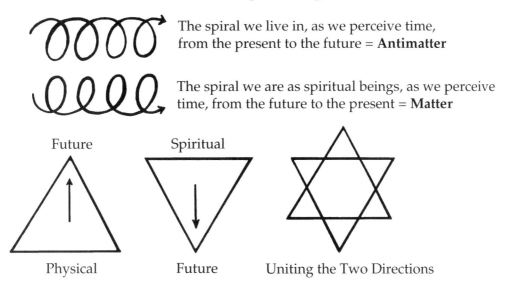

The spiral we live in, as we perceive time, from the present to the future = **Antimatter**

The spiral we are as spiritual beings, as we perceive time, from the future to the present = **Matter**

Future   Spiritual

Physical   Future   Uniting the Two Directions

Figure 15 The Secret of Light: Two Directions of Light

Kenneth Killick offers an explanation about the energy existing in two tetrahedrons or the human energy body.

"Light travels in two directions of the electron spiral. The spiral we live in, is antimatter. Time goes from past to future. When the electrons spiral in the other direction you are in the world of Matter. Here time goes from the future to the past. As we have said before, the pyramid is an antennae that refocuses light into its two directions. Light is synonymous with time. Light and time have two directions. In the physical pyramid, time goes from the past to the future. In the spiritual pyramid time goes from the future to the past. This is the symbol used by man when he unites the two directions of light or time. The Jewish people use this symbol as well as the founders of America. The symbol was used in the Essene villages where Jesus was raised. Its meaning for us is the uniting of the two directions of light so that one can pass on into the spiritual world. The first step one must take is to develop his sensing abilities to see and hear light. At this point he has begun his initiation into the higher levels of consciousness…If one is to look into the universe, one can easily see it express itself into the two directions of light. Everything in the universe is a spiral. Two directions of light moving in, and two directions moving out. The electrons are in constant spiral around the nucleus. The moon is in constant spiral around the earth, the earth around the sun and so on. The sub-atomic particles of light are moving in and out as they make up the energy field of the universe. It is in these energy fields that the power of the universe is expressed, tachion energy." (15)

As coincidence would have it, this same terminology called tachion energy (a proposed theoretical, but not yet discovered type of energy), is frequently used by *Star Trek* writers. For instance, in a *Star Trek Next Generation* episode called "Redemption, Part II," a series of 22 tachyon pulse beams (spelled differently) are cohesed into a tachyon detection grid to detect cloaked Romulan ships passing through a security net in space set up by the Federation, a governing organization for all planetary members. Tachyon pulse beam energy, mentioned in many *Star Trek* episodes, is used to power several spaceship technologies. In the original *Star Trek* series filmed in the late 1960s, the starship Enterprise was powered by matter/antimatter reactions in the ship's engines. This combustion process is said to power all Enterprise spaceships in *Star Trek* programs.

Bob Monroe has helped to create a similar reaction in the engine of the driver who is starting out to tour non-physical reality on the Interstate, by using a combination of Resonant Tuning and REBAL to launch consciousness into the non-physical realms. (See Figure 16.)

Theoretically speaking, tachyon energy is created through the dynamic use of three planes of consciousness. The force going straight up and down in the Star of David symbol is the force known in some bodywork and martial arts systems as the microcosmic orbit. This is a circuit of energy running vertically up and down the body. As Killick explained, there is the force going clockwise and a force going counterclockwise. In a Focus 15 experience, I was guided to learn that adding a third circling movement to the REBAL would change the energy from a standard Hertzian Wave to a standing columnar waveform which is tachyon energy. This movement was what was portrayed in the film, *Contact*. I began practicing this in my own meditative practice and instructing participants in advanced skill-building classes on how to activate the energy field so that tachyon energy is produced.

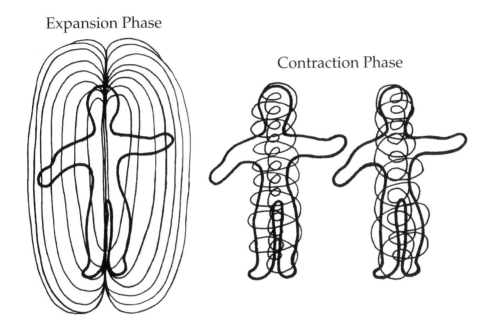

Expansion Phase

Contraction Phase

Figure 16 Creating Tachyon Energy in the REBAL

When adding a third turn to their REBAL, participants now report a noticeable change in their perception during Focus 10 and beyond. Monroe said during our Gateway Outreach Training Program, "If you get a good lift into Focus 10, it becomes the launching pad for all the other states." I have taken that to heart and do three movements during the creation of my REBAL which often produces an incredible "lift." I have discovered there are other times where tachyon energy can be inserted into the experience of other cities as well.

A recent newspaper article revealed that antimatter is now physical fact. Physicist Walter Oelert, with his team from Erlangen-Nurenberg University in Germany, produced antimatter atoms in Switzerland at the European Laboratory for Particle Physics known as CERN.

"Ordinary atoms are made up of a number of electron particles in orbit around a nucleus. Antimatter atoms have the same basic structure, but are made up of antiparticles. Every subatomic particle is known to have a corresponding antiparticle. Scientists say the fascinating quality of antimatter is that when it meets matter, the substance that all things on Earth are made of, the two substances annihilate each other, releasing a burst of energy." (16)

The collision changes duality into light. Thus, as the light increases in the energy body, the perplexities and karma of this Earth life transmute into creative intelligence or information. Light energy contains information. This discovery could provide a *Gateway* to a completely new anti-world, similar to the wormhole which is looking more and more like the tiny door Alice in Wonderland went through in her dreamtime activities.

The last skill-building in Focus 10 involves learning what Monroe called **Function Commands**. These are memorized sets of words sometimes coupled with a symbol to encode an experience while in a particular Focus state. The Function command or encoding process is similar to hypnotherapy and Silva Mind techniques known as anchoring. I refer to the Function Commands "triggers" because they retrigger a learned event much like a laser ruby opens a hologram record of information. During the Focus 10 experience, Monroe gives instructions for the five Function Commands. The first is an anchor for **memory**, a second is an anchor for becoming **awake and alert**, the third is an anchor to **spontaneously "pop" or trigger the REBAL** at any time or place, the fourth anchor is to **spontaneously trigger Focus 10** to use in waking reality without the Preparatory Process and without meditating, and the fifth anchor is to **return safely to physical reality** or what Monroe calls "C-1" consciousness. These are stashed to use whenever necessary in subsequent travels down the Interstate. Many participants have said these are very useful in everyday situations as well. (For further information on the use of these instant triggers, refer to the end of Chapter 5 under Gateway Excursion Examples.)

THE ROLLERCOASTER EXERCISE: INTRODUCTION TO THE CITY OF FOCUS 12

Tuning the dial to around 104.1 FM brings the exit sign of Focus 12 into view — the city of expanded consciousness. Typically, the first experience of Focus 12 is accomplished by experiencing a rollercoastering effect, that is to enter a state of non-physical reality then fairly quickly phase into another, then back into the original state. This rolling back and forth technique provides a sharp awareness of the new state posed against another state to measure the difference or change in perception. The experience of actually being able at will to shift phase from one state of consciousness to another is quite exciting for it provides the traveler with the idea that the consciousness is the vehicle that is changing phase, not the body. The traveler is the consciousness doing the changing, not the sounds, nor Bob Monroe. This is proven by practicing the shift phase without the aid of Hemi-Sync guidance. There is a distinct sensation that accompanies the change of perception into Focus 12; thus, when participants search for words to capture these sensations associated with expansion or contraction of perception, they get quite creative in their choice of words. (See Appendix A.)

Because Focus 10 is, as one participant puts it, "more stringent" than Focus 12, Monroe has participants follow their Preparatory Process through the five steps; the Ocean Surf relaxation phase, using the ECB, saying the Gateway Affirmation, constructing the REBAL, and lifting to Focus 10 using their Function Commands when needed during the process. After clearly experiencing the unique characteristics of the split state of Focus 10, he uses precise sound patterns to help the individual shift the consciousness to a wider perceptual window, that of Focus 12. When the experience in the change in consciousness in Focus 12 is achieved, he instructs the move to Focus 10, then back to Focus 12, then back to Focus 10 and to C-1 consciousness or physical reality. This is called rollercoastering. In Focus 12 the second time, he helps the participant to encode an anchor to spontaneously shift phase into Focus 12 without the Preparatory Process and for use in waking reality separate from any meditation practice. He also gives instructions for creating an anchor for Focus 12 problem-solving in waking reality, called the **One-Breath Focus 12 Problem-Solving Technique**. This, too, is to be used as a separate technique outside of meditative practice for making decisions in everyday reality.

ANCHORING THE CITY OF FOCUS 15

The exit to the city of Focus 15 is found near 102.1 FM in metaphorical terms. Monroe asks participants to do their Preparatory Process and then move on to Focus 10 by using the Function Command triggering the awareness for Focus 10. Then he asks the traveler to shift phase into Focus 12 by using the anchor that unlocks the experience of Focus 12. After the characteristics of Focus 12 are experienced, he guides participants to Focus 15, again using distinct tones to locate this city. After a time when Focus 15 is experienced, Monroe helps to anchor this city in consciousness by asking participants to think of a symbol representing a blissful, unconditional loving experience along with the actual vivid picturing or feeling or hearing of that experience. After the encoding is completed for Focus 15, participants stay in this city to explore its environment and are asked to notice how they are perceiving this place. Then they are guided through Focus 12, 10, and out at C-1 consciousness.

THE COLOR LADDER EXERCISE TO THE CITY OF FOCUS 21

After doing the Preparatory Process and phasing into Focus 10, then 12, then 15, Monroe then points out the Interstate sign for the next city. Close to 100.1 FM is the road sign for the exit to the city of Focus 21. This is achieved by using a series of colors assisted by different layers of Hemi-Sync sounds to move to the edge of the time-space continuum as we know it. Participants are asked to get acquainted with this city — its culture, its language, its peopled entities and most of all its energies — then are guided through the other Focus states back to waking consciousness.

The use of progressively deeper layering of Hemi-Sync sounds facilitates sequential training processes through to Focus 35. After each Focus state is firmly anchored, exercises demonstrating how to use the Focus states for personal growth are taught. The exercises can be used in meditation or as freestanding techniques. At times, the participant is asked to practice phasing into a group of Focus states while in a waking state, in order to integrate the skills and the encodings and to help transfer these skills and encodings for use in everyday life situations. In turn, this helps facilitate the development of Knowns for non-physical reality.

LEARNING HOW TO USE THE CRUISE CONTROL: GETTING CREATIVE

Are you interested in getting creative on your excursions? An interesting approach is to learn how to use the cities of Focus 10 through 21 and the skills in the Preparatory Process while standing on your feet in everyday situations. This combines the powers of the "Me" and the "I AM" aspects of consciousness. (See Chapters 5 and 6 for real life examples of people using this combination.) In addition, each of the Focus cities can be used by themselves or they can be combined with Human Plus Function Commands. (See Glossary.) This is where the dimensions come into play. Focus 10, being a city of consciousness with perceptual cues similar to earth-like existence, can easily be used for everyday events. By either doing the Preparatory Process privately or by using the Focus 10 trigger (Function Command), Focus 10 can be achieved in minutes while talking on the phone, sitting around the dinner table, or at a staff meeting etc. Specifically, Focus 10 can be triggered in moments of sadness, intimidation, or frustration for the purpose of ventilating, problem-solving, making decisions, or weighing options. For this reason, it's important to develop an awareness of the general characteristics for each Focus state so that they can be effectively used for specific life events. Here are some illustrations.

USING THE FOCUS STATES STANDING ON YOUR FEET

+ The crystal-clear clarity often found in Focus 10 will be beneficial for those events requiring clearheadedness, physical results, physical processes, emotional clearing, brainstorming, decision-making, problem-solving, and goal-setting (patterning).

+ The "body asleep" symptoms of Focus 10 will prove useful for events requiring body cooperation and synchronization such as childbirth, surgery, chemotherapy, dialysis, giving blood, running in marathons, or getting stitches.

+ The expansiveness quality associated with Focus 12 will be useful for events necessitating wide open, conceptual thinking such as storyboarding, imaging, creative brainstorming, locating trends and patterns, strategic planning, or synthesizing thinking such as coordinating organizational projects having many tasks, linking resources, or identifying combinations that will produce a new product.

+ The timelessness aspects of Focus 15 can be used to access other time periods for a history exam, to determine cultural or environmental impacts, to project ahead in planning for the future or to discern spiritual purpose.

◆ Focus 21 is well-suited to larger issues, moral challenges, right livelihood, learning about the universe, the cosmos, and beyond, developing a relationship with entities beyond this time-space continuum, and other approaches as mentioned in Chapter 2.

USING THE HUMAN PLUS ENCODINGS AS HOLOGRAPHIC KEYS TO JUMP START THE ENGINE

In the late 1980s, the Human Plus tapes were developed to help people gain and maintain control of their present day lives. Currently there are 28 variations on a theme of Function Commands on the Human Plus tapes, plus more on the Mind Food tapes which can be used in the Focus states at strategic times to create a specific response. Each Human Plus encoding tape is centered on a particular feature of physical, emotional or mental body components of everyday life. Examples: The H+ tape, "Let Go" is to release overwhelming feelings and emotions; and the H+ tape, "Tune-Up" is to learn to perceive, adjust, and heal any part of the physical body system; and the H+ tape, "Wake/Know" is to learn to use the sleep state to solve problems. Before attempting to use the combination of a Focus state and a H+ Function Command, a H+ tape should be selected and encoded according to the desired result. The first side of the H+ tape is a "dress rehearsal" to prepare the energy field for encoding, and the other side is the actual encoding process. After using the H+ tape to encode a Function command once or twice, the tape can be shelved or given away because the Function Command is all that is necessary. Once the 30 minute encoding process is completed and the more the Function Command is used, the more actualized the response becomes.

SEQUENCING HUMAN PLUS ENCODINGS TOGETHER CREATES CRITICAL MASS

Sequencing of Function Commands is advised especially for "stubborn" or "difficult" Function Commands to be coaxed into working. Sequencing, or combining several Function Commands together, puts the brain and energy field into a critical mass state called overdrive. This is a state whereby energy builds up in potential in order to help the traveler break through into a new perception and dimension. A popular sequencing combination many people use when they are in an emotional crisis is to first use the Focus 10 anchor to access Focus 10, wait until the Focus 10 signs arrive, then add these three Human Plus Function Commands one after another: H+ **Attention**, H+ **Relax**, and H+ **Let Go**. Focus 10 is used to clear up the mind and detach the body. H+ **Attention** is used to tell the mind to focus in on the overwhelming emotional event without being distracted by other events or people. H+ **Relax** is used to then tell the body to keep relaxing and get the endorphins going despite the emotional pull. H+ **Let Go** is used to let go of the emotional thoughtform. I call this particular sequencing approach "poking a hole in what's awful" because it helps stop the draining pull of the emotional experience while at the same time supporting the ability to pay attention to what's important in a crisis situation. Usually it's very difficult to stay sane during a highly emotionally-charged event. Numerous clients report how powerful this H+ sequence has been for them. Another approach is to access and use Focus 12 for wide open perceptual expansion. For instance, at city council meetings, in a courtroom, or during family dinnertime, use the Focus 12 instant Function Command and then insert the Function Commands of H+ **De-Hab** to break up a particular habit triggered in these tense group settings. Then use H+ **Mobius West** to shift behavior into a more desired pattern. There are actual life stories from clients using H+ Function Commands and their results described in Chapter 5.

Putting these tools together, the Focus state and Function Commands, can produce very creative outcomes since there are hundreds of combinations using the 13 Focus states, the 28 H+ Function Commands and the encodings on the Mind Food tapes. However, as said before, the specific intention of the person at the wheel determines what the actual outcome is. If a person has a purpose with a third dimensional perspective, most likely, exiting will occur in a "downtown" neighborhood. On the other hand, if the intention comes from a fifth dimensional viewpoint, then an "uptown" neighborhood response will occur. Using the first example, if there was a third dimensional "intent" driving the vehicle, travel would exit into a logical, reasonable, physical, "black and white" form; whereas, if there was a fifth dimensional intent behind the wheel, then travel would result in a abstract, symbolic, form most likely with a pure and simple answer. What is created *by intention* when saying a Function Command in a Focus state will create the results.

DON'T FORGET TO DROP THE TRAINING WHEELS !

Many people who use the Focus states gradually forget to use these cities regularly in their everyday lives. Instead, they think this is only for special meditation moments, not for practical, commonplace use. On the Voyagers List, which is a TMI sponsored online service devoted to Hemi-Sync fans, I suggested that the Focus states be used for real life situations. Many people across the globe expressed surprise and resistance. Unfortunately, people stick to the tapes, limiting themselves to what is suggested in the exercise and then forget about using the Focus states without the tapes or CDs.

Rather than being a set of magic bullets, think of Hemi-Sync as being a set of training wheels. Bob would often suggest that we move away as quickly as we can from these training wheels so that our consciousness can take off on its own and use its own creative juices. A way to wean yourself off the tapes is to use a piece of Metamusic in the background to support your efforts to enter and sustain Focus State experiences. Then loan or give away the tapes to someone else so that your vehicle can be driven under its own power.

TRAVELING IN RAIN, SLEET , NOISY CONFABS, OR SNOW

There are conducive environments that support Interstate travel but there are also "Grade B" conditions that aren't so helpful. A few years back I remember conducting a class, which I called the "20,000 Mile Brain Tune-up," at a large Cleveland NASA facility. The purpose of the class was memory enhancement which involved encoding the H+ **Imprint** tape. Between 50-60 individuals attended who were jet plane pilots, engineers, statisticians, and researchers. During the encoding, when everyone was deeply relaxed, a rapid sequence of several noisy jets took off down the runway, blasting and shaking the metal quonset hut we were in. That was not fun! My anxiety level rose and hovered precipitously. Later on, during the deep sleep phase of the tape, I suddenly thought to myself, "What if a lot of these people fall off their uncomfortable steel chairs all at once during the last part?" (When most people fall deeply asleep!) To make matters worse, I was the only one awake in the building. They all were seated at long tables. One by one, several heads fell gently onto the tables. Meanwhile, my anxiousness rose like one of those jets taking off! I began to worry about whether the encoding was going to "take" at all. Seeing things building, I quickly triggered my H+ **Relax**, **Let Go**, **Think Fast** Function Commands to get beyond my panicky preoccupations. I knew if there was a lot of skeptical energy including my own in the room, we weren't going to have good individual and group scores on the memory test to show a change in memory and recall abilities. I worked to clear away my anxiousness and return to a relaxed state using these Function Commands. We did the post-test memory exercise with the memory recall anchor. I breathed a sign of relief when both the individual and group scores indicated a change over the pretest scores despite the jet noise and being jammed into a cold, small metal hut with a lot of skeptical individuals.

FINDING PRIVACY TO TRAVEL TO POINTS UNKNOWN

This same situation can be found in family homes or shared living situations where there are constant loud interruptions, banging doors, blaring music, neighbors fighting, phones ringing, and doors blowing shut. Many a parent of young children has asked me, "Where do I find a place to do this stuff?" Try asking for privacy, briefly explaining what you are doing in simple terms, and being persistent about your use of personal time. Probably the best story I heard was where one couple strapped on their Walkmans, escaped to their boat stored in the garage, made themselves comfortable, and turned on their Hemi-Sync tapes!

RETURNING TO THE REGULAR WORLD

Besides the actual environmental space factors, the energy of the people around the meditative, learning space should be considered as well. For example, one time I was facilitating a Gateway Excursion a few years ago in a large well-known suburban motel in the Midwest. Everything went quite well during the sessions on Friday and Saturday. The participants were asking especially insightful questions, and we all were feeling very supportive of each other. This smooth ride continued into Sunday until we hit the first restroom break, when another world literally came upon the scene. In the restrooms we were besieged with Mary Kay cosmetics conventioneers dressed in their finest, smelling of heavy perfume, made up like movie stars and of course, networking loudly like a gaggle of geese circling over a corn field. Needless to say, it was a dramatic change of pace from the comfy, cozy, quiet atmosphere we had enjoyed the first two days. Because there are a lot of breaks on the Gateway Excursion due to energetic cleansing, we had to face the stars every hour on the hour. The blast of their energy versus ours was very difficult to overcome.

This sudden barrage of hitting the real world after doing Focus state work in your special area can be equally unnerving. Suggest to family members or housemates that you require time to regroup just as they do after taking deep catnaps. Easing back after doing Focus State work requires a few moments of time to readjust to the regular world.

OVERCOMING 'TWO THUMBS DOWN' TRAVELING PLACES

There are prime meditative areas and then there are "two thumbs down" spaces. Many of my clients have reported more Grade B environments than prime spaces. An ideal place is a quiet carpeted place with no phones, no loud elevator noise, no opening and shutting of squeaky doors, no clicking on and off furnace noise and no loud, hissing air conditioners or blowers, no rattling windows or shades, no loud birds cawing outside, no cars or delivery trucks coming and going, and no loud jet planes taking off into the wild blue! Having experienced all these delicious aiding and abetting factors, it's sometimes hard to work around them. If you have difficulty finding a quiet, peaceful place and time to meditate, I suggest wearing your calm, happiness, and sense of balance that comes from doing Focus State on your shirtsleeves more prominently. This has helped create more cooperation than a list of demands nailed to a locked, bedroom door. Afterwards meditating, strike up a little conversation about the experience in general terms. These comments can be reassuring and a little educational for the family or household.

It is so important to set aside and maintain a prime time special meditative space. This can have considerably more longterm payoffs for you than having a best friend who takes care of things when you are on vacation. As you use your prime area in the home over and over, it becomes a mini-energy vortex center. Eventually it will feel like an old, comfortable car that you love to sit in, perfect for traveling to points unknown.

REVIEWING THE TRIP TICKET:
TRACKING THE RESULTS OF TRAVEL EXPERIENCES

Was the trip enjoyable? Was it worth it? Too often, when people go to the near and far territories of consciousness, they come back and quickly push themselves into the harried world without knowing if the trip gave them something of value. This makes the experience a Disneyland trip once removed. Is there a real urge to find out the meaning of life in this part of the Interstate? Is it worth something to you to stop and make the connections about what was experienced?

Two approaches can be used to evaluate what happened. One is to become more aware of what happened as a result of traveling into non-physical realities (taking ownership of the experience), and the other is to make a conscious effort to take non-physical learnings back into everyday life (integrating what was learned).

THE 'FLY ON THE WALL' APPROACH

As a travel agent over the years, I've noticed the tendency of workshop participants to get so absorbed by the trees, they don't take time to develop their ability to view their own forest. Monroe, at different points in his three books, encouraged his readers to develop a third person perspective, a "fly on the wall" view to look at the bigger picture. This, in part, was possibly a role for his ISH or his Inner Self Helper which appeared throughout his books.

To do this means to imagine seeing yourself having the experience as though you were a third person watching yourself. This is done by dialogging with yourself saying such things as, "she poured herself into the Resonant Tuning and then halfway, lost her focus and didn't make an effort to stay with it," "Eddie launched himself quite well into Focus 12 and experienced this…" or "Nancy experienced a mystical union with a bright light form and kept wondering how she created that and what it meant." Developing objectivity helps to see and understand the subject matter of what is going on but also the process one used to gain that meaning.

Using the "fly on the wall" during and after traveling jaunts makes patterns or trends become more obvious. Sometimes you are so close to the answers you don't see them. The patterns reveal larger meanings that will gradually grow into Knowns. This produces unique and gratifying travel experiences. Sometimes the patterns or trends are known, but not registered with intent or feeling, so they get lost in the newness or the entertaining aspect of traveling. Here are some approaches to see the bigger picture of what's happening and to coach yourself into being more aware of the results.

IDENTIFYING THE BIGGER PICTURE

• **Tracking Dreams**. Keep a dream journal and go back over it from time to time looking for patterns or trends. Pay attention to repeated topics. Assign a label to a dream such as "Baby Dream," "Beach Dream," "Falling Dream," "Learning to Assert Myself Dream" so that tracking of patterns is easier. Observe for not only repeated themes but also for repeated processes such as going down the same street, getting lost in maze after maze, eating something over and over or experiencing various types of sensations. Cultivate an intuitional ability to scan through dreams looking for connections by freely letting the eye center on important written phrases. Try highlighting one phrase or word, then use free-associating method to uncover the pure meaning. This is done by letting any descriptive word after word come out until something clicks to announce the right meaning. Then gather up the "clicks" and look for connections.

Find the peaks and valleys in the dream plots. Be especially objective about these highs and lows or positive and negative areas, for they indicate places where big decisions or solutions are being played out. Don't look for the obvious meaning. Dream subject matter is abstract and symbolic in nature. Consider taking the opposite approach or developing an idea that would be totally contrary to what would ordinarily feel right. Look at any crazy, off the wall dream components, characters, or scenes as if they might be the sanest moment in the dream.

• **Re-experiencing an Intriguing Element.** Days or months after having a traveling experience, reread your notes about your jaunts onto the Interstate. This lends a fresh viewpoint and brings to mind things that were de-emphasized at the time. To recapture an experience, the use of drawings will help reexperience the dynamics of a particular approach. These drawings contain opportunities to identify a Know-How formula ("How did I do that?") that is beginning to form. Doing a painting, a watercolor, an acrylic or a sculpture of an important element or entity from a particular Focus state experience will reveal hidden components of unique personal content or process. Using the arts to reexperience non-physical wisdom validates the objectivity encased in its memory, so that it flows out into the physical, ready and willing to be incorporated into everyday life.

◆ **Observing Personal Energy Changes**. Tracking personal energetic changes can be a powerful source of information. Observe the subtle nuances in behavioral routines or rituals, such as watching voice impressions, rhythm, pitch, or the power behind words. Watch hand movements, observe sensations in the hand. Subtle growth changes in the hand can show how the body moves and supports the changes going on. Talking to yourself in the mirror can identify facial changes and body posture changes. Moreover, as the waveform of you who, minute-by-minute, rearranges your beauty within, these tracking activities help anchor a sense of worth, value, and self-love. This is learning to stay in the body.

◆ **Examining Belief Systems**. Ask the question, "What would (insert your name) had to have believed in order to have this experience (he/she) just had?" Repeating this question three or four times in a row will often get to the core belief underlying the experience. The first few times the ego will reply with a status quo belief, then eventually the unconscious mind will release the truth underneath. Secretly held beliefs then pop up which bring to light parts of the unknown Self. Using H+ "Contemplation" and "Let Go" during the process will put extra momentum behind the question. This exercise will help you get to the core of your personal philosophy and belief systems. This kind of traveling on the Interstate challenges beliefs all the time. They *often* require modifying or eliminating. Remember Monroe's words, "Essentially, we are a waveforms of energy."

◆ **Asking for Feedback From a Traveling Partner**. Develop and maintain a supportive relationship with a traveling partner who is also traveling the Interstate of Consciousness. Meet on a regular basis. If it's not physically possible to locate a person with similar interests, ask in Focus 10 or Focus 12 to manifest such a person. Be willing to use the phone, email or carrier pigeon to carry out this relationship. Be open to innovative means to support each other, and open communicative possibilities such as remote viewing and remote healing projects to increase skills and Knowns. Take some trips together either at the same physical time and place or at different times and places but with the same intention. Share content and process, help each other through the use of objective empathy, that is maintaining individuality while being able to understand the other's point of view and experience. Develop wonder about the waveform of another, watch his or her unique Divine Design pattern unfold.

INTEGRATING BACK INTO EVERYDAY REALITY

All the learning, insights, and skills achieved in non-physical reality can be transferred back into everyday life situations. Unfortunately, this is something many people forget to do. Maybe this comes from the ingrained belief that "My physical and non-physical life should remain separate." This is similar to the thinking that church and state, boss and co-worker, parent and child, are apples and oranges, and thus, there is a line that should be drawn. On the contrary, as within, so without. If a skill is learned in an expanded, non-physical reality, the "within" in physical reality will be definitely be changed.

To consciously recognize and take responsibility for that change means there will be an identity shake up. That's where the hesitation comes from — claiming the new identity after energetic releases, rearrangements and new insights. The beta-based ego, who lives in incoherency and who wants to maintain a status quo, no-growth situation, is the culprit. This part of Self has to be coaxed in small ways to realign with the growing, changing energetic Self.

Here is an actual example of how to coach parts of the Self to catch up to the changed, energetic whole Self. Oprah Winfrey, talk show host, received so much mail on her permanent weight change and its effects on her listening audience that she created a program in the summer of 1995 on that topic. Later, in November of the same year, she had a segment in which she reviewed the most popular people for the previous year on her talk show. Receiving some of the highest caller responses for one of the most popular was a woman named Judy. She confessed that she was no longer the loyal fan she had been for years. This was due to Oprah's overall identity changes. Judy gave the following example. She said she would have been very willing to invite Oprah into her home for a cup of coffee when Oprah was heavy, she now would feel awkward and unwilling to do so.

Not only was Judy accurately describing the collective belief about the physical body stereotype during weight loss changes, she was also making a statement about changes in the energy field (REBAL) which individuals radiate and how it can intimidate those who have the same issues.

At first, upon hearing this confession, Oprah admitted she had a lot of difficulty understanding this woman's point of view. Later on, after sorting it out, she became angry with her because the woman had attempted to place blame on Oprah for Oprah's lifestyle changes. In the program's closing moments, Oprah eventually accepted this woman's opinion, but felt compelled to say she was not going to return to her former self. She confessed that her excess weight had represented a gigantic need to protect herself from the heavy issues of abuse, neglect, and abandonment she had experienced in her life. It was the jettisoning of this abuse addiction, not the calories, that shifted her weight. As a result of these inward changes, she declared she would continue to step away from the traditional talk show format in order to be lighter and happier despite the ratings drop and the loss of certain friends and professional allies. When making changes in everyday situations, Oprah is an excellent example of how to take baby steps to firmly retrain the ego Self to support the new change learned in non-physical reality.

Next step on this journey is hearing the stories of people using Hemi-Sync while on the road and how they have carried their learning into their daily lives.

HOW TO PUT THE PEDAL TO THE METAL

From the first M-5000 TMI workshop weekend to
understanding the Frequency Following Response.
While decoding the human hologram,
tuning the radio brain to different cities of consciousness,
adding H+ to cruise and not forgetting to evaluate the trip,
it all works out.

DOWNSHIFTING TRAVEL EXPERIENCES
INTO THE GEAR FOR EVERYDAY LIVING

*"Just as ships without rudders are at the mercy of the wind,
so our minds are at the mercy of our moods...
Suppose we could direct our minds the way rudders direct ships.
We can. The rudder is called Hemi-Sync."*

Ronald Russell, *Using the Whole Brain*

ROUTE 5

TAKING SYNCHRONICITY ON THE ROAD

Childlike wonderment, increasing calmness and growing spiritual identity move in as travel on the Interstate of Consciousness progresses. Over the years, there have been many people who have shared their traveling experiences with me, some through individual coaching, others who attended the Gateway Excursion, still others who are TMI graduates and are part of the monthly Explorer Support Group meetings that I have been facilitating for many years. I have met these people through presentations in adult education classes at colleges and universities, elementary through high school programs, in neighborhood centers, outreach prison programs, church child care centers, corporate wellness centers, holistic organizations, hospital continuing education programs, civic/social groups, and through professional referral. More often than not, individuals decide on their own to use this tool rather than being encouraged by professionals or family members. People who seem to be the most satisfied and encouraged by their results are those who open to the larger, unknown possibilities, who are comfortable with abstract ideas, and who are aware of their lives changing on several levels. Following is a gathering of stories from people who have used Hemi-Sync as a key to open their doors of adventure whether it be of a chilling, thrilling nature, a nice bedtime read, or a mystical, unifying experience. On the other hand, I have also seen people use Hemi-Sync to close other doors that represent eliminating diseased, dying organs, brutal life chapters, or unsatisfying jobs. These real life narratives represent non-ordinary adventures on the Interstate. The first story shows a broad comprehensive picture of using various Hemi-Sync tools (Gateway Experience Series, Human Plus, and Mind Food tapes) for physical skill change and spiritual growth for both the client and myself.

WILL I SEE LIKE NORMAL PEOPLE SEE?

Sally: We began to work together in January of 1990. We seemed to switch roles somewhere early in the 18 months we were partners using Hemi-Sync. At first I thought if I could use Focus 12, I would magically redevelop physical sight which I had for a few hours when first born. Being two months premature, soon after birth my retinas were burned away by too much oxygen left on in my incubator, creating total blindness. Inspired and challenged after hearing a radio interview with Patricia describing her Hemi-Sync work, I phoned her and asked if she could help me rebuild my self-confidence and increase my attention span. Up until now, at 35 years old, I had been unemployed, and undecided about many things and generally losing interest in life.

Patricia: When I made my first house call, I soon found myself foundering, searching for words. One of the reasons was I felt intimidated by Sally who represented something unknown, literally someone who lives in the dark side of herself. The first time we met my fears came packaged in all kinds of concerns, but I kept them on the back burner. I was worried that she wouldn't be able to remember one tape from another because she couldn't see them and I couldn't rely on the catalog to reinforce my explanations. There wasn't any braille marking system available to help. I realized we both were in the dark in many ways.

On my second visit I let go of my confusion and intimidation, got brave and asked Sally if she would guide me into her world of darkness. I let go of my traditional, intellectually biased, therapeutic approach and told my intuition to be my guide dog. I listened carefully to Sally's health care history which was highlighted by diabetes and narcolepsy (overwhelming attacks of sleep) diagnosed in high school days. To help her with her scattered energy and self-esteem, I showed her how to encode the **Human Plus** (H+) tapes of **Attention** (to focus) and **Off-Loading** (to release restrictive behavior) for daytime use. To increase her efficiency and attentional energies in the afternoon when her sleepiness increased and her Ritalin medication wasn't helping her enough, I encouraged her to use the tape **Concentration** played on an auto-reverse cassette player for periods when she typically got sleepy. In the radio broadcasting studio during the day where she was a student, Sally had to be physically and verbally quick on her feet so she also encoded **H+ Speak Up** and **H+ Reset** to use there.

Sally: In the intervening weeks, I remember telling Patricia about a discussion I had with my mother on how she felt about my using the Hemi-Sync tapes. She told me she was skeptical and had reservations about the results. I began to feel very anxious and so I said the encoding to Off-Loading ("fade, fade") and minutes later through my tears, I found myself saying very emphatically that I wanted to feel the eagerness for life that I had felt as a child despite her misgivings. Maybe it was how I said this, but from then on, it was my Mother who kept noticing little things about me that were changing. Changes were really happening! For instance, when I used **H+ Attention**, it was like someone opened up the top of my head, breathed fresh air inside causing all my senses to snap open. What a great, refreshing change!

Another thing that happened was during Easter services at church. Previously, my pastor asked me to give the Palm Sunday children's homily on "Blessed are the blind" by describing what it was like for me to be blind. He also asked me to sing a favorite song of mine for the congregation. When it came time to do that, I silently used **H+ Attention** , **Speak Up** & **Off-Loading** during my talk in front of the kids. Having taken singing lessons for a long time, I felt my breath control ability amazingly expand like an endless balloon. I didn't have to use hardly any stagger breaths to regain control. I just kept talking smoothly, and easily; whereas in the past, I wouldn't have had the courage, the words, or the breath to do this.

Patricia: Sally was diagnosed with Carpal Tunnel Syndrome (numbness in the wrist due to habitual overflexion and nerve damage.) Having two other surgeries in the past year which caused weight loss and hypoglycemic episodes adding to her general feeling of losing inner control, Sally began to dread the surgery. She asked me to use the **Surgical Support Series**.

Her results were similar to other clients who had used these tools. Sally gained the support of her orthopedic surgeon, her anesthesiologist, and nursing team and negotiated to have a local anesthetic despite recommendations by her surgeon to have general anesthesia. After the surgery Sally underwent significantly less pain, used no pain medication for the first six hours, ate heartily in the Recovery Room and did not have any nausea and vomiting, nor cyclic constipation for four to five days post-operatively. Typically her weight went below 89 pounds with the other surgeries due to these problems, but this time she did not have any weight loss. At the first dressing change three days post-op her surgeon remarked how clean and clear her suture line looked which is unusual for diabetics to heal so fast and well. Throughout this surgery, Sally expressed a great amount of pride in being more of a partner in her healing process. Instead of assuming her old passive behaviors during a life-threatening event, she said she was gaining a stronghold inside and feeling more inner control. As a result of these changes, she found it necessary to decrease her Ritalin dosage and use less insulin without any negative effects.

Sally: I asked Patricia to help me start the **Gateway Experience Series** of tapes for my own spiritual growth. Inside my dark world, I knew I had sight in some way. Somehow I wanted to make it more apparent to myself so I began on a regular basis to use the encodings without the tapes to access and sustain Focus 10 in my everyday situations. One day while grocery shopping with my Mother and my Aunt, I distinctly heard a little inner voice like my Uncle calling me on the phone to say he was going to pick up his wife that next day. At the checkout I told my Mother what I heard. That evening he called and said exactly the same words I heard in the store earlier. Patricia asked me where on my body I felt sensations when I received his message in the grocery store. She explained that as we grow our third eye abilities, progressive sensations in various parts of the body signal input. First sensations of early intuitional skill center in the abdomen, then as the skill matures, the point of vibration moves gradually up the chakras and eventually settles in the third eye. I had experienced a quivering sensation in my heart area. Later on, I had another intuitional experience involving a close friend which seemed to vibrate in my third eye area, leaving that area warm and somewhat tingling. This gave me proof that I, indeed, was seeing more than I had ever looked for. This kind of intuitional skill might be a distinct advantage for other blind people to use in their lives because it will be a trustworthy friend as it is now becoming for me.

So Patricia and I sort of took each other's hand and crossed into each other's worlds. I became more physically self-assured as I now know more clearly what's out there because I am trusting my intuition more and more. I have become gainfully employed for the first time in my life, and I feel much more alert and eager for life again.

Patricia: I bumped and bumbled around to discover the workings of third eye sightedness through Sally's inner eyes. Surprise of surprises! Besides helping me to gain a new perspective, it helped Sally enrich her sense of self-esteem and my own. Along the way I found out how to drop my sighted expectations and work collaboratively with her and in so doing, walked or was led, I don't know which, into seeing beyond the physical plane.

S.L., Cleveland, Ohio and P.A.L.

ROAD STORIES FROM GATEWAY GRADS LEARNING TO USE THE FOCUS STATES

IT ALL STARTED WITH A FEW MOMENTS OF SURF

September 1994, my level of dissatisfaction increases to a fever pitch as I contemplate my so-called life at 42. President of a small (too small) computer technology company. Suburban house. Overworked wife. Cranky kids. Cranky me. Seriously depressed. What is wrong? I've been shedding my bad habits over the years. Stopped drinking (did the AA thing, it worked) but all this God talk all the time; I cannot relate. I must find my own answers. God doesn't talk to guys like me — except to say something like "figure it out, dip shit." I'm not drinking but what's left is the empty glass. I need to know more. The last thing I want is an organized religion. It's why I skipped out on sticking with AA. It's just too much judgment and control for me. And can I read another self-help book or listen to a tape and NOT blow my brains out? I need actual experience, not another book.

Wandering around the Internet looking for something interesting, there's a mention of The Monroe Institute; further investigation reveals interesting technology and a non-religious approach. This appeals to my empirical mind. So naturally I blow the whole thing off.

October 1994 — I wander into a small bookstore and see a copy of the Surf tape from TMI. Why not? That evening I lay down in my bed after work, dim the lights, flip on the tape, and there's the sound of syntho-surf, seagulls squawking, waves washing. Underneath, a faint pulsing rhythm. A couple of minutes later it's over. Except it's been a half hour. Hmm.

I've been listening to the tape once a day for two weeks. Using it, I have no thoughts — which has a potent effect, since my mind runs on a nuclear burn constantly. Physical things happen. The body feels tingly, like it's full of some kind of energy. Sometimes it feels very heavy (which it is, of course). Frequently all body sensation drops away and all that is left is pure awareness. These were very deep experiences, Focus 12 they call it.

I meet up with Patricia in Boulder, converse with some people on line, pick up the first series of the Gateway collection, and plunge in. I achieve deeper and deeper states of 'relaxation' for want of a better term. I have many personal realizations. Some call this guidance, voices from the nether worlds, angels, whatever. Personal insight is a good description for me. What are some of them? I learned the capability of achieving calmness and relaxation. Something that I use constantly. My co-workers have asked how I've become such a different person, so suddenly. This alone has improved my relationships with the family more than I can describe. I see that my thoughts are images that I make, as are my emotions. They are not me. They are my creations which allows me to see that they are controllable. I've become the watcher behind the person and the voice that everyone sees and hears. An important distinction. Before I wasn't that fully in my body.

I know that I am not a body. I'm an energy being. Ok, I could say spirit, but I still have my aversion to traditional religious lingo. I know this because there is a specific, clear difference between the energy I feel during a tape session (dare I call it meditation?) and the physical metabolic energy of my body. Do smiling light beings answer all my questions? Do I fly to far away places and see beautiful things? Do I dance across the Milky Way, talk to my dead grandmother, or bounce photon balls with friendly aliens? Alas, none of these things occur. But I wouldn't trade my new life for any of that regardless of the entertainment value.

D. H., Denver, Colorado

BECOMING THE WAVEFORM

On the Gateway Excursion Weekend I had quite an experience in Focus 12 while listening to its high intense sounds. I knew it was Focus 12 because of the intense feeling sensations and wide open perception. In the beginning I heard ocean sounds while visions of blue, green, and black patterns danced before my eyes. I sensed that this was water. Sometimes it felt like surface water, sometimes it felt like deep water. Then there were waves. Beyond that, I was both the water of the wave and the transparent droplets of the splash of the wave. Soon after, it seemed the water was rushing over me and I became the riverbed. Then the water began moving faster, faster and started to swirl and erode deeply into me, deeper and deeper into what seemed like a canyon. Then I realized it was not a canyon, but a deep artesian well, bubbling up with effervescence. Again another insight came, I was that bubbling water!

For me, Hemi-Sync is helping me to expand my awareness on other planes and provides many new avenues for solving problems, avenues that are simply not available in the ordinary plane of my human consciousness.

In these heightened focused levels I am obtaining insights which are powerful tools to carry during my daily work in this life. The part about me being water in that focused awareness really does translate that I am more than my physical body. I can see this so clearly in these Focus States. This is where I realize the true word or my truth. My truth of who I am in part is no longer a belief, it is now a Known.

H.A., Las Vegas, Nevada

DISCOVERING WHO AM I IN FREE FLOW FOCUS 12

In level 12, I asked who I was and where I was before I came into this body. Who am I really? I was surprised to see a beautiful, billowy, opalescent angel floating down, carrying a white form. I knew the form was a soul being delivered to a body and that I was both the angel and the soul. I felt a sense of awe and deep peace. Afterwards I felt very precious and innocent.

Later that evening and the next day more understanding and more knowing came to me. I understood that my angel is Divine Innocence and that as the angel carried the soul to its new body, the angel projected its innocence into the soul so that when it was born it would feel innocent once again. I know now why I love babies so much and why I have always felt so close to angels. I also understand now that I came to earth to experience that which I am not. My innocence has been taken advantage of repeatedly throughout my life but now I have gained the knowing that my innocence is important to be here in human form at this time and that I go where my innocence is needed.

B. C., Steamboat Springs, Colorado

USING FOCUS 10 THROUGH 21 WHILE WALKING ON A GRAVEL ROAD

This happened while I was at a Gateway Voyage at TMI. We were instructed to go out beyond the training center and our CHEK units to test our newly developed skills by walking around the grounds and putting ourselves sequentially through the Focus states to experience their effects, all the while with eyes opened. I used the Preparatory Process to lift myself into Focus 10 and noticed that my seeing and hearing abilities were significantly enhanced while my body seemed to be somewhat detached and easily syncopated in its walking rhythms. I moved into Focus 12 then observed that I was perceiving a halo-effect of light around the pine tree needles and tree branches. I stuck my fingers into the halo area and sensed a quivering warmth of energy moving in that area. Moving into Focus 15, I walked along with seemingly nothing happening for quite a while, then all of a sudden my foot wouldn't go down for the next step. It was frozen in place. I changed my balance, my posture, my muscle alignment and pushed harder. Nothing worked. I decided to make the best use of this experience so I forgot about my frozen right leg hanging in mid-air and put my attention on a large pine tree. There was a bird high in the tree on a branch almost at the top which was about 15 or 20 feet above me. I willed my consciousness to be on an even level with the bird and found myself stretching upward. I looked at the bird face to face and felt the grain of his feathers as my sight flowed over him. He began to chirp and another bird in the distance returned his call. When the chirp came back, a vibration went through me on its way to the bird who sent a chirping sensation back. I blessed both of them for showing me how they communicate, then I willed myself to return to the road and without warning, my right foot touched the ground with an abrupt, loud thumping noise. In Focus 21 I walked along the perimeter of the ridge and looked straight onto the deck of a beautiful brown cedar home. There were noisy, chattering birds perched on a bird feeder. I absorbed the exquisite peacefulness of this sight that seemed to reach over the ridge into the mountains like it was a palatable vitamin perfectly designed for me, and then I moved back to C-1 consciousness. Literally since then I have been acquiring more and more peacefulness in many aspects of my lifestyle and eliminating the elements that use a lot of struggle, effort and drama.

P.L.M., Erie, Pennsylvania

INCREASING SYNCHRONISTIC EVENTS WHICH ARE MESSENGERS IN MY LIFE

Having explored a number of different spiritual systems, including various forms of yoga, meditation, mysticism, shamanism, astral projection etc., I was quite intrigued by the Bob Monroe material and the Gateway Excursion Weekend. His work seemed to integrate and honor so many other disciplines, while being completely unique at the same time. It was possible to achieve states of deep, meditative consciousness through the

Focus states with greater ease and celerity than through other approaches. I had previously assumed that a more rigorous, disciplined and lengthy practice was necessary to arrive at such enhanced states of being.

After going through the process several times, the order and ritual of exercises that leads you into the Focus states starts to feel sublimely well-orchestrated. It takes on an otherworldly familiarity as you begin to personally cultivate each region and nuance of the experience. Focus 10 is one of the most profound states of physical tranquility that I have ever entered. It becomes remarkably easy to achieve. The sheer concept of training your body to be deeply asleep while your mind is simultaneously awake and alert is a brilliant stroke which seems to have major healing implications as well as providing a launching pad or *Gateway* for more advanced spiritual work. The feeling is remarkable and quite attainable; a split level of consciousness, not unlike the left and right hands of an adept pianist or like a dreamer who can walk into the mundane, terrestrial world. In fact, on the first night of the Excursion Weekend, I had one of my most vivid and powerful lucid dream experiences, becoming quite conscious and in control in my own dreamscape. The sequence lasted for quite a long time relative to previous episodes of lucidity and contained quite a few Castaneda-esque elements. I felt certain that the Bob Monroe work had helped to facilitate access to these conscious dream realms, which are usually quite elusive, only occurring at very infrequent and seemingly random intervals.

Spending time in the Focus States tends to increase synchronistic activity as well, or at least the awareness of its occurrence. While in Focus 10, there were several flies moving around the perimeter of my body intermittent touching specific spots on my skin, if only for a moment. Each incident of contact seemed to relate intimately to thoughts I was experiencing at that instant, using parts of my body symbolically as the syntax for some etheric form of communication. As odd as it sounds, messages of personal significance seemed to be relayed by this whole exchange, whether the flies were unwittingly operating as some sort of conduit for information, or they possessed some version of intelligence, or whether it was all an acausal concurrence to which I ascribed my own particular meaning. The fact was, my sensitivity and my receptivity to such minutia had been heightened in the Focus States.

A few weeks after the workshop, Patricia, who had done such an excellent job conducting the entire weekend, called me on the phone. I had been playing rather wild electric guitar into a Rockman, a device that allows you to play through headphones at a decibel level that would surely disturb the neighbors if played through an external amplifier. I was playing through an array of sound effects to color and enhance the signal — primarily echo, chorus (slightly de-tuned doubling) and reverb. I had been playing in this sonic nether world for about an hour when I heard the phone. Immediately upon lifting the receiver and uttering my first sentence, Patricia remarked, "You sound funny; like your energy is doubled or reverberating somehow. As though your energy field is not entirely coherent." I was so astounded, not only by her sensitivity, but by the possibility that playing music in that form could actually alter my subtle energy fields. Sure, it seems plausible conceptually, but to have such an overt experience of it was a bit startling. I've been playing acoustic guitar almost exclusively since the incident.

More peculiar still, was a day where I entered into Focus 12, which is a state of receptivity and awareness unlike any I have ever known and where slowly pulsing amorphous gray blobs create the entire "mindscape." On one particular occasion I reached a certain non-verbal serenity that I had come to associate with Focus 12 and the now familiar gray shapes began to appear, more still than usual this time. Once I had settled in, I recognized the shape of a face which was not fully formed, but still recognizable as a woman who I knew but had been out of contact with for several months. I thought it odd for her to show up in such a deep state for me, because we were never really that close. Her face was the only remotely anthropomorphic image in my scope of awareness. Later that afternoon, my live-in girlfriend arrived home from a fair she had been to. "You'll never guess who I saw at the fair." Amazingly, not only had she run into the woman whose face had appeared in my Focus 12 state at approximately the same time, but the woman had done a portrait of my girlfriend as well. When she showed me the painting, the most characteristic detail was the fact that my girlfriend's face was not fully formed or well-defined around the edges, the same kind of underdeveloped countenance that the woman's face had had in my Focus 12 state.

Many wondrous events have occurred in my life in the four months since the Gateway Excursion Weekend and although they cannot all be traced to a singular experience, the work we did that weekend seems to have been some kind of integral component or catalyst for much has followed.

F.E., Boulder, Colorado

INDEED WE ARE MORE THAN OUR PHYSICAL BODIES!

Surprises! The totally unexpected! These are cliches for TMI experiences but, for me, they best describe what occurred at my PREP session during a Guidelines Residential Program I attended at The Monroe Institute in June 1993. The PREP Program (Personal Resource Exploration Program) was initiated in January of 1989. The PREP session took place in a sensory isolation booth in the Research and Development laboratory at TMI and lasted approximately 90 minutes, beginning with an interview. This was followed by a guided exploration session through the various Focus states and ended with a debriefing session with a Monitor who explained computer reports of physiological monitoring done during the PREP session.

Lying on the bed, I was floating in and out of various altered states of consciousness. I "opened" my eyes and to my left and down by my feet were several creatures who were ant-like in structure. They looked to be slightly smaller than human size, not standing up or erect at all, but seemed to be on the same level of me lying down. They were pale brown in color, neither translucent nor opaque. I could sense more than one entity and focused on the one in my foreground. All had faces similar to one on the cover of Whitley Strieber's book *Communion*. One entity, slightly in front of the others, and I struck up a brief conversation which follows. It should be noted that the dialogue was completely non-verbal, a mind-to-mind telepathic type of communication.

RBR: Who are you?

ALC: You are one of us.

RBR: If I am one of you, what am I doing here?

ALC: To learn so you can teach us.

At that point I spoke into the overhead mike to the Monitor to relate my experience. I started to say to her, "This is a real kick in the pants! You aren't going to believe this, but there are some ant-like creatures in here with me." This inadvertently broke the contact. I remember that I had no fear throughout this experience, just wonderment. Afterward, I knew this experience tied a lot of experiences together from my childhood. As a result, I discovered a certain kind of peace inside of me because I now had a piece of the overall picture of me. I am more aware of who I am which carries a certain responsibility. It further chips away at any remaining fears I have about about being human and being here.

R.B.R., Boulder, Colorado

OVERCOMING BEDTIME FEAR: USING HEMI-SYNC WITH CHILDREN

My six year old son, Peter, was going through his "monster phase," something I believe to be a normal process for children his age. For months he had been growing increasingly frightened of going to sleep. His fears predominately manifested at bedtime, when he perceived monsters to be under his bed, having come up though the floor from the basement. Reassurance, extra snuggling, flower essences, a night light, and the family dog posted as guard had little effect to alleviate his fears.

After consulting with Patricia, I tried some approaches she recommended. First I suggested he call upon his guardian angels to help him with the monsters. He seemed quite open to this idea. Second, I played the Hemi-Sync Bedtime stories and Sandman Suite tapes for him at bedtime, spacing them out over about a ten day period. About a week later, Peter mentioned very casually at breakfast, "I made friends with the monsters." About two weeks later, the following story complete with illustrations appeared in Peter's journal at school:

> "The house of colors is very beautiful. One day a little boy came to the house of colors and knocked on the door. A monster opened the door. The little boy was very scared and he ran far away and you can be sure that he never went back. The monster had never seen a person. He was very interested and he followed the little boy all the way to his house. The monster knocked on the door. The kid's Mom opened the door. She screamed and slammed the door and locked the door. The monster hid next to the door. After a little while the Mom looked out of the door and the Mom didn't see the monster so she went for a walk. The monster opened the door and the monster told the little boy that he was a nice monster and they played together. When the Mom came back from her walk and saw the monster she screamed but the little boy calmed her and told her that he was a nice monster and he stayed for a guest."

Two months have now passed and monsters have not been mentioned by Peter, nor is he afraid to go to sleep now. What's more, his story was published in book form at his school for all to see and enjoy.

Polly Tifft, Boulder, Colorado

OFF-ROADING CHALLENGES: USING HEMI-SYNC IN LIFE-THREATENING TIMES

Next, five clients describe their experience using the Hemi-Sync tapes called the **Surgical Support Series**. They add a few descriptions about the reactions of friends and relatives to whom they loaned these tapes. These stories provide a way to understand what unusual abilities were tapped during their operations and how this affected their life following surgery. Note how each person, in his or her own way, describes how they became able to take control of their healing process.

FOUR WEEKS OF VACATION INSTEAD OF RECOVERY FROM SURGERY

These are the impressions that I have following surgery 1/21/91 for a third repair of a ventral hernia. I listened to the pre-op tape two times prior to surgery. The last time was while I was waiting in my room to be transported to the operating room. This event represented my sixth surgery that can be categorized as major. This, as well as the last surgery two years ago, qualify simply because I had a heart attack in 1988 and this complicates the process. I was quite apprehensive about this surgery as I remember how much pain was involved with the others. The doctor had promised that this could possibly be the worst of all of the hernia repairs because it would be difficult technically. The incision is approximately 14-16" in length and was closed with 34 staples. My history as a patient is not one of patience. I always think that I am doing well, but there are those who would disagree with my assessment. They contend that I am cantankerous, ornery, difficult, etc. I, of course, am none of these things. I am kind and considerate as well as cooperative and compliant. In a word, I do as the medical staff asks and am very sweet to be around. Now you ask, why in the name of God is he telling me all all of this? I am telling you this because I can say that after this surgery, both myself and my observers agree that I did as well as I say that I did and acted as well as I say that I did. I attribute this to the use of these tapes. Now for the specifics.

The surgeon, anesthesiologist, and surgical/recovery room nursing staff were all very cooperative. I briefed the nurses beforehand that I would be listening to a tape during surgery, and it would need to be changed in the recovery room to another tape. This posed no problem. The surgery lasted for two hours, or so so I heard the Intra-Op tape probably about twice. I had a player with automatic reverse.

I awoke with no pain in the recovery room partly due to the injection of a local anesthetic in the suture line and partly due to the tapes which had been changed to the Recovery tape. I distinctly remember looking around as I awoke and when I regained control of muscle, I waved at people as they acknowledged me. (I work at the hospital so people know me.) The tape indicated that I would be fully awake when the count had gone from 1-10 and as I listened to this dialogue, I almost felt compelled to be awake at the last number. The nurse in the recovery room was amazed that I woke up so fast and was so coherent. She remarked about it several times. My blood pressure and pulse recordings seemed to be more stable in the recovery room and I believe all during surgery.

I returned to my room at 7:00 pm and had no trouble moving from the stretcher into the bed because of the local (anesthesia) and the tape. I was surprised that I did not go to ICU as that was the pre-op plan. I was wide awake and carried on an intelligent conversation without drowsiness. This was a truly amazing sight to both my wife and our priest. Neither of them could believe that I was that well. Both remarked that it was like nothing had happened. This would become a common comment.

I listened to the Recuperation tape that night and several times the next day. Pain was very controllable, and it was done with Demerol and Vistaril as opposed to the Morphine which is what has been necessary for me in all previous times. The pain meds worked well with less than what I normally require. Using the "55515" embedded code I learned on the tape worked to control the pain. I also continued to listen to the Recuperation tape and the Energy Walk tape periodically. The anesthesiologist asked how I felt about the tapes and I told him that they worked well and that recovery was the best I had ever had. He seemed to be pleased with the process although he did not say so. He did indicate that he may need to use them the next time that he has a bleeding ulcer.

I was released on Friday which was the fourth day post-op. I could have gone sooner except the Doc was being real conservative and did not remove the drains until Thursday. My at-home recovery has been rapid and without incident. There has been some pain but not like I have experienced in previous surgeries. I have been very mobile since Wednesday after surgery. This is the fifteenth day post-op and I am way ahead of the other surgeries.

In total, I have remained very calm and peaceful throughout this process. I was initially apprehensive of having another surgery, and the peacefulness is due to the tapes. I listened to them as instructed. I can not say enough about how they affect the mental and thought processes during this normally difficult time. Surprisingly enough, I now have four weeks vacation instead of four weeks of recovery to look forward to.

R.E., Middleburg Heights, Ohio

SIGNIFICANT FEELING OF BEING IN CONTROL
DURING & AFTER SURGERY

I found the tapes very helpful. This experience for major surgery was very different from any previous inpatient or outpatient one. Overall, I felt more in control, clear about my boundaries, and used the hospital routine to my advantage. I found the "55515" (pain control) command useful in controlling pain and used it prior to any use of the pain machine. The difference for the pain control physician was that he had to be called 3-4 times to reduce the amount administered because it made me sick. Third day post-op I was off all IV's and pain med except Motrin 600 mg prn (whenever necessary). Over the course of the first two weeks I think I took a half dozen pain pills tops. My husband found this hard to believe. I was discharged without a major pain med. Prior to surgery, I used Advil, Motrin, Fiorcet, or Ponstil on a fairly regular basis. Obviously, the surgery cured the cause of pain. I'm sure the relaxed state I was in from the tapes minimized the muscle abuse and tenderness one usually experiences from this surgery. The healing of the incision was fairly rapid. My energy was very high, almost frightening. I slept better in the hospital and very little the first few nights at home. I didn't do the nap routine much, as a matter of fact, indeed felt so good, so energetic, I overdid! For several weeks I did have difficulty staying focused mentally, my attention span, be it conversation, TV or reading, was short. There was sort of internal hyperness, don't know how else to describe it.

Much to the surprise of the staff, I was discharged early on the fourth day post-op. Because of my positive experience, I since have shared the tapes with two friends, one for a similar surgery. She had surgery two years prior so her experience was still vivid in her mind. She found the tapes helpful as well, was up and about unusually fast with lots of energy and recovered quickly, same mental issue for a while. Maybe this was the anesthesia effect. The literature research indicates it takes women on the average of 14 months to recover from this surgery versus various other types of surgery. Well, at four weeks, I was back to teaching and by eight weeks, I was up and running full force. Sure I get tired but to date, thank God, no worse than before. If I get any discomfort I still use the 55515 pain command.

On 3/19/91, I found a good friend going in for a D & C (this is a female exploratory surgery), dreading it because of how long and horrible she felt with the last one. This person travels a lot with her job and can't afford to be down so I suggested to her to use the tapes. I dropped her at hospital admitting at noon and received a call to pick her up at 2 pm. She is feeling really well, felt the tapes helped her relax. She used the first one and the recuperative tape. They wouldn't let her take the others into surgery but she was fully awake by the time she got into recovery. All vital signs were perfect going in even though she was apprehensive. I spoke with her three days later and she said she felt fine and much better than last time. She feels the recuperative tape helped her stay relaxed and let her get a good sleep which she doesn't normally do.

T. L., Rocky River, Ohio

WENT HOME SAME DAY OF EMERGENCY GALL BLADDER SURGERY

Almost nine months ago I experienced a most unusual phenomenon. Early in January I began feeling acute pain in the stomach area which eventually turned out to be a severe pain leading to emergency gallbladder removal, a cholecystectomy I believe. I was fortunate to have an experienced surgeon perform the procedure and even more fortunate to be acquainted with a trainer of a technique called Hemi-Sync. This technique helps to organize and integrate the processes of the both sides of the brain, hence its name. Since I had recently learned the primary Hemi-Sync techniques on a Gateway Excursion Weekend, I had no reservation in using the Surgical Support Series of tapes that is designed for such occasions. On a near moment's notice, I was able to obtain these tapes from my trainer, Patricia Leva. She also gave me detailed instructions as to their use. After the initial listening to the first tape, I entered the pre-op room and informed the attending anesthetist of my intentions to use the other tapes during the actual operation and in the recovery room. The surgeon and the anesthetist complied with my wishes and even assisted in the process. Even though I was a good candidate for the newer laser surgery techniques, I was aware that I may have had to undergo the conventional method of surgery. As it turns out the procedure and the recovery room experience was much less traumatic than one would expect. As a matter of fact, my surgeon told me right in the recovery room that everything had went so well that I could go home that same day if I desired. Although I am a strong and healthy 39 year-old male, I owe plenty to the Hemi-Sync techniques for making the experience almost pleasant.

G.S., Kent, Ohio

NURSE NOTICES THE BODY ISN'T SO "SNOWED" AFTER SURGERY

I was very impressed with the **Surgical Support Series** of tapes. I used them before, during, and after reconstruction surgery, after having had a mastectomy. I found I felt very good on awakening from anesthesia. I required much less pain medication and my recovery and healing were quite remarkable. The plastic surgeon was amazed at how quickly my incisions healed. I used the tapes for several weeks after surgery which helped greatly in my recuperation process. In the past when I had surgeries I was quite nauseated the first two days, and was mostly unaware of what was going on. This time I was awake and hungry! I would highly recommend them to anyone having surgery.

My brother in Houston, Texas also used the tapes for his surgery for cancer of the prostate. His recovery was also remarkable. He was wide awake after returning from recovery and required very little pain medication. He went home after 5 days with 7 being the usual minimum. All the hospital personnel in OR Recovery and on his unit were impressed with how well he responded. The unit head nurse is going to purchase the tapes for other patients to use. Going into surgery in a relaxed state is wonderful. Much less medication and anesthesia is necessary and thus, the body is not so "snowed" afterwards making healing rapid and a happy experience.

C.R., Westlake, Ohio

OVERCOMES FEAR DURING MAJOR JAW RECONSTRUCTIVE SURGERY

I am writing to tell you of my recent experience in using the **Surgical Support Series** prior to and after my recent surgery. My friend lent me her set of tapes about two weeks before I was scheduled for lower jaw surgery in September. She knew that I had actively been preparing myself for several months, dealing with my fears, learning how to reframe pain, learning to take more time to nurture myself, etc. I immediately began to listen to the tapes at night before I went to sleep. Initially, I "previewed" all of them and then used the "Pre-op" tape primarily, while occasionally using "Recovery" and "Recuperation" for general health maintenance and pain control (have orthodontic braces). I found that in the two weeks prior to surgery, I had no trouble sleeping at all, including the night before surgery!

My surgery was scheduled at 8:00 am and I reported to the hospital at 6:30 am that morning. While I was nervous and dealing with some "grief" emotions, I did not feel panicked which, in the past, was my experience over very scary experiences. At the hospital, I had expected to receive a tranquilizer that had made the IV easier to deal with. Well, times have changed and hospitals no longer give surgery patients tranquilizers as a matter of course so I experienced the insertion of the IV with no chemical help at all. I was surprised at how calm I was during this (minor) but painful procedure. I stayed calm when the nurse had to remove it from one site and insert it in another. I felt as though I was "witnessing" the pain, not reacting to it. The surgeon, who was watching the whole thing, even commented on how well I was "taking it." I believe this to be due to my ability to relax and minimize the pain, an ability the tapes helped me learn. I chose not to use "Intra-op" because I had discussed with my surgeon things I wanted him to do during the operation: his choice in music, reframing the pain, reframing nausea, positive verbalizations about how the surgery was going. This agreement supported what I felt would fit my needs at the time.

In the hospital I was moved to "post-anesthesia care" where I was for a longer period of time instead of being observed in Intensive Care. Our beds were lined up in front of the desk, no tables. My husband and I had decided to make the decision about when to use the "Recovery" tape once we saw what the situation post-op could be. Since I had jaw surgery, communicating was difficult. I was quite aware of what was going on in "Post-op," I remember first waking up and certain details, even my thoughts which included how good it all felt.

Once I got into my room, I immediately asked my husband to get me the "Recovery" tape. The headphones had to be put over the huge bandages around my head and the volume turned way up. From that point on, I used "Recovery" to help me sleep and deal with the pain (which wasn't really pain but tremendous pressure) continuously the rest of that day and all night long. I also used it the next day in the hospital. This tape was very effective in helping me sleep, helping me turn the pressure in my jaws down, helping me feel "in control" of the situation. I did not ever feel anxious or worried about anything all night.

The next day, I was released from the hospital about 5:00 pm. At home I continued to use the tapes, specifically "Recuperation." I probably used this every night for two weeks! I had very little swelling in my jaw, barely noticeable bruising and more people who saw me couldn't believe I had surgery. Both my surgeon and my orthodontist expressed amazement at my recovery. I enjoyed working with the tapes so much I am ordering my own set.

C.M., Akron, Ohio

USING HEMI-SYNC TO BUY A CAR & TO SEE THE ROAD

The following are two stories of individuals that illustrate the creation of new realities by programming for specific results using the tools of Hemi-Sync. Bob Monroe liked to substitute the word "pattern" for goal-setting for he preferred to think in terms of wholes rather than pieces. When developing Hemi-Sync approaches for goal-setting and achievement, he encouraged people to design a pattern or a set of energies. Along these lines, the first is a description of acquiring a few necessities to make life easier and the second story is a description of making the transition into a new lifestyle over a year's time.

LEARNING TO USE HUMAN PLUS ENCODINGS

I decided to use a few of the Human Plus tapes to make some changes in my life, changes that I had been procrastinating about for several years! A surprising thing happened with the H+ tape called **Mobius West**. I have been looking for a Honda very seriously for about a month and was getting discouraged. During my search, several situations happened to make me think I wasn't supposed to buy a car, much less a Honda. Last Sunday the Honda I thought I was buying (having made an offer to the owner) was sold before I got there. I said in a firm voice, "By next week, I will find a car that I like, in good condition, and at a price I can easily afford!" Then I said the Mobius West Function Command, "change, change" and went on doing other things and forgot about it.

Monday when I looked at the paper there were no new Honda ads. In the evening I went to the Morley Library, and parked behind a silver/beige car, a hatchback Toyota. I thought it was beautiful, probably too expensive for me. I said to myself, " I wished I could find a car like that one." Back home I looked at the paper again and decided to call a Toyota ad having a Mentor phone number near where I live and made arrangements to go see it the following day. I had no idea what a "Celica" looked like. When I pulled in their driveway, I saw that the car for sale looked similar to the one I had seen in front of the library. It was real sharp. I knew it was what I wanted. I made an offer, and she accepted it. At the bank getting a loan was easy. The actual transaction went smoothly. While waiting for my plates I talked to the woman who sold me the car. I asked her if she ever went to the Morley Library. She said she was there Monday night. I was extremely surprised to find out that it was her car parked in front of mine that night and I bought the exact one I wished for!

After the success with Mobius West yesterday, I had an opportunity to try it again today. I went back to the eye doctor hoping to exchange, for free, contacts that had turned yellow two weeks after I purchased them. While waiting for the manager, I repeated to myself, "I will get a new pair free" then I said the Function Command, "+Change, change" right afterward. I argued with the manager for quite a while but the best she said she could do was to give me a new pair at half price. I got very angry and left. Back home I found a message on my answering machine saying they didn't want to lose me as a customer and to come back to get a new pair FREE. So, for me, Mobius West is getting exciting to use.

L.M., Cleveland, Ohio

PATTERNING FOR A NEW LIFE

I want to share the results of my use of the One Year Patterning tape. I've been in school learning to be a massotherapist for the last few months. I began using the Gateway Experience tapes about two years ago. On

April 1,1995 I attended the Gateway Voyage at TMI. My "desire or goal" for the Gateway Voyage was to remember what my work was to be. After fifteen years as a Banker (Commercial Lending & Real Estate V.P.), I was ready for a change. My three children were grown, they had completed college and the last one was married, so as a 51 year-old, single parent I felt I was at a place where I might do something different which was less stressful, more healing and incorporates my whole self. The entire Gateway Voyage was wonderful, but it wasn't until the last two hours before I was to leave, during a body massage I finally learned what I was to do. In the middle of that massage I found myself saying, "I can do this. I can be a massage therapist."

When I arrived home I began to determine what would be necessary for me to accomplish this "knowing." I started with the "**One Month Patterning**" tape in the Gateway Experience Series and during the encoding I envisioned I had all the necessary information and ingredients (training, location, $ etc.) completed that would enable me to become a massage therapist.

By the 4th week of May I had the location picked out where I was going to conduct my business, although it was not zoned for an office. On June 1st I visited a massage therapy school and enrolled for the September class. I had determined I had enough left in my profit sharing to support me for one year without an income. I began to use the "**One Year Patterning**" tape. While using this tape, I saw the training complete, the business open and successful.

On August 15th I resigned from the bank effective Sept. 8, 1995. On Sept. 11th, 1995, I became a student again. In Anatomy and Physiology class (600 muscles — origins, insertions, actions & 206 bones with all their landmarks), there were times of feeling overwhelmed after 30 years out of school, but I would simply go back to the One Year Patterning tape and see the completed product again to remind myself this was already finished on the vibrational thought plane. On March 1st I graduated from school.

On March 19, 1996 the variance hearing for me to operate the business in my chosen location took place. The proposed business location was next door to one church and across the street from another which happens to be my church. The churches wanted to purchase this particular property and make it into a parking lot. This would require tearing down the house on this lot, but we told them the house is not for sale. Both churches had about 45 people there to object to my request for a variance. The Board of Adjustments, comprised of 5 members voted 4 to 1 in favor of approval on

March 29th. The churches appealed the approval to the courts. When I heard this I was upset. But after an hour or so I reminded myself that it was all set and as long as I kept my focus it would work out all right. And I again focused on the completed pattern and surrounded everyone with love and light and joy and harmony. Three days later I suddenly was certain the churches would withdraw their objections. One week ago, I was informed by my attorney the churches had written a letter dated April 26th withdrawing their objections. I got my business license that same day. I also spent a lot of time in praise and gratitude and giving thanks.

The business "Horizons Therapeutic Massage Clinic" will be open in one week. This is one year from the time I began using the patterning tape.

Betty N., Boston, Massachusetts

EXAMPLES OF APPLYING GATEWAY EXCURSION SKILLS TO EVERYDAY LIFE SITUATIONS

One of the last activities during the basic foundational Gateway program called the Gateway Excursion Weekend is to go over the seventeen skills participants have acquired during the Excursion and discuss how these can be used in everyday situations. In the months after the Excursion, graduates have reported back to me about how they have put the Excursion skills to use in their lives. Following are descriptions of how they have actually used the Focus states and the encodings with all kinds of people in various settings in very innovative ways.

OCEAN SURF RELAXATION
(PURPOSE: RELAXATION)

When I am stressed out I have recalled the ebb and flow of Focus 3 waveform energy heard at the beginning of each Hemi-Sync experiential learning experience. Sometimes I have used this for stress management at work...as a helpful clarifying memory tool...to withdraw from a chaotic dinner meal...to lower high flowing feelings of anger, fear, anxiety, rage, grief during a funeral. Sometimes it's as simple as wanting to find a moment of peace and balance. Using the memory of Ocean Surf helps me to feel this peace.

ENERGY CONVERSION BOX
(PURPOSE: DIRECT & MAINTAIN ATTENTION WHERE DESIRED)

I have used the ECB outside of meditation as a sleeping pill before bed by putting all my aches and pains, worries, concerns into ECB and sliding into sleep. This really works. I have put phobias of any kind into the ECB to convert anxiousness into a neutral balance. At times I have put off-the-wall, personal quirks of friends or acquaintances, the annoying mother-in-law, boss, or tax auditor into ECB. In order to be able to do the hard jobs that are things I procrastinate like mowing the lawn, balancing the checkbook or dumping the diaper pail, I have deposited the easier jobs in the ECB first then I am able to attend to the more difficult ones. To get beyond writer's block, I have put any kind of resistance in symbolic form into the ECB. It usually works very well.

RESONANT TUNING
(PURPOSE: CHARGING UP, CLEANING OUT DULL ENERGY)

I have used RT to gain high energy. To release co-dependency or addiction while doing resonant tuning, I pull in prana and push the symbol representing the addiction or co-dependency out. To release any upsetting dreamwork I like to do RT in the shower before the day's beginning. Before or during dull meetings or family dinner hour, I do resonant tuning in private. After a deep catnap I do RT; and before meditating or praying I do RT which seems to really clear out things.

RESONANT ENERGY BALLOON
(PURPOSE: SECURES & PROTECTS, SAVES & CONCENTRATES ENERGY FIELD)

When co-workers are obviously sick I establish my REBAL and stiffen it or pull it in to become a germ barrier or when in situations such as a restaurant where hygienic techniques are not being used, I use it the same way. I have "popped" my REBAL to defend against unwanted thoughts or feelings of others. I have used the REBAL during jogging to protect myself against threatening dogs or people. At times I use the REBAL before going into very important meetings with the boss to concentrate my energy. During occasions where people are drinking or smoking heavily, I use the REBAL to protect my energy field so that their energy does not drain me. I have also done the opposite by using the REBAL to invite a new relationship, money, or a new project into my life by visualizing the new change and expanding the energies of the REBAL out to that symbol and bringing it to myself. I have added specific colors to the REBAL when constructing it to gain and or change the surrounding energy or to add a degree of specific protection when this is required. Using the REBAL usually gives me great energy!

GATEWAY AFFIRMATION
(PURPOSE: DEFINING INTENTION OF A THOUGHTFORM)

When I say a special affirmation before doing something, I know I am disciplining myself to a certain purpose. Then my ego has to take a back seat. I have surprised myself because the Gateway Affirmation is a personal parenting thing I do for myself, like a permission I give myself to explore non-physical realities or even to broaden my regular life. I have used this before sleeping to design a particular dream for decision-making or for problem-solving by telling my dreaming self to play out a particular scenario. When I am feeling flighty, anxious or scared, the words of the Gateway Affirmation help to recenter me or help me become fully present. Sometimes when I say the Gateway Affirmation, but I don't fully believe I have the capacity to carry it out so when I detect that I am hedging I will also ask for the capacity to achieve the full purpose of this affirmation.

FOCUS 10
(PURPOSE: MIND AWAKE & BODY ASLEEP)

I have used this focus state to relax in times where I need a split state with the mind clearly alert and the body deeply relaxed like the time when I gave blood or I had a tooth pulled. I know it could be used at other times like during the labor process of delivering a baby or after seeing a car accident happen. I have used Focus 10 to figure out what the real truth was during the many confusing, high-powered meetings I have to attend at work. I have used Focus 10 to tune into fresh, clear thinking power when I am feeling dull. As a student I have used Focus 10 to help me understand things when I am studying. I have used Focus 10 to focus my attention totally on a specific event when things seem to be chaotic. I have used this for about 10 minutes to re-energize myself at hairy times like between work appointments, between planes, between meetings, during the time-out periods with my children arguing and also I have used Focus 10 to be more intuitive which really works.

RETURN TO C-1 TRIGGER
(PURPOSE: GROUNDING, RECENTERING)

I have used the C-1 encoding to come back out of a daydream. When I am feeling threatened, scattered, or dull, I use this trigger. I have used this technique to help me create feelings of safety, centeredness and security in myself. I find it can be especially helpful when I have heard surprising or shocking news.

MEMORY ENCODING TRIGGER
(PURPOSE: INSTANT REMEMBERING)

I have used this for all sorts of things, for dream recall, remembering lost items, small pieces of information, remembering names or faces, money deposits I forget to write down or to remember phone numbers I see on service trucks, billboards, email addresses, home shopping network ads, and license plate numbers. Putting my hand up to my forehead is something easy I can do and people don't seem to notice that I am doing something different to remember more. I find that the memory encoding helps me to increase comprehension and retention when I am trying to learn something or during a surprising event. For dream recall, I have constructed a *Dream Mail Box*. I use the Memory Trigger right before going to sleep saying that I will automatically put a copy of each and every dream I have during the night in the Dream Mail Box. Then, right away in the morning, I say the memory trigger as I check my mail box for the dreams. I have increased my dream memory a billion percent using this technique. Works for remembering problem-solving plots during dreaming too.

REBAL ENCODING TRIGGER
(PURPOSE: INSTANTLY SAVE AND SECURE ENERGY FIELD)

I have used the REBAL encoding when I have needed instant protection and/or energy concentration; i.e., during martial arts training, physical fitness workouts or when competing in athletic events. This really works for me! When I have been in threatening or confusing situations, I have used the REBAL — for example when I had to change a flat a tire along a very busy interstate or when I recently had to do a presentation for the first time in front of my new boss and his supervisors.

AWAKE & ALERT ENCODING TRIGGER
(PURPOSE: INSTANT AWARENESS & ALERTNESS)

I have used this Function Command to stop drowsiness and stay alert during long drives, intense study, between planes, waiting in doctor's offices, and even during a tax audit. I have used this before doing the memory trigger to sharply focus my attention before trying to remember or recall something. I have found it has been helpful to use during visits to the doctor because it seems to increase my hearing capacity. It also has helped me pay attention during boring lectures, meetings or when I am in a involved teleconference with people in several cities.

RELEASE & RECHARGE
(PURPOSE: RELEASING EMOTIONAL BODY OF FEAR)

When there have been unpleasant thoughts or disturbing actions building up throughout the day on a subtle level and I am feeling heavy, I will use the **Release and Recharge exercise**. When I need to deliberately off-load those constant worry thoughts and get a fresh perspective, I will use this. When I have to be very juicy, very creative and light, I have purposefully used this exercise before big meetings. I put a special part into the Gateway Affirmation so I use this exercise to uncover my real qualities and real true powers. Sometimes I have surprised myself by discovering hidden talents I forgot I had. I have used the cleansing part of this process to strip away puzzling elements of a situation. It is like washing that "man out of my hair" so I can know what it is like to feel free of what has become a crusty, dirty feeling around me. I don't think this has happened until after I have done the exercise and feel so much lighter and easier about the situation. I have even lost weight with this process!

FOCUS 10 FREE FLOW
(PURPOSE: TO CREATE A FREE FLOWING FOCUS 10 DATA STREAM)

I have been doing Free Flow Focus 10 when I have wanted to be very creative, to have lots of insights, or to expand problem-solving options, or to test choices for problem-solving. Surprisingly this Free Flow Focus 10 state can be a rich environment for doing past life regressions or future progressions because when I have tried it without the Focus state, it doesn't seem as simple and clear. I have used this to do a healing in Free Flow Focus 10 by drawing in a flow of particular color and focusing this color on an injured or painful area of either myself or another person. The free, light mind quality of Focus 10 has been an absolutely perfect place to congratulate myself on a job well done when I haven't really received this from others.

MOVING BETWEEN FOCUS 10 AND FOCUS 12
(PURPOSE: TO VIEW A SITUATION FROM TWO DIFFERENT NON-PHYSICAL PERSPECTIVES)

Looking at a situation from two points of perspective can enable goal-setting and decision-making situations to become more productive and targeted at the most useful outcome. The rollercoastering process enables the need to ventilate, to brainstorm, to reconfirm or clarify a solution for its here and now aspects and its bigger picture implications.

FOCUS 12 PROBLEM-SOLVING
(PURPOSE: TO USE THE UNIVERSAL PERSPECTIVE OF FOCUS 12 FOR PROBLEM-SOLVING)

I have used this to gain a larger, holographic perspective on a problem by shifting my awareness into Focus 12 while standing on my feet in regular situations. I have used this to determine the real cause of a problem and to know the larger connections, patterns, or trends that might be hidden. I find that the environment of Focus 12 gives me an opportunity to become well acquainted with other entities or systems that are helpful to times where I have needed to do some problem-solving or learn new ways of communicating, on a different level, to know my Divine Purpose and ways to achieve that purpose.

FOCUS 12 ONE BREATH TECHNIQUE, ENCODING
(PURPOSE: INSTANT PROBLEM-SOLVING IN FOCUS 12)

I have found that this instant remembering process helps me to gain quick answers, numbers, data, names, places, options, and solutions all the time. One of the most amazing encodings that I have used!

FOCUS 12 FREE FLOW
(PURPOSE: TO CREATE A FREE FLOWING FOCUS 12 DATA STREAM)

Free flowing in Focus 12 is useful for me when I want to increase my awareness about my Knows, about maintaining balance in my life, learning about unconditional love, on the right use of will, and to explore what the state of grace or inner peace means for me. I have found that using this Focus state in a free flowing, free associating way gives me the opportunity to explore and become familiar with a beginning state of timelessness, what that is like. I have used this very creatively, to stretch myself out into a universal perspective to solve problems and to learn how to intuit associations, conflicts, and feelings that I would not be able to do in regular life.

On the Gateway Excursion Weekend I offer training using the DEC tool. This is also learned at TMI Gateway Residential Programs. **DEC** stands for *Dolphin Energy Club*, which is a group of people who are encoded with the ability to do personal healing and healing of others using the symbol of a dolphin representing universal love energy. Using guided imagery, construction of an energy bar tool is achieved. This is very similar to the light saber that Luke Skywalker used in the *Star Wars* movie. During the initial construction of the energy bar tool, the bar of light is given several properties similar to a laser instrument such as the ability to pulsate, to wobble, to contain various color frequencies, and to cleanly change/and or charge energy. In addition, the intention of moving or changing energy flow where there is too much or too little energy is attached in the human energy field is attributed to the DEC tool. Another added feature to the DEC tool is the ability to heal (rebalance) each of the three lower bodies of energy: the physical, emotional and mental bodies. This is done by asking the dolphin imaged in the dominant hand to rebalance each energy body, one-by-one. An active DEC group coordinated by TMI has existed since 1991 throughout the world which includes an online DEC group. Its members receive postcards with names of people who have requested healing within a certain time frame. The results are tracked and referred back to the DEC members. Please contact TMI for further information on DEC. In addition, there are some online DEC groups offering healing service to humankind.

DOLPHIN ENERGY BAR TOOL
(PURPOSE: TO HEAL SELF AND OTHERS)

I have used the DEC tool for personal healing by working specifically with my physical, emotional, and mental bodies and also to do absent or remote healing with others This works surprisingly well with my husband! I have discovered that the the dolphin tool can cut, slice, and magically change things like King Arthur's sword, Excalibur. For example, I adjusted it by turning a specific glowing color and I've used it to shift and/or cohese energy in meeting rooms, the operating room, around our family dinner table, in the family car or to offer healing to Third World countries, underprivileged children, homeless people in shelters, and prisoners. It can be used in many circumstances because a lot of abilities were encoded within it when we first encoded ourselves with DEC; light pulsation, changing the amplitude, wavelength, color, shape, etc. This is a very creative tool to use.

THE TMI PROFESSIONAL DIVISION ROAD CREW
AN ALL-SERVICE INTERSTATE OASIS

Literally hundreds of concrete practical applications are documented in several Hemi-Sync books (see Appendix C), the *TMI Journal*, a newsletter of the Professional Division of TMI, doctoral dissertations, and articles published in magazines, newspapers, and professional journals throughout the world. The *TMI Journal* was first published in 1983 under the name *Breakthrough*, then it assumed a greater cope of research and reporting of projects using Hemi-Sync technology; thus, in the Spring of 1990 a name change was instituted. As a pivotal resource demonstrating wide utilization of Hemi-Sync technology, the *TMI Journal* offers articles written by professional practitioners in all walks of life using Hemi-Sync in a variety of settings with all kinds of people and also articles written by people who have personally used TMI tools. Individual theme packs called *TMI ToolKits* containing numerous testimonials from Hemi-Sync tape and CD users including children and adults are available from TMI. These center on broad usage categories such as Wellness, Children,

Learning, and Surgical applications. An annual professional seminar, sponsored by the Professional Division during the summer, brings together practitioners from over the world to discuss their research and work using Hemi-Sync technology. Various modalities in conjunction with Hemi-Sync are demonstrated at the seminar such as Reiki, Holotrophic Breathwork, Qigong, and biofeedback. Over its nearly 30 years of existence, this consciousness expansion tool has been used in thousands of lives involving people, animals, plants, and the planet upon which we live.

These real time stories of travelers give us an idea of what it is like to use Hemi-Sync for various reasons and how they have been affected. The next destination on our Interstate expedition is to explore 30 very provocative stories of Interstate travelers who describe their adventures in detail.

WE ARE ONE

Living blind but knowing, becoming that bubbling water,
You'll never guess who I saw at the fair,
I bought the exact one I wished for! I used it as a germ barrier.
You are one of us, an all-service oasis.

EVOLVING CONSCIOUSNESS:
ON-LINE CONVERSATIONS

We live at the most marvelous moment in history...
we are at the dawn of "conscious evolution," when the creature human first
becomes aware of the processes of Creation and begins to participate deliberately
in the design of our world. "

Barbara Marx Hubbard, *The Evolutionary Journal*

ROUTE 6

CYBERSPACE CONVERSATIONS: PERSONAL CONSCIOUS EVOLUTION POSTS

The information highway in cyberspace has become a source of support and encouragement for many who are engineering their own conscious evolution. Numerous home pages (locations of agencies or private individuals offering advertisements, products, and services), newsgroups (public message boards), and mailing lists (specialized interest groups) are developed for this kind of information exchange. The Voyager Mailing list (VML), sponsored by The Monroe Institute, has, in its short history of two years, been a forum for intense exchange of stories, ideas, philosophies, and techniques about consciousness with Hemi-Sync as a focal point. Following are posts from VML members with various international addresses who are sharing their Interstate experiences, asking for help, comparing notes, and supporting each other. These on-line conversations are rich with detailed illustrations of how people conduct their own consciousness research project using unusual experimental methods and open-ended possibilities. Here are actual examples of people throughout the world trying to achieve deliberate, full consciousness on their own. Their original online words are used to preserve the purity of their experiences. Notice the Voyagers cross back and forth on the Continental Divide of Consciousness by describing experiences involving both everyday reality and non-ordinary reality. The first section covers several themes called "threads" in cyberspace. These threads range from helping each other to do the tapes, having vibrations, changing sound perception, changing time perception, doing lucid dreamwork, having OBEs and helping others through the death process.

VML MEMBERS HELPING EACH OTHER

SUBJECT: TODAY WAS DIFFERENT (PERCEPTION OF TIME)

Hello Everyone, Today was slow for me. I mean by that, I did a lot of things, but I didn't feel rushed. When I thought it was one o'clock it was still before noon. My sense of the time passing had to do with the things I accomplished. Still, I didn't feel rushed. It was like being a kid again when time seemed to stand still. Only this time I enjoyed it. I needed to share that with someone who might understand.

John B.

A day later...

SUBJECT: RE: TODAY WAS DIFFERENT

John, I think that we all experience this, but for whatever reason fail to really take notice. I have experienced this phenomenon many times as well as the reverse. One of the things I have tried to do is be more aware of where I am and what I am aware of at all times. This started me thinking and brought me to the realization that time is not linear as we have been led to believe (from a personal perspective). When I am in a very balanced condition mentally and physically, I seem to accomplish more than I would otherwise in the same amount of time. Time is an element of the physical universe we live in, but we can choose to move slower or faster than physical time. What I think you experienced (as have many of us) is actually moving "faster" than physical time. This seems to be in conflict with our experience, an illusion. This is a hard concept to try to explain and I still have some trouble with it. It appears as if time is moving slower, when in actuality it is moving at the same measured rate, and we are moving faster. I hope I have thoroughly confused you.

In time and out, Rick S.

A month and many messages later...

SUBJECT: THE SIMULTANEITY OF TIME

I won't include all the traffic on this thread; I just wanted to relate a story Joe McMoneagle told at a Gateway program this summer. I don't know if he talks for every group, but he did for ours and it was a most fascinating presentation. He was talking about his ability to "time slide" while remote viewing — viewing a particular location and running backwards and forwards in time. At some point while trying to explain how he thought that works he just stopped, looked down for a moment, took a step forward, and said, "Look, this is how it is; everything that ever was, is, or will be, every possibility, every physical, non-physical, or otherwise reality or dimension or universe, everything any being has ever thought or imagined…just is." He walked over to the easel, lifted sheet of paper up and continued, "Everything just is. If this sheet of paper represents that — everything that is, is contained on this sheet. Time is what we use to string together individual experiences based on our intention. There is no such thing as past lives, it's all simultaneous. I am, right now, standing in this room talking with you; I am also a centurion in the Roman army and a lot of other stuff. Our lives are just groups of individual experiences strung together like a thread in this sea of what is, and we have many going on at the same "time." Oops! Business calls.

Reed M.

◆ ◆ ◆ ◆ ◆ ◆ ◆

SUBJECT: FRUSTRATED!

Hi All

How do I put this? I guess this post has been two weeks in the making. "Why so long?" you ask. "I'm glad you asked," I say excitedly. The thing is that for me it's getting really frustrating when working with these tapes (started about two months back with Wave I). I just don't seem to get anything out of them! OK, went through tape 1 (no problem), listened to tape 2 for weeks (don't think I ever came close to F10), went on to tape 3 when I could no longer stand the boredom/frustration when listening to 2. Now when I listen to tape 3, I'm getting these same feelings. I'm starting to feel like these tapes work for 99.99% of the population and I'm part of that .01% who stand outside watching the rollercoaster go by and seeing how much fun the people on it are having. (Skip parts of message.)

So why am I posting? I guess it is to ask if there are any other people on this list who have had similar experiences/frustrations, and how they solved them, or at least worked around them? Also, what does Focus 10 FEEL like? It's described as 'Mind Awake, Body Asleep,' but what does this MEAN? Does the body feel numb, do you feel ANYTHING at all, is it something like when you sleep on your arm and can't move it afterwards due to lack of circulation, does it feel the way it feels when you are asleep

(I don't know 'cause I'M ASLEEP), or what? Newbies, old-timers, your comments will be appreciated.

Fred Albrecht

SUBJECT: RE: FRUSTRATED...

Hello Fred,

I don't know if I qualify to give anyone advice. I am a complete newbie at this, currently up to Tape 4 in the first GE series. But I can maybe help a bit just by describing my experiences so far. There's been nothing earth shattering, but I went into this expecting little because I had never before even gotten to a point of being able to relax at all using any other method.

Well, for me I was really surprised when listening to the first tape that I could actually see a box!! I am not good at visualizing anything and chose something I had seen before to start with, hoping that would make it easier. And I actually could see the old "hamper" we still have that once came with a vacuum cleaner. It's simply a rectangular box with a thick padded lid that you can sit on. I imagined it as being very strong and made of metal inside. So, since then it has been my Energy Conversion Box. And it seems to work just fine.

I did feel some effect from the Hemi-Sync signals on the tape from the beginning, so I was pleasantly surprised by that. And at the exact same point on that first tape, every time I listened to it, I would experience a rather violent twitch in the large toe on my left foot, as well as various other tingles, twitches, etc. in other parts of my body at random times. So, these were signs for me that the tapes were going to do something.

I had read a lot about others having felt cold at times during the tapes. I normally tend toward having cold feet and hands most of the time. So I was a little surprised that, beginning at the surf sounds early in that first tape, I began to feel an odd warm spot on the bottom of my left foot, near the base of the toes. As I listened to the tape this gradually spread until by the end of it, both feet, ankles, and my calves, almost to the knees, had this same odd feeling of warmth. It's difficult to describe, but it was almost hot, but not, and almost a numbness, but not quite that either. It was not unpleasant at all, but sort of on the verge of being so.

Going into Focus 3 later in the tape was a sort of odd, barely there, sort of pressure in my head. I wasn't at all sure it was really there, but at one point, I did see something rather odd; I seemed to suddenly be looking down at a baby in a crib. It seemed like an older crib, and the child was dressed more like a '50s baby might have been. I've never seen this baby before that I can recall, but I knew she was female. She was up on hands and knees and I had the impression that she had just managed this for the first time, ready to begin to crawl. She looked up at me with a large smile and twinkling eyes, rocking just a little, very pleased with herself. This only lasted a few seconds, and suddenly I snapped back with a jerk. Nothing like this has happened again, and I have no idea what it meant, or who the baby was. I don't think it was anything much, but I did see it, as clearly as if I were standing beside her crib. I was back in C-1 (physical reality) and Bob began to say to wake up. That never happened again and I listened to the first tape several times, never really sure if I'd even gotten into Focus 3. So, finally I went on to Tape 2.

In Tape 2 nothing remarkable happened except for one thing. The first time through the tape I found out what Focus 10 feels like, or at least I think so. I'm not really sure I had ever fully relaxed before in my life. But I certainly did then. By the time the countdown was done my entire body felt very heavy, not numb but just barely there. As an experiment I tried to lift my right arm. I could do so with effort but it was a dead weight and the instant I relaxed it dropped like a stone! So, I assumed I was in Focus 10 for sure. I hated to wake up again at the end of the tape.

I didn't know how many times I should listen to each tape, so I went through Tape 2 several times as well. About that time I had a very bad sore throat and began to cough myself silly from it. That lasted nearly two weeks. I could get nowhere because it's impossible to do any deep breathing when you bend over coughing every couple of minutes. So I was delayed a bit in using the tapes due to that. But, once the coughing began to go away, I redid Tape 2 and went on to Tape 3. As usual, the first time listening to the tape had the greatest effect. I was easily able to drop into F-10, though, not really as deeply as that first time, but very relaxed all the same. A few strange things began to happen in my room on that third tape. I clicked out a couple of times, that was a first, but I could see there's a difference in that and falling asleep. They aren't the same things at all. And about three times my TV turned itself on and off again, that was really odd. I took it as a sign that something was happening and just waited for developments. When I finally decided to go on to Tape 4 I thought I would listen to Tape 3 one more time, and then try Tape 4 right after. About halfway through Tape 3, the tape suddenly stopped and all the electricity to my room had failed. I was barely able to come out of it enough to reach for the master switch on my computer power center before it came back on. So it was only off for about 10 seconds. But on checking, I found that only the two circuits going to my room had failed, not the rest of the house!! But it wasn't a fuse or breaker because it came back on by itself!!

Well, needless to say I didn't try Tape 4 that day, in fact I avoided the tapes entirely for a couple of days. I still seem to be stuck on Tape 4, more things I need to get rid of, I suppose. But I did try Tape 5 once and couldn't even get fully into Focus 10, let alone go to sleep. So I'll take it easy for a while and see what happens next. Considering that I had found myself going into Focus 10 automatically whenever I would start Tape 3, and was able to enter Focus 10 at will almost any other time, and even managed to pop my REBAL while chatting with someone on the net before, I'm sure this is only a minor setback. More will come when I'm ready. As for the odd electrical things I just told myself that there was some reason for it, they seem to have stopped, and I still don't know if there was a connection.

Well, that's enough, but I hope it helps a bit. I learned early on not to expect anything, just wait and see, continue and be surprised if something unusual happens. I remember reading somewhere that in this you should expect only change, and the form that takes will eventually be what you need it to be. So keep it up, just go on, assume that things are proceeding as they should. That's what I'm going to do.

Alleycat

SUBJECT: RE: FRUSTRATED...

First off, I'd like to say that I enjoyed this post of Alleycat's. It brought me back to some fond memories from when I started. It is good that Alleycat has learned not to expect things in this early stage of his tape experience. I learned this, too, but not until Tape 5 of Gateway Experience (Discovery album) when I experienced a real consciousness shift from the physical. I found myself floating in the room and then shooting out through the window.

I had many "different" kinds of things happen before that doing the other tapes, but it took this experience to make me see something. That something was that when I was doing tapes and had things happen before that it was when I was not "trying." I knew that then because when I had that shift occur I was definitely not trying to do anything. I was just doing a tape to be doing a tape. I had no expectations whatsoever at the time and "bang," I got something most pleasantly surprising. After that experience I thought back and realized that all those other things had also happened when I was not trying. It just took that one time to connect not trying with results. Since that time I have never tried or had expectations, but that can trap you too. I found myself trying not have expectations, and since I was trying, I was held at bay again. So it's sort of hit and miss.

To all who are starting this adventure I would say not to think about anything at all and not judge events as they happen. Save the judgment and comparisons for after a tape session. Also I advise keeping a journal of each experience. It won't seem to be very important at the time, but later on you can look back and see some very interesting trends, and you can link your effort level to your "success" rate. You will be glad you went to the trouble. Now, if I could just take my own advice!!!

As for how many times to do a tape, you will know. I never really thought about how many times I would do a particular tape. I just did it until I knew it was time to move on. If you find that you think you should not have gone on to the next tape, just go back, no problem. I hope newbies (can we think of another word for this?) will benefit from this, my perspective after nine months of Hemi-Sync work.

Michael Smith

• • • • • • • •

SUBJECT: SOUNDS

Hi All: This subject reminded me of an experience that I had in August of this year. I'd awakened suddenly during the night (due to the heat, I think) and I'd gone into the living room to watch TV. While channel surfing, I remember coming across one of those late night religious programs. Now whether I fell asleep or was in the twilight between sleep and consciousness, I don't know, but I saw myself lying on the sofa, and then I heard a buzzing sound so loud that I remember glancing at the TV to see if it had gone off the air! At that moment, I felt an almost electric sensation beginning at my crown and continuing all the way down my body. The energy had a liquid quality to it, and I distinctly remember sensing a golden color. At first I admit that I tried to fight it but sensed that the experience was okay. And if this wasn't enough, I heard a voice which seemed to come from behind me (I was on the sofa, which was against the wall) saying "I am delivered!" The message was in the first person — not "you are," or "They are," but "I am…" I immediately sat up on the sofa, and was more energized and felt lighter than I had in quite some time. I must admit that at that time, I'd been under a great deal of stress and had been praying for resolution or at least some help. Your observations/experiences on this would be greatly appreciated. Thanks much for listening.

Lois Douglass

Two weeks and many posts on this topic later…

SUBJECT: RE: SOUNDS

Hi Barry, Hi Luca,

About this subject, I think I have something to say although I'm not an "experienced voyager." Yet I've been spontaneously out-of-body a lot of times for the last six years, and as the experience repeated itself along this time I could perceive the very subtle signs that happen before my "non-physical body" is fully out. It has always begun to happen while I was lying but awake, many times at 4 or 5 a.m. after having slept. Some time before the OBE happens I feel something like electrical discharges inside my brain (it seems to be right in the center of it). These "discharges" make some very low sounds and keep increasing in intensity (seem to grow stronger). On one occasion they were so strong that I saw a kind of light; it resembled a storm with lightning and thunder. Then something happens in my brain, and I'm in a different state (like a transition between one state and another). At the same time I begin to hear a strong, continuous sound inside my head. In the beginning of my experiences, it seemed to be in the ear, but now I perceive it in the brain itself. Immediately after this, I can move my "other body" and come out-of-body. It gives me the impression that it's the sound that makes this possible. I've heard the sound in every experience, although in the first experiences I didn't perceive the electrical discharges. The time between hearing the sound and being able to move the extraphysical body is about five seconds. Many years before this, beginning when I was 18 (I'm now 42) I've heard this sound but didn't know what it was and thought I had some problem in the ear. I have consulted a doctor but didn't have any problem. Only in 1989 when my first experience took place I came to know by myself that the sound was the beginning of an OBE. When it is a "partial projection" as we call it here in Brazil, I mean, only a leg or an arm (a part of the extraphysical body) goes out of the physical body, I keep on hearing the sound. The sound only stops when I'm completely out of the physical body. I haven't usually heard it on the return as some people report (it happened only once).

Another thing, it never happened during the day while doing everyday things. Sometimes I hear a sound during the day that lasts a few seconds, but it is a completely different thing from what I described above. So Barry, I think you have been very near to having an OBE and the conditions were good as you were in a relaxed state meditating. Don't worry, the sound is completely harmless. If it happens again don't do anything, just keep on hearing and let it lead you away…out. Don't be afraid or anxious; keep on trying and good luck. I'd also like to hear from other people. Hope to have helped in some way.

Tania D.

◆ ◆ ◆ ◆ ◆ ◆ ◆

SUBJECT: SEEING

I have been working with the Gateway tapes for almost a year. Several times now, I will go through the preparatory process and into Focus 10 then 12. I then visualize myself lifting out to about 3-5 feet above my body. On a couple of these occasions, I will "feel" like I am out. This feeling is generally one of bilocation, that is, I am both in and out at the same time. Sometimes I am more out than in. However, I do not "see" my body or the surrounding environment. This raises several questions. Am I really OBE, or just imagining it? Is it possible to be OBE but unable to see and hear? I would appreciate any suggestions.

Regards, Tim B.

Reply, one day later…

SUBJECT: RE: SEEING

Tim, what I think you are experiencing is the projection of your consciousness to a point outside the bounds of your body. First of all, you've made a big step. I believe (with info I have gathered during OBE's etc.) that OBE's are simply a situation where our consciousness is mostly focused outside of the physical. We don't actually leave our bodies, as we really never are in them. We are only focused in them. What we really are, is on the outside of the physical system. It has been said that to the real us, our physical lives are the dream, and this agrees with my experience. In the TMI focus levels, the higher the number, the less we are focused in the physical system. I guess that an OBE could be considered focus 100 (totally arbitrary number, don't quote me on that!). As far as seeing/hearing, you're probably still a little too close to the physical to have separate perceptions or senses. Try just thinking that you can perceive, as opposed to seeing or hearing. When I am OB, my perceptions do not parallel the physical senses. It is much more true-all-encompassing "knowing." When I touch a wall, I have a complete knowing of the wall down to the smallest bit of energy (matter) that makes up the wall. It is a truly wonderful way of perceiving.

Rick S.

A month later going further into the idea of seeing in other ways…

SUBJECT: RE: OPEN EYES WHILE WORKING IN THE FOCUS STATES

John, Matt, Steve, Mike and others…

I'd like to comment on using open eyes during the various Focus levels, but only from personal experience. By now readers of this list have probably seen comments about the "no tape" and "silent walk" exercises during the residential Voyage and Guidelines programs. In my case on my walk outdoors I assure you I made it all the way to Focus 21 with my eyes open and walking around…it is a VERY different world in that state, much more visible energy and "knowing" about oneself. It is truly a beautiful experience. This comes toward the end of the week so you have spent four days doing five tapes a day and not having a care in the world, so you are quite familiar with the focus level states and how to get there on your own. (I think) this exercise is included to make sure you understand that you do NOT need the tapes to achieve these altered states of consciousness, only practice and patience.

During Guidelines, I also had the experience of opening my eyes numerous times and still "saw" what I was having visual imagery of during the tape experience. Sometimes I could see this as if it were "dual vision" where I saw my CHEC unit with the image overlaid, and sometimes I no longer saw much of my CHEC unit. Several of these experiences were quite profound. Many times I have given much gratitude for these experiences. Hope this helps. Like I said up front, this is not an experience using a particular method on how to do this (like the Buddhist one you mentioned), but it is just something that happened to me.

Richard Madaus

◆ ◆ ◆ ◆ ◆ ◆ ◆

SUBJECT: MY FIRST VIBRATIONS

The other night I had my first experience with RAM's "vibrations." I got so excited that I almost lost them then and there, but I forced myself to relax and they stayed, but then as I lay there, they just started to fade. Could someone please tell me what I was doing wrong? I started to pay close attention to the vibes, but they just faded.

Matt G.

SUBJECT: RE: MY FIRST VIBRATIONS

Hi Matt!
I don't think you did something wrong. It takes some time to get used to the vibes (IMHO). Depending on conditions which I don't know at this time, sometimes the vibes lead to OBEs and sometimes they don't. Now there is something more to consider. The vibes can be felt on leaving and entering the body (at least in my experience). So it could be you just got conscious on entrance to your body from your night or sleeping activities. And that is why they went down instead of up. Let your inner self decide when to make you conscious of the OBEs, but keep the motivation or desire to do OBE. This can be accomplished by wishing it to happen for a specific purpose, be it helping humanity, exploring yourself, or anything else that comes to your mind like the TMI affirmation. Hope this helps.

Jorge L.

◆ ◆ ◆ ◆ ◆ ◆ ◆

SUBJECT: 100% LUCID DREAM

Hi to all, I'm very happy because Friday night I had a 100% lucid dream. I read all day some material from the Web, I read one technique, seeing your hands in a dream will help you to be aware of the dream. This is incredible, but when I went to bed and started dreaming, I was in my high school running, I was being chased by someone. During this, I was running very fast, suddenly I saw my fist closed and remembered the technique (about seeing your own hands), so I stopped and saw my hands (both hands open).   In that instant I began to see more clear all my surroundings, it was amazing! I realized that I could do anything I want, so I decided to run very fast, and I did, when I felt that I was losing consciousness. I moved my hands up and saw them. I did this in all the dream, I was consciously aware that it was very long the dream; so I decided to stop (a stupid decision). So I woke up and wrote all my dreams down. Well, I would like to know if anyone else has had these experiences.

Your friend, Jonatan

Next day, several messages later…

SUBJECT: RE: 100% LUCID DREAM

Hey, man, congrats on your lucid dream success! Once you start having lucid dreams, it's easier to have them again. But don't get discouraged if you have dry spells. I go on dry spells for a few weeks at a time. I don't think I'm trying hard enough. Anyway, you'll learn that there are many different types of lucid dreams. I will describe them using percentages of your conscious mind. In a lucid dream where you have 80% consciousness, your dream occurs in real time. You can feel time passing and there are no gaps in your experience. Sometimes in a lucid dream where you're only 50% conscious, you may do things and change things, but sometimes you slip into normal dreaming for a bit and then come back to lucid dreams. One thing I noticed is that usually once I start having lucid dreams during the night, they keep coming back. Sadly, my lucid dreams are typically short, but usually once one lucid dream fades out, I start one up again as soon as I go back to sleep. If you're having lucid dreams, don't move a muscle in your bed. Remain still. Do whatever you can to NOT disturb your body. Also, you're on the right track. In lucid dreams many people have to focus on some object, like your hands. I did this myself without ever reading about it. When you focus on an object, you then focus your lucid dream clarity and perception. Try finding someone to talk to about this.

Brian

Same day…

SUBJECT: RE: 100% LUCID DREAM

Well, I've been wondering a lot about the difference between lucid dreaming and OBEs lately. Mostly because I have found two major distinct types of lucid dreamings among my own experiences. The main differences are:

Type I
- I do have quite good left brain activity; I can analyze, I can plan actions and follow my plan, I'm not distracted easily by events occurring.
- Perception is stronger; colours are more vivid, places visited that are also present in the physical world are almost identical.
- Surroundings and situations are much more stable; I can alter them at will, but they don't change because of random thoughts or associations.
- I have a high level of consciousness (I'm almost always 100% aware that I'm not acting in the physical).
- The dream is stable (after an initial instability), it ends when I will it to end, not earlier.

Type II
- Left brain activity is low, analyzing abilities are poor, I can hardly make coherent plans and don't stand a chance to follow them through. I'm distracted by almost everything (which makes plans impossible).
- Perception is mostly like in my ordinary dreams, strength of impression is somewhat lessened (colours e.g.), feeling of emotions is stronger.
- Surroundings and situation are unstable and change with random thoughts and associations. I almost never am in any localities that have a counterpart in the real world.
- The level of consciousness is generally low and unstable.
- The dream is unstable and sometimes vanishes with heightened consciousness.

These differences are strong enough by far to make this distinction into two separate categories. The two types feel totally different. And Type I reminds me stronger of the spontaneous OBEs I've had. Maybe the question is just the level of awareness of the situation. This, of course, is a similarity between OBEs and lucid dreams, you first have to realize that you are not in the physical/waking world.

Regards, MaX

◆ ◆ ◆ ◆ ◆ ◆ ◆

SUBJECT: ROLL OVER
(PART OF A PROCESS FOR INITIATING AN OUT-OF-BODY EXPERIENCE)

Hey There, I have a question about Tape 5 of the Discovery album. When Bob tells you to roll out of your body like a log, do you try to do it physically, or is it a mental command? I would think it's a mental command (imagery). But, in one of Bob's first OBEs, if not the first, he was lying on his bed drawing patterns on the floor with his finger, waiting for the vibrations to go away. Now, before his hand went through the floor, he must have felt like he was in his physical body because he didn't feel any different except for the vibrations. So this leads me to believe that I could try to roll physically. What do you think?

Thanks, Dan W.

Two hours later...

SUBJECT: RE: ROLL OVER

Hi Dan, There is a subtle technique here. The roll out, which is my favorite, can only be successful if you attempt it when you have reached the stage where you no longer feel your body. At that point you do it physically. As the energetic body is already detached from the physical, it responds by rolling out on the floor and this completes the separation process. The physical body remains asleep in bed. One good indication that you have reached this stage is the feeling that you are paralyzed. It can be a scary feeling, but once it is understood, it is a gateway to a full projection. If the roll out is attempted before this stage is reached, you will only succeed in moving your physical body and waking yourself up.

Good Luck, Michael N.

SUBJECT: RE: ROLL OVER

Hi Dan,

Just thought I'd add my own 2 cents about the roll out technique. In my experience the roll out can be and most often (90%) is successful when the strong vibrations are present, even if you can still connect/feel your physical body. Actually I've only failed in this technique recently, with the vibrations only present and very light lately otherwise I'd have given it 100% success rating. But the vibrations I'm talking about are not the quaint fuzzy vibrations of Focus 3, but rather a strong electrical type of vibration accompanied by sound and in various locations not so diffuse over your whole body like the fuzzy vibes of Focus 3. And at that time I actually try to roll my physical body over and guess what, only my light body moves, resulting in an OBE. Hope this doesn't confuse you with the divergent opinion, but you must remember all of this is very relativistic.

Skywalker

SUBJECT: RE: ROLL OVER

Hi Everyone,

The questions and comments about rolling out of the physical are great! I am glad to get the information that it is like trying to roll physically, except it only works when your body is asleep. I had that impression but had not proven it to myself yet. On my only successful conscious OBE, I was truly body asleep/ mind awake. I did not use the roll out. I was doing Tape 5 and when Bob said to try to float up, I had the feeling of separation but could not see. When I said I wanted to see, I could see!

The interesting, great, weird, etc. thing about that time for me was that I was paying attention to the tape, and I figured that I was very deeply relaxed, if not asleep. Then I started to hear some really weird sounds. As soon as I listened, they went away. Then they came back, and I had the most profound strange feeling as I identified the sound of me snoring! This comes after 13 years of swearing to my wife that I DO NOT SNORE. (I haven't told her. It would ruin the fun.) I just laid there and listened for a while. It was like listening to someone else. I had to "change," to retune into myself in order to go in and stop the snoring. I was able to stop snoring and retune to where I was. Very soon after that is when I separated. If only I had known how fast I would go through that window.

If only I had kept my head and not been startled by how high above the driveway I was. If only, if only…Well, next time I am not going to be that way, I hope. I guess my first time out lasted all of 30 seconds. I just wanted to bring up the subject of snoring. Anyone else hear themselves snore? Or are you also unwilling to admit that you snore?

Michael Smith

◆ ◆ ◆ ◆ ◆ ◆ ◆

TMI Residential Program Trainer Franceen King responds.

SUBJECT: AWARENESS IN SLEEP STATES

First of all, one of the purposes or effects of any kind of consciousness work is expanding awareness. During sleep, the human brain is several times more active (as measured by electrical activity) than during waking states. So one question which emerges is what is going on or what are we doing (in the sleep state)?" Normally during sleep people are unconscious or unaware. We know that there is a typical 90 minute sleep cycle during which the brain cycles through various brain wave patterns.

Until the 1970s, it was generally thought that humans could not be aware when the brain was showing the kinds of patterns that occur during sleep. With all of the interest in consciousness these past 30 years, we have learned that this is not true. In fact, through disciplined meditation, Hemi-Sync, and a variety of other brain/mind tools and practices, it has been shown in many labs around the world that people CAN be trained to generate the kinds of brain wave patterns normally found in the various stages of sleep and still be aware. One way of looking at the Hemi-Sync training program is that we are learning to extend awareness into those states that we normally only experience during sleep. This takes practice. That is one reason why people often fall asleep or "click out" — go unconscious when they first start listening to the tapes.

The basic "launch pad" state that TMI teaches is called Focus 10. This refers to a state of awareness, although it is characterized, or can be recognized by a specific brain wave pattern. As many people on the VML and elsewhere have reported, in this state they sometimes even hear their body snoring. The body is doing its "sleep thing," but the mind is still aware. So, being aware of your breathing as you sleep sounds to me like a Focus 10 state (unless your awareness is a result of sleep apnea, a condition in which people stop breathing during sleep and are awakened by the body gasping for air). "Listening to yourself, listen to yourself" definitely represents an expansion of consciousness into what is often referred to as an observer mode, but is a higher or more developed kind of awareness, a new level of self-awareness.

As we gradually continue to extend awareness into this domain (sleep), we become aware of many things. For example, we suspect that all people have spontaneous OBEs all the time during sleep. We just don't remember them because we haven't yet developed the ability to stay aware in those states. Dreams are another kind of awareness. Lucid dreams represent another kind of awareness — the ability to be aware of both the dream and that we are dreaming, and the ability to exercise conscious volition within the dream. The Night School experiences that Joe and others have been writing about are examples of other kinds of experiences in the sleep state and there are so many possibilities.

Hope this helps, Franceen King

SUBJECT: SHARING OUT-OF BODY EXPERIENCES

I'm sending this unsolicited OBE experience. My first and only OBE occurred some years ago. Its content was validated on the same day that I had it! I was asleep in my bed about 6:30 a.m. in Oxford, Mississippi, when I was suddenly on the Mississippi Gulf Coast, in Long Beach, 325 miles away from Oxford. I had no body, but I was floating backwards at head height. I saw my old high school friend, Pat, and his wife, Martita, walking toward me carrying suitcases. They were in a corridor connecting their bedroom wing from the rest of their house. It was not like a dream at all. Their personalities were right there, and I was there with them. I got so excited that I woke up, back in my bed in Oxford.

Throughout the day this experience remained on my mind until 5 p.m. when the phone rang, and it was THEM calling from a service station. Before that day, I had not heard from them, or even thought about them for quite some time. I asked the wife, who is from Panama, and whose father was head of medicine at a hospital in Panama City, "What were you doing at 6:30 this morning?" "Carrying our bags out to the car," she replied! They'd had airline tickets and a room reserved in Las Vegas, but, as they walked down the corridor where I had seen them, he said, "Let's not go to Las Vegas, let's go somewhere else." Eventually they settled on driving in their daughter's Porsche to Fayetteville, Arkansas, where he had been born. He wanted to see the place. As they drew abreast of Oxford, they were reminded of me and decided to visit. When I told them of my experience, Martita exclaimed, "Oh, Billy, your dream must have called us up here!"

Since then, I have had a couple of extremely vivid night visions (one of my dead mother), but no more OBEs. Also I've had some daytime, eyes-open visions. As to my psychological stability, I have held a university faculty position for over 30 years. I welcome all kinds of psychic experience. I read RAM's original book many years ago.

Bill Wilkes

SUBJECT: FIRST REAL OBE

I remember the excitement when I thought I had my first OBE a few months back. I felt a "surge" or "woosh" of energy go through me and exit out my feet — like a rubber band it snapped back within seconds. I was sure — my first OBE!!! Except last night I had a real one, so I'm wondering what that energy whoosh was before. Last I remember I was doing the Hemi Sync **H+ Contemplation** tape which I had started about 11:40 pm. It was about 12:30 am when I was awakened from a very light sleep with what I know now are THE "vibrations" everyone has been talking about. I'd always thought I knew how they felt - until I felt the "real" ones last night. It was like going over a "speed bump" which are grooves in the road and when your tires on the car go over them your car vibrates, only this was about 20 times stronger a vibration! It was almost as if I could "hear it" also. Anyways, it was very strong (intense) and startled me to a fully conscious state of mind...I was laying on my side at the time but when my second body started to separate, it felt as if it was separating from a body that was laying down flat. This was an odd feeling. For me it was just like I've seen in movies — when people have Near Death Experiences — it was a very graceful exit...and I was totally half separated from my physical body all the way to my neck! I remember thinking "Wow, this is it" and I was ready!!!! I remember thinking that I MUST decide where I will go once my body was completely out...it was floating over my real body but there was a sensation that part of me had not separated yet, and I just needed to complete that. Soon as I began to contemplate where I would go once I go out of my body totally, I drifted back in. I was SURE I could recreate it, to no avail. I'll never forget it. I was fully conscious during it, and when I settled back in I got up and wrote down the date and a brief summary of what had happened.

Mimi

A reply & another OBE description…

SUBJECT: RE: FIRST OBE

Mimi,

Congratulations on your first OBE! What a wonderful gift! The first time I had an OBE was in Montana in 1975. I was meditating and it was close to midnight. After 20 minutes or so I was very deep into the process. I started seeing something. Hmm, I thought, is this a mystical revelation of some sort? I looked closer to see what it was and realized that I was looking at a man sitting in a chair who appeared to be asleep. Not very mystical, I thought. Still, there was something about the person I was observing that seemed vaguely familiar. I peered closer and much to my delight realized that it was me! I was also aware at that moment I was floating or hovering up next to the ceiling across the room from where I was meditating. Wow, I've finally done it! I'm out of my body! As soon as I thought that, BAM! I was pulled back into my body with a loud CLICK! in the back of my head and my excitement turned to sorrow when I realized that I had caused my non-physical body to reconnect with the physical before I was ready. It was a long time before I had another OBE but I always knew it was possible because I had done it. Converting that belief into a known was a powerful experience for me, and I always carried it with me. Once you've done it no one can take that experience away from you. Again, congratulations!

Greg Collins

SUBJECT: RE: FIRST OBE

Congratulations Mimi. Now that you know what you're looking for and what to expect when the real vibrations hit. It may be easier for you next time; the first times are not always so easy, for you or me, it takes a lot of will power to fully separate. Don't think about your physical self at all, just think hard on getting out and enjoy. I have had occasions of not getting fully separated. It's like an elastic band stretching between me and my body. Even after separating this pull is felt. During my last OBE I started using affirmations like "total freedom and awareness NOW!" or just "Clarity now," something I learned from William Buhlman's book *Adventures Beyond the Body*. These affirmations helped me to stay out longer and go further than before, so try to use commands and think in absolute positives. It may be that we are somehow so used to our physical reality that it holds us like glue. It's up to us to unstick ourselves by affirming and using our imaginations and creative minds to get us where we want to be. Good luck and keep it up!!

Terry Thayer

◆ ◆ ◆ ◆ ◆ ◆ ◆

SUBJECT: WAVE III TAPES 1 & 2 (REMOTE VIEWING)

I continue to be amazed at the potential which I am sure exists in all of us. A week ago yesterday, the wind was howling and resulted in a power outage that lasted four hours. Alone in the house, I decided to get back to the tapes. For the last few weeks, I had been working with Tape 1 of Wave III (Gateway Experience Series) with only limited success. Kept falling asleep. This time I managed to stay awake. As suggested, I formed my REBAL, expanded it and floated. The tape repeats this exercise a number of times, changing the degree of expansion to develop control of the REBAL. On the last two repetitions, the night sky came into view. There was a constellation that stood out prominently, but not sure which one. After the tape was over, I went outside and looked up. You guessed it. That constellation was directly overhead! I had a sense that this may have only been my imagination because I had no sensation of the winds which were present, but still found it interesting.   After more thinking, I concluded that the wind only has an effect on physical things, hence the absence of this sensation could be possible.

With the lights still out, I rummaged around and located Tape 2 of this Wave. I didn't have a chance to read through the printed description, but went on. For those of you not familiar with this tape, some explanation is necessary. This is a tape for exploring the ability to do some remote viewing and obtain a validation of the event. (I learned this after doing the tape.) As I listened, RAM suggested taking my Energy Bar Tool (See Chapter 5 under Dolphin Energy Club, "DEC") and turning it into a tube, charging it, and stretching it out to the envelope at the target, entering the envelope, and perceiving the numbers written inside. Because I didn't have a pre-established experiment staged, I couldn't do this. I did, however, stretch out the tube to a target (work associate) and attempted to perceive her. It should be noted here that she and I had agreed that it would be OK to drop in on one another during meditation. I perceived "snapshots" of the location. In one perception, my work associate was sitting on a couch watching TV. During the next phase, I perceived a second "snapshot" where, how can I put this…well, let's just say it was a very intimate moment between her and her husband. These snapshots were very vivid and clear, and there may have been some motion evident, but I don't recall it.

OK, so I have these two mental snapshots of something now. I am still thinking that this must be my imagination or something. And, based, on the content of the latter snapshot, I had a sense that validation would be a little awkward. Last Monday I arrived at work, and after some rehearsal, spoke to my friend. At that particular time, on that particular evening, she said that she and her husband were watching a naughty movie and…well, one thing led to another…and…well, you get the picture (actually, I hope you don't get the picture!). More to the point, although a little embarrassing for both of us, it seemed validation had been obtained. Or had it? I still wasn't convinced.

Later in the week, I suggested that we explore the validation issue a little further. So I presented a couple of the generalizations in the second snapshot to her as specifics. These were also validated. NOW I am convinced. I apologized for invading her privacy. She does not have any experience with TMI's products; nonetheless, she indicated she has made visits to me as a target on a couple of occasions. The first one I could not validate for her (no recollection), but I was floored by the other. She said about 6 pm on December 18th she visited me. She asked me if I remembered what I was doing at that time. I thought about it, recalled where I was, and nodded. She then proceeded to give me an exact description of the events. She said I was in front of my computer and appeared to be writing a letter to someone. Check, but it was not that unusual for me to be doing that. Next she said she couldn't be positive, but thought it was a letter to a lady, and that the letter had something to do with her (associate). Check again. In fact, she said that she tried to contact me, but I was too preoccupied with what I was doing (yep, that's me). At that particular time, I had been working on a letter to Patricia Leva, and it, in fact, had something to do with her. OK, you get the picture again.

For me this RVing was very different from an OBE. There were no vibrations, and no sense of motion. In subsequent conversations, my associate and I discussed how we saw what we saw. She said her "seeing" was more like a movie than a snapshot. I asked if she was seeing through my eyes, but she indicated that she had been in a corner of the room watching me and could move around. This was the case with my snapshots, too, sans the motion. We agreed that it would be fun to set up the Wave III tape 2 experiment between us. She seemed to think that it would work, and I heartily agree. I'll keep you posted. Any explanations or thoughts from anyone on VML would be most welcomed.

Bob K.

SUBJECT: RE: WAVE III, TAPES 1 & 2 (REMOTE VIEWING)

Hi Bob,

You posted this at the perfect time for me. I have some time off that I can do some things that ordinarily I can't do. So I have included some RV fun in my holiday plans. Thanks for the reminder.

I loved the RV tape in Wave III. I saw into the envelope, though it was fleeting, and I got three of the numbers. VERY real! Later on I tried visiting my son, Jon. The times that I was most successful he was in school. I got more than a snapshot, but less than a video. I'd call it a video clip minus sound. I was able to describe his teacher and what she wore that day and the fact that she is rather theatrical in her style (waving her arms about in various attention-getting gestures). Jon confirmed all of this for me.

Why I have not done more of this is beyond me. I have used the energy bar tube at lunch time here at work (no tape) and am pretty sure I viewed some happenings at our biotech division, but had the presence of mind not to try to validate any of it. Do keep us posted on the project. I have a willing 'other participant' here at work that lives 40 miles away, but have never done the RVing of that envelope/cotton ball thing (Tape 2) except with Jon downstairs in my house.

I have never experienced the vibrations in doing this. Actually, the vibrations are rare for me, although I have had very profound experiences where I know I was tuned into a different place and experienced being there. I am sure that the vibrations are not a prerequisite to OBE, but am not sure why they are sometimes present and other times not. Still a mystery to me. I think that this experiment could generate a lot of interest if enough people on the list gave it a try.

Michael Smith

◆ ◆ ◆ ◆ ◆ ◆ ◆

SUBJECT: THE PARK
(TRANSITIONAL STATE OF CONSCIOUSNESS AFTER DEATH, FOCUS 27)

When my wife's grandmother died we were all there three days before. Someone was by her bed the whole time (one of her dead sons or daughters). About two days before she died she started talking about visiting with relatives that had died years before. Everyone was very accepting of this and they enjoyed trying to puzzle out who everyone Grandma had seen.

Rylan R.

Next day a post in return…

SUBJECT: RE: THE PARK

I just wanted to add some information to "The Park." I have heard about it for two years. I work in hospice as some of you know and before someone dies, usually about three days before, they are escorted to "The Park" for a visit. I always thought this must be heaven. Many times when discussing death, and I have many opportunities to do so, the near death experience would come up. I have always used the "white light" as "The Park" analogy. My argument is, if, when someone is dying they see a white light merely because of lack of oxygen then…how can so many of my patients that come from all walks of life, different ages, sex, and nationalities, describe the same place??? During these trips, my patients walk, run, climb trees, and are away from their pain. They are usually escorted but not always. They return to say their goodbyes and tell me about it. I provide the opportunity for them to express this safely. They are wonderfully surprised to hear that others have been there too. I only have read Bob Monroe's first book about eight weeks ago. When I read the part about "The Park" I literally dropped the book! This is a big deal in hospice work. How validating!! Not that I did not believe any of it, I did. As I said, I thought it was heaven and now it seems like it is a wonderful receiving area. I cannot wait to see it myself. I would prefer to see it first while still in this physical journey.

Nancy S.

VML MEMBERS SHIFTING BELIEFS INTO KNOWNS

SUBJECT: FENCE WALKING IN FOCUS 12

Boy, it is one thing to experience it and quite another to articulate it in words. That night, a week ago now, I laid down in bed and decided to do the thing I have been trying for months. Frank described it a while back, recommending you "lazily" allow yourself to drift off, but retain conscious awareness. Well, this is what we do with the tapes, right? But I think this goes a little beyond Focus 10 or 12. Maybe not, but it was different to me than being in 12. I can get to 12 without tapes, but not very easily yet. 10 is easy for me without tapes. I know that 10 is what I have accessed for all the years that I tried to do Harold Sherman's relaxation techniques. The only thing I lacked, thinking back, was the higher frequency signal to keep my awareness "active." Once I had had the experience I could (can) replicate it. That is why the tapes are called tools, right?

OK, the hard part, the actual perceptions I had. I know I had made it to 10 and was concentrating (in a lazy way) on further letting go of the physical body signals. It was like going down stairs. I would sense different levels of physical signals. After a few steps I would stop and try to stay awake, because I knew that if I went down one more stair, I would be mind asleep and would have failed. Well, doing that always brought me up a few steps toward physical body awareness. So the process was a long one. I would descend three steps, then stop and regain control, which would cause me to go back up two steps. I would then start my decent again, three down, stop, two up. This went on for quite a while. Occasional sound interruptions had to be dealt with, which is probably the single most significant deterrent I have had to deal with.

A few times I would, while stopped, try to calculate the time since I started the procedure. After a while it became difficult to get a feel for elapsed time. Having the thought that I should ignore passage of time and not be concerned with it sent me back up the staircase many steps, eroding much progress. But having that thought also enabled me (I believe) to descend the staircase farther and faster than I had ever done previously. Actually, from that point on I do not have any reference to time at all that I can recall.

I had just reached Focus 12, I believe. I felt that way because when I get to 12 with a tape I have a very pronounced perception of my visual field and my awareness expanding 'outward' in all directions. I liken it to the difference between peering through a hole at a scene and then having the hole get big enough that I can stick my head through it, and when I do, I have peripheral vision that covers a much wider field of view. I feel that it is happening with all of my senses, not just vision. Maybe this is like a "knowing," or at least a change that enables me to perceive beyond what I can in "normal" state or even Focus 10.

I felt as if I had arrived "'somewhere." Somewhere is not a good word at all for it, but it will have to do. It was like I stood at the edge of a chasm, not having any fear of falling in. I knew that venturing beyond where I was would be ok, that no harm could come to me. Even so, I stayed on this edge for a while. I just wanted to be there for a while to get the feel of it. Probably I wanted to become familiar enough to be able to return via an easier, less arduous path. I hope that ability is something I will attain eventually.

I felt very light. Or I felt very mobile, I don't know which. It was as if my thought would become action. That is what I was thinking as I willed myself to step out, over the edge of the abyss. Having that thought, at that time, brought me back as soon as I stepped off. I decided that this is not the time to be thinking. Just go with whatever happens seemed to be the thing to do. Just float away without thinking. I started again to float away. I thought "Hey, this is cool." THAT brought me back. Damn! I could go on for a long time recounting all the attempts and all the thoughts that kept bringing me back, but you get the picture, right?

I tried another approach. I "leaned forward," like I was going just stick my head in and look around. It seemed to work because left brain could analyze and not bring me back doing this. I thought I must be fooling myself into thinking I was still anchored in familiar territory, but able to see beyond. It was about then that I felt like I was within a misty cloud or a fog that was dense enough to not see your feet in. Like that theatrical fog they flood the stage with in the cheapy movies. Bear in mind that I really have no visual input all this time. I tried to get a visual a number of times and got nothing. At the same time, I felt that I did not need to relate to anything visual to be able to perceive my surroundings. My thoughts went to RAM, floating in INSPEC territory, waiting for contact. Having that thought promoted a desire to make contact with my INSPEC, or my EXCOM, or GUIDES. Gee, everyone else can do it, why not me? Well, I think I can, I just don't know the mechanics of it. Perhaps this experience is the base upon which I can build my repertoire of "tricks" that will enable me to access the states that I need to access in order to truly break free and explore the dimensions, the rings, whatever.

I get somewhat hazy from this point on. It really is my last stop on this voyage. I do remember deciding to erect my signpost. My signpost looks like a yield sign in height and shape. The writing on it is my initials (taken from Rick's idea) usually with a number under it. I didn't know what number to assign to this, so I put a question mark below the initials. Signpost erection is sometimes very difficult for me. When I do it I usually hear Rod Sterling's voice saying "There's a signpost up ahead," and I hear the doo-dee-dooo-dee-doo-dee-doo-dee of the Twilight Zone theme song. I have to wonder if anyone else's thought life is as weird as mine. You guys seen my sign? If you spot it please tell me where I left it. :-)

I feel like I stayed in the mist for a while and then I must have fallen off of the fence. Had no dream recollection in the morning, but this was (is) burned into my mind. I have spent all this week thinking about it. Actually, I was fearing that I could not describe it. I probably did a rotten job of it, but when I sat down here to compose this it flowed out of me without too much time spent contemplating how to word it. I am glad that I did not jump in and write this a few days ago like I intended to do. Don't think it would have made any sense at all. I am sure that this is the process that takes place that allows us to fully integrate an experience into our knowledge/belief/known base.

Well, that's it. I can't describe the feeling I have. I have been given *something* that is priceless that nobody can ever take away from me. Thanks to all of you for journeying with me. And thanks for letting me drive for a while. Someday I'll chuck this learner's permit and get my license. Then nobody on the interstate will be safe. :-)

Michael Smith

SUBJECT: ODD ENERGY EXPERIENCE

Back in the 1980s, a friend of mine was trying to do some "regression" therapy with me as an experiment. I was lying on a massage table, well covered and warm, a thick cloth across my eyes, soft pleasant music in the background. He was doing some kind of hypnotic droning, then he began to ask questions. In each case, I had no answer, I told him that the questions had no meaning. This went on for what felt like a half hour, but I was so comfortable I didn't mind. Then it felt as if my whole body began to tingle, as if every cell were beginning to vibrate, slow at first, then faster and faster. It was a very pleasant sensation, and I just lay there and enjoyed it. When my friend asked me what was happening, I was able to describe it in precise detail while it was happening. Soon the vibrations were so rapid, I perceived my body as being made up completely of blue light. This continued for some time — five or six minutes I estimate, though "time" did not seem very real. Then something spoke through me and said, "There are only two valid states of awareness. The first is *Knowing*, the second is *Not Knowing*." I lay there for a bit, then I said, "What did I just say?" My friend repeated it back to me, and it began to have an impact on me. He said, "Then what is everything else?" The "something" spoke again, "Everything else is ego." I just lay there for quite some time, enjoying the blue light sensation which slowly calmed down until I was just a "meat" body again. The words spoken through me gradually changed my life. I no longer felt the need to convince anyone that I knew things or had experience. I would either give an answer about which I was certain or I would simply say, "I don't know." It took a huge load off me and gave me a great sense of peace. What I know, I'm certain of. All the rest lies in the wondrous realm of Not Know, only one short step from Know. Just thought I'd share this with you all.

Eric B.

A month later, on the same topic but with a change…

SUBJECT: MY METAMORPHOSIS FROM MAN TO HUMAN, THE CONTINUING JOURNEY

Finally, I think I've found a forum where I can present this. and those that read it will be able to relate, at least I hope they can. It was just about a year ago, on a rainy Saturday afternoon. Things were just starting to settle down after a very stressful summer (my wife and I had buried our respective fathers within two weeks of each other, both had been ill for a long time). We went shopping and had swung by the library to return some books. I wandered over to the "New Books" section to see what there was. Maybe a new Harold Robbins book or something. A book caught my eye. It had an interesting title, *Ultimate Journey*, by some guy named Monroe. I picked it up and scanned it briefly. Having always been a fan of that paranormal stuff I checked it out. Looked like it might be interesting. I scanned it a little more thoroughly at home (I admit that I never did read that book). I found it somewhat confusing, and a lot of what he professed was kind of beyond belief. Some of what he said conflicted strongly with my belief systems. I asked my wife to return it.

About 5:15 am, I decided that I had better try to get some sleep so I could function at work the next day. I went back to bed and shortly thereafter I had another "weird dream." This time it wasn't a frightening dream, just weird. Something about me driving car around the top of a four-sided mesa-like structure (man-made, though). The problem was, as I approached, I couldn't tell what was over the edge (to drive over it and get off the top of this place). I wasn't alone, my wife's girlfriend accompanied me in the car?? After driving around in circles for a long time, looking and not being able to tell what was over the edge, I decided to throw caution to the winds (conscious decision!) and I drove the car over the first edge...a road, relief, smooth ride — CLICK — back on top again, I drove off the edge again, this time stairs and a bumpy, but not unpleasant, ride down — CLICK — around again except this time I started to wake up, sort of, awake but not awake.

Three weeks later something unusual happened. I went to bed about 11:30 pm on a Sunday night. I had a startling (frightening) dream. I don't remember what it was specifically, but remember that there was an older man standing on my patio looking in through the glass door. (I woke up screaming, "no-no," adrenaline flowing big time at about 2 am. Seemed so real, not like a normal dream). I didn't recognize the old man. He appeared to be mid-to-late sixties, about 6 feet tall, not heavy but not thin, and dressed in comfortable-looking casual clothes. And, as I remember it, he could have done with a shave. But there was an odd element as well. As I looked at him and repeated (yelled) "no-no," he got sort of a sad look on his face, turned to his right and walked away slowly with his head hanging down. Like his feelings had been hurt. I was so shook that I got out of bed and went out to the living room to see if the old man was out there. He wasn't visible to me. I had a cigarette and did a few crossword puzzles to relax.

Thinking like I was awake (mind), but still asleep (body). I remember seeing a faint light (blurry) which appeared to be very small or way off in the distance and was not symmetrical. In my mind I was trying to figure out the source of this light. Then things got really weird. For some reason, I thought, "Oh, what the heck, let's roll out, go up, and have a look around.

What followed must have taken all of about 30 seconds, but it's 30 seconds I'll never forget. Without any prior sign or warning I felt a tremendous pulling outward and up from my chest/abdomen (below the breast bone in an upward direction, angled about 45 degrees toward my chin). I rolled from right to left (like a scuba diver's shoulder roll when entering the water from a boat) and fell off of the bed and onto the floor (thud!). I remember hitting my head on the nightstand, but it didn't hurt, sort of went through the nightstand. Almost immediately I felt tremendous and very coarse vibrations, a really loud buzzing too. Thoughts came fast. Dying? Heart attack? Electrocution? Loud noise, vibrations, will wake my wife, will she be shocked too? Don't touch her. I got up (stood?) and gave a small jump upward (may have had company/guide/helper but didn't see or feel any). This resulted in a tremendous sense of speed. Couldn't see while traveling but could sense things going by very fast. Thought still coming, what's the noise…too loud…how'd I get through the ceiling?…traveling too fast. I remember thinking, "Need to stop." No sooner thought then done. Thought, "should look around." Again, done, was able to "see" but things were not clearly in focus…what's that?…green and blue? A garden with a lake?…must be the one Monroe was talking about…but it's round and there's nothing attached to it, isolated…must be an island or something…why can't I focus? Sense of motion again…vibrations are smoothing, fading, fading, noise is gone too. I slowly opened my eyes and looked around. Still alive, in bed, wife's asleep, all my pieces appear to be where they're supposed to be. I looked at the clock, time to get up and get ready for work, time is 6:17 am.

As the day wore on I noticed two strange things: 1) My vision had improved. I could see very clearly, able to focus without strain, without my glasses, but this wore off within a day or so. 2) I wasn't the least bit tired. In fact, I felt better than I had in along time in spite of the lack of sleep. Not just better, I felt different, more alive maybe (this, too, has worn off, unfortunately). I was very confused about the noise and vibrations. They were impossible to put out of my mind as was the whole event. I chose not to tell anyone about it at first. I wasn't sure what to make of it myself, how could I talk about it to others? Maybe all the stress of the recent months had finally caught up with me. In short, I was confused and a little afraid, but at the same time excited.

After a couple of days I shared what had happened with my wife. The conversation started with, "You've got to believe me, and I'm not crazy, at least I hope I'm not but..." To my surprise and joy she didn't think me odd (no more than usual anyway). After she heard my story, she offered unlimited support. She suggested that the island I had seen may have been the earth from a great distance. She was, of course, correct. I know now that's what I saw on my brief, but memorable and unforgettable journey.

Although my first trip was spontaneous, I'm looking forward to developing the ability to go OOB, at will, and with control, so I can get a better understanding of who I am and where I'm from. A big change I've noticed, is my ability to understand the difference between "believing" and "knowing." I guess until my journey, I really didn't fully understand the distinction. I sure do now. I know Monroe not to be the crackpot I first thought he was, but rather a teacher/explorer and more. I wish I had had the opportunity to sit and talk with him face-to-face, maybe I still can. Needless to say, my belief systems have undergone some changes, I have too. I find I am much more aware of my surroundings, sensations in my body, waking and sleeping, and having NVCs with something or someone that I perceive as trying to help me into a greater understanding of myself and my role. I've been able to dump nicotine, once and for all, after almost 30 years of two to three packs/day, and I'm learning to listen for and tune into my intuitive feelings. I'm a lot more open to what's possible than before. I am seeing more of the good in things, people, society and the environment. Life has become a pleasure again, like when I was a little kid. It's clear that I have started (or am continuing) my metamorphosis from man to Hu-man (physical to spirit). It will be a pleasure having you all around as I evolve further. Sorry this got so long — had a lot to say for a long time. Thanks for your patience.

Bill K.

Three days later, Eric posts a message back to Bill...

SUBJECT: RE: MY METAMORPHOSIS FROM MAN TO HUMAN

I think you've struck right to the core of this, your beliefs, and therefore you have changed and there's no going back. Let me share an insight which was channeled to me about ten years ago. "There are only two valid states of awareness, Knowing and Not Knowing. Everything else is ego." When you Know something, there is neither an explanation for "how" you know it, nor any need for one. And unless you do know, you're in Not Know. The neat thing I realized afterwards was that Not Know, which we've been trained (to think) is a terrible place to be, is actually never more than a brief millisecond of awareness away from Know. All it ever takes is a slight shift of viewpoint, a realignment of data, and you suddenly have that "Ah Ha!" It removed the need to "know about" or "I've experienced that." You either Know or you Not Know. Takes away a lot of the bs.

Eric B.

Bill returns with another post...

SUBJECT: RE: MY METAMORPHOSIS FROM MAN TO HUMAN

Eric, You should know I was not attempting to go OB, in fact, I had convinced myself that that would be the last thing I wanted to do, rather it just happened. The bottom line is this: My belief systems which I carried with me for more than 40 years have suddenly been shaken to their foundations. I was comfortable with my belief systems. They provided a structure I could hide inside. They sheltered me from the unknown. Now, I've got a whole new set of rules to deal with because I Know. Except, I'm not sure what the rules are or if there are any for that matter. I'm exposed and I feel vulnerable. I'm not comfortable with this new knowledge, I just don't know what it all means yet, and I am having trouble understanding why I didn't wake up sooner. I Know, absolutely that I am changing and probably for the better.

Bill K.

VOYAGER MEMBERS ON EMERGING NEW KNOWN:
"I AM MORE THAN MY PHYSICAL BODY"

SUBJECT: UNIMPORTANT WORLDS

I've read a couple of Monroe's books. Gonna start chewing on the third one. Anyone ever think, or maybe in passing thought, that under the philosophy that Monroe's books imply…that is, that this physical existence is but one and that we are much more. Does anyone ever feel that things that go on in this life are just not as important anymore? Let me explain myself. I'm not talking about the learning experience of this life. I'm talking about other things, like death. With complete certainty in what Monroe has experienced, does anyone place less importance on say, a family member dying? Do you think I'm being too drastic? Or maybe taking this too seriously? It's like the entire world has been reduced in intensity, like going from sunlight to shade. Mind you, these are just thoughts. I'm not withdrawing from my life. In fact, I've become more interested in it. But these questions seem important to discuss, and I'd sure appreciate your views on it!

Brian

SUBJECT: RE: UNIMPORTANT WORLDS

Life on earth is just a small bandwidth on the spectrum of consciousness. Life here can be very important, if this is the only aspect of life you are aware of. Once you become aware of the broader spectrum, human aspirations become secondary, and you often trigger an intense sense of alienation, depression, or more appropriately, "homesickness." I don't grieve over the death of any friends or family members. Death is simply a transition in consciousness, and I do everything possible to help them make the transition smoothly.

Actually, you are not being drastic enough, and you should consider this matter more seriously. Once you cross that threshold where you attain certainty on your personal immortality and your role as a tourist here, there is no turning back. You will find yourself very much a stranger in a strange land, physical reality will be much less solid and you'll probably question your own sanity. Thank God this type of insanity seems to be spreading!

Joe H.

Michael responds…

SUBJECT: RE: UNIMPORTANT WORLDS

I find it a lot easier to say, "It just doesn't matter." If someone goes berserk on the freeway cutting people off and acting like a fool, I don't get upset as I might have when I was twenty. I can see that they are obviously on a different path than I am and let it go. I do get the feeling that was mentioned in one of the posts of being a little outside of things by knowing how much more there is than just this.

When I was a child, I must have had some sense of this because I can remember making my mother cry with an honest comment. At the time I was three or so and going to Sunday school. My father was a food salesman; we weren't rich. I stood in my bed that still had rails on it and looked around at my bedroom which was the living room. I told my Mother that I couldn't wait to die. She was shocked, of course, and asked why. I said, "If this is all that there is, I can't wait to get to heaven." Now this wasn't really a death wish. It was a wish to limit the time spent on what looked like an uninteresting, unproductive experience. You know, and get on to the good stuff.

Mike T

◆ ◆ ◆ ◆ ◆ ◆ ◆

Two weeks later Brian comes back with a new twist on this post...

SUBJECT: SO LONG HUMANITY

Nooo-o, this isn't a suicide note! It's about what happens to you when you Know that Monroe was right and so are all these other people following along similar paths, and that we're much more than what we can perceive in waking life. I believe Monroe and I believe there is more to existence, despite not having had an official OBE or any sort of spiritual contact. I only believe because I find it impossible to believe that Monroe was crazy and so are a lot of you out there, and luckily I've had a few minor experiences that provide some glue to keep everything form falling apart into uncertainty. So, here I am, reducing my ego much faster than I was before I knew of Monroe. I believe that there is more to myself. However, I feel like I'm becoming less human. I look at life in a more objective way. I've basically become less human because I don't believe that human existence is IT (all there is). Like, "OK, I'm a human being, and I experience this existence. But I'll participate in it only to a degree. I can't take it very seriously." A lot of what we think of as being typically human has a LOT to do with a person believing that human existence is the only existence in the universe.

So, what do we think of this? Does increasing your awareness naturally lead to a decrease in your human qualities? Also, I'm not sure if anyone else relates to this, but it's important not to use mind expansion as an escape or a way to be different. This would be really bad, if you used mind-expanding as a means of being special. I can say this because I've thought about this myself. I have always been a quiet outsider, and for a long time I would rationalize this as "I'm special," so I would use my behavior differences as a means of being better than other people. It's just a thought. It came out when I asked myself, "Why have I gotten into this stuff? It screws up everything." Again, I don't want to fool myself. Thanks for listening.

Brian

After many messages to him, Brian says...

SUBJECT: SO LONG HUMANITY

Well, thanks for all the replies! Thanks to those who gave me leads to more info on this subject. When I said, "less human" I knew I would get some response to that. I suppose I don't really mean less human. I guess it once again goes back to how a person behaves when they believe that their current physical existence is the TRUE and ONLY existence they have. So with that, they really get into the role of being human — developing human patterns. Also, they view every human experience as if it's all-important. I guess when I sort this out, you don't really become less human. You become a different human. You just don't think of the world in the same way and it becomes less important and less worrisome. Because you know you are more than your physical self, you tend to take matters lightheartedly. So, this lightheartedness is what I'm describing, I suppose. In a sense you are less human. You're less interested in many human affairs, so you are sometimes more withdrawn under certain circumstances. That is all.

Brian

Brian receives one more reply from the metamorphosing Bill.....

SUBJECT: SO LONG HUMANITY

Maybe not less human, just (growing) more spirit, and (achieving) a different ratio between the two, possibly? I can only speak for myself, what I've been able to learn, how I've changed. Try this on and see if it fits.

- I'm less concerned about "being better" than those around me.
- I'm less impatient with people, I'm alert for anything I can learn from them, even how not to be if that's the lesson.
- I've learned to be much less "closed" with people, allow them to see a side that I may not have (willingly) shown before.
- I don't get angry anymore or upset, such a waste of positive energy.
- Likewise, I don't worry anymore (about dying, about being cheated, about being belittled etc.) I just don't take that stuff seriously any longer, no point to it, interferes with the real job at hand, it's really not important. I don't fret over things I have no control over and I've learned to determine when that is.

These are human qualities that I've lost, glad I did, wish more humans would too. I laugh a lot more and am enjoying this life more than ever, but I know there's a lot more to it. Do I owe this to the tapes? To TMI? To RAM himself? No, although they have helped me on my journey and for that I will be eternally grateful, but they are not the cause of my enlightenment. That comes from a much larger power than Hemi-Sync. I'll learn where this larger power resides with time, I hope my $0.02 helps.

Bill K.

Our next sojourn is to explore various CEVs (consciousness expansion vehicles) in educational car dealerships across the country and develop a sharp awareness of how to choose the right vehicle for your voyage. Included are various selection methods and a maintenance plan for the care and feeding of the CEV.

GOING TO THE NET: IT'S A LOVE/LOVE GAME

Voyager time, sounds, light, vibration, seeing, dreaming, dying
Odd energy experience
Or are you also unwilling to admit you snore?
Yet metamorphosing, Knowing and Not-Knowing,
Thank God, this type of insanity seems to be spreading!
Congrats, adding my 2 cents, I hope I have thoroughly confused you,
Good Luck; And that's all.

TRANSPORTATION VEHICLES

"…man's chief delusion is his conviction that he can do…but actually nobody does anything…out of himself a man cannot produce a single thought, a single action. Everything is dependent on everything else, everything is connected, nothing is separate & everything is going the only way it can."

Georges Gurdjieff

ROUTE 7

SHIFTING GEARS: FROM THE OLD TO THE NEW PARADIGM

When Neil Armstrong stepped through our biosphere into outer space and planted an American flag on the moon in 1969, a world belief began to self-destruct. This straightforward and exhilarating televised event entered popular awareness at full speed. Immediately filed inside, the resulting paradigm change was so great, it didn't just shift, it jumped giant steps the moment we saw the flag planted and heard the words spoken, "One step for mankind." In those seconds, a mental leap was made, ending the belief that man was the center of the universe. Immediately, a new paradigm opened shouting that humankind was a mere speck in an immense universe.

We, on Gaia, grew so large at that moment we are still mystified by its impact. In terms of consciousness training and personal growth, it is no surprise that, over 30 years later, educational specialists still are unable to keep pace with their own futurists. As a result, education and training methods used to enhance the new paradigm aren't as yet supported in our everyday culture. Physicist Erwin Schrödinger observed long ago that scientific findings move very slowly into the world. He estimated a lag time of 50 years passes by before actual behavioral changes occur. (1)

In the field of consciousness education and training, this gap has just begun to be bridged. The majority of people who still pursue old beliefs often come from the paradigm perspective that humans, being the center of the universe, are separate from the elements that make up the universe. They would say tools for consciousness expansion exist outside themselves similar to the "magic bullets" physicians prescribe to alleviate symptoms of an illness or disease.

IS SOUND A MUTE DUMMY?

In the same manner, many a traditional teacher or trainer has described Hemi-Sync as a learning "aid and assist" tool. Pause for a moment. Is sound a mute dummy? As a universal, energetic element, sound possesses creative intelligence. When I learned about becoming the waveform, I came to understand that sound was a living, breathing entity. This learning enlivened my act of merging with or becoming the energy of the sound. More than just manipulating it to achieve a change in consciousness, or better yet turn the channel to another source of entertainment, I dove right into my own waveform literally. I became the vehicle that transports itself down the Interstate.

When people take medications prescribed by a doctor, many know, on some level, of the creative intelligence of what appears to be an inert substance. The multitudes of half-filled prescription bottles in bathroom cabinet are testimony to the fact that the majority of all prescriptions which are filled are not totally consumed. There is something shifting in the collective unconscious that knows that unless one merges with an antibiotic and its life-giving essence, the appropriate healing will not occur. The "magic bullet" effect is lessening daily.

CAN YOU GUARANTEE I WILL HAVE AN OBE?

When the old paradigm is well-entrenched in individuals, they treat Hemi-Sync or any other consciousness expansion vehicle as a object to be manipulated either on a conscious or subconscious level so as to experience the instant Whiz-Fizzes and Wham! that some mind tools can deliver. Understandably, this phenomenon-seeking behavior is rampant today because the world is hanging in-between a local (selfish) and a non-local (selfless) perspective. If I had a dollar for all the requests from clients (in the local mode) who have said to me, "Can you guarantee an out-of-body experience if I do Hemi-Sync?," I'd be a millionaire! My approach is to bring them down to earth by describing how the sounds of Hemi-Sync are not magic bullets to have OBEs. Truly, it is the unique partnership between these sound elements or any other consciousness expansion vehicle, physical or non-physical, and the individual that creates a change in consciousness. Simply speaking, there are no magic bullets provided and no OBE guaranteed, as we create uplinks to non-physical reality. It takes a few 500 mile trips on the Interstate to detune the body and tune into non-ordinary consciousness!

CHOOSING A CAR:
A CONSCIOUSNESS EXPANSION VEHICLE (CEV)

Just as the automobile industry has flooded the marketplace with a tremendous selection of cars to choose from, far too many consciousness expansion vehicles (CEV) are overwhelming many people seeking a reliable, dependable, safe trip on the Interstate. Hundreds of mind machines, audio tapes, books, videos, software, and nutritional supplements are flooding the marketplace. They do not include the natural CEVs right at your fingertips — the water, the air, and the sky above. Typically, when looking for a car to buy, it is commonplace to turn to Consumer Reports and the bluebook in order to narrow down the options, but this isn't required when choosing a CEV. All that is necessary is to figure out what particular energy is "on tap" or dominant in a person's life. To discover what CEV might be best to drive, do a little personal research by using one of the basic tools that have been around for a time such as astrology, I Ching, the Myers Briggs Indicator, the Native American Medicine Wheel path or Ayurveda approaches. (See the following CEV Tip Sheet to identify dominant driving energy.) These will show the primary energy powering the spirit of the driver behind the wheel. By matching the dominant form of energy in a person to the energy of a particular CEV, there will be a natural partnership. This knowledge will help an Interstate traveler choose the most appropriate wheels from the many car selections available today. In this manual the CEV is considered as both an internal and external means of transportation. Eventually the driver and the car become one. Underlying the choice of the right CEV, is the idea that all vehicles are created from material goods which are essentially blobs of energy forms. Let's look at the five basic energy forms.

THE FIVE ESSENTIAL ENERGIES

Using the Ayurvedic model, Dr. Vasant Lad explains that "Ancient seers of truth, the rishis, perceived that consciousness was energy manifested into five basic principles or elements: Ether (space), Air, Fire, Water, and Earth. From the soundless Aum came the first element, Ether, and from its ethereal movement came Air. From Ether came friction, light, and the element of Fire was manifested. Then Ether dissolved and liquefied into Water, then solidified into Earth. All came from Ether which came from the soundless sound of Aum. All five manifested in the energy from the Force, all five are present in all matter in the universe; therefore, energy and matter are one." (2) Each of the five basic elements have correlates in the five senses of humankind.

Ether - **Hearing**
Air - **Touch**
Fire - **Vision**
Water - **Taste**
Earth - **Smell**

The word Ayurveda is a Sanskrit word which means "science of life." Ayu means "life" or "daily loving" and Veda means "knowing." (3) Sound, the first sense to arrive in the newborn and the last sense to leave in the dying person, is the Ether coming and going, enfolding and infolding. As it comes it creates the other four senses and as it goes, life as we know it dies. Sound, as Ether, is a resonating tool. Air or Ether in action activates the mental body, Water activates the emotional body (also known as the astral body), Fire activates the causal body, and Earth activates the physical body.

There are literally hundreds of CEV vehicles available to choose from. They can be divided into five categories according to the five elements that make up the universe. Each offers a chance to partner either with Ether, Air, Water, Fire or Earth; although, each element contains all matter, therefore all energy. This pertains to the intention of the person who is driving the vehicle.

PARTNERING WITH THE ELEMENT OF ETHER
Those consciousness expanding vehicles which incorporate *sound and/or speech* whether it be audible or inaudible will be useful cars for those who prefer to use Ether as a convenient mode of transportation.

JOINING WITH THE ELEMENT OF AIR
Those vehicles which use the *sense of touch* involving the skin, which cause large muscle movement of the body or stimulate pulsations of the heart, expansion and contraction of the lung, movement of the stomach wall, intestines, the cells, and the Central Nervous System will be beneficial for highly mental types, those who like to use Air as a means of transit.

ALLYING WITH THE ELEMENT OF FIRE
For easy traveling, those people having a fiery nature will find it advantageous to use *vehicles of light, heat, or color* as well as things that

stimulate metabolism of the body, the brain, the feet, the eyes, and the enzyme system.

LINKING WITH THE ELEMENT OF WATER

People who like the *taste* of good things will want to use vehicles that stimulate the abundant (80%) watery nature of their bodies such as immersing themselves in watery environments and/or have experiences that stimulate the secretions of the digestive juices, the salivary glands and the mucus membranes. The Water element will be their most beneficial mode of transportation.

PARTNERING WITH THE ELEMENT OF EARTH

Individuals, whose consciousness expansion vehicle stimulates the *body's solid structure* such as the bones, cartilage, tendons, nails, muscles, skin, hair, and teeth, will prefer traveling with the Earth element as their CEV.

EXAMPLES OF CONSCIOUSNESS EXPANSION VEHICLES*

Using one element as a CEV is referenced here as requiring a one-car garage. Those who want to combine two elements are referred to requiring a two-car garage.

* These listings are not meant to be the author's recommendations but only examples of many available resources.

USING ONE CAR & TWO CAR GARAGES FOR THE CEV

FOR THE ONE CAR GARAGE OWNER

ETHER VEHICLES

Self-generated Sound: toning, overtoning, omming, singing, crying, humming, chanting, clicking, sniffing, yawning, yelling, and talking etc.

Generated Sound: music (recorded or live), Tibetan bowls, crystal bowls, gongs, drumming, rattles, Hemi-Sync, sound tables, tuning forks, holophonic audiotapes, primordial sounds (example: Ayurveda, Dr. Jeffrey Thompson), music with animal sounds (Paul Winter), hypnotherapy tapes (Dr. Milton H. Erickson, Dr. Lloyd Glauberman, Changeworks) guided imagery tapes, self-talk tapes.

AIR VEHICLES

Breathwork such as omming, resonant tuning, chanting, rebirthing, holotrophic breathwork, dancing, aerobic workouts, all physical sport activities, spinning, air purifiers, tachyon products, GSR Meter (galvanic skin response), BioCircuits, magnets, massotherapy, anesthesia, negative ion generators, alternate nostril breathing, hugging, flying, hands-on healing (Reiki, therapeutic touch, touch for health, craniosacral therapy, Rolfing, chiropractic therapy), yoga, and crystals.

FIRE VEHICLES

Strobing lights, broad spectrum lights, chromotherapy, violet ray, laser, virtual reality, colored sunglasses, candles, aromatherapy, potpourri, software (Axel Bruk's Mind Art system), fire walking, sauna, sweat lodge ceremony, walking, stereoscopic training (Magic Eye cartoon), video games, virtual reality games, some recreational drugs, alcohol, color therapy, and vision training.

WATER VEHICLES

Flotation tank, crystal energized water, blood, showering, swimming, diving, cleansing or fasting, sexual intercourse, nutrients (spirulina, blue-green algae, wheat grass), activated water, miraculous water, mineral baths, and holy water.

EARTH VEHICLES

Walking, running, jogging, smelling, sonar, horseback riding, bones, teeth, skulls, shells, wood, cement structures, salt water swimming, digging, overtoning, chanting, playing the violin, vibrating beds and chairs.

FOR THE TWO CAR GARAGE OWNER
(TWO ELEMENTS COMPLEMENTING EACH OTHER)

FIRE & ETHER VEHICLES (LIGHT & SOUND)

TENS (Transcutaneous Electro-Nerve Stimulator), Alpha Stim products, MindsEye products, The D.A.V.I.D. Paradise, The Dreamwave II.

EARTH & ETHER VEHICLES (SOUND & BONE)

Using the human voice in acts of singing, toning, overtoning, talking etc. sets up a resonance which vibrates both the body and the skeleton of the body. Information accumulated through the ages located in the boney skeleton is released; thus, toning on a mountainside or near an energy vortex is a means of communicating with Mother Gaia's skeleton and receiving her age old knowledge. For this same reason, in ancient Egyptian Mystery School initiation ceremonies, the ankh (crux ansata) was used as a resonating tool by placing it next to the third eye of the initiate and using sound to transfer sacred knowledge.

EARTH & WATER VEHICLES

Dirt and water as mud packs or in mud volleyball, water and stone in sweat lodge ceremony, playing with shells in the ocean surf, doing Jungian sandplay in creek streams, rebirthing in water, open eye meditation with the full moon.

FIRE & AIR VEHICLES

Fire and water in sauna baths, swimming in bright sun, using the MindsEye in a flotation tank, gazing at a candle, strobing cloud/sun images, laser light shows.

THE CEV TIP SHEET

Want to buy the best car? Here are tips for locating the right CEV having built-in intelligent technology and smart aerodynamics to travel the Interstate of Consciousness. Because the CEV is a perfect match in elemental energy for you, it will be the best car designed for your traveling requirements. Its sophisticated safety systems, a 14-gauge steel chassis and frame, coupled with the power of an available V-8 energy engine, will enable you to drive through places where the only other vehicles seen are eagles, helicopters, and your Total Self.

ASTROLOGY

On the birth (natal) chart there is an indication of the number of planetary signs that an individual has in each of the four elements which are earth, air, fire, water. The element having the most signs indicates the dominant element which will be the most natural CEV selection. Example: according to the Tropical method, there are a total of 10 planets displayed on the natal chart, each representing an element. A person could have 1 fire, 2 earth, 3 air, 4 water; therefore, water will be the most beneficial CEV with air being an appropriate second vehicle.

NATIVE AMERICAN MEDICINE WHEEL

A Chippewa (Ojibwa tribe) Indian medicine man, Sun Bear, says (4) a person is born into one elemental clan. This represents the elemental energy having the easiest and most important relationship of the four elements. Being related to a particular element means there is an important responsibility for caring for that element. The elemental clan shows the common characteristics shared with other members of the clan as well as the strengths and weaknesses. Four clans exist which are symbolized by a totem animal; they are turtle clan (earth), frog clan (water), butterfly clan (air), and thunderbird clan (fire). Some elements complement each other; they are frog-turtle (earth/water) and butterfly-thunderbird (fire/air). These would be suitable for two CEVs. Those clans opposite each other can, in the long run, become complementary, but in the short term, they usually have difficulties. These are butterfly-turtle (air/earth), butterfly-frog (air/water), thunderbird frog (fire/water), thunderbird-turtle (fire/earth). These two CEV combinations would be helpful for working to release stuck energy. In nature *like attracts like*, thus it's natural to first work with the clan one was born into, known as the *totem animal*. Refer to Sun Bear and Wabun's book to determine the dominant totem energy.

AYURVEDA CONSTITUTIONAL TYPES

In this system of understanding energy, an additional element is included as previously explained which is ether. These five elements combine to form three basic principles known as *doshas*. As *prana* (ether) gets absorbed into the body, it is transformed into *kapha* (water & earth), then *pitta* (fire & water), and then *vada* (air & ether). Each person is seen as a combination of these types with a preference toward one or more. To determine the constitution, please refer to an Ayurveda practitioner or physician.

MYERS BRIGGS TYPE INDICATOR

This is a Jungian questionnaire for finding out how one constructs a picture of reality or how ideas are gathered (perception) and how these are used to make decisions (judgment). The MBTI is based on the four elements of earth, water, fire and air. Information from the questionnaire is used to sort out how energy is used, and the values given indicate a dominant energy, an auxiliary helping energy, a tertiary energy, and an inferior energy which forms the shadow, better known as the energy having low quality. To determine the type please refer to a Jungian practitioner or educator.

KINESIOLOGY

Among its many practices, kinesiology has a simple muscle test that uses the body's wisdom to denote balanced or unbalanced energy. There are various approaches using various muscles to indicate energy flow or disruption. Where there is an energy flow, a "yes" response is indicated, where there is a weak response or a brokened response, a "no" answer is given. Either the deltoid muscle in the arm or the fingers of the hand are typically used.

A simple exercise can be done to indicate whether a particular CEV should be used at any given time. First, relax the body and develop a clear intention in the form of a question such as, "Is it in my best interest to use this mind machine at this time?" Then extend the dominant hand and begin to gently rub the thumb against the index finger or the third finger and feel if the sensation between the finger and thumb is either smooth or sticky. If smooth, then a "yes" is indicated, if sticky or hesitant, the response is a "no." Other finger tests are explained in *Behaving As If The God In All Matters* by Machelle Small Wright. The kinesiology process is explained in the book, *Your Body Doesn't Lie* by John Diamond, M.D.

Whether it be through the use of an astrology birth chart, the totem animal in native American terms, the constitutional type in Ayurvedic terms, the MYBI dominant element, or muscle testing, it is important to note that identifying the primary elemental energy will automatically provide vehicles that will deliver ease, high comfort and accelerated growth. Unfortunately, when many people choose a CEV, the vehicle is often selected for quick starts, fast acceleration times, entertainment value, and satisfaction of phenomenon seeking-needs. Thus, a particular vehicle such as a light-color machine might not be the best selection for an individual whose elemental energy is not compatible with light elements. Just as one would research the merits of buying a particular car, so should the selection of a CEV be equally considered, if not more so.

THE VEHICLE OF HEMI-SYNC: A TECHNICAL SKETCH

As an Ether vehicle, the sounds of Hemi-Sync can assist the traveler in using the other elements of Air, Water, Fire, and Earth because of Ether's all-around transportation feature. This characteristic is enhanced by the technological features of Hemi-Sync which use tonal patterns incorporating gamma through delta frequencies associated with all the brain states.   Skip Atwater, Director of the TMI Research says:

> "The trademarked term Hemi-Sync signifies a process, a procedure in which individuals willfully participate by listening to a combination of multiplexed audio binaural beats that are mixed with music, pink sound, and/or surf and by focusing attentional processes. In most cases the Hemi-Sync process also includes breathing exercises, guided relaxation, affirmation, and visualization." (5)

Bob Monroe developed this refined binaural beat technology coupled with well-known relaxing techniques to induce and sustain brain balance in individuals. He described this auditory-guidance process on the TMI tape called *The Way of Hemi-Sync* by demonstrating how the listener hears a tone in one ear and a different tone is heard in the other ear. He called these tones "carrier beats" because they carry a signal from the ear to a sound processing center (the superior olivary nucleus) located deep in the brain stem. This auditory sensation is transported neurologically to the reticular activating system (RAS) and at the same time, conducted to the grey matter, the cortex, where it can be concretely measured as a frequency-following response (FFR). Each hemisphere has its own sound processing center. When these two centers vibrate by means of nearly similar but different carrier beats, the brain detects a phase differential between these signals. The differential of the two carrier beats, known as a binaural beat, is heard by the listener as a vibrato tone or a wobbling sound. For example, when singing a tone in a large but quiet cathedral, a vibrato resonating tone will be heard by the singer.

THE PARTNERSHIP BETWEEN THE LISTENER & HEMI-SYNC

By itself, the binaural beat is not mechanically produced by the listener, but is the result of the combination of the two slightly different carrier beats coming together in the field of the listener. This outcome can be understood by applying quantum mechanics theory which incorporates the listener as well as the outside carrier beats in the reception of Hemi-Sync tones. *The listener and the outside Hemi-Sync tones act as partners to produce the binaural beat.*

Quantum mechanics takes the view that every factor is taken into account in any given event. This includes both the tangible and intangible. When studying the ether in 1887, classical physicists and Michelson and

Morley studied only tangible elements, whereas when developing Hemi-Sync, Monroe took into account the listener in this technological process. Thus, Hemi-Sync or hemispheric synchronization is literally created through the use of precise sound patterns perceived by the listener AND the listener's energy in tandem.

"Quantum mechanics," says John Wheeler, "has led us to take seriously and explore the view that the observer is as essential to the creation of the universe as the universe is to the creation of the observer." (6) This places new emphasis on the value of inner conscious awareness of the observer as a cause of reality. Formerly, scientists would have denied or discounted the listener as a key player in the design of causal reality. This is why on-ramping procedures are so important because the listener's intention plays a key meaning-making role. "Meaning may be the missing link between matter and energy" says physicist David Bohm. "It may be the connective tissue that joins the apparently abstract realm of mind and the 'manifest' physical world in a continuum." (7) The key here is where attention is focused. If, for instance, the RAS is consciously noticing theta binaural beats, it can attend to these in physical reality by altering consciousness and detuning or tuning down the "noisy" audible elements encased in the physical body.

FOCUSING THE PICTURE OF REALITY:
THE WORK OF THE RAS

Here is an example of how the RAS operates in physical reality. A person walks into a room and sits down to read. She begins to notice a noisy grandfather clock. Its insistent tick-tocking sound seems to fill the air because she has directed her RAS to attend to it. As she decides to focus on the book, the ticking sounds become barely noticeable, gradually diminishing altogether, despite the fact that the clock is still ticking away.

The RAS goes where it is consciously directed. This function of the RAS in the listener plays a key role in explaining how Hemi-Sync works. One of the most important features of Hemi-Sync is that it provides information, not normally and consciously accessed, to the brain's RAS which controls attention, awareness and arousal, all very important elements of consciousness. *Hemi-Sync helps the RAS alter consciousness so that we can attend to non-physical, formerly inaccessible, information.*

THE IMPACT OF RESONANCE ON THE PHYSICAL BODY

Another feature of Hemi-Sync is found in its resonance properties. In 1980 Hugo Zuccarelli (8), an Argentine, obtained a patent for his technology called Holophonic sound. In order to develop this sound which produces the equivalent of a live performance, he realized that the spatial perception of sound must be reliant on a coherent sound source just as a coherent light source or laser reference beam is necessary to construct a hologram. This requires the human ear to be an instrument capable of broadcasting a tone. In 1981 the *BrainMind Bulletin* reported the curious finding that the ear can broadcast a tone with some individuals emitting a tone loud enough for others to hear. Manfred Clynes, (9) a neuroscientist and concert pianist in Australia, after decades of experiments with sound, discovered a phenomenon he called essentic forms or primary emotional responses, which sculpt a subtle energy pattern into a sound for a period of two seconds. He suggested it is the subtleties of amplitude and duration that give music its particular meaning. In similar fashion, the instrument of the harp and the bowed psaltry are especially suited to generate music with feeling because their resonance is focused through the back of the instruments directly onto the body. This, in turn, broadcasts the partnership of bone and feeling tone through the sound being played. Which leads one to ask if this is possible through the human ear?

The body may contain resonance qualities encompassing an individual's lifelong learning experiences. It may be that, under certain circumstances, these experiences can be released into direct consciousness by sounds directed at the physical body and particularly the boney skeleton. The resonance of binaural beating as evidenced by the frequency-following-response (FFR) (10), described earlier, may be amplified by bone conduction. If this is the case, altering the spatial orientation of the binaural beat into a figure-eight, or a horizontal, or vertical pattern may change its influence on the brain. For example, when the movement is vertical, there is a significant resonance sent through the corpus callosum or the middle neural network of the brain containing 80% of the nerve endings in the brain. When these 200 million nerve fibers connecting the right and left hemispheres are stimulated by a particular binaural tonal pattern, circumstances may be just right to release those embedded lifelong learning experiences into direct consciousness. The response is, of course, predicated on what binaural tonal patterns are being used coupled with the conscious and unconscious intentions of the individual. Over time, similar responses can be repeated again and again by the individual without the aid of the binaural training wheels using the TMI encoding process of learning that is known as Function Commands.

MULTI-PLEXED LAYERS OF HEMI-SYNC SOUNDS

During the last 40 years, numerous tonal patterns (signal layers) have been researched and developed by TMI to help individuals locate various non-physical states of consciousness, each having different "power" or Force level. The signals for locating each Focus state vary. In addition, the signals change within a Focus state in order to achieve a particular goal for a specific activity. The encodings are used to anchor that activity so that it can be repeated within that Focus state at a later date without using the sounds. As the Focus states increase in balancing quality, the layering of Hemi-Sync signals increase and so does the coherency and information of the sound field increase. For example, in Focus 10 there can be as many as six layers of Hemi-Sync signals and in the tapes used at TMI for Guidelines and Lifeline Residential Programs, there are as many as 20 layers of signals, again each experiential learning activity varies in signal layers according to the purpose for that exercise.

RESONANCE: THE KEY THAT UNLOCKS COHERENCE

In the last ten years, brain mapping studies at TMI using precise Hemi-Sync tonal patterns have indicated increasing electrical activity throughout the brain and increasing coherent brain patterns as one progressively advances through the Focus states. The coherent brain patterning effect produced by this technology and the listener is a very important element to consider. During the waking state usually a random, incoherent state of consciousness prevails, i.e., scattered attention represented by low voltage indicators throughout the brain. *Various Hemi-Sync tonal patterns producing increasing levels of coherency can be acting as laser-like reference beams to decode the human and universal hologram template enabling an individual to exit into various cities on the Interstate of Consciousness at will.*

Increasing hemispheric synchronicity where the right brain "talks" more coherently to the left brain is reflected by increasing electrical activity throughout the brain. On a continuum, Focus 3 presents a kindergarten level of balance or coherency of energy, whereas Focus 21 presents a college level of coherency. Recently, a popular book suggested we have learned all we need to know in kindergarten which is, relatively speaking, true. Thus, the opportunity to dial into a Focus 3 station of coherency relates to a relative quality of experience.

DESCRIPTION OF THE BRAIN STATES

Let's use the element of water as an example to explore how the coherency of energy changes through the brain states. (Refer to Figure 17.)

Figure 17 Beta, The Waking State: Random Brain Activity

This shows the **beta brain state** as a incoherent, random state where very little joint electrical activity is present. There are only small blips of electrical partnership between areas in the cortex creating an environment wherein the left side of the brain doesn't know what the right side is doing. In brain mapping studies being conducted at TMI using customized computer software and a 24 lead neuromapper, there is sporadic electrical activity of low voltage in various remote areas of the brain in a primarily beta-based state.

In the beta brain state, water is an icy solid (Earth element) where minimal activity is occurring. The molecules are randomly locked in a very slow moving state, vibrating in place with little or no attraction between them. Unfortunately, this is our waking state where most of our traditional learning and most important life experiences take place. Because the brain is only using one half of its central nervous system, and the grey matter is only using one of its two hemispheres explains why there is a lot of physical effort and struggle involved in daytime acts of communication, memory, attention, decision-making, problem-solving, conflict management, etc.

Figure 18 Alpha, The State of Imagination:
Beginning Brain Coherency

When a person daydreams, the brain moves into the **alpha brain state**. (See Figure 18.) This is equivalent to the latent fire element inherent in water beginning to move, melting the ice into liquid water. The brain liquefies itself, metaphorically speaking, in alpha wherein the molecules have a weak attraction for one another, they slip freely over one another and begin to be closely aligned. The neural network begins to go beyond the autonomic functions of the body and touchs itself through the other half of the CNS or the parasympathetic nervous system and possibly the ventricles of the brain. Here it (consciousness) begins to understand what is being communicated and is able to sustain it for some time. A classical example of using alpha energy is the act of daydreaming which typically lasts from one to ten seconds. In the daydreaming state there is fluidity of thought, vivid and clear, and appealing imaginative quality. But as fast as we recognize we are daydreaming, we are unable to hold that window of consciousness open to use it at will, and the window slams shut. We haven't yet trained ourselves to stay conscious in alpha very long. Those who have learned how to use NLP (neurolinguistic programming), Silva Mind Control, accelerated learning, biofeedback, active imagination and guided imagery know how to stay suspended in alpha long enough to use this brain state at will.

Figure 19 Theta, The State of Peak Performance: Mutual Brain Accord

When water begins to bubble, it eventually turns into steam (Air Element) which is like the **theta brain state**, simmering, percolating, then erupting into the air. (See Figure 19.) There are audible frequencies of sound in theta, and there are inaudible components. In this state, all parts of the body and mind are beginning to come together. Cooperation is occurring on almost all fronts.

Before competitive events, some athletes use this state to program themselves for specific peak performance behaviors. This is fairly easy to do because one can stay awake in a light theta state and program a particular goal.

Theta is the twilight phase experienced before going into deep sleep and before waking up. Like a bubbling creek, deep states of theta exhibit very lucid, knowing moments which feel like greased lightning. This is the "zone" that athletics talk about, where almost everything is synchronized and moving well. This is also the experience I touched when I relaxed into my spinning as a child and felt an overwhelming, incredible, enfolding comfort. Yet my body with my head attached was saying, "You're going to fall, crazy you!" or "You're going to lose consciousness (yourself), be careful!" As a child I had been already taught to deny my ability to consciously go into theta, feel and use its power, and allow myself to transport back. When I went to the Adirondack woods, I took a long time to relax enough into Mother Nature's theta rhythms and cycles in order to go into theta and enjoy myself. Now I can distinguish the Force in alpha and concretely sense the Force in theta experiences. However, as with all brain states, it is somewhat difficult to isolate purely beta, alpha, theta, or delta brains states as there is a natural movement all the time of energies in the brain and the rest of the body interacting with energies in the environment. In actuality, what is designated as a beta brain state is a state where the majority of frequencies are beta.

Figure 20 Delta, The State of Being: Bioenergetic Coherency

As water effervesces, its energy becomes luminiferous (light-carrying) Ether as it evaporates into space. (See Figure 20.) This is the **delta brain state** or what we know as deep sleep. Delta has the capacity to bridge the move from body-connected consciousness to spirit-connected consciousness.

THE NULL POINT OR THE ASSEMBLAGE POINT

Anesthesiologists know there are over 20 states of delta, the deepest appears to be death-like in nature. Monroe described this point of deepest awareness (or profound change of state) as the **Null Point**, at which point the body polarity has the potential to reverse. (11) It is the point at which the electric field of the body registers zero movement and exhibits no polarity. Gregg Braden calls this **Zero Point** and has described this unpolarized state in detail. He notes the geologic record has shown that the magnetic fields of the body of Earth have shifted into the Zero or Null Point at least 14 times in the last 4.5 million years. (12) Interestingly, the element of water has a Null Point equivalent known as the "triple point" where water exists simultaneously as any of three states — solid, gas, or liquid.

HOW ATOMS OF GAS ACT WHEN AT THE NULL POINT

Here is an illustration of how physical elements may be demonstrating a Null Point state in physical reality. In June of 1995, Carl Wieman and Eric Cornell at the University of Colorado, (13) discovered that atoms in extreme cold, 40-billionths of a degree above absolute zero to be exact, take on new properties. Absolute zero is -459.7 degrees Fahrenheit (F). For a way to understand this measurement, water freezes at 273.15 degrees Kelvin or 32 degrees (F) and it boils at 373.15 Kelvin or 212 degrees F. Normally, atoms in a gas move at about 1,000 miles per hour in a random manner. However, at near absolute zero they inch along at barely 6 feet an hour. Usually they remain separate when they move, but at snail's pace, they merge, creating what is called the Bose-Einstein Condensate, after S.N. Bose and Albert Einstein, who predicted this outcome 70 years ago. After studying the properties of the condensate, Wieman discovered that the frozen blob was a strange new form of matter. Since the background temperature of the universe, in the empty space between the galaxies, is 3 Kelvin, there is now a possible picture of what atoms are doing in the Delta brain state.

The merging of atoms, I suggest, could be the substance that creates the bridge between two states of consciousness, a highly coherent, yet malleable "different form of matter." Usually normal atoms move in random patterns, but when slowed to this degree, at near absolute Zero, they line up together in a lock-step fashion, looking surprisingly like a laser reference beam. As Dr. Gerber suggests, laser-like, coherent reference beams of energy are capable of opening the human holographic template containing all knowledge. Coincidently, there is a saying at TMI, "*Focused consciousness contains all the solutions to the questions of human existence.*"

THE NULL POINT & THE OUT-OF-BODY EXPERIENCE

According to Monroe, the Null Point might be the place where spirit-connected consciousness separates from body (human) consciousness, where out-of-body experiences begin. Don Juan Matus taught Castaneda how to move the Null Point which he called the **assemblage point** (AP) from the right side to deep inside the left side of the energy body to evoke an OBE or the beginning of pure, spirit-connected consciousness. (See Chapter 8 in the section on don Juan and Castaneda for more AP descriptions.) He also taught Castaneda many variations on a theme of moving the AP to create what he called "separate realities." The assemblage point looks like a star and is a concentration of energy similar to the wormhole in *Star Trek* terminology. It is a vortex of energy, a portal existing between physical and non-physical reality. Ken Eagle Feather, apprentice to don Juan for ten years and former TMI staff member, calls the AP, the **Focal Point**. (14)

One of the key characteristics of an OBE is that the consciousness is totally separate from the physical body and views the body apart from itself, literally where spiritual consciousness and human consciousness are in two different places. The OBE is similar to air evaporating into space, losing form and being itself in totality, a transpersonal element with intelligence. During lucid dreamwork, primarily a theta experience, there is a subject/object-oriented experience whereas in mostly delta experiences, there is a unitive experience. Presently, with our limited brain functioning ability, our collective consciousness has not been trained to stay conscious in delta. There are instances at TMI during the Residential Programs when participants have reported such abilities. Senzee and Litvak discussed how the infrastructure of the brain has been storing potential over the last 150,000 years. Perhaps one of the reasons is to support humankind's ability to transport back and forth between physical and non-physical reality.

THE ILLUSIONS OF BETA-BASED REALITY

If we learned to stay conscious in delta in the physical world, we would say that beta is an illusionary state, full of waxy, heavy, sticky experiences whereas delta provides pristine, pure, and exquisite experiences. Workshop participants, upon learning how to transport themselves from physical reality to Focus 12 (a state which has very little earth-like characteristics), often talk about the immense heaviness of the body and its bodily functions upon returning to physical reality. Upon retuning to physical reality, the perception regains its forgetfulness about the illusion, snaps back to a limited picture of reality, then denies the heaviness and distortion in physical reality. In some stages of deep delta, the coherency of this energy resembles a laser-like reference beam which can be used to open the universal hologram record of information in the energy field.

DECODING THE HOLOGRAM OF REALITY

In *The Holographic Universe*, Michael Talbot (15) suggests what is perceived as solid, physical reality might be holograms constructed by the holographic mind operating within the narrow confines of explicate order. Explicate order is another way of describing that which is relegated to the narrow band of life we call physical reality. The opposite, implicate order, he defines as that which is attributed to the deeper order of the universe. Likewise, the opening lessons of the Course of Miracles (16) suggest we live in an explicate world of illusion. These lessons give the student sledgehammers to crack open this tightly-held holographic picture we all maintain. *Coherent, balanced beams of mind-body energy are the sledgehammers that decode the hologram of physical reality.*

If we were to combine our waking abilities with our sleeping state abilities, would we not know the truths of our universe? Instead, we get stuck. We sleep in our waking experiences, bathed totally in beta frequencies, while trying to live full lives, actualize our potentials, and pass on our humanness to our children who arrive living most of their early days in delta. How amazing! The reverse is true as well. Weirdly, we lie fully awake in our sleep, staring blankly at our dreams as if these contain strangers acting out our practice lives!

The various blends of tonal patterns of Hemi-Sync signals could be unique reference beams to decode the holographic universe. The Human Plus blend to encode the ability to contemplate (**H+ Contemplation**), or to sufficiently eat right and metabolize well (**H+Eat/No Eat**), or to learn to increase natural healing ability in emergency situations (**H+ Emergency: Injury**) are examples of Hemi-Sync applications to help decode the human hologram. The blends of sounds associated with Focus 3 through Focus 35 may be seen as examples of helping to decode the holographic universe and beyond.

MAINTENANCE PLAN FOR THE
CARE AND FEEDING OF THE CEV

Just as a car must be maintained over its transportation life, so does the physical body and energy (light) body require a preventive maintenance plan. Soon the two will be working together as one to support the emergence of new galactic beings. In preparation for that time, there are a few required service calls which will assist in the joining of the two. During and after traveling, some individuals show adjustment signals on the car dashboard as their light Force capacity outstrips their physical body suspension. The groans and shudderings of the physical body come in the form of palpitations (without attendant feelings of anxiety), quick intense energy waves, momentary vision blurring, bilateral sweating (rings of sweat encircling the chest area), intense thirst, concentrated urine, and voice changes. For the most part, these are due to central nervous system stress as the unused DNA, unused brain capacity and unused chakras come on line.

As the light Force increasingly animates the human body, former ways of being human shift all pictures of reality involving relationships, organizations, family, lifestyles, philosophies. What was once considered illness and tragedy will soon be considered a blessing in disguise. For example, where the medical establishment and churches have taught us that inflammation and family conflicts are a symptom of breakdown , the light-Force-animated body will teach us that inflammation, cancer, AIDS or divorce are symptomatic of a breakthrough process at hand. These stressful events represent significant opportunities to change the way we are thereby acquiring regenerative and restorative abilities we have lost.

THREE PREVENTIVE MAINTENANCE SERVICE PLANS

To strengthen the physical body suspension of the driver so that it can accept the infusion of the light Force, three key components of a preventive maintenance plan can be used when necessary. Now available at your favorite dealerships in the service departments are the **5,000 Mile Mind-Body Tune-up**, the **50,000 Mile Mind-Body Tune-up** and the **Mega Major Overhaul**.

5,000 MILE MIND-BODY TUNE-UP

At the **5,000 mile marker** of the Interstate of Consciousness, it becomes evident that a significant nutritional adjustment must be made as a result of the following symptoms: overall sluggishness and downright fatigue, blah appetite, out-of-the ordinary reactions to medications/alcohol/sugar intake, and general system backups, e.g., excess gas and noxious fumes, numerous headaches, creeping low blood sugar symptoms, increasing high blood pressure, and gaining weight. These come on line as the car frame is not able to keep up with the energetic demands. As more expanded frequencies are held in the energy field, there will be a need for more sleep due to deeply held emotions being processed during this time. As the physical structure gradually becomes adjusted to the new cellular frequency, the physical body will require less sleep. Thus, changing sleep habits cycles could be a symptom of advancing consciousness expansion. Sleeping patterns are a good indicator at the 5,000 mile marker of how things are changing energetically in the field.

There are food elements in nature that provide remedies for those disruptive symptoms. Considering that all processed foods, canned or frozen, contain minimal or "dead" energetic fuel for the body, then eating raw, steamed or minimally processed foods helps to increase the light Force quotient of the physical body. Likewise, these alive foods contain more of the cosmic life force which the human body, especially the nervous system, requires at this time. Consciously eating fresh plants, herbs, and grains gives the body the nourishment of 2 billion years of evolutionary forces of Nature. This is excellently described in zho-do-Rah and Zon-o-Rah's book called *The InterGalactic Cafe Guide to the Care and Feeding of Your Light Body*. (17) Not only do they offer recipes using biogenetic foods (foods containing light Force), they show when specific foods can be eaten to complement natural body metabolizing rhythms which are described in Marilyn and Harvey Diamond's book entitled *Fit For Life*. (18) They point out how important it is to learn to respect the natural digestive and absorptive rhythm so that food energies can be most efficiently used according to the body's three eight hour cycles:

Intake: noon to 8 pm
Integrate: 8 pm to 4 am
Eliminate: 4 am to noon

Ayurvedic approaches offer many other nutritional strategies based on an individual's constitution stemming from elemental types discussed previously. (19)

50,000 MILE MIND-BODY TUNE-UP

At the **50,000 mile marker** on the Interstate of Consciousness, more adjustments to the physical body vehicle may be necessary as a consequence of energy surges, raw energy inputs, and Photon Band influences affecting the internal combustion of the engine of the driver. Hence, an engine tune-up most likely will be required due to these higher light energies now impacting Earth.

What is the Photon Band? By means of satellite surveillance, the Photon (Light) Band was discovered in 1961. Shortly thereafter, Americans landed on the moon and saw the vastness of space and the beauty of planet Earth. The astronauts saw the Photon Band and began to acknowledge its presence. A photon is the smallest of electromagnetic particles with no mass, no volume. As Deepak Chopra says, "The similarity between thought and a photon is very deep. Both are born in the region beyond space and time where nature controls all processes in that void which is full of creative intelligence." (20) Our solar system returns to visit the Photon Band every 11,000 years and bathes in its light for 2,000 years during its 26,000 year orbit around the galaxy. The effects of the returning Photon Band became apparent in 1987 primarily through emotional body clearings, and in March, 1994, the physical body clearings intensified to make room for more light capacity. (21) This infusion of photons will impact our planet by periodically playing havoc with electrical systems and all the mechanical applications that use electricity. This challenge will increase public demand for the inventions of the late Nikola Tesla and others who work with electricity and magnetics. (22)

As a consequence of these energetic shifts in the electrical system of the body, some of the physical body short circuiting indicators will be: experiencing short eye flashes (electrical white or colors), ear ringing or buzzing (usually, not always, one-sided), momentary surges of raw energy as evidenced by watch batteries going dead quickly, electrical appliances having serious problems or going dead, TV reception interruptions, etc., and intense or mild vibrations in the lower trunk (or hands and feet) felt when going to sleep and/or upon waking. Some alternative remedies that have been useful for people at the 50,000 mile marker are the use of superoxygenation, superlumination, water therapy, body cleansing or fasting and emotional and/or mental clearing techniques. For further description see zho and Zon's graphically clever and very humorous work as well the contribution of Linda Rector-Page, N.D., Ph.D., (23) who has extensively described complementary body healing approaches, such as cleansing, healing juices, drinks, sea vegetables, green super foods, and the use of food grade hydrogen peroxide. These elements contain frequencies more closely aligned with the light body frequencies.

With the increasing energetic shifts and clearings, symptoms of body wisdom frequently appear.

BODY WISDOM SYMPTOMS

- Goose bumps on skin
- Body shivers
- Ringing in the ears, one-sided or both ears
- Shallow respiration
- Fast pulse
- Instant knowing without emotional charge
- Perspiration in one particular body part or laterally across the body

Any of these symptoms indicates correct, insightful information from the Total Self has been received. Body wisdom symptoms show themselves fairly quickly and dissipate soon thereafter. They are a sign of an energetic release of body knowing which indicates a true connection has been made. Trust the connection. Pause, don't think, and observe the connection made to gain the conscious knowing. When a body wisdom symptom appears, it is an indication of a path of right information or right action.

MEGAMAJOR OVERHAUL

Further down the Interstate might come the transpersonal crisis, sometimes known as a spiritual emergency. This generally requires ascended master intervention in addition to sensitive and adept earthly assistance. For this reason, what might be called a **MegaMajor Overhaul** of the vehicle-driver will be required in these cases. The term "spiritual emergency" is used to indicate that a critical turning point in the progression of consciousness growth has been reached. A transpersonal crisis is a developmental occurrence where the physical body experiences so much quickly changing energetic pressure that it sends signals indicating its physical mainframe is out of joint or worse, still, rusting at point of wear and tear. The story in the Bible of the apostle Paul being hit by a bolt of lightning is another way of describing the energy surges associated with a transpersonal crisis. We read about his life dramatically changing from that point on as a result.

THE AWAKENING OF KUNDALINI ENERGY

If the mainframe on which the driver rides is experiencing a radical realignment in the form of a transpersonal crisis, various pictures of reality will be mixed in with the leap of consciousness pictures, creating what seems like a weird mixture of symptomatic changes. Without any warning, transpersonal crisis symptoms can suddenly occur or they can be triggered by numerous stressors, e.g., an accident, disease, childbirth, etc. But the initiating factor that seems to be involved is that prior to the transpersonal crisis, the individual has been meditating for a period of time. It is important to note that not everyone who experiences unusual states of consciousness and subsequent heightened awareness is going to have a transpersonal crisis. Some who experience these energy surges sometimes called *Kundalini* move into a more expanded state of being with ease. Here is an account of awakening Kundalini energy as described by a member of the on-line Voyager list.

SUBJECT: SPIRITUAL EMERGENCIES

Hello Fellow Voyagers,
There have been a few messages in the last few days regarding Stan and Christina Grof and the subject of Kundalini. Christina Grof suffered through 12 years of spiritual transformation; in fact, it was through her Kundalini experience that she met her husband, Stan. There was some talk here as to doing holotropic breathing to push or nudge the Kundalini energy to rise and therefore gain a transformational experience. From personal experience I would not recommend that anyone try this on their

own. You must be with people who know what is going on and what can happen to you during this process. Yes, it is true that some awakenings are very peaceful and truly wonderful; however, the majority of cases are not without problems and some of them are very severe. As a person who has been living this experience for the past two years, I can tell you that if I had not had a doctor who was aware of spiritual enlightenment, I do not think that I would be here today. As a good friend, he supported me (and still does each and every day) during the days when my energy was out of control and I was bouncing off the walls. He saw to it that I educated myself on what was happening by loaning me all of the books he had on Kundalini awakening written by the Grofs, Gopi, Dr. Bonnie Greenwell, Dr. Yvonne Kason and others.

Kundalini earns its name, "spiritual emergency," very well. It can turn your life inside out and change you completely. Throughout the whole process which can last for years, you may require constant loving support and sometimes mental and physical care. Now change in itself is not bad, but if you have a family that is not really understanding or really aware of what is happening, it can be quite a challenge. Try explaining to parents and spouses about psychic gifts arriving. Since my Kundalini awakening, I have healing abilities which I am channeling into Therapeutic Touch and I also now have clairsentient abilities. Since this has happened my life goals and focus have changed. I have difficulty explaining these new goals to my family and trying to explain these changes are not part of some growing mental problem. One time I tried to share a very special meditation experience and all I got in return was blank stares, head shaking and laughter. I have learned very quickly not to share my insights and growth since it disturbs them. In fact, I just choose to love them where they are, knowing that a higher power is at work with and through me.

Jane B.

SYMPTOMS OF KUNDALINI RISING

Awakening Kundalini symptoms vary, but generally involves a near frazzled nervous system. The odometer on the car dashboard looks like a bunch of spinning 0's, literally. Accordingly, the transpersonal crisis manifests symptoms, in part, that look like a "nervous breakdown" and also simulate a variety of medical disorders (e.g., a heart attack, Jacksonian epilepsy, incipient multiple sclerosis, an impending CVA). Unfortunately, traditional psychiatry and medicine have not yet developed the ability to recognize the difference that exists between psychotic, physical and spiritual experiences. Christina and Stan Grof, M.D., (24) well-known for their expertise in this area, have described signs of the transpersonal crisis that differentiate it from psychiatric illness. This not only includes symptoms that Kundalini energy is coming forth but symptoms indicating a transpersonal bridging to a higher state of being is occurring. In regard to the former, the Grofs say:

> "The awakening of Kundalini energy is accompanied by sensations of heat and energy rising up the spine along with shaking, hyperventilating, tremors and twisting movements. Sometimes there is involuntary laughing, crying, chanting of mantras or songs, talking in tongues, emitting animal sounds and assuming spontaneous yogic gestures (mudras)and postures (asanas)." (25)

All these can be interpreted by the psychiatric community as signs of a psychotic episode, yet when identified with symptoms associated with awakening Kundalini energy, these are indicators that a spiritual change is occurring rather than a psychotic breakdown. In addition to psychological and energetic symptoms, there are other signs associated with transpersonal crisis. (For further descriptions of the Kundalini process please refer to the writings of Stan Grof who has an extensive bibliography in his books.) He and Christina oversee the *Spiritual Emergence Network (SEN)* which supports individuals experiencing transpersonal crisis. (26) In many instances, the changes associated with Kundalini energy awakening evoke the development of dramatic and amazing skills that are expressed through a powerful enhancement of intuition and other psychic talents such as Jane described. Kundalini represents a leap in consciousness expansion, one that adds significantly to the growing capacity to enjoy daily life.

The next traveling stopover on our journey is to meet with six inspirational teachers who helped design a map for the Interstate of Consciousness and who were the original travel agents in the field of consciousness development and training.

POST CARD FROM SUNNY FOCUS 21

Taking the CEV out and revving it up,
To travel in style with the snazzy top down.
Come beta, now alpha, theta and Blitzen
Dash away, dash away,
Having a ball.

Traveling the states and the far-out cities,
Humming my om, twirling my REBAL,
Popping Focus 10 & swelling to 12
Poised on leaping off the Edge of Here and Now.
Wish you were here.

MAP MAKERS & TRAVEL AGENTS

"I was going to 'seek the miraculous.' I already knew then as an undoubted fact that beyond the thin film of false reality there existed another reality from which, for some reason, something separated us. The 'miraculous' was a penetration into this unknown reality."

P.D. Ouspensky

ROUTE 8

MAPPING OUT THE INTERSTATE OF CONSCIOUSNESS: GEORGES GURDJIEFF AND P.D. OUSPENSKY

As parents and as babysitters, we have found ourselves reading the fairy tale, *Alice in Wonderland*, to children before they go to sleep. The meaning, enfolded within its words, contains the idea that we can enter non-physical reality through the dream state. Perhaps Lewis Carroll developed the character Alice as a means of expressing his own non-physical memories. Vicariously through Alice, he showed us how he might have traveled into the Wonderland (worm) hole leading to a larger universe.

The field of early consciousness education and training embodies people who literally have fallen down Alice's rabbit hole and *awakened* to their own non-physical memories. These are the cartographers and early navigators who have been lighting the dark passageways appearing in many of our own dreams. Bold and brash, these people were committed to teaching us how to get into that conduit and swiftly move into Wonderland. Of the many who led the way, six pioneering travel agents, Gurdjieff, Ouspensky, Monroe, don Juan, Castaneda and Roddenberry stand out.

Georges Gurdjieff and Peter Ouspensky have described the general lay of the land on the other side of the hole. They are best known for their descriptions of the non-physical sections of Interstate and how consciousness expresses itself either as matter or as energy. Robert Monroe came along and mapped out the various cities located along the Interstate and provided the concrete means to differentiate each city. Don Juan and Carlos Castaneda entered the picture and developed the basis for energizing the vehicle to do the traveling. They also provided opportunities to learn how to recover various perceptual skills supporting unlimited voyaging on the Interstate. Then came Gene Roddenberry, the most famous of all the travel agents, who educated the general public about space travel through various dimensions. Despite a cultural milieu that emphatically said "Eh, you're really far out, man!" these map makers and travel agents have had the courage to describe the wider realms of consciousness and to teach us the worth of these extended realms.

Recent studies have indicated that 25% of us acknowledge we have had some form of out-of-body experiences. (1) This implies that the average person admits to being far out and waking up to the larger meaning of Alice's *Adventures in Wonderland* written by Lewis Carroll back in 1865. Carroll's imaginative writings captured the idea that there was a dreamtime world inside each of us that people know and use. While generations upon generations saw this entertaining fairy tale as a means to get kids to sleep, a few tenacious energy teachers knew this trip had more meaningful implications.

Back in the early 1800s there was one person who was awake to the night side of ourselves and that was Georges Gurdjieff, then an editor of a Moscow paper. Besides having a talent for writing, he had a reputation for leading groups to study what was known as "occult" at that time. Gurdjieff, a Greco-Armenian, had an Indian (Hindu) manner, but looked oriental. Before coming to Russia he visited remote Tibetan monasteries, experienced the Sufi Schools in Persia, in Bokhara and Eastern Turkestan, and traveled extensively throughout the East. His lifework became a striking tapestry of experiences woven from various cultures. Gurdjieff authorized one of his students, Peter Demianovich Ouspensky, to write about the teachings and experiments that he offered to his students during the years 1914 through 1924. Shortly thereafter, Ouspensky ended his relationship with his mentor and went on to become well-known for his book, *A New Model of The Universe*, published in America in 1931, the last of four books he authored. Gurdjieff and Ouspensky both devoted themselves to the question of life beyond physical reality and how to access this kind of existence. Together they became a student-teacher team which was to repeat itself over a hundred years later in the partnership between don Juan Matus and Carlos Castaneda.

This foursome had differing perspectives. Gurdjieff and Ouspensky made use of Christian, Eastern, and Theosophy teachings whereas don Juan and Castaneda drew their work from one specific Indian tradition, the Toltec teachings which originated in South America. Ouspensky, having a mathematical inclination, tackled the consciousness question from a geometrical point of view, while Gurdjieff addressed this question primarily from an existential philosophy perspective. Ouspensky stayed ensconsed in the literary field while Gurdjieff became a controversial educator. Because they brought to their work various inclinations, their diverse approach laid down a basic but solid foundation which still stands today. That foundation centers on the realization of the importance of energy and how this works through the universe and beyond. Alive in groups known as *The Fourth Way*, Gurdjieff's followers around the world continue the experiments and practices he started over 80 years ago.

On the Interstate, these two men were responsible for three important highway markers. These road signs are still used in the field of consciousness education and training today. They are: **Interstate Barricade** (the belief system that humankind essentially views its Self as a machine), **The Entrance to Interstate of Consciousness** (how energy works according to the Law of Three and the Law of Seven sacred geometry teachings),and **Non-Stop Ramp** (whirling dervish Sufi dances to learn the rhythm and natural order of universal energies). More will be said about these road signs and why they continued to be important hallmarks for this journey.

FOUR STATES OF CONSCIOUSNESS

One of the most important contributions at that time to the emerging field of consciousness education was Gurdjieff's idea that there were four states of consciousness possible for humankind. He proposed that the ordinary person used only two of those states (*waking* and *sleeping*) while the other two were only momentarily accessible in flashes. He thought this poverty of awareness came about because, essentially, people believed themselves to be machines; therefore, they acted automatically and irresponsibly. Gurdjieff described the third state as the state of *self-remembering* or self-consciousness of one's being and saw the fourth state as an objective state of consciousness, the state of *enlightenment*, where humans see things as they truly are.

SELF-REMEMBERING: SELF-CONSCIOUSNESS

Gurdjieff proposed that the only way to realize objective consciousness was through the development of self-consciousness. (2) This was to be achieved by experiencing acts of self-remembering. After a critical mass of self-consciousness had been reached, the individual awakens to other states of consciousness within and this causes all surrounding life to take on a different hue at an essential level. This is similar to the Me and the I AM presence discussed in Chapter 2. Gurdjieff explained that along the way there will come a point when there seems to be two people inside a person, the one who is called I AM and the other who is called by various characteristics such as "Patricia," "Leva," and "PAL." At this point it will become important to acknowledge there is a passive observer, the I AM and the active "I, the doer" who is the personality. Then, with more and more self-consciousness occurring, the I AM gradually becomes the overriding element or the essence. Robert Monroe would call the I AM essence, the Core Self or the Total Self.

ESSENCE: THE CORE OF BEING

While don Juan led Carlos Castaneda through experiences which helped remove his personality (ego), Gurdjieff went in the opposite direction by helping his students discover personal essence as if it were a physical, concrete component. He believed that the act of making the essence concrete could provide an indelible, core home base quality of self worth. "Essence in man is what is his own. Personality in man is what is not his own...(personality is) what has come from outside, what he has learned, or reflects...A man's real *I*, his individuality, can grow only from his essence." (3) Overdeveloping the personality, the Me at the expense of the essence, the I AM, leads the driver straight into an **Interstate Barricade**, that is, feeling and performing like a Tin Man machine, a robot dragging through life.

THE FAMOUS 'EGO DESTRUCTION' EXERCISE

To regain a firm sense of essence, Gurdjieff suggested an experiment to his students. This involved learning how to stop identifying with anything, especially that which resembled a personality description. For example, he asked them to remove the pronoun "I" from their conversations. Years later don Juan instructed Castaneda to take the same approach by learning to remove the accumulated identity which comes from identifying with outer things, academic labels, and material goods so as to loosen the connection with physical reality cues. This was accomplished by what don Juan called recapitulation (explained later).

- At this point, stop a moment and try to describe yourself without using the pronoun "I." Be aware of when you forget and say "I" and how that shifts awareness away from beingness to doingness or from wholeness to separate "me-ness." This me-ness is the personality or ego regulating your picture of reality. The ego is a constructed, invented identity, a partial identity.

* Now, by deep breathing to recenter yourself, shift your awareness from the past "who you think you are" descriptions chattering in your head, to focus only on the present moment of observing who you are. Get fascinated with who you are this moment. Let no dialogue or discussion of who you take over. Just keep observing. This is the I AM essence of you. This is the act of self-remembering.

Gurdjieff also asked his students to walk down the street using the art of self-remembering. To understand what this experience creates, Ouspensky described one of his own self-remembering experiences,

"I saw that self-remembering gave wonderful sensations which, in a natural way, that is, by themselves, came to us only very seldom and in exceptional conditions. Thus, for instance, at that time I used very much to like to wander through St. Petersburg at night and "sense" the houses and trees. There was no "imagination" in it, I did not think of anything, I simply walked along while trying to remember myself and looked about; the sensations came by themselves...we do not remember ourselves; that we live and act and reason in deep sleep, not metaphorically but in absolute reality...if our memory really is alive only during moments of self-remembering, it is clear why our memory is so poor." (4)

Here is an example of one person's act of self-remembering demonstrating his first steps toward self-consciousness. (This post appeared on the Voyager's mailing list as part of the ongoing discussion on consciousness.)

SUBJECT: WAKING REALITY

I suppose I'm writing this because people here on VML understand and I don't have to explain all these little details that I would if I talked about this with someone unfamiliar with this whole deal that we discuss in various forms. I'd like to know if anyone has been in my situation and what they did about it. I feel like for most of my life I haven't really looked at reality and my existence in their faces. It's like I have been living in a dream world. Although, here I am, aware of my existence, I have never felt like I am actually existing. It's kinda like when a crisis or emergency occurs in your life…that weird feeling you get when you think something like "Geez, this is really real!" It's like this crisis has made you more aware of your life or something. That's kinda like what I feel I'm in or coming out of. Well, I'm aware of it, anyway. I believe that this feeling, next to fear, has limited my growth. Although I feel like I've only touched a grain of sand on an infinite shore, I can at least recognize that something MUST be going on under our physical noses.

Brian

In this post Brian offered a striking example of wanting to go beyond the robotic, machine way of living which has become the standard in our world. Obviously he, like many of us, has had some experiences which have provoked memories of who he really is, what Gurdjieff would call self-remembering. Recall the description with Figure 9, The Road to Everywhere. This described the last 12,500 years as a phase of forgetting and how we are collectively moving into a phase of remembering more of who we really are.

Gurdjieff's star pupil Ouspensky asked him, "How do you define consciousness?" and he was told, "Consciousness is considered to be indefinable. You can know consciousness only in yourself. Observe that I say that you can know for you can know it only when you have it. And when you have not got it, you can know that you have not got it, not at that very moment, but afterwards…You can define the moments when you are nearer to consciousness and further away from consciousness. But, by observing in yourself the appearance and the disappearance of consciousness you will inevitably see one fact which you neither see nor acknowledge now, and that is that moments of consciousness are very short and are separated by long intervals of completely unconscious, mechanical working of the machine." (5) Fifty years later Bob Monroe would develop a tool for learning how to extend the moments of consciousness at will.

GURDJIEFF ON THE LAWS OF ENERGY GOVERNING THE CREATION OF THE UNIVERSE

Gurdjieff became famous for his Middle Eastern-influenced *Law of Three* (6) and *Law of Seven* sacred geometry teachings underlying the creation of all phenomena. These explain how energy works. Gaining understanding of this road sign, **Entrance to Interstate of Consciousness**, makes it fairly easy to move into the flow of creation rather than just sitting, spinning wheels, and grinding gears.

THE LAW OF THREE

The Law of Three says that every event is the result of the combination or the meeting of three different forces. Typically we recognize two of these energies, that of the positive and negative forces in our lives, but unfortunately we put more emphasis on the latter than the former. As we become self-remembering individuals, we begin to become aware of the third force which is a neutralizing, knowing force. Three examples of this Force have been identified so far in these writings. In Chapter 2 there was a description of a *third neutralizing force* that appears in the void of consciousness called the place of I KNOW and it makes itself known as the soul's promptings, a little voice tuning the I AM to the Total Self urgings. The same Force was also described as found in the third phase of resonant tuning, following inhale and exhale when unity occurs through self-consciousness and in Chapter 4 the third force was described when adding the third spiral to the REBAL.

THE LAW OF SEVEN

Gurdjieff went on to describe a larger energetic pattern very prevalent in our universe by outlining the Law of Seven or the Law of Octaves. This is comprised of two sets of threes plus an interval which appears irregularly in the pattern of 7. He supported the viewpoint that says vibration is discontinuous and has its chaotic moments. (7) Until the last decade, we Westerners have insisted that vibrations are continuous, creating the belief that what goes up must come down or that the best motion is upward and onward at all costs. Just recently, theorists are beginning to address the worth of the chaotic and disassociative events as these create various life experiences and off-beat elements of the universe. For instance, we like to think there is balance in nature which many of us take as an organizing principle for life, but this is a myth. Remember the book, *When Bad Things Happen to Good People* by Harold Kushner? He was acknowledging the Law of Seven at work in our lives. Other examples of this law in action are in regard to how the chaos created by fire and germs is viewed. Forest fires are now considered nature's way of rebalancing its environment, whereas in the past, forest fires were to be stopped. Having a bad case of the winter flu is considered the body's way to rebuild its immune system, but in the past the winter flu bug was Mother Nature's way of revenge.

When we allow for and work with the mysterious element of chaos (the interval), we recognize the nature of actually being a waveform of energy. In Chapter 2, the discussion of the waveform introduced the possibilities that many deviations in our energy occur both above and below the Continental Divide of Consciousness and that nothing stays the same. Most of us are ready and willing to recognize that change, lots of it, is here to stay. Up until the 1980s, predictable static, status quo jobs, marriages, and lifestyles were the norm. Recognizing the interval in the Law of Seven, we are just beginning to accept change as part of our landscape. Investigating the Law of Three and the Law of Seven in our own lives helps to explain how energy works on the Interstate of Consciousness.

SYMBOLS: ELEMENTAL ENERGIES IN ACTION

Gurdjieff described how energy worked as a dynamic force through his explanations of the Law of Seven. He took this further by showing his students how symbols, which are variations of the octaves in themselves, create energetic communication or universal enneagrams, the essential forms enfolded in sound, light, water, earth, and fire. (This is discussed in Chapter 8 on selecting transportation vehicles.) "The mere simple symbols, or the numbers 2-6...possess a definite meaning in relation to the inner development of man; they show different stages on the path of man's self-perfection and of the growth of his being." (8) (See Figure 21.) Gurdjieff explained that energy in the cohesed form (symbol) of a number has a certain resonant frequency. For example the number 2 is the symbol for the dualistic phase of humankind which evolves into the number 3 representing the joining of three forces or the Trinity of humankind and so forth. Along these same lines, in Chapter 2 the five universal symbols were discussed as they relate to discerning Focus 12 experiences. This is the Law of Seven making an appearance.

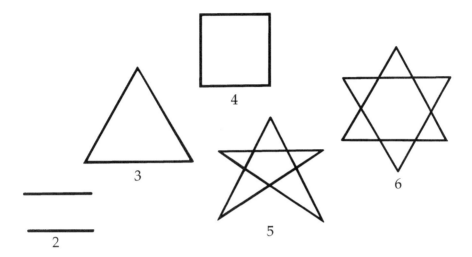

Figure 21 Symbolizing the Growth of Humankind

Gurdjieff extended these teachings to what we call inanimate planetary objects — the sun, the moon, the stars. He talked as if these were living, conscious beings, each in their own time moving through various forms and possessing possibilities of development and movement to other planes of being. He said, "the moon was a 'planet in birth' (and had) not yet reached the degree of intelligence possessed by earth...(and) the intelligence of the sun is divine." (9) His remarks were light years ahead of his time!

LEARNING THE MOVEMENT OF ENERGY
THROUGH SUFI DANCING

In accordance with these two laws, Gurdjieff contributed a third highway marker, that of the **Non-Stop Ramp** road sign. This came from his Sufi experiences and the *spinning phenomena* which I, too, have innately used. Many experiments in body movement were conducted by Gurdjieff with his students to demonstrate physical reality powers within the Law of Three and the Law of Seven. Besides the whirling dervish movements, his students were taught to move according to the two laws and then to use their instinctual body wisdom to note the perceptual changes that resulted. After my spinning events, I recalled the dizziness that overtook me and the disorientation that followed. I used the confusion I felt to suppress any changing perceptual cues that followed because I rationalized that disorientation was producing a fear of losing myself. When I gradually was able to experience the fear yet continue spinning through the building disorientation — which feels like building surface tension — I let go into a freedom flight in the Adirondack woods and into my I AM essence as witnessed by the daisy symbol which popped out in the center of my Indian shield at that same time in my life.

The roadsigns that Georges Gurdjieff and P.D. Ouspensky constructed were symbols of their devotion toward mapping out this part of the Interstate of Consciousness. Anticipating that there might be a few wrong turns or a tendency to drive in circles, they left luminous lanterns hanging on the road signs for other travelers to follow. Their visionary work remains strong and brilliant almost a hundred years later.

LOCATING THE CITIES
ON THE INTERSTATE OF CONSCIOUSNESS:
ROBERT MONROE

About the same time Gurdjieff was becoming a famous educator in Europe, another rabbit hole risk taker arrived in the United States. Scorpio-born on October 30, 1915, his name was Robert Allen Monroe. He came into the world big (twelve pounds), left-handed, grew to be over 6 foot tall and very adventuresome. His early days were spent growing up in Lexington, Kentucky, with his sisters, Dorothy and Peggy, his brother Emmett, his mother, Georgia Helen Jordan and his father, Robert Emmett Monroe.

MAJOR HOLE TRAVELER

During a taped TMI interview about his life Monroe hesitantly confessed, "I could have killed myself any number of times, but I didn't tell my parents." Here is an example of one his escapades. As a big, but skinny nine-year-old, he slithered down a tunnel and became stuck a couple of times in its narrow, sweaty, cold cradle; then, like a snaking slimy eel, he plopped down onto the bottom of a cave where he sat for what seemed like forever; all the while, brewing pure, white fear. Little "Bob Allen" felt lost and panicky. As the darkness cleared, he saw stalactites and stalagmites. Slowly he realized he had to use his willpower to find a way out before his parents started looking for him. He sat in the dark until it became less scary. Then he shouted out, "Where in the heck is the light?" Gradually, a soft light appeared as if leading him upward and out. Bob stressed this was a pivotal experience for him, an event which set things in motion for other similar rabbit hole side trips. In looking back he saw how he was guided to learn things which seemed wholly disconnected in his childhood, but by young adulthood those fragments were adroitly weaving themselves together in preparation for things to come.

By age 13 Bob already had his first airplane ride, been stunned by a lightning bolt, suffered through a life-threatening bout of scarlet fever, acquired a thirst for music and writing, and showed an innate mechanical ability. He got his pilot's license at age 17 and left home for the wild blue yonder. He entered Ohio State University to major in mechanical engineering, flunked out, and took to the rails living the life of a hobo for a time. When he returned to college, he transmuted his thirst for excitement into entertaining audiences. Writing an overnight play, *The Lantern*, he won second prize in a playwright's contest and, in amazement, saw it performed before a large gathering. "I knew by their silence they were being affected by the play. Eight hundred people! It was the first experience I had of communicating with an audience...That something like this could happen, such rapport with an audience! It deeply affected my life." (10)

STEPPING STONE TO SOUND LEARNING TECHNOLOGY: RADIO BROADCASTING

Graduating with a degree in English, Bob went off to New York City in 1938 to write, direct, and produce his own radio shows. For good measure, he also wrote and scored music for radio and designed sets for TV programs. By age 35 he had risen to the pinnacle of showbiz, married three times, in between commuting back and forth to Hollywood to produce radio shows and was maintaining his own company, Monroe Productions in NYC. For good measure, on weekends, he flew a four-seat, 175 horsepower, low-wing Navion. Flying and sound were destined to become all-important mediums for Bob to express his intense passion for life.

Soon after the Hollywood/New York producer hit it big with a weekly program called *High Adventure* that ran for seven years featuring interviews with everyday people who had experienced high risk events during WWII. Over 40 years later he was to use that same name and theme for one of the TMI Residential Programs designed to support individuals in their own quest for bold journeys. Next came the era of quiz shows and the Monroe company joined the bandwagon.

WHERE THE HUMAN PLUS SELF-REGULATION TAPES HAD THEIR BEGINNING

Unfortunately, this heavy work load took a toll on Bob's physical well-being for he developed ulcers, which he fought for years through diet and medication. Faced with surgery, Bob decided to go after the cause of his ulcer and came up with a surprising insight, "A hole in the stomach is a hole in your mind." (11) In his highly ambitious manner, he took care of the hole in his mind, and his ulcer healed within three weeks. This valuable self-healing lesson set the scene for producing future self-regulation and healing tools for thousands.

While the rest of the media world was progressively moving into the medium of TV, Bob resisted moving into this arena because the kind of car he liked to drive was sound. To keep his company increasingly productive, he turned gradually toward the technical aspects of musical production and invented ingenious devices and gadgets.

AGAIN, CHASING HOLES IN THE NETWORK OF LIFE!

After a trip south to Ecuador to investigate an oil concession venture, Bob had a prophetic dream which he described in his very entertaining biography, *Catapult*, authored by Bayard Stockton.

> "The year before I started to go Out-of-Body, I had a recurring dream which was exasperating. I dreamt I was taxiing my plane and taking off. I just barely got off the ground, but I was stymied by wires overhead. I'd fly along them, looking for a hole, but I couldn't find one...I tried maybe a hundred times...tried to get free. Once I had my first OOB, I never had that dream again. Maybe that was the last barrier...trying to find the hole in that wire-energy network." (12)

It seems the holes (the circle as an energetic signature) in his life were mounting up.

DEVELOPING EXPERIMENTAL SLEEP TAPES

It was about this time, around age 42, Bob began noticing signs that mid-life questions were nagging at him. To keep these at bay, he decided to begin another adventure to keep his business exciting and strategically postured. Intriguing research begun in the 1930s in Germany, then advanced by the Russians, provided Bob with data and some technical approaches for developing accelerated learning sleep tapes. (13) In a small research lab, Bob and several of his friends used themselves as guinea pigs to study the effects of various sleep tonal patterns. During this period, in a CBC (Canadian Broadcast Company) radio interview, Bob said he must have listened to the prototype tapes over 100 times. He attributed this as one of the big factors that caused a massive leap through the "wire-energy network" to a second, new life. However, a few of his close friends thought differently. They told him it was his habit of sleeping under a pyramid-shaped copper-covered roof in his home in Westchester County, NY that provided an accelerating boost to propel Bob into the non-ordinary realm. Whatever the case may be, Bob was in for the ride of his lifetime.

THOSE VIBRATIONS, CAN'T CONTROL THEM!
AM I GOING CRAZY?

In April of 1958 Bob experienced intense involuntary vibrations in the muscles below his ribs lasting five to ten minutes. Just like you and me, he became very upset. Initially he thought he was dying or at the very least, losing his mind, but after being examined by several professionals, he knew there wasn't any medical or psychological explanation for the vibrations nor was he dying in any physical sense. But his old life was, indeed, coming to a close.

That September on a Friday evening, after deciding to go sail-planeing the next day and seeing himself gliding in and out of perfect weather, Bob settled in for a night's rest. Again the vibrations started. He tried to be patient, waiting them out. The next thing he remembers was feeling his shoulder bump hard against something. When he rolled over he found himself hovering on the ceiling of his bedroom looking down at the chandelier, and then he saw his wife in bed with a man who was, by a quick deductive glance, himself. Next he remembers finding himself sitting up in his physical body, on the bed, very shaken.

Unable to find much OB research in Western literature or with those people who had OBEs, Bob surmised that he would have to do his own research. He constructed a small quonset hut behind his 27 acre home and began to research the effects of the OOB experience on the brain using an electroencephalograph (EEG). This machine tracks the electrical fluctuations in the brain after amplification of more than a billion times. He discovered the brain shows electrical activity in deep delta ranges when an OOB event is occurring. This inspired him to research the dynamics of how this occurs and why. Bob then went on a mission to identify sound patterns that would induce the OOB state so that he could learn more about himself, how to control his OBEs, and perhaps help others who were in the same situation.

THREE LOCALES: PREDECESSORS TO THE FOCUS STATES

By 1959 with his OBEs continuing under his own power, Bob had conceived of the idea of Focus 10, the mind awake/body asleep state. He called the places he visited "locales" and assigned numbers to differentiate between the various states of consciousness. These were the predecessors to the Focus States which were more discrete Locales. In his early days he described **Locale I** as closely aligned with physical reality, having people and places that actually exist. He suggested the perception of the traveler was distorted when Locale I has strange beings, places, or events. Bob described **Locale II** as having characteristics of a vast, non-material plane with laws of motion and matter differing from the material world, and it was occupied by various entities with varying intelligences who had communication abilities. **Locale III** was closely related to our own physical world. In this environment were trees, houses, businesses, all the accouterments of an equivalent physical world, but the scientific means to support this lifestyle was not the same as in our physical world. He noticed there weren't any electrical devices in this place, rather different kinds of mechanical power was used.(14)

By then Bob had determined that he had three bodies. Besides the **physical body**, he called the next, the **first non-physical body**. Perhaps this is the etheric body because in his description he says he was able to move his consciousness, but not his body. He called the next one the second non-physical body (the astral or emotional body), and later he shortened this to the "**second body,**" preferring not to use the phrase, "astral body" or "astral travel." He was able to move this body great distances using his mind and noted having any stray thoughts would cause a quick change in his planned destination. Traveling in his second body seemed so fast to him that time was for all purposes ended. He could also travel back and forth in time by using his thoughts to direct where he wanted to go. (15)

By 1965 the Monroe family had moved three times going from Croton, NY, to Richmond, VA, and then on to Charlottesville, VA. Interestingly, it was during this time of turmoil when Bob had his first experience of Focus 27 which he later called "The Park," its early predecessor being Locale III.

OUT-OF-BODY TRAVELING RESEARCH WITH CHARLES TART

Into Bob's life came Charles Tart, Ph.D. in 1968 who had arrived at the University of Virginia Medical School to teach psychiatry to medical residents and later, became a lecturer in psychology at Stanford University. With their common background of working in radio stations as young adults, they quickly became close friends. Charlie took Bob's OBEs seriously and set up experiments whereby Bob, while OOB, would travel to a location where Charlie was located and afterwards be asked to validate his OOB experience by describing specific elements of the location he had visited. It was at this time Bob began writing *Journeys Out of the Body* which included descriptions of these experiments as well as EEG studies at University of Virginia researching his OOB events. Charlie went on to become known for his classic book, *Altered States of Consciousness* (16) which attempts to differentiate various states of consciousness other than waking reality. Truly a champion educator and researcher about non-physical reality, Tart continues to bridge the gap between psychology and parapsychology and between science and the practice of hands-on consciousness experience. He would later, in the '90s, become instrumental in the development of the **Going Home** tapes in conjunction with Bob Monroe and Elisabeth Kübler-Ross, M.D.

The year 1971 was a year of immense changes and challenges for Bob. His gear box began to shake and rattle while traveling at supersonic OBE speeds. He had a second heart attack followed by a carotid artery repair and was forced to surrender his pilot's license due to vertigo symptoms which continued after the coronary. There were other landmark events that year. He married a close friend, Nancy Penn, who had four children of her own (Penny, Nancy, Cindy and A.J.), purchased Whistlefield, an estate just outside of Charlottesville, and had his first book, *Journeys Out of the Body*, published.

PARTNERING WITH THE I AM

With all this furious activity, the engine of his vehicle blew a gasket. The "me" juice in his waveform could go no further. Bob realized this and made some needed changes in his Interstate travels by switching over to his "I AM" juice. He described this important change:

> "In the Spring of 1972, a decision was made that was the limiting factor. The limiting factor was my conscious mind. Therefore, if the OOBE decisions were left up to that part of me, as they had been, I would remain just as I was. I was too much in control — this left-brain "I." What would happen if I turned this decision-making process over to my total self (soul?), who was purportedly conversant with such activities. Believing this, I then put it into practice. The following night, I went to sleep, went through two sleep cycles (about three hours), woke up and remembered the decision. I detached from the physical and floated free. I said in my conscious mind, the decision to do is to be made by my entire self. After waiting for what seemed only a few seconds, there was a tremendous surge, a movement, an energy in that familiar spatial blackness, and there began for me an entire new era in my OOB activities." (17)

For several decades a group of volunteers calling themselves the Explorers had been working closely with Bob as informal adjunct faculty members. Perhaps as an outer manifestation of Bob's decision to trust higher forces, he wrote the Gateway Affirmation and encouraged those participating in Gateway Programming to make this public. Giving the Gateway Affirmation airtime changed things significantly and brought new opportunities to the Whistlefield group, one of which was an invitation by The Esalen Institute to do an intensive Hemi-Sync training weekend in

California in 1973. In 1976 with the Whistlefield Research Lab losing money and the need for training space advancing, Bob and Nancy began a search for new land which was found near Charlottesville. They moved to Roberts Mountain Farm in 1979. This became **The Monroe Institute for Applied Sciences,** later shortened to **The Monroe Institute**. After a long germination period from the late '70s, the mystical *Far Journeys* was published in 1985. In November of 1987, Bob announced the Human Plus program, a new component of the business to provide an easy but powerful set of tools to the public. Human Plus is a belief-free tape series to help empower individuals to make pragmatic changes in their lives at their choosing. He called the H+ tapes, "a set of tools to help tune-up your thinking machine." This same year he set about writing a third book, *Ultimate Journey* and periodically released several excerpts from the book in the *TMI Focus*, a quarterly membership newsletter.

TAKING LEAVE

Teaching her husband and soon to be thousands about the spiritual aspects of the death process, Nancy Monroe left this plane in August of 1992. Her last years inspired the legacy of the Lifeline Residential Program, and the Going Home tape series. After a long incubation, *Ultimate Journey* was published a year before Bob passed over after a short bout with pneumonia on March 17, 1995. While he was reluctant to talk about the spiritual aspects of his journey in his lifetime, curiously, in his last earthly decade, he embodied the monk of his last physical life, a person who lived in a Coshocton monastery in Pennsylvania. (18) Knowing this, there isn't any wonder why his eyes were ultra-sensitive to bright lights throughout his life. To many, those unusual eyes were the dominating feature of his whole countenance. By developing the Hemi-Sync tool for experiencing the full reaches of consciousness, he helped illuminate the way into the rabbit hole using his own unique and brilliant light essence.

THE HOW TO'S FOR INTERSTATE TRAVELING: DON JUAN & CARLOS CASTANEDA

To learn how to penetrate non-ordinary realms, a fascinating, but controversial individual having large, brightly lucid eyes, apprenticed himself in the summer of 1961 to a 70 year-old Yaqui Indian sorcerer by the name of don Juan Matus of Toltec heritage from Sonora, Mexico. Carlos Castaneda described his outrageous experiences with don Juan in ten books written over a period of 30 years which inspired thousands around the world to explore new levels of consciousness beyond the physical. Having traveled during his adult years throughout the Southwest, don Juan's knowledge of non-ordinary realms came from many sources anchored within Indian traditions spanning the globe. Through complex rituals, enduring tests, and numerous disorienting experiences designed to unravel the way Carlos perceived the world, don Juan taught him how to access other levels of consciousness which he called separate realities. Don Juan orchestrated exercises that helped Carlos learn how to widen his perceptual skills either by over-saturating his attentional abilities so these would shut down or by enveloping Carlos in experiences that repeatedly demonstrated cues about the nature of various non-ordinary realities. At the end of each experiential event, don Juan taught Carlos principles enabling him to access these realities at will. Where Bob Monroe was succinct in his approach to help the learner identify various cities along the Interstate, don Juan emphasized the driving skills necessary to do the traveling.

At first, through several years of training, Carlos did not grasp the idea that there were separate realities accessible by merely shifting his attentional abilities. Under the guidance of don Juan, Carlos ingested medicinal plants as learning vehicles, but as Carlos described throughout the first three of the nine books, he remained clueless as to who was doing what to whom and where it all was taking place.

> "Why did you make me take those power plants so many times?" Carlos asked don Juan. He laughed and mumbled very softly, "cause you're dumb." I heard him the first time but I wanted to make sure and pretended I had not understood. "I beg your pardon?" I asked. "You know what I said," he replied and stood up. He tapped me on the head as he walked by me. "You're rather slow," he said, "and there was no other way to jolt you." "So none of that was absolutely necessary?" I asked. "It was, in your case…to be sensitive is a natural condition of certain people," he said. "You are not. But neither am I. In the final analysis sensitivity matters very little." (19)

Until his apprenticeship, Carlos had been taught that all learning required effort. Over and over he took copious notes as a dutiful sociologist would, then he spent long hours analyzing his experiences in conversations with don Juan trying to figure out what happened and how it occurred. Repeatedly, his experiences didn't make sense. His confusion came as a result of the means he was using to access these states, his acts of thinking. By using the act of thinking (internal talking and reasoning) to open his mind to these cities, Carlos kept himself clueless. Later on don Juan showed him how to retrain his thinking so that other skills would be available to support his ability to access full consciousness. (See Figure 22.) In order to perceive and use full consciousness, don Juan explained that he would have to develop the attending skills of will, seeing, feeling, dreaming, first reflexive and second reflexive skills. These skills are described in Ken Eagle Feather's book, *Traveling With Power*. (20)

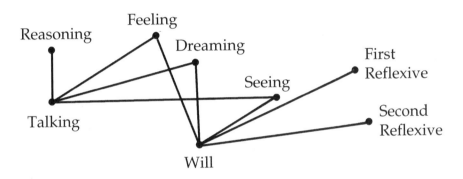

Figure 22 The Eight Attentional Skills of Consciousness

In day-to-day living our overdependence on speaking and reasoning, which rely on the five physical senses, causes the other attending skills to be sacrificed. Unfortunately, this is a case where our enculturation process has cut the nose off to spite the face. We are at the point where we don't know what we have lost. To support the majority of our life in the Me portion of the waveform, we have sacrificed the I AM abilities. In so doing, we have depreciated the six other attending skills which literally would balance out our picture of reality and open us into full consciousness. Talking and reasoning make use of thinking. Thinking and perceiving are two entirely different attentional states but we have been taught to lump them together as if they were identical twins.

THE TONAL & THE NAGUAL

Thinking belongs to what don Juan called the **first attentional state** (the tonal) and perceiving (the nagual) belongs to the **second and third attentional states**. The first attentional state has to do with experiences in physical reality, the second attentional state involves experiences in non-physical reality and the third attentional state incorporates both physical and non-physical reality or states of "free perception," the unitive or mystical states.

THE DIFFERENCE BETWEEN THINKING & PERCEIVING

Don Juan continually stressed the importance of making the distinction between thinking and perceiving. He suggested that when thinking is stopped, the idea of the physical world stops, so does physical identity and all that was constructed from and about that identity. If we stop thinking such and such then the world will stop being that which we have thought. If we shift attention into a wider perceptual field, then the world takes on broader meaning and helpfulness.

BEING ROBBED OF MY SELF-IMPORTANCE

One day as a young mother I was shopping in a crowded department store while pushing my youngest child, Katie, around in a bulky stroller. For one moment my eyes left my child and the next moment I noticed my purse was gone from the top of the stroller. At first I thought it had fallen to the floor somewhere so I and several other people searched frantically for my purse. It was nowhere to be found. Inside that purse were numerous important keys, credit cards, licenses, car registration, money, phone numbers, family pictures, etc. After that event I went through weeks of total shock, anger, disbelief, and grief realizing what had happened about losing the contents of that purse. This was totally disarming to me; it really had upset the apple cart!

Months later I began to question why I had such an adverse reaction to what was a relatively minor event in the scheme of things these days. Bit by bit I discovered that I was very attached to the things in my purse, so much so that I had constructed an identity in which I and the items in my purse were one and the same. Before the event I didn't know that I thought this way. When all of these items suddenly evaporated, I wasn't Me for days. I literally felt strange to myself, weird, not me anymore. Little did I know I had constructed a picture of reality through which I and the things were bonded, like identical twins. I did this through my constant thought patterns, thoughts such as "Who was I now that I couldn't prove who I was?" and "Why did I leave so many valuable things in my purse?" In similar fashion, this same ego destructuring phenomena is naturally occurring throughout the world in the sudden loss of job, house, car, child, marriage, and health.

Don Juan pointed out the internal chatter that goes on over and over inside our heads throughout the majority of each day drains valuable energy which otherwise might be used for non-ordinary consciousness. We think this is so and that is so, then we come to believe that is true without the slightest verification in our own experience. We come to base our lives and relationships on limited pictures of reality. These pictures were created from our past, but aren't necessarily true in the present. *This constant construction of current reality based on past thinking and maintaining that picture of reality sucks up a lot of energy.* Don Juan recognized Carlos' dilemma. Since traveling the Interstate of Consciousness requires high octane fuel and because Carlos was a master at thinking which devoured that kind of gas, don Juan then switched his tactics from dramatic jolts to subtle, nourishing practices. This new tactic helped Carlos learn how to build up the right kind of fuel by redeveloping his six lost attending skills.

RECOVERING THE LOST SENSE OF SEEING

In the second Castaneda book, *A Separate Reality*, don Juan created a lengthy experience on the first lost skill, **Seeing**, which Carlos couldn't understand or sustain. Monroe would call this skill **Knowing**. In many ways, we are like Carlos, we know how to talk and reason, but most of us don't know what the benefits of seeing are because we have forgotten what it does. Like Carlos, in our frenetic, robotic lifestyles, we don't have enough gas to access and sustain the second attentional skill of seeing.

THE DIFFERENCE BETWEEN LOOKING & SEEING

Don Juan said, "You don't understand me now because of your habit of thinking as you look and thinking as you think." (21) He went on to explain that looking is not seeing. Looking has thoughts involved, seeing does not. Training our eyes to see certain things is looking and looking is an automatic, robotic act. On the other hand, *when we learn to see, then we realize that we can no longer think about what we are looking at.*

Typically, we train our eyes to attend only to the densest of our energy fields, the physical elements of our world. As a result, we don't see the other higher vibrating fields that are simultaneously present. Acquiring the skill of seeing means stopping the automatic response, stopping the thoughts especially the ruminating thoughts about feelings and self-importance and softly focusing the eyes while perceiving with the whole instinctual body. When this is achieved, seeing reveals that nothing is more important than anything else because there are no longer familiar features in the world, everything seems new and luminous when seeing. An excellent illustration of this is Richard M.'s message on "Seeing" in Chapter 6. Ken Eagle Feather, who has been an apprentice of don Juan and a TMI staff associate, says:

> "Part of the training is to completely let go and know you don't know a darn thing. The more you know that you don't know anything, the more abstract your individual awareness becomes. Because you have reduced self-importance to such a degree that you no longer reflect the world but are the world, you are totally being in the world. You no longer think about yourself. You have molded your energy into a state that's so abstract and also has such great integrity behind it that you don't need to continue thinking and reflecting about yourself. You just are yourself." (22)

Both don Juan and Gurdjieff taught when we are seeing, we experience the oneness of everything, the essence of ourself, the truth of reality, and how all is connected.

RECOVERING THE LOST SENSE OF WILL

Don Juan described **Will** as the force that comes from within, from the solar plexus and attaches itself to the outer world but seeing was different, it was a means to get through things. This is likened to the difference between a driving power or a force, and a static beingness. He defined Will as a power that can be dynamically used but that it was not a thought, nor a wish or an object. The act of Willing is described in Chapter 2 in Focus 15 descriptions (subway scene in the movie, "Ghost") and also in several stories from Gateway participants in Chapter 5. Here is a striking example of the use of Will coupled with Seeing.

> "Don Juan held my arm and pushed me up on my feet again. "You have to walk," he said, "the same way you got up the other time. You must use your will." I seemed stuck to the ground...I intently tried to recollect the actions I had performed on that occasion, but I could not think clearly...the thought occurred to me that if I said, "up" as I had done before I would certainly get up...Nothing happened..."Your life is getting complicated," he said. "Get rid of whatever it is that's causing you to lose your temper. Stay here quietly and rearrange yourself." He walked away. My first impulse was to fret again, but I could not gather the energy to work myself into it. Instead, I found myself slipping into a rare state of serenity; a great feeling of ease enveloped me...It was my little boy...I must let him go. I began to weep. My eyes filled with tears...Suddenly I had a great urge to get up and look for don Juan to explain to him about my little boy; and the next thing I knew, I was looking at the porch from an upright position..."Good, good work," he said reassuringly. At that instant I became aware that something extraordinary was taking place right there...When I stood up and turned around I saw don Juan; 'the don Juan I know' definitely walked toward me and held me. But when I focused my eyes on his face I did not see don Juan as I am accustomed to seeing him; instead, I saw a large object in front of my eye...The strange, luminous object in front of me had to be don Juan's face. (23)

Willing, like seeing, requires no thought. Its energy becomes available by sending an energetic force (second attention) from the solar plexus (for some, the throat area or the third eye for other people) and manifesting that which is desired. As don Juan suggests, anything that is in the way of this force such as emotional concerns, limiting mental beliefs, or physical expectations must be released so there is *serenity* as Carlos experienced in the place where Will resides. It becomes especially important when attempting to use Will energy to clean and neutralize the emotional body before using Will energy. This can be done through don Juan's **recapitulation technique** (discussed later) or Monroe's **Release and Recharge technique**.

DISTINGUISHING FOURTH DIMENSIONAL WILL ENERGY FROM THIRD DIMENSIONAL WILLPOWER ENERGY

The Will center, known as the Tan Tien in Eastern teachings, is about 3 cm or 1.25 inches below the naval. It lies about one-third into the body and is said to be the seat of an energetic brain. Will is to be distinguished from willpower, a cognitive force which isn't helpful in non-physical reality as Carlos found out in his early escapades with don Juan. Recovering alcoholics discover the limits of willpower when they use 'cold turkey' methods to eliminate drinking alcohol. The same goes for obese individuals who try to push away from the table and the refrigerator using food sacrifice and exercise to carve off the pounds. Unfortunately, the addiction often returns in another form until the consciousness force of Will is used. Most likely, Will energy is what Oprah Winfrey and Richard Simmons have been using to change their physical forms. Beginning in 1983, Ceanne DeRohan channeled numerous books, the first of which was called *The Right Use of Will*. (24) These are helpful resources for understanding the historical roots of this non-physical skill and how its loss has affected humankind throughout the ages. Notice in Figure 22 that the Will jointly works only with feeling, dreaming, and seeing which helps to produce second and third attention pictures of reality. In addition, Will is used as a partner with first and second reflexive skills.

RECOVERING THE LOST SENSE OF FEELING

The attending skill of Feeling develops by using feelings as a source of data. Feeling is a second attentional skill; however, most of us confuse thinking with feeling so we intellectualize when we want to express feelings. There's quite a bit of confusion existing in our manner of speaking about feelings. We have been conditioned to use the phrase, "I feel" when we mean "I think." Watch people talking. When asked, 'What are you feeling?" they will reply with their *opinion* not their feelings. The converse is true as well! When giving an opinion, a person will begin by saying, "I feel this way" and then state his or her ideas. We run away at high speed from actually naming our feelings in conversation. This behavior illustrates feelings are not being valued as a source of data, nor does the person feel serene enough to express feelings.

LETTING THE FEELING BODY TALK

To name a feeling is to go within, slow down or turn off the thinking and perceive a sensation coming from body wisdom. As a general rule, the majority of us have a difficult time naming feelings because we have been so accustomed to spouting off answers quickly, meaning giving our opinions using talking and reasoning. This keeps us in a first attention picture of reality. But to reach in, stop the thinking, and the worldview based on the past, feel the feeling and label it requires shifting the perception to another less black and white place. People around a circle who express feelings put the atmosphere of the group into a more expanded data base. Gradually as this attention skill of feeling is valued and used more, telepathic skills as well as intuition increase and that extends out into having deep unitive experiences with elemental energies such as native spirits and devas. Developing the skill of feeling was very difficult for Carlos to do because his thinking left brain frequently got in the way.

RETRIEVING THE LOST SENSE OF DREAMING

Don Juan used the term, dreaming body, when talking about the second attentional skill of **Dreaming**. He explained how the dreaming body becomes activated by illustrating how the nature of the dreaming content progressively changes. Initially, dreams seem to have a vague, fragmented quality, then they take on more vividness and connectedness. Soon after they become more lucid in form. This activation process is like cleaning a dirty window. In lucid dreaming, when the window is clean, the dreamer knows he or she is dreaming. Physical reality and non-physical reality are beginning to merge. Another way of saying this is the dreamer and the dream unite. At that point inner control of the dream is possible. (Discussions by Jonatan, Brian and MaX in Chapter 6 on "100% Lucid Dream" are examples of the control that is possible in lucid dreamwork.)

Many people do not remember their dreams. On some level, this is a choice not to remember this component of themselves just as they could choose to forget making a Freudian comment. Other people would notice and remember the Freudian slip, but the unconscious individual using first attention slips right by the off-handed comment. Recalling a dream is not a thinking event, it is a *perceiving* event because it comes from a second attentional state. Many people want to recall it in a deductive (logical) manner instead of inductively accessing it or drawing it out.

As physical awareness becomes connected to the non-physical awareness, literally a person is able to move, at will, into the dream state and gain control of dreaming. For example, before going to sleep a person can ask a question whose answer is unknown in physical reality. He begins to dream, recognizes he is dreaming, enters the scene consciously and plays out the scenario in full control. Then he awakens knowing what went on during the entire dream, why it occurred, and is able to apply the solution in everyday reality.

DREAMING SHIFTS THE ASSEMBLAGE POINT IN THE ENERGY FIELD

As the dreamer and the dream become the same event, something very interesting happens in the energy field. Under the control of the dreaming person, a localized star of condensed energy, which don Juan called the **assemblage point** (AP) or what Ken Eagle Feather calls the **Focal Point**, gradually shifts from the right side in waking reality to the left side of the energy body during sleep states. (See Figure 23.)

DESCRIPTION OF THE ASSEMBLAGE POINT STAR

The AP is the place where the luminous energy body and the energy of the physical body meet, a portal. It looks like a brilliant, fiber optic star about the size of an orange with a halo surrounding it. Its natural location is about two feet below a person's right shoulder blade, but conditioned as we are to stay most of the time in a beta-based brain state, the AP will be often be found on the right side of the energy field. Going from waking to sleeping states, the AP easily becomes displaced on its own into the left side of the energy field. If the AP is moving constantly, disassociated images will be seen similar to what schizophrenic and hallucinating individuals report. On the other hand, if the AP becomes fixed at a certain spot, then cohesed perception results. No AP is visible in a dead person's energy field because the AP is the stamp of consciousness. Don Juan explained to Castaneda that throughout the ages various apprentices were given the gift of certain APs containing Rotes of information about specific skills. These APs were then passed down throughout the lineage of sorcerers.

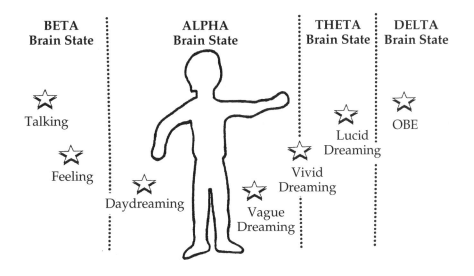

BETA Brain State   **ALPHA** Brain State   **THETA** Brain State   **DELTA** Brain State

Talking

Feeling

Daydreaming

Vague Dreaming

Vivid Dreaming

Lucid Dreaming

OBE

Figure 23 Shifting the Assemblage Point in the Energy Field to Change Perception

THE GIFTS OF MONROE & CASTANEDA: SHIFTING THE AP AT WILL

As one of their most important teaching objectives, both Bob Monroe and don Juan taught individuals the means to achieve conscious movement of the AP thereby achieving the ability to shift consciousness at will. What Bob Monroe called the Null Point was the equivalent to the AP in don Juanian terms. While Monroe did not stress energy and how it changed, his system of progressively moving into more expanded states of consciousness using a dynamic anchoring system supports this perspective. He developed exercises which centered on moving into the Null Point, the purpose being to reverse polarity or to totally shift phase. The Focus states are like minuets, little waltzes that build up to an interval shift. To digress a bit more, the wormhole concept in *Star Trek* plots represents the same idea. Don Juan was not as specific with his traveling lessons as Monroe was; nonetheless, he preferred the traveler be conceptually adept at using energy to shift the AP to produce various separate realities.

UNDERRATED BENEFITS OF DREAMING

Inside dream characters, plots and endings devised by the dreamer is Total Self intelligence. This suggests that the skill of dreaming is vastly underrated as source for living a full life, for in dreams there is content, the stuff that innovative decisions could be based on. Inside our dreams there are interesting life options played out, creative resources are used, and possibilities not imagined are experienced in near physical reality. The most recent of Castaneda's books, *The Art of Dreaming* (25), focused entirely on developing this skill.

THE LOST SENSES OF FIRST & SECOND REFLEXIVE SKILLS

First and Second Reflexive skills have to do with the use of pure Will energy which reflects back what is sought. As Eagle Feather describes, first reflexive skill has to do with the nature of relationships, structure, and organization, whereas the second reflexive skill involves the void that is comforting and enfolding as opposed to the void of nothingness that is endless and empty. The void that is full has a I AM nature that moves and participates in the development of creative experiences. This is the beginning development of co-creative abilities which will be mentioned in Chapter 10.

By no means does this description of the eight attentional skills of consciousness cover the full range of extrasensory abilities. This is merely the tip of the iceberg. There are more resources which empower the retrieval of extrasensory abilities listed in Appendix B. In addition to the Toltec tradition, other cultures have passed down their oral traditions which keep the memory of the lost skills alive. Look within your own heritage to retrieve these lost skills; these memories might be right under your own nose!

DON JUAN'S BASIC PRINCIPLE:
EVERYTHING IS ENERGY FIRST, THEN MATTER FOLLOWS

Returning to the Toltec tradition, another important teaching of don Juan's is that *we are fields of energy not bodies.* In Chapter 1, Carlos' idea of having enough gas or available "free" energy was discussed as being a prerequisite to travel the Interstate. Carlos, in his early experiences with don Juan, did what many individuals do, they use their thinking skills. In so doing, a projection of who they think they are comes back to them mirroring their intention. But when perceiving skills are used, second attention abilities reflect back the "I-thou" experiences. This kind of sensitivity takes into account the consciousness of other elements such as animals, rocks, clouds, and non-physical entities. James Redfield in *The Celestine Prophecy* suggests this when he gives instructions on how to read the energy field of plants. (26) When a person accesses Focus 12, the second attentional state becomes the operating base in order to enjoy the full benefits of this city. Any analysis (thinking) done during Focus 12 experiences will cause a phasing back to Focus 10, a state requiring first attentional skills for the most part.

THE CONCEPT OF IMPECCABILITY

If we operate from the premise that we are fields of energy and not bodies, then don Juan suggests we have to drastically change the way we make choices by becoming very careful and mindful. Choices either support the enhancement of energy or the loss of energy. He called this **impeccability** or the strategic control of behavior. Don Juan suggests that impeccability is developed by either being a *dreamer* or a *stalker*. The difference between the two is one of process. Dreamers use a right brain, abstract approach whereas stalkers use a left brain, concrete approach. Generally, stalking involves focused, determined first attention actions that keep the physical body in integrity regarding efficient use of energy while dreaming makes use of expansive second attention activities enabling one to create and achieve large gestalts of learning. Castaneda was a stalker who enjoyed being systematic and precise, while Monroe, a dreamer, used his creative juices and his dreamtime to create his picture of reality. It has been frequently said that Monroe was "out more than in" on this earth plane.

RECAPITULATION:
THE ART OF UNDOING STUCK ENERGY IN THE FIELD

To help retrieve energy lost when the identity is developed by focusing entirely on the past, don Juan taught Castaneda how to take back the energy stuck to limited pictures of reality. This involves retrieval of all memories associated with the development of a false ego self and breathing techniques to release the stuck light body energy in order to regain power. This is his well-known technique of **recapitulation**. Many recapitulation groups now exist across the nation for the purpose of recovering original powers. Monroe developed a similar approach, originally called the Cleansing exercise, now known as **Release & Recharge technique** which primarily centers on releasing stuck energy in the energy field associated with emotions and feelings. The stuck energy builds up in places in the light body (known as "The Egg" in Castaneda terms) forming what Monroe and don Juan both called encrustations or knots of energy. Recapitulation and cleansing techniques loosen and peel away the encrustations so that energy can flow again and become available for non-physical travel. When these techniques are done, quite literally a loss of weight can be experienced due to the release of heavy aspects of the stagnant blocks in the energy field. Both the Monroe and don Juan exercises have the same goal, to reclaim the original energetic, flow state before limiting perceptions diminished the flow and thus, personal power.

Don Juan through Castaneda's writings made many other contributions available to the traveler to learn how to make the grand tour of the Interstate of Consciousness. Both men substantially added their knowledge and experience to the field of consciousness training. In recent years, several other people have begun to describe their training with don Juan as well. Ken Eagle Feather has written two books which have helped to decipher Castaneda's work especially with regard to the eight attending skills of consciousness. His first book, *Traveling with Power* described both his TMI experiences and his experiences with don Juan and his second book, *A Toltec Path*, (27) distinguishes the unique features of the Toltec tradition as this applies to consciousness expansion.

TRANSLATING CASTANEDA CONCEPTS INTO PRACTICAL APPLICATIONS

Victor Sanchez is another person who has significantly helped to unravel the confusion associated with Castaneda's works by demonstrating how to apply the don Juanian principals in everyday circumstances. His early life was spent living primarily with indigenous Nahuas and Huicholes, then using these experiences to teach groups how to live purposefully. After 13 years of studying the Castaneda books, he found many similarities between what he knew and don Juan's approach. Sanchez decided to streamline the don Juan teachings while honoring the tremendous depth that the Toltec possessed. In his book, *The Teachings of Don Carlos* (28), he reviews the core don Juanian concepts then offers numerous practical exercises to understand and integrate the concepts in everyday life. As the teacher teaching the master's ideas, he achieved his purpose quite well. Two other people in the tradition of don Juan's group also have written of their experiences. Using a descriptive form, Florinda Donner, the dreamer, and Taisha Abelar, the stalker, have written first-hand accounts depicting the growth of their spirituality (29) in less of a warrior stance than Castaneda uses. In addition to numerous resources now entering the reading marketplace, the don Juan work is now becoming a part of the experiential training arena in form of programs co-led by Abelar and others. The more visible programs called *Tensegrity* (an architectural term meaning the creation of balance), also in video format (Vol. I-III), primarily teach body movements, known as sorcery passes, to relax and shift energy in the energy body in order to retrieve energy and to loosen the encrustations in the light body similar to recapitulation. All these works are evidence that more and more people are remembering and triggering their original state of beingness.

Thanks to these early cartographers and many others, the arena of consciousness training has been gradually transforming itself. Once a quiet underground movement circulating around indigenous people who passed skills and knowledge by oral tradition, the larger global audience has now joined this search for knowledge by gaining and sharing information in cyberspace, in personal growth literature and educational events, and through intensive cross-cultural shamanic training. The quick spread of this exploration implies that a tremendous consciousness shift has happened. Quite simply this represents a leap to embrace the lost skills of our full heritage.

OPENING THE PUBLIC'S EYE TO SPACE & BEYOND:
GENE RODDENBERRY

A rebel from the word "born," the creator of *Star Trek* arrived on August 19, 1921 as a "veiled baby," an omen portending unusual life circumstances that lay ahead. Folklore had it that when a piece of the placenta covered the baby's head and shoulders, the baby was destined to have psychic abilities to see far into the future. This omen certainly came to be true in the later years of Roddenberry's life. Born to Glen and Eugene Edward Roddenberry, "little Gene" had a brother Bob, and a sister, Doris Willowdean better known as "Willie." True to his birth entry, one of his early childhood friends, Pat Bradley, described him as being very quick-witted and introspective. "I always thought Gene's personality was operating in its own field. When I would talk to him, he was most pleasant, interesting, making appropriate remarks, but he truly was in a little bit of a world of his own making." (30)

Embracing his nature as a self-effacing and shy fellow to the fullest, the masterful storyteller, throughout his life, gathered around him people who would craft his scripts into hundreds of other world plots focused on exploring "Space: The Final Frontier." These words, now a household phrase permanently inflected with a lilting, edgy, interval pause, are synonymous with Roddenberry's mission: teaching the public about the value of using our lost skills. His purpose wasn't just to entertain us, but to conduct weekly televised classes on the possibilities that could emerge in our own near future using our superhuman, non-ordinary skills. Nearly three decades of teleconferenced instructions via episodes involving places of no-time, no-space and beyond the time-space continuum have contained thousands of ideas, and dress rehearsals for the future. Roddenberry's space is inhabited by Vulcans, Klingons, Romulans, the Borg, Ferengi, and other mysterious races. These characters have nudged us into thinking about what life might be like on other planets and in other galaxies with different kinds of people and other lifeforms. For a long time Earth was thought to be the center of the universe. Thanks to Roddenberry and his team of writers, citizens of Planet Earth are exploring the far reaches in the passageway called the universe and beyond.

THE BIRTHPLACE OF STAR TREK

The *Star Trek* series had its beginnings in the voluminous reading habits that Gene had while growing up. He would often spend long hours soaking up pulp magazines, radio programs and ten cent movies about his favorites such as Flash Gordon, Tarzan, Buck Rogers, and John Carter of Mars. His ability to fantasize his heroes' adventures stored up a lot of material for the future writer-to-be. Following in the footsteps of his father who was one of his important role models, he went to work for the Los Angeles Police Department and while there, wrote television scripts in the 1950s under the pen name, Robert Wesley — Wesley being his middle name and Robert being his brother's name. When he made sergeant, he met another probationary sergeant by the name of Wilbur Clingan who was the inspiration behind the Klingons, a fierce warrior race first appearing in the classic *Star Trek* segments. William H. Parker, the LAPD Chief of Police at the time, was the role model for the well-known half-human, half-alien Mr. Spock. In June of 1951 a children's radio program called *Space Patrol* attracted a large audience and went quickly into TV production due to its overnight success. Its format became the pattern from which *Star Trek* was conceived. The plot was that the *Space Patrol* had been designated by the United Federation of Planets to fight space pirates, mad scientists, and evildoers around the galaxy. (31) Gene sold his first script for a Ziv Productions program, *Mr. District Attorney* that was filmed and broadcast in 1954 while he was still a LAPD officer, so his on-the-job experience became very useful in his role as a technical writer for Ziv. Now enjoying a second income, Roddenberry turned to what he loved best, writing science fiction stories, but it was ten years before his science fiction work would hit pay dirt.

Not all good things start well. The original *Star Trek* pilot on NBC-TV failed in a fall line up opposite 30 other programs. Production on the second pilot originally conceived in a Roddenberry script called, *Where No Man Has Gone Before* started in July, 1965. The first *Star Trek* episode, *The Man Trap*, starring William Shatner as Captain Kirk, was aired in September, 1966, ran for three seasons and it, too, was canceled due to low ratings. Over one million viewers protested so loudly that the campy *Star Trek* was renewed. A second series was introduced in 1987 called *Star Trek: The Next Generation* (STNG). As the series progressed, a character known as Wesley Crusher, grew to manhood during the 178 *STNG* segments. Coincidentally, another character had appeared earlier in a classic *Star Trek* segment by the name of Commodore Robert Wesley. *STNG* took on a bolder, more diverse format and ran for seven years followed by *Deep Space Nine* (*DS9*), which premiered in January, 1993. Some 303 episodes aired before the latest series *Voyager* began in January of 1995. According to Paramount TV research, by then these shows had garnered a weekly audience of more than 20 million Trekkies throughout the world. With more than 63 million *Star Trek* books in print and six *Star Trek* movies earning nearly $500 million at the box office, (32) Roddenberry's work had become a stellar hit.

The *Star Trek* stories have evolved from a stilted, uptight vignette format into a slick, feature series leaving an almost too-smooth, utopian impression in the eyes of many viewers. In this format the stories have substantially contributed toward the public's understanding of the paradigm shift in planetary consciousness taking place, teaching the difference between a competitive and a cooperative stance. Throughout all the *Star Trek* programs, the United Federation of Planets, an alliance of approximately 150 planetary governments based in San Francisco, coordinates the activities of all *Star Trek* characters. Roddenberry has used what is known as the Prime Directive to get an important concept across to his audience. Known as General Order #1, the Prime Directive states that all Starfleet Federation personnel and space craft are prohibited from intervening in the normal development of any society they might encounter. Some of the *STNG* plots centered solely on the difficulties in performing according to the Prime Directive which simply boils down to a question of maintaining balance so as to not do any harm.

RODDENBERRY TAUGHT HUNDREDS OF CLASSROOM LESSONS ABOUT SPACE

With an uncanny sense of the educational baby steps that John Q. Public required, Roddenberry designed and paced *Star Trek* plots to reveal the idiosyncrasies about space travel, time travel, and relationships in space as if he has had a recent, long, first-hand experience of this himself. Using some old ideas that appeared in the pulp magazines, he spun out incredible story lines that propelled our minds into the future so that we might have a dress rehearsal for what is to come. Through his mainstream TV programs, Roddenberry developed hundreds of classroom lessons to expand consciousness beyond physical reality. Among the more important concepts he taught was the idea of wormholes connecting various quadrants of the universe and beyond, the advantages and practical use of intuition, how energy manifests as matter and antimatter, the practical uses for the materialization and dematerializational properties of energy, multidimensionality (past, future and parallel lifetimes), group consciousness as a lifeform expression, and the possible abilities of a God-like creature. Some descriptions follow illustrating these key educational lessons.

WORMHOLES IN SPACE

Most of the action in the *Star Trek* learning classroom mainly took place on either one of six versions of the starship, *Enterprise* or an old Cardassian mining space station which Starfleet retrofitted and renamed *Deep Space 9* (*DS9*) commanded by Benjamin Sisko or, most recently, the *Voyager* starship. In the first episode of *DS9*, a Bajoran wormhole was discovered linking the Bajor system with another in the far distant Gamma Quadrant. Take note that space, as the *Star Trek* writers envisioned it, was divided geographically into quadrants having names associated with most of the known brain states (Gamma, Beta, Alpha, and Delta), an interesting coincidence.

Just as NASA is readying an actual space station, the *DS9* space station has fascinated the viewing public for years. By means of the *DS9* programs and many of the *Voyager* plots, Roddenberry taught the public about the energy of the void, the Einstein-Rosen bridge, and how energy implodes on itself and changes polarity which, coincidentally is the very same dynamics that occur during an OBE. At one point in a *DS9* plot, a runabout (a small starship for short-range interstellar travel) has to be carefully maneuvered by Captain Sisko through the Bajoran wormhole using strategies that come strikingly close to don Juan's attending skill of Will or what was used in the subway scene of the movie, *Ghost*. Again, a vicarious thrilling classroom dress rehearsal for what is to come.

THE LOST SENSE OF FEELING IN STAR TREK PLOTS

Periodically through the *DS9* space station windows, viewers see gaseous stars, multihued planets, and odd-looking lifeforms, some of which have telepathic communication abilities. This is strikingly similar to Focus state experiences where gaseous blobs or pulsating grid-like formations appear at times. As in the Focus states, telepathy is sometimes used in the *DS9* plots as a means of communication for these experiences. For example, in the original classic *Star Trek* series, Captain Kirk meets with Sylvia, a space entity who has expert telepathic skills. She was the first character to introduce the skill of seeing as described by Castaneda. Portrayed as having immature, raw talent, she used her ability to read the minds of others in order to manipulate reality to keep her power intact. Later on, the *STNG* character Deanna Troi, the ship's counselor, was Roddenberry's way of showing the importance and usefulness of full-blown telepathic skills in various circumstances, be these friendly or threatening. He had Deanna originating from a race called the Betazoids who were skilled empaths. She was given a key role in the majority of *STNG* plots using her empathic skills such as intuiting the true intent of other races during negotiations, to telepathically read the environment of alien cultures, and to help resolve subspace cultural wars.

Roddenberry and some of his writers have been able to tap into their memories on some precognitive level for these kinds of extrasensory skills. Uncanny renditions of my experiences and those of other Interstate travelers I know have been portrayed in the majority of *Star Trek* plots. An instance of this appears in the opening episode of *Voyager* when an accident occurs which sends the Enterprise crew traveling at incredible speed. As a result, they become lost in space in the Delta Quadrant. Again this is curious because the delta brain state where all known physical characteristics disappear and where lost supernatural skills start to reappear. The entire *Voyager* series then unfolds on the theme of trying to get home. How blunt can this get? We'll have to tune into the *Voyager* series in the future to see if they actually return "home." Interestingly enough, this "lost in space" sensation oftentimes occurs in Focus 15 and beyond until a new map of the locale is outlined. Perhaps the master storyteller has, indeed, charted this area of space very well.

MATERIALIZING AND DEMATERIALIZING

Roddenberry introduced the concept of energy in the form of matter and antimatter to the public through the introduction of high-tech gizmos in the plots. For example, the warp drive (the main engine) in each *Enterprise* starship is described as powered by a matter and antimatter reactor. In several episodes the warp drive is near a warp core breach, then what often happens is that various changes to the warp drive engine have to be made in order to overcome some aspect of the plot. Similarly, many changes must be made to the engine or the mind of the driver during Interstate traveling in order to continue to be the waveform, such as being able to use the various forms of consciousness by adding a third spiral to the REBAL to change the waveform force to tachyon energy. Throughout the *Star Trek* series, the starships are often shown traveling at speeds up to 9.99 warp suggesting what it might be like to break the constraints of time and space in a vehicle.

In the hundreds of *Star Trek* episodes, three differing kinds of matter conversion devices introduce the viewer to the idea that solid matter can be changed into non-matter and back to solid form. The first of these was the transporter (a matter-energy device which briefly converts an object or person into energy, beams that energy to another location, then reassembles the subject into its original form). Another was the food replicators on the Enterprise which created instant food on board the starships and still another was the cloaking device (an energy screen generator used to make an object invisible, often a space vehicle). This was first introduced through the cloaking technologies of the Klingons and the Romulans who had an alliance in the early episodes but became warring races in later plots. The Aldea cloaking device was shown to be so powerful as to make the entire Aldean planet disappear.   All these materializing and dematerializing features of the *Star Trek* plots suggested to the viewing audience that not only will future technology but also human beings have the possibility to carry out this function. Roddenberry explored the hard edge possibilities and also showed the benefits of developing these abilities.

THE MOST FASCINATING STAR TREK LEARNING TOOL: THE TRANSPORTER

As a ten-year-old listening to Buck Rogers radio programs or reading the comic strips, Roddenberry became enthralled with a stupendous outlay of electronic gadgetry displayed on this program such as anti-gravity belts and disintegrator rays. The first transporter, created when Gene was a child, appeared on the *Buck Rogers Radio Show*. With Roddenberry at the helm, the *Star Trek* programs advanced into the 24th century revamping the transporter concept several times over. It grew into a terrifically famous teaching tool well beyond the televised series. Now, at the more than 200 annual *Star Trek* conventions, the transporter exhibit is, by far, the most popular attraction for both adult and young alike. Over the years, these "museum-on-wheels" conventions have served thousands of space thirsty viewers by offering hands-on learning exhibits to study technological possibilities of the future in space such as voice security devices, tricorder communication devices, the holodeck virtual reality simulator, and many advanced healthcare devices — all originating with *Star Trek* plots. At these conventions it's especially wonderful to see how the children far outnumber the adults in their intense, passionate enthusiasm for this kind of classroom experience.

RODDENBERRY SHOWED HOW PARALLEL UNIVERSES MIGHT IMPACT OUR REALITY

Many questions concerning parallel lives, past lives, and future lives are raised throughout *Star Trek* stories to further explore overlapping pictures of reality. For instance, in one episode Jean-Luc Picard, Captain of the *STNG* Enterprise, lives an entire lifetime in 20 minutes by means of time travel in another parallel place. He brings back a silver flute that he learned to play in that parallel place as proof that he had another life, a life where he was married and had two children. In an early episode of *DS9*, when Captain Sisko is new in command of the space station, he experiences a series of time travel flashbacks. Sisko relives the traumatic death of his wife, Jennifer, and in so doing, receives more information about that part of his life. This frees him to carry out his new duties with less grief and stress and considerably more authority. In an episode of *STNG*, the character played by Whoopi Goldberg, known as the 500 year old sage Guinan, possesses an unusual perceptive sense of being able to intuit beyond the time-space continuum. She uses this ability to tell another character, Tasha Yar, that Tasha is dead and belongs to what is called an "alternative time line." Since Tasha had already died in a previous segment, this infers that she was living in another parallel universe, and that the plot was taking place in that parallel universe. Guinan, able to foresee the future, tells Tasha that she will again die. Knowing this, Tasha willingly sacrifices herself to achieve resolution to a problem at the program's end.

THE CONCEPT OF GROUP CONSCIOUSNESS: THE BORG

During *STNG* programming the concept of group consciousness as an alternative lifeform expression was introduced by means of the Borg, a powerful race of enhanced humanoids from the Delta Quadrant who had implanted themselves with cybernetic devices having various hardware for different tasks. A *STNG* writer named Maurice Hurley derived the name "Borg" from the term cyborg (cybernetic organism). Each Borg was wired into a sophisticated communications network forming the Borg collective in which the idea of the individual was seen as useless. The Borg's typical day was divided into three components: assimilation, implementation, and regeneration. In the latter they reattached themselves to the communications system and received technological reprogramming for the coming day. For the purpose of improving the quality of life in the galaxy, the Borg took on the mission of capturing unfortunate space travelers and assimilating them into the collective consciousness of the Borg. Several plots in *STNG* involving the Borg collective and the huge cube-shaped ship were among the most popular of the *STNG* programs. One of these was a program in which Captain Picard was captured at the beginning of a warring offensive by the Borg and assimilated into the Borg collective, becoming one of them. By introducing the notion of group consciousness through the Borg race, various facets of homogeneity and the power of collective consciousness as a whole have been explored by the large *Star Trek* audience. High attendance records for the recent *Star Trek* movie, *First Contact*, has again demonstrated the public's intense and continuing interest in group consciousness issues.

EXPLORING THE POSSIBILITY OF GOD IN SPACE

In the *Star Trek* episodes, the concept of God or higher intelligence was treated in somewhat of a bipolar manner. Two *STNG* characters are metaphors of higher intelligence, intelligence that often begins in early Focus state work in the form of intuition and knowings. The character of Q, played by John DeLancie, is portrayed as an immensely powerful multidimensional entity from the Q Continuum, an extradimensional domain. Supposedly all Qs have supernatural powers. In the many plots Q has appeared in, both his godlike and childlike qualities repeatedly disrupt the current train of thought and then provoke large leaps in consciousness for those about him. Known for his magical abilities to appear and disappear, to create and uncreate events, Q, in a very entertaining way, demonstrates some of the lost non-physical skills for all to see. For example, the last episode of *STNG* centers on stopping time, going into the past (to the first program which was 177 episodes earlier) and reinventing an element that develops a more effective future while impacting all of creation. And who was the master wizard in that time-space mystery but Q! The viewer sees the dilemmas and the benefits that would occur through Q's eyes if time travel and highly developed creativity were possible. When traveling the non-physical focus states, this is possible through out-of-body travel, remote viewing, and bilocation techniques as suggested in the plots involving Q. The other godlike character, called Traveler, who only appears in three segments of *STNG*, is an amorphoric humanoid from a distant planet able to manipulate space, time and thought as if he were a "lens" though which all these are focused. To Hemi-Sync individuals, he is a multidimensional metaphor for achieving progressively more and more focusing abilities as one travels the Interstate of Consciousness, but to the Trekkie, he is merely an all-knowing, but mysterious, far-distant being. The Traveler is attributed all the qualities that Q doesn't possess, those of gentleness, unconditional love, trustworthiness, and above all, a keen sense of knowing. Both Q and Traveler are able to instantaneously appear and disappear at will and manifest anything they wish at any time — the Genie in the bottle routine.

The non-physical equivalent of this godlike creative intelligence appeared in the movie *Star Trek Generations*. The crew came across a large energy mass looking very similar to a ribbon, and they gave it the name Nexus. Being fearful about entering the Nexus, a few of the crew accompanied a guest who felt compelled to visit it and found, while they were in it, an ability to manifest all their desires instantaneously and experience a mystical state of bliss. Coincidentally, this sounds very identical to mystical experiences that come after learning to totally surrender to what Monroe called the Total Self (the Nexus) or as some would say, God.

Shortly before his death in October, 1991, Roddenberry was interviewed by Terrance Sweeney, a Jesuit priest doing research for his book, *God &* (33) and was asked the question, "Who is God to you?" His reply was:

> "As nearly as I can concentrate on the question today, I
> believe I am God; certainly you are, I think we intelligent
> beings on this planet are all a piece of God, are becoming

God. In some sort of cyclical non-time thing we have to become God, so that we can end up creating ourselves, so that we can be in the first place. I'm one of those people who insists on hard facts. I won't believe in a flying saucer until one lands out here or someone gives me photographs. But I am almost as sure about this as if I did have facts, although the only test I have is my own consciousness." (34)

OTHER MEDIA MOGULS CRAFT STORIES ABOUT SPACE & BEYOND

Many other media travel agents, namely Ron Howard and Steven Spielberg, have offered less accelerated, more leisurely trips on the Interstate of Consciousness. The epic film, *Cocoon*, caught our eye and taught us about our luminous or energy fields that contain the physical body while the film *E.T.* grabbed our hearts, showing how children, closer to their memories of being in their light bodies, can communicate with light entities. The films *Always* and *Ghost* wrapped us in chills as they explored the passage of the physical body into light and the abilities gained by being in a light body after death. Too, there have been numerous other travel agents who have looked into the nooks and crannies of this thing we call consciousness.

Perhaps the growing crowds who seek *Star Trek*-like experiences and flock to these films represent a yearning to know what it is like to consciously transport over millennia just as the soul has done and to experience the freedom of having a light, all-knowing body. This is the search for the "miraculous" as P.D. Ouspensky put it, the quest to understand the shape shifting and healing abilities of shamans, yogis, don Juan and other indigenous people who have OOB experiences. This symbolizes the desire to return home and the "good life." In normal life, Roddenberry would suggest, this is done all the time when prayers are answered, when a simple seed reproduces itself, or when a man and woman create a child. Likewise, the food replicator, the transporter, and cloaking devices are fancier versions of the small miracles created in physical reality every day. Not surprisingly, the miraculous has been available at our fingertips all the time!

Voyages onto the Interstate through the eyes of the cartographers and travelers lead us beyond the frontier of human consciousness and into a new land of full consciousness. What does full consciousness encompass? How does it manifest itself on the dashboard of the driver? This is the subject of the next destination on our journey.

HALT, WHO GOES DOWN THE RABBIT HOLE?

Map makers & travel guides all rolled into one
Brandishing REBALs, tricorders, transporters and luminous eggs.
Whirling into spinning dervish dancing
By sound, by self-remembering, by seeing
To break the tribal veil between the worlds
outside.
There sits the Cheshire Cat all prim and pretty
Smiling back at you who's very dizzy and dirty
From falling down the hole that the map makers found
Which leads to the middle of the universe
inside.

THE CONSCIOUSNESS FORCE:
WHAT IS IT?

*"Now millions are attempting direct personal contact
with a deeper creative reality through meditation, prayer, yoga…
We want to feel the Force. We want to work with the Force.
We want to become the Force."*

Barbara Marx Hubbard, *The Evolutionary Journal*

ROUTE 9

THE ITINERARY OF THE CONSCIOUSNESS TOUR: THE TRIP OF A LIFETIME

Around the world the popular movie phrase, *"E.T.: Phone Home!"* triggered a deep, resonating chord in the hearts of many. The overwhelming reception that particular movie received, plus the now constant theme of extra terrestrials in all kinds of media, indicate millions are now beginning to seek a deeper, more sustained contact with a reality, one not associated with a tangible place. This desire appears in many variations. For some, journeying to a larger, spiritual home is seen as recovering a Paradise Lost and for others, it means a New World is beginning. Whatever the case may be, the ultimate goal of their trip represents the idea of becoming wholly conscious and fully capable of using the Force of consciousness. Phoning a (spiritual) home symbolizes experiencing contentment as a full being.

We are in the honeymoon stages of the search to go Home, symptoms of which are twofold. On the outside, we absorb anything and everything we read, hear, and experience that sounds remotely supernatural or out of the ordinary. On the inside, we tentatively tweak around trying to explore the possibilities of full intimate relationship with our conscious Self. Even so, we view consciousness as a separate entity, a Force outside of ourselves. As a consequence, our exteriors are increasingly interested in angels, apparitions, and astronomy, but our interiors go experimentally in and out of meditation, prayer, and the exploration of the dark, unknown sides of ourselves. Unfortunately, it often takes a crisis to propel us into these obscure, inner sacred areas. If this polarizing, "leaking tire" approach continues, Home will continue to seem far off in the distance. Nonetheless, emergency roadside help is available from the tour operators and cartographers.

This help comes in the form of some basic ideas about what it is to have full consciousness. Besides Eastern mystics, the journals of the travel agents, Interstate travelers, and research scientists have been addressing the issue of what is consciousness. In the first chapter a basic definition of consciousness was offered — an energetic Force of constant movement; a creative, intelligent energy which aspires toward wholeness by making use of a group of Knowns that provide the means for its growth.

DEFINITIONS OF CONSCIOUSNESS
FROM A DIVERSE GROUP OF PEOPLE

Now it's time to revisit that definition introduced in the beginning. Let's look at the travel notes of the cartographers and theorists to see what they have had to say. For starters, Charles Tart talks of Frederick Spielberg, an Indian scholar, who says Sanskrit has about 20 nouns each translating into "consciousness" or "mind" in English. In sharp contrast, we Westerners use the words "mind," "brain" and "consciousness" interchangeably as if they were one and the same word. (1) This is very telling situation. Let us take a look at a variety of definitions and descriptions about consciousness from people with diverse occupations.

University of Iowa neurologist Antonio Damasio says, "Consciousness is a concept of your own self, something that you reconstruct moment by moment on the basis of the image of your own body, your own autobiography, and a sense of your intended future." (2) Seminar leader at the Esalen Institute Nick Herbert, who was a member of Berkeley's Consciousness Theory Group in the 1970s, says that consciousness must be considered as an elemental force of the universe, on the same level with such fundamental phenomena as gravity, light, mass, and electrical charge. (3)

In his characteristically entertaining and provocative style, Stuart Wilde favors an esoteric view. He describes the Force as,

> "...an energy that experiences evolution. It is massive, exhilarating, magnanimous beyond description — perhaps, you might want to call it God. It is not stagnant, as some would have you believe; it is growing, dynamic, and has an inner drive or desire to become more of itself. To achieve this, it divides itself into more and more separate parts or definitions, and it does so because it knows that, by dividing and spreading out, it will have more power and, having more power, it will grow. The Force is a part of each and everything in the physical plane. This includes our planet, the stars and galaxies, and the physical universe, as it stretches out in space, beyond our perceptions. By its very nature, the Force is immortal and never-ending and, because it is the inner light or 'livingness' within all things, we call it universal. The more life force a thing expresses the more complicated or greater is the extent of the Force within it." (4)

TWO TYPES OF CONSCIOUSNESS

In a slightly more pragmatic manner, Western mystic Dennis Holtje goes into much more detail using the same premise as Damasio. He describes consciousness as any level of awareness or state of attention in which the seeker lives each moment. He thinks consciousness can be divided into two parts: outer or **human consciousness** in which a sense of reality is created by dependence on the physical senses and inner **spiritual consciousness** which creates true reality through contact with the energies known as the *Audible Life Stream*, or what Wilde terms "the livingness of all things." Of the five energetic bodies within the physical body that make up full consciousness, Holtje says four of them are concerned with the human state of consciousness: "the *physical body* and its needs; the *astral body* (also known as the emotional body) and its desires and feelings; the *causal body* with its karma and propensity to be continually creating through thought, word and deed; and the *mental body* where thought originates, and we use reason to solve our problems." (5) The fifth human body he calls the *soul body* which involves spiritual consciousness. This description is a general picture of the luminous body or the Egg that don Juan helped Castaneda to discover and use. Like don Juan and Monroe, Holtje differentiates between attentional states, but simply generalizes them into the lower and the higher planes (bodies). Human consciousness involves awareness cultivated from a lower plane and this tends to create dependent, unclear, uncertain and uncommitted behavior more often than not, whereas spiritual consciousness using higher plane awareness combined with the senses of the soul creates the ability to know and see truth.

Like McMoneagle and Monroe, Holtje says there is often a head-on crash between human and spiritual states of consciousness when there is an opportunity to discover higher truth or to examine and test out a new recognition. Holtje explains that "spiritual consciousness is the awakening of soul, the state of awareness that lies beyond the mind that all seekers yearn to experience. Awakening of soul means that soul is totally aware of its own existence, no longer encumbered by the various viewpoints of the four lower bodies and their incessant concerns and demands." (6) Whether it be through human or spiritual consciousness, we have the power to create experiences that satisfy the desires of both the lower and higher bodies. Holtje would say that unique power is consciousness. In support of Holtje I would suggest that achieving balance of satisfying both human and spiritual consciousness is being fully conscious of "making Home" on earth. Another phase commonly used for "Making Home" is "creating heaven on earth," that of merging or fusing the higher and lower planes of existence while living on this earth.

THE CONTINUUM OF CONSCIOUSNESS: VARIOUS SETS OF AWARENESSES

Using a communication system analogy, Bob Monroe describes consciousness as sets of awarenesses along a continuum.

> "In our focused wakefulness, we as Human Minds employ that part of the consciousness spectrum limited to space-time. This is made possible by the device we identify as a physical body, with its five physical senses. This physical body permits us to express externally our mind-consciousness through physical activity and communication. When this focusing is affected for any reason, our mind begins to drift along the consciousness spectrum away from time-space perception, becoming less aware of the immediate physical world. When this happens we become conscious in another form. The fact that we often have difficulty in remembering correctly our participation in that other part of the consciousness spectrum does not negate its reality. The problem lies in perception and translation, diffused and distorted as they are by the use of current time-space systems of analysis and measurement. The spectrum of consciousness ranges, seemingly endlessly, beyond time-space into other energy systems. It also continues 'downward' through animal and plant life, possibly into the sub-atomic level. Everyday human consciousness is active commonly in only a small segment of the consciousness continuum." (7)

Monroe adds another twist by likening the process of consciousness or the ability of the radio mind to tune into various states of consciousness, first in an unconscious, student-like way, then in a willful manner. He suggests the end product of perception is directly related to the tuning ability of the perceiver. Like Gurdjieff, he adds to the definition by saying that all the elements in the universe are connected from the grossly obvious ones to the invisible elements. This was quite a statement coming from someone who was very skilled at using mechanical and physical objects in his life.

Deepak Chopra (8) carries this thought a little further by saying there is a universal connection to each other as individuals as well as to patterns of intelligence that oversee the cosmos. He suggests that our bodies are part of a universal body and our minds a component of a universal mind, sometimes known as the cosmic mind. He would agree that both human mind and body and the universal body and mind are inseparable.

WHAT GIVES CONSCIOUSNESS LIFE?

What makes consciousness tick? What is the nature of consciousness? Both Holtje and Wilde give us possibilities by saying consciousness or the Force is the same as the inner light or livingness of all things. This assumes there is a creative intelligent energy animating consciousness. It begs that old question, "What kind of force am I dealing with?" It is here that we Westerners would stand up, yell, and shout big objections. Immediately, our old beliefs would come quickly to the surface because we were taught that the Force just is, always was, and always will be. A static, rigid element. This creates the head-on crash of lower and higher consciousness perspectives that McMoneagle likes to talk about. The so-called big and little guns going at it.

A DYNAMIC RATHER THAN STATIC FORCE

The experiences of the travelers are a far cry from dealing with a motionless type of energy. On the contrary, their feedback represents the experiential, moving side of the equation, the place where Knowns are discovered, certainly not the dry, theoretical beliefs that form the body of knowledge of the field of human consciousness today. Their betwixt and between stories follow Nobel Prize recipient Ilya Prigogine's thoughts that the physical universe is more like a creative, unpredictable enterprise than a steady-state machine. (9) From Prigogine's viewpoint, it then follows that since the physical universe, being matter, is dynamic energy so then consciousness being either energy or matter is also dynamic in nature. Individual consciousness appears, as depicted in the travelers' stories, to act like a dynamic, moving breathing entity. Aha! Doesn't this sound like the waveform?

LIGHT & SOUND FORMS OF CONSCIOUSNESS

Through his experiences, Holtje has discovered that pure or full consciousness does not exist in physical form as the Materialists would suggest, but rather in the soundless sound or, as Gurdjieff suggested, *in the space between the sounds in the void*. He and many others call this space, the **Audible Life Stream** (or **Sound Current**), the place where the emanating sound of creation lives. Ayurveda defines this as the *Ether*, the mysterious thriller element with which Michelson, Morley and Albert Einstein became involved. Holtje defines this further by saying the Audible Life Stream divides itself into two components, a visible (Light) form and an audible (Sound) form. (10) The stories of many travelers would support this for they have described both auditory and light form experiences that seem to contain vastly different form and intelligence from what the brain/mind perceives with light and sound in physical reality.

DIAGNOSING DASHBOARD INDICATORS OF THE FORCE: LIGHT (MATTER) OR SOUND (ENERGY)

In early efforts of working with meditation or Focus 3 and Focus 10 states of consciousness, my clients have reported that visions frequently permeate their field of perception. Little blips of flashing lights, lightning-like flashes, streaks of rainbow-hued light beams, colorful, swirling, gaseous forms, or fleeting faces appear in these states. This is one of the energy manifestations of the Audible Life Stream which some call the River. When he named his hit tune, *River of Dreams*, Billy Joel could be referring to the Audible Life Stream of energy that animates or gives life to our very being. In the same way, the Midwestern middle school kids in the Hemi-Sync class in 1992 that I taught knew this without question. Among the 52 personal growth classes offered during a two-day seminar in the large rural middle school, this class was the second most popular and evaluated with the highest grades. Over 120 kids filled to capacity the two classes I taught. We had to turn people away. I was very surprised at how they enthusiastically jumped right into this topic of consciousness. They knew it was about what animates life, what is on the other side of physical reality.

All forms of physical matter reflect this Light manifestation including the ultraviolet and infrared light we cannot see. When spiritual consciousness begins, when the soul awakens, fascination with light emerges, fascination that seeks information and knowledge about the hidden meaning of Light manifestations that appear while working with spiritual consciousness in meditation.

PLAYING WITH MY LIGHT BODY

The following is an illustration of my experiences with Light. Some time ago I remember being very interested in a peculiar light around me after I laid down to sleep at night. With my eyes closed, I first thought it was light reflections bouncing off objects as moonlight came in the bedroom window. Looking again, it was my whole body that was the source. I played with the sheets, fluffing them up and down to see if I could stop or cover up the light, but it continued. In fact, the light around my body stayed no matter what I did. When I drifted off to sleep, the light would begin to disappear. During meditation in the darkened room, I noticed this same light coming from all of me as if I were a phosphorescent object. Just as before, I rationalized it as light coming in from under the door behind me and bouncing off the door to illuminate me, but when I shoved a towel at the door to block the light, the light remained. I noticed if I tried to mentally figure this out, the light would disappear, and if I sat and observed it while staying very relaxed and centered, I could play with it to make it stronger or weaker and to move it out and in. Then I began noticing moving light forms beyond me and tried a form of telepathic communication with them. This turned out to be a lot of fun. In meditation a few years later my playful period of using the light ended on its own, and things changed dramatically. I became worried that I had done something to erase the Light. I finally learned that this was a normal progression of events. Many a night I sat in the dark getting acquainted with this type of light. During this time, as previously described, I was inspired to drop the outer things that had formerly guided me and do what seemed right, trusting that I would be guided into the right experiences.

INTEGRATING MY LIGHT BODY:
SPIRITUALIZING MATTER

At this point I am reminded of John Denver who, at the height of his career, decided to drop all his orchestral support and backup singers for his concerts and go it alone on stage with only his guitar and his voice. Or Elton John, who dropped all his costuming, fantastic glasses, and background effects to do his concerts just as he was. Similarly, one of my key experiences was surrendering to the Force in the Adirondack woods, another was assigning much less importance about how to meditate, how to work my business, how to use I Ching etc. These "I'll do it my way!" statements indicated I was switching from being a student to being the Total Self, the waveform. My friends at the time became very protective and anxious when I made the statement one day, "If it doesn't have anything to do with energy, I won't do it!" They replied, "How will you live?" "How are you going to support yourself?" "Have you gone crazy?" Little did I know my statement was going to tremendously affect the rest of my life.

Invariably at some point in consciousness education and training workshops, clients want to figure out the meaning of the "lights" and the entrancing visions in their Focus state experiences. So I teach them how to discern the language of Spirit (Audible Life Stream) at this point. This is the *Window of Opportunity exercise*. Much appreciation goes to Sheri Klingler who originally taught it to me in 1988. (See Figure 24.)

Window of Opportunity

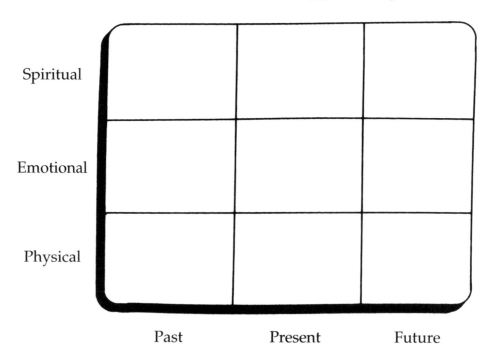

Figure 24 **Discerning the Light Language of Full Consciousness**

READING THE LIGHT GRIDS IN THE LIGHT BODY

It is possible to discern the meaning encased within the language of Light, if the window of perception being experienced is divided into observable components. Please keep in mind that all matter is composed of light, and light has its own creative intelligence so it can communicate meaning from certain placements in the energy field. Going from left to right horizontally, the first section is where **past** thoughtforms are located, the middle section is equated with **present** thoughtforms, and the far right section is for **future** thoughtforms. On the vertical axis, the bottom section is associated with **physical** thoughtforms, the middle section relates to **emotional** thoughtforms, and the top section is where **spiritual** thoughtforms tend to be.

Using this grid, one can "read" the presentation of both visual scenes (e.g., several people in a familiar scene) or mere symbols as they appear in the field of perception or the window of opportunity. For example if a red ball appears in the center section and up in the second or middle box, the information relates to a present, emotional event, factor, or issue of the person who is experiencing the red ball. Furthermore, the red color denotes that the first chakra is involved which means a certain degree of physical action or physical component is being requested. (Refer to Angeles Arrien's symbols for information about the circle which is also an element of the red ball.) Moving visuals can be interpreted using this grid as well. It would be beneficial to learn the associations and meanings of the seven primary chakras, the five universal symbols, and to learn how to trust what is discovered when the information presents itself.

Keep in mind that some visuals are made up of several symbols. For instance, the form of a chalice typically uses several circles and two triangles with a square as the stem. In Focus state experiences it is beneficial to use the "memory" encoding and the "awake and alert" encoding to record the vision while it is being received and continue experiencing whatever there is until meditation is completed. Analyzing information after the experience is ended is a wise use of energy. This exercise can be used for understanding light emanations seen in physical reality as well as "reading" other energy field emanations, that of the astral and mental bodies. Once this approach has been easily used, a fourth horizontal layer between the emotional and spiritual can be imagined. This adds the mental body input. But when first starting out, a threefold grid helps keep the learning process simple.

AS EXPERIENCES WITH THE SOUND CURRENT INCREASE, FASCINATION WITH LIGHT FORMS DECREASE

As practice with the Audible Life Stream advances, fascination with light forms diminishes. Likewise, depending on astrology, I Ching, Runes, psychic readers, and other outside sources of light information lessens. As the Sound Current becomes more audible, the lights on the dashboard of the vehicle begin to dim and the sounds beneath the hood begin to take precedence.

As the Light component of the Audible Life Stream completes its work, the Sound component takes over, not in actual physical sounds, but through soul promptings (audible soul communication). This takes the form of *inner hearing, inner seeing* (the same as Castaneda refers to), and *inner knowing* or the senses of the soul. In regard to the inner hearings, my clients have reported all kinds of hearings — noises such as bees buzzing, tinkling bells, rushing and swishing water, harps and heavenly music not heard on this plane — all sounds that others do not physically hear. Conceivably, the tones heard by certain people living in the area of Taos, New Mexico are a manifestation of the Sound component of the Audible Life Stream.

Holtje says, "All the outer worlds of God, as well as all the inner planes of experience, reverberate continually with the Divine Melody…Almost all great religious texts and sacred writings refer to the audibility of spirit as it flows from the Godhead to give life and consciousness to the creation." (11) But do we listen for our own Divine Sound(s) communicating songs of home? In Chapter 6 Tania and Lois described their experience with the signs of the Sound Current in their lives. Here is TMI Program Trainer Franceen King again, describing her own unique growing partnership with the Sound energies of the Audible Life Stream. This was a post on the Voyager Mail List on the Internet.

SUBJECT: SOUNDS

As a "concerned citizen," or maybe just a curious white woman, I spent 2+ hours on Monday watching and listening to Louis Farrakhan's talk at the Million Man March. Somewhat to my surprise, I experienced it as both inspired and inspiring, despite what most of the news reports have said. Much of the talk was about the need for black men to go within and reconnect with the One God who is their true source of power…and to reconcile their relationship with God.

I was particularly interested in a portion in which he talked about the various meanings of the word "atonement." Most of us know, for example, that atonement means "at-one-ment." Farrakhan went letter by letter through the word and through various combinations of the letters to give his interpretations of meaning. During one part he talked about the "A tone." To summarize, he said that "A" is the first letter and the symbol for one or oneness. The A tone in music is 440 cycles per second. When you go within and hear the "A tone" it is an indicator that you are connecting with the One.

I normally hear many sounds within. Most of the time they are in the background, although I am aware that they are always there. Sometimes they are very loud, e.g., in various altered states, OOBE's etc. There is a background of what I call "fizzy, crystal chimes" — fizzy because by focusing on them I can easily begin to feel the effervescent sensations which we usually call tingling or vibrations. Within this background are discrete tones — sometimes individual tones, sometimes chords.

Yesterday, after doing some breathing exercises, I was very much aware of the sounds which were very loud. There was one clear tone which was very pronounced. Remembering what Farrakhan said in his talk, I decided to go to the piano to see what note it was. (Although this idea has occurred to me in the past, I've never acted upon it, I'm not a musician.) Sure enough, it was the A tone. I thought this was interesting.

Franceen King

The A tone is the tone of the crown chakra.

CONSCIOUSNESS AS BOTH MATTER & ENERGY

Coming in as both Light and Sound manifestations, the Audible Life Stream differentiates itself into **matter or energy**, that is, either particle or waveform depending on the attending skills of the driver traveling down the Interstate. This is the remembering (implicate/infolding) and forgetting (explicate/enfolding) movement of energy previously mentioned. Energy pulsates or breathes in and out on both the micro- and macro-levels as we understand it in our physical plane of existence. We have forgotten our better half, the non-physical or waveform part of ourselves and chosen to remember only the physical or matter component of ourselves. Being a particle (matter) translates into using human consciousness to experience the physical reality of Me. Being the waveform (energy) translates into using spiritual consciousness to experience the I AM aspect of the River, the Audible Life Stream. (See Figure 25.) In actuality, the Me and I AM are one and the same waveform, but on a planet that experiences polarity, a dual aspect of the Sound Current appears to pulsates in and out of form. When the waveform and particle become one, unified balance or pure coherence occurs. Don Juan would call this "third attention" also known as the state of transcendence. Mini-moments of this occur naturally in our daily lives. We call them *coincidences* or synchronistic moments.

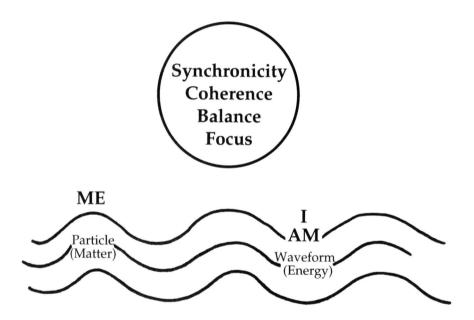

Figure 25 Experiencing Balance Between Energy & Matter
on the Interstate

THE ILLUSION OF SPACE

Traveling the cities along the Interstate of Consciousness using both human and spiritual consciousness, the driver can do some journeying into all kinds of cities of matter, of timelessness, of spacelessness, and beyond the time-space continuum. As traveling days increase, it becomes apparent that there are more cities of spacelessness and beyond as opposed to those of matter. To those of us who are students of Sound, we have noticed that there is illusion lurking in the guise of preoccupation with the matter side of life these days. Why has the Force demonstrated this pattern? Why so much space for void possibilities? In the micro-matter of things, why, in the last 150,000 years, has the brain been rearranging its matter to provide space for more personal processing? Why is there more room for energy than matter in consciousness?

Perhaps the answer may come from the lessons we have cultivated from this journey. Consider Joseph Chilton Pearce's remarks; "Truly big energy, the evidence from quantum mechanics suggested, comes not from matter at all, but from the empty spaces between the particles of matter — within the spaces of an atom, or in spaces without atoms, quantum physicists said, lie far larger fields of energy. The most comes not from the least, but from nothing at all." (12) Since it seems apparent that places of nothingness are the places to be in the future, Roddenberry was right, space is the final frontier!

Repeatedly, Monroe, Gurdjieff, Tart, Wilde, Holtje, the ancient elders of indigenous peoples, the masterful Yogis, and the Ayurvedic rishis all have said that consciousness is able to divide itself into more and more separate parts in order to actualize more power. For now, the power place on earth is *in* the space of things:

> in the aftermath of a terrorist bombing,
> right after a baby is born,
> after downsizing has occurred,
> in the silence after a fight,
> in the void in meditation,
> in the pause that refreshes,
> after inhaling and exhaling,
> after toning,
> after sexual orgasm,
> following a tornado or an earthquake, and
> waiting for an answer.

As a corollary, consciousness map makers have consistently said there are three states of consciousness (waking, dreaming, deep sleep) meeting the need to satisfy the goal of experiencing the lower plane of existence. In various ways, they all have identified the fourth state of consciousness or *the silent witness state or the observer state.* This is the state of Not Knowing described by many travelers and travel agents as the seat of the Total Self, the place the place of full consciousness. For as fast as Not Knowing occurs (while in balance), Knowing occurs instantly. Throughout this manual, Not Knowing was described as:

> ...the fifth dimensional neighborhood,
> ...the skill of knowing using the Total Self (Monroe),
> ...as the skill of seeing (Castaneda),
> ...the art of self-remembering (Gurdjieff),
> ...mastery of merging in the journey of the soul and
> ...HOME.

When at home, the Total Self is a single point of consciousness, not divided, content in itself, having no likes and dislikes, enjoying and making the most of the present, or fully encased moment and feeling totally at home.

Consciousness as either matter or energy communicates creative intelligence. In order to appreciate how matter or energy communicates information, it is important to understand the context in which information is received and how this environment is formed.

INTERPRETING TYPES OF ENERGY SIGNATURES ON THE DASHBOARD

There are three kinds of energy environments that appear during travel experiences, each of which can be present within a single non-physical event. William Buhlman explains these habitats as consensus, nonconsensus, and natural environments. (13)

The **signature of a consensus reality** leaves the impression of a firmly molded, solid and stable environment intact because it was developed and is maintained by the thoughts of a group of individuals. Thoughts, no matter how focused, will not affect this environment, but will affect the personal energy field of the traveler. For example, thoughts of flying will enable us to fly, but will not change the consensus habitat. The Interstate cities having exits closest to the beginning of non-physical reality will have consensus reality features that closely resemble earth-like structures such as Focus 3 and 10. Buhlman says, "This energy environment is so physical in appearance that most people believe they are observing the physical world. In reality, they are observing the first inner dimension of the universe. Since this dimension is closest in frequency to matter, it is often seen and experienced during out-of-body experiences." (14)

The **nonconsensus signature of a reality** is like a chameleon, it has unstable features and frequently changing scenes. Because this locale is not firmly shaped by a group thoughtform, it contains random, incoherent, form-containing energy which can be shaped at will. Most dream experiences contain this signature where one scene shifts into another scene. Changing scenarios are the key feature of this environment. They restructure according to the conscious and unconscious intentions present which shows how singularly important it is to learn how to focus, control, and direct thought. Within this habitat, a single, highly coherent thought will remold the situation in seconds. Did you notice that the nonconsensus reality was the one most frequently described by the travelers in Chapter 6? It is the one most commonly experienced in non-physical reality and also the one we will be become most familiar with in the next decade in physical reality. Buckle up and hang on!

The **signature of a natural energy environment** is one where no definite form or shape exists. The cities of Focus 12 and beyond more often than not, exhibit this signature where the landscape seems to have a gaseous, blobby, smeary, floating quality and certain areas contain empty, spaceless voids having white, grey, silver or golden clouds of energy that constantly change. Because this environment is very responsive to intention, it can be a playground for the traveler to study the effect of various degrees of focused intent with instant feedback. The attentional skill of Will is easily learned in this environment due to its raw energy quality.

Personally speaking, when I identify what kind of environment I have entered by spending a few moments to observe and interact with the energy, I gain a sense of security and solidness about where I am, what the environment is capable of returning to me, and what kind of intention I may use to get a response. I highly recommend learning how to interpret the signatures so that travel in non-ordinary reality becomes easy and satisfying.

SYNCHRONIZING THE GEARS: SHIFTING BETWEEN WAVE & PARTICLE

Just as Bob Monroe fell into a dark cave and had to find his way back into the light of day using non-ordinary skills, I strapped my old, beat up roller skates onto my mercurial feet and pushed myself into spinning over and over, learning how to find my way through the whirling air into a larger perceptual field. He and I learned how to shift back and forth between satisfying lower and higher body desires until we achieved balance. Spinning for me was my own pivotal teaching tool, my creative intelligence taking me to the edge of a new frontier and giving my Me and I AM the opportunity to learn how to hang in space without physical support, with only my soul existence in hand. I had to develop my own Know-How to leave the comfort of being physical matter to become the waveform in order to create balance. Frankly, I'm still learning that "hang in there" approach. I suppose that's why I moved to the Colorado Rockies to learn to create balance while "getting out there" on the mountaintops. My agenda was to learn how to go from matter to energy or from particle to waveform of energy and back again. Spinning was the avenue I used to transport myself.

SPINNING, A CEV VEHICLE THAT MANY ARE DRIVING

It is entirely possible that the spinning phenomena is impacting the world at large in a major way. Witness the growing fascination in amusement parks internationally for spinning entertainment. The roller coaster arms race is an incredible growth industry on its own, packing millions of crazed coaster junkies into its thrill-a-second vehicles and sending them off screaming into the bright skies, only to return to earth talking endlessly about how fast and furious they flew on the rails. Using state-of-the-art electromagnetic catapults to attain 100 mph, the *Superman: The Escape* coaster made its debut in May, 1996, at Six Flags Magic Mountain in Los Angeles, CA. It was designed to race along a flat stretch of track, reach top speed in a mere seven seconds, then it curves 415 feet straight up, giving riders a sense of weightlessness for 6 1/2 seconds before plunging backward to the starting gate. Breaking the barrier of 100 mph on a rollercoaster is a dramatic statement about the gigantic urge to shift not only external but internal group consciousness from mundane to total pleasure and flying freedom.

SPINNING & FLYING DREAMS

Listen to Fred who, in a VML post, talks about how he experiences spinning. His memory of the vividness of these kinds of dreams demonstrates how close spinning consciousness is to the surface of physical reality. Since many of us have flying dreams, could this be evidence of the collective consciousness expressing itself toward some end — the urge for total freedom and/or having the ability to fly — into wholeness?

SUBJECT: FLYING DREAMS

Thought I'd like to share this with you. When I was in my early teens I had these dreams in which I could fly, or more accurately "ride the air currents." These dreams were always fun, and very realistic in the feelings and sensations I felt while flying; things like the wind on my face, the air currents on my palms when I cupped my hands into the wind to gain height, the heat of the sun on my back, the sense of height while flying, etc. And when I woke it was always sad to know that it was only a dream. But it was always so real that during the dream it felt as if there could be no other world except the one in which I was flying. One of my favourite ways of achieving "lift-off" was to take out my can of "flying spray," spray some on my back, take a running leap, fall into the wind, and soar. About ten years ago these dreams stopped. Lately they started up again.

Now I find that my dreams are becoming more and more realistic. While interacting with people in my dreams it's like I'm doing so in real life. At that time to me it is real life. And when I wake up the images are still crystal clear. There were even a few nights that I did not want to dream because of the realism of my dreams and knowing that it will all be gone when I wake up. In one dream I "met" somebody that I knew who I have forgotten in this everyday life, but I had to let go because at this moment she is not part of this reality

My flying dreams are back. I've had several over the last few weeks. It always feels so strange to be able to feel the wind and direct my flight by pushing on the air, or guide the wind in such a way that I go in the direction I want to. Flight paths are true and stable, and the feelings associated with flying are getting more and more intense.

Last night's flying dream was awesome! I was flying along the coast (I'm close to the sea) enjoying the freedom of flight. I wasn't paying much attention to the rocks below me. All of a sudden a huge wave slammed into some rocks directly below me sending up an incredible amount of spray and water, shocking me with its icy chill, leaving me breathless. A wave of air slammed into me, and I was flung out of control high into the air. This really surprised me with its intensity and the reality of the sensations I was feeling. If I could package those few instants and share it with you it would be the best rollercoaster ride you'd ever experience. After flying a bit more, the dream ended. And the reality that I was stuck in bed unable to fly slammed home.

Before I die one day I want to fly like that…for real. :~)

Fred

The beat of spinning goes on and on. In general, the public possesses an increasing fascination with the weather and its swirling patterns whether it be the changing jet stream, inland tornado forecasting, water spouts in the Great Lakes and the oceans, or the sport of tracking tornadoes and hurricanes. The hugely successful box office movie hits, *Backdraft* and *Twister* are testimony to the viewing audiences' sensational thirst for revolution.

PERSONAL CYBERNETIC FORMS OF SPINNING

Other slightly less popular spinning forms exist in our culture; e.g. break dancing, virtual reality simulators, airplane take offs and descents, air surfing, some video game formats, ice skating, snow boarding and over-indulging in alcohol and recreational drugs. Consider, the build-up of power on a coaster ride is easily equivalent to the power build-up experienced going from the wave field of Focus 3 to Focus 10 and lifting off into the wave fields of other consciousness realms. Likewise, the power build-up experienced in an airplane getting ready to take off and break through the clouds is easily the equivalent to the Preparatory Process taught to phase into Focus 10, the launching pad for all the other Focus state experiences. Monroe knew what he was capturing as he inserted the experience of spinning into every Hemi-Sync experience. He knew how important this was because he had hands-on experience with spinning in both physical and non-physical realities. The potential power of revolution, of the Force of consciousness, is housed in the energy field of an individual just waiting to be tapped. As previously mentioned, this is the spirit or fire of the individual, the relative horsepower which propels one forward. Spinning literally engages the potential to be thrust forward. Likewise, Bob Monroe helped us develop the clutch to engage the Force at will.

HOW SPINNING INFLUENCES THE ENERGY FIELD

Engaging the clutch engages the gears in the energy field. In sacred geometry terms, the two tetrahedron-encased energy fields, collectively known as the MerKaBa, make up the energy body. The energy body exhibits two different phases, one being a static form, the other a dynamic form. When sitting, the field remains in a static position; when riding a rollercoaster or merry-go-round, the fields become activated and begin to spin! At certain ratios and speeds, the fields start to flatten, creating a saucer-like form. The two tetrahedrons then merge, neutralizing one another, and create a united form. This third form contains the potential for full or unified consciousness. Perhaps the rollercoaster mania has, as its roots, the mystical urge to become the dynamic form of the MerKaBa. (15)

Looking at that clutching action a littler further, the potential power of the waveform is encased in a field of energy, a continuum of energy having no localization, no place. Doesn't this sound similar to the cartographers' comments on full consciousness? On the other hand, the particle (the physical body) is the physical manifestation of energy, a very localized expression of the non-local field. The wave field does not have physical form and does not exist as a measurable time-space event. Physicists say that the wave field underlies all particles of energy. They say the more compact the wave itself, the closer together its peaks and valleys, the greater the power inherent within that wave spectrum. This implies in everyday life if there is a repetitive action with frequent balancing of lower (human consciousness) and higher (spiritual consciousness) planes of existence, then there is a lot of potential power building within that continuum. (16)

THE ROLE OF THE ETHERIC BODY: THE BATTERY UNDER THE HOOD

The etheric body, sometimes known as the light body or the luminous body, initially appears to the neophyte traveler as a one to two inch halo of yellow-white energy surrounding and passing through the physical body. It can be perceived by the physical eyes using a soft focus as if pretending to see from the back of the head. This is especially observable in highly emotionally charged situations having either a black or a white background. The etheric body is a wave field of energy composed of infinite threads stepping down or transducing energy from the Primary Source to the physical body and providing a medium for the exchange and transmission of energies back and forth between the physical body and the Primary Source. It determines and conditions the physical body and keeps its energy coherent. (17) When disease sets in the physical body, energy in the etheric body becomes incoherent or out of balance. The threads of energy in the human etheric body are connected to all aspects of manifested life in every kingdom in nature through the etheric bodies of these creations. Lines of light pass energy from form to form in constant exchange. The objective of all these connections is to promote the unfoldment of consciousness in all elements. (18)

SCIENTISTS RESEARCH THE ETHERIC LAYER
OF THE LIGHT BODY

Scientists for the last ten years have been investigating in earnest the Light component of the Audible Life Stream. Polish physicist Janusz Slawinski says, "Although we cannot yet measure and reproduce these fields, the electromagnetic nature of consciousness cannot be discounted. Out-of-body experiences may be the result of a temporary separation of the 'electromagnetic consciousness' from the physical body. Could this field, which contains energy, internal structure and information, be a supreme factor in the organization of life? Light is more basic than time and space." (19) Slawinski believes that the light waves hold a tremendous amount of information.

His conclusions came as a result of studying the **deathflash** of a dying person, an emission of light from the top of the head at the time of death, its intensity and duration reflecting the rate of dying. Throughout life, all living organisms emit low intensity light (photons) which can be measured either as particles, by "photon counting" or as electromagnetic waves. During the death process all organisms emit a radiation that is 10 to 1,000 times stronger than that emitted under everyday conditions. West German scientist and chemist Fritz-Albert Popp has been studying the light emitted by cells of living things and found radiation in the range of infrared and ultraviolet light. After a series of tests, Popp concluded that, "DNA is the essential source of the photon emissions from biological systems." (20) The implication follows that DNA has consciousness, and if this is so, then DNA is linked in some fashion to the etheric body. When death occurs, the etheric body is the first to leave and within its folds, consciousness returns to the Primary Source to begin another unfolding of life.

EXPERIENCES AT THE DEATHBED OF THE DEATHFLASH

In my nursing career I have witnessed several death bed experiences involving both sudden deaths in emergency room settings and lingering passings. Soon after graduation from nursing school, I went to work in a new, well-equipped hospital in California just over the border from Tijuana, Mexico. One day I had to fill in for a emergency room staff member who had gotten sick. An American tourist brought in by American consulate personnel was assigned to me for care. I followed protocol for serious heart problems, gave him pain medication and awaited a visit with the cardiac attending physician. Suddenly he turned blue, clutched his chest and stopped breathing. I started manual CPR on him. Very shortly the cardiac physician arrived and pronounced the man dead due to a massive heart attack blowing out the posterior muscle wall of his heart.

A huge knot of doubt arose in my heart. I had a very hard time believing this man had died because every time I pushed on his chest he would turn pink. I was told to stop my efforts and to cover him up with a sheet and move on to another patient. The cardiologist explained that when I was pushing on his chest I was circulating what blood remained in the upper aortic system and this was why he turned pink. But something else nagged at me, and I didn't know why.

Begrudgingly, I returned to the other patients. Several times I went back over to him, picked up the sheet off his face to check to see if he was breathing and found he wasn't. Over and over something kept drawing me back to him to place my hands on his chest and to stay with him. My supervisor sternly told me to leave him alone and assist with casting a fractured bone which I eventually did. That night I dreamed that I was still there holding my hands on his chest for some unknown purpose. Intuitively I knew that the etheric body of this man was still present keeping the consciousness physically connected to the body for some time after his physical death. I didn't know that consciously at the time, I know that now. I hadn't developed the abilities I have now in regard to seeing the light body in action. But I knew something was not right in letting this man die in this manner under these circumstances.

Perhaps families and funeral home directors would consider a longer death process similar to what some indigenous cultures carry out to allow for the etheric body to complete its journey.

When I was a student nurse, I had an especially close relationship in the hospital with a older gentleman who had no friends. What little family he had also abandoned him. I cared for him at intervals throughout a year of repeated hospitalizations as his cancer slowly progressed. He sank into a coma and stayed in this state for weeks. Nonetheless, I would talk to him and continue to do the special routines that he came to love. One morning, despite the fact I wasn't scheduled to work until evening, I had an urge to go up to visit him. He was surrounded by machines and several staff members because his vital signs indicated he was in the stages of dying. I took his small, fragile hand into mine, whispered goodbye and wished him happiness. I was amazed that Russell squeezed my hand and moved his lips to form words I didn't consciously hear. Then he passed over. I turned to leave the room and had an urge to look back once more. What I saw was astounding. A blinding, very bright, momentary light ripped from the room. At that time I thought I was hallucinating, but what I saw was the deathflash, the sign that the etheric body was leaving.

If the etheric body is the container for consciousness and the physical body, it becomes important to establish a direct link with the wisdom of both so that when there is unbalance or encrustation building up, a radiator flow test can be run to determine what will be necessary to reestablish energy flow. This can be done by learning how to access and use the wisdom of the Force present in the Focus States, merely by asking questions and receiving answers.

SHIFTING GEARS FROM LOCAL
TO NON-LOCAL PERSPECTIVE

We all experienced ourselves as the Force in full flamboyant color when, by means of the spaceship Challenger, we blasted out into outer space to see pristine, mind-boggling pictures of our cobalt blue planet from outer space. This gigantic leap into the unknown witnessing the higher plane forced us to all shift from a primitive, terrestrial, self-centered perspective ("We rule the planet!") to a non-local, selfless, universal perspective ("Who goes there?") For generations we were priming ourselves for this moment, sheltering a modicum of humility somewhere deep inside, as we grew our bloated egos to gigantic proportions on the outside. But deep inside a tiny tendril of humility kept a warm place open for the next interval to occur much like the Wall Street Stock Exchange undergoes corrections in a bear market. Just as silently, our consciousness abilities had quietly sneaked along on two attending skills (talking and reason), as if we had to be deliberately unconsciousness in order to "get it" during the next burst of significant self-remembering or self-correction.

In the silence of the noisy world, we now have begun to develop the capacity to participate *deliberately* in the creative mindstream we call Life. Looking back on the "good ole days," this baby-stepping process without the lost skills seemed endless and ever so subtle until one day an interval leap suddenly broke the veil of agreed-upon earth reality, and all things changed immensely. Now, as we go merrily along, at the most unexpected times, the best of what we would call the worst of life options happens. This is the Force at its most perfect macro point beautifully demonstrating the Law of Octaves hard at work in our universe.

FROM THE SPORT TO THE PROCESS OF GIFT-GIVING

Here is an illustration of this paradigm shift in the large collective environment. In the Course of Miracles there is the idea that one cannot give what one does not already have. Just two decades ago, in the former octave before we saw ourselves from outer space, there was a deeply held belief that when giving gifts, the giver was the loser. People were either winners or losers in the giving game. In this game, the giver usually selects and gives away the gift he or she wants. As a result, a deep loss is felt in the wallet and/or in the mind by judging if the gift was the right gift. Until recently "Give until it hurts" was a favorite password of charitable organizations looking for a donation.

Today, the sport of gift-giving is starting to change. It is now becoming a process of gift-giving from the heart. People are more careful of giving because they know there are feelings involved, whether it be feelings for themselves or for others. There is a growing recognition that the "gift of giving keeps on giving," that is, by dividing up what is owned and giving it away, there is a continual feeling of giving through memories, through the spirit of the gift, and through the merging of energy between the giver and the receiver that the gift represents. This is similar to the growing idea that consciousness divides itself in order to gain more identity and power.

In the former selfish-forgetting phase, we recognized only one part of the threefold equation, that of being the giver. Rarely did we focus on the receiver unless it was to measure his or her reaction to see if our role as giver was enhanced. In the new octave, not only are we giving something of ourselves, but realizing it is the combination of the giver and receiver which is so powerful. This produces the embodiment of a third force exemplified by the binaural beat, the state of balance (the Tao), the peak experience, the "aha!" insight, the orgasmic moment and the mysterious void. These are all experiential third force manifestations.

The act of giving was formerly a purely mechanical, dutiful act, and it is now becoming a purposeful joining of two people to creatively create a power larger than themselves as individuals. The old octave local existence was based on consciousness focused on itself to gain identity separate from the Primary Source. The new, non-local existence converts the selfishness to selflessness incorporating a universal perspective, a perspective that we are now becoming citizens of the cosmos with all the accompanying responsibilities and pleasures.

MAKING HOME IN A NON-LOCAL UNIVERSE

Here is another case in point on a personal level. My freewheeling, spinning days in the Adirondack mountains tweaked my old forgotten wisdom and knowledge about the magnitude of my non-local abilities. In the woods, I had learned to pace myself according to Mother Nature's rhythms and to honor her sense of order. Thank goodness I had the luxury of experimenting with the synchronicities of a Walden Pond environment and like-minded people without the stimulus of TV, radio, cars, newspapers, shopping malls, and a responsible job. Before coming to the woods, I acquired a certain sense of humility, an openness to again wonder and be curious without analyzing things to death. This set the scene for something that occurred one day in 1991 while at a TMI residential program.

EXPERIENCING THE KNOWN,
I AM NOT ALONE

In the middle of our training week, we were shown a movie in the conference room entitled, *The Powers of Ten*. We weren't told the purpose of the film other than some simple statement about exploring the possibilities that exist in this Universe. This film suggests the feasibility of making a leap from a tiny earth perspective to a larger universal perspective. It achieves this by using the format of clicking off seconds and minutes traveling at the speed of light out into space. It begins with a scene of a couple enjoying a picnic somewhere on Lake Michigan in the United States. At first the overhead camera focuses close-in on their delight and then begins to move farther and farther away from them, all the while time is ticking off in a small box in the upper right hand quadrant of each movie frame. The couple quickly become a tiny speck and disappears. The outline of the United States through clouds becomes visible, then continental boundaries appear which melt into the larger planetary globe draped in brilliant, dark blue with smears of white. Traveling further out, other planets reveal themselves. Going beyond, into space, nothingness pervades. As traveling continues through the nothingness, there appears a few more planets and asteroids clustered together, then there is nothingness. The clock stops, the end of time, the end of space as we know it. Quickly the camera retraces its motion backward and the pattern of regular form spaced among irregular intervals makes itself even more obvious. The movie ends.

In silence we are instructed to go back to our CHEC units and wait for instructions. After a few minutes of soothing music over the headphones, Bob gives us instructions to follow his coaching to go into Focus 15. While there he asks us to expand our awareness beyond earth and then to look back at the earth, the sun and the surrounding planets. He calls our attention to the clustering pattern effect. After a lull, he asks us to again travel outward by going into the blackness, to see other stars, planets and note their formation. What I saw were three shimmering, yellow-white planets grouped in a horizontal plane, two as if they were stars, the third much larger. Bob then suggests we embrace these planets using whatever means possible and then listen for a message. After I expressed appreciation to the three planets before me, I felt a tremendous welling surge of familiarity. Then I heard, "Welcome home, Patricia, we are your creation, welcome home!" I asked where I was and I was told "Sirius, the Dogon group." This made no sense at all, I had never heard the word Sirius; in fact, I heard these words as, "Serious, the dog-gone group!"

I came back from that experience in an overwhelming state of confusion with a sense of pressure building inside me. I remember walking outside to clear the globs of clouds in my head, asking myself, "What in the heck was that all about?" The words had no meaning. I let myself begin to cry and let go of the tremendous tension I was feeling inside. As I did this a tiny sparrow jumped out onto the path and firmly planted its feet deep into the gravely dust. As I approached, the bird didn't flinch but stayed nailed to the spot where it had landed. What was the bird trying to tell me?

In the debriefing session with the other participants, I related my experience and as I did, in a snap, I became aware of the implications of what had just happened. As I talked about being able to move my consciousness "out that far" or "expand that much" and still communicate very well, it dawned on me I had a natural ability to leap that far while staying who I was. Finally I had the answer to my question, "If I let go will I lose me?" That was the answer to my little world question, but the experience triggered another set of questions, the flip side. To the other voyagers I wondered out loud about how a planet could communicate, and why was it that I received this message from this group of planets. Furthermore, how was I their creator and how was I connected to these particular planets?

As quickly as I asked these questions, a knowingness in the form of a Rote came over me having to do with the all-at-once aspect of this experience, that is, being limited in a human body, but also at the same time being a spirit which is able to quickly expand, by intention, to that place of deeply felt connection and safety. My answer came in the form of the infinity symbol (a figure eight) which popped into my perception. I knew this connected immediately with the clustering pattern I experienced traveling. At that time I knew nothing of the Law of the Octaves and how it demonstrates the path of energy. It would be four more years before that conscious knowledge and experience would have physical and practical meaning for me.

Soon after I returned to Cleveland, in the newspapers there was a raging debate going on about the Gaia Theory started in the late 1960s by a British scientist, James Lovelock. This, coincidentally, came to the forefront, not before I went, but after I returned from training at TMI. Lovelock, later joined by Lynn Margulis, expressed the idea that Earth was a living organism having a complex but mutually beneficial relationship with all elements inhabiting the planet, a symbiotic relationship. It didn't take much to apply this theory to the questions I had about my Focus 15 experience because the Dogon group sure acted like they had sentient consciousness.

CHANGING FROM A CONSUMER TO A PARTNER

Before having this experience, I was merely a mute bystander consuming Gaia's resources, and her life's blood and standing aside from the natural order and rhythm of her energy and my own life. Frankly, I had been treating the planet like it was an inanimate object to be used. After the experience, I took a much different approach, one that was more respectful and curious. I found myself gradually moving into a proactive partnership with Gaia by participating with others in full and new moon ceremonies, moving toward more sustainability in my life, trying to take full advantage of her hibernation, spring reactivation, growth and harvesting cycles throughout the year, and through conscious use and recycling of her resources. The *Elation Universe* learning experience at TMI was a life-changing event for me. I was able to re-establish bonds with energies that felt very familiar and supportive, energies of a non-local nature and in so doing, became more solidly connected to my present reality.

As I gained conscious experience and Knowns for a broader perspective, I became empowered to contribute my sense of balance to others and to the whole planet. The same holds true for all of us. Making ourselves at home in a non-local atmosphere will serve to add solidity to the ever-increasing sense of fluidity that we are feeling in these days of change.

SYNOPSIS OF THE DRIVER INSTRUCTION MANUAL ON CONSCIOUSNESS

By experiential reporting and discussion from the cartographers and Interstate travelers, what we have heard described throughout this manual is that full consciousness is an energy having two components, a human expression and a spiritual expression. Popular press and research has emphasized the human component while downplaying or out right denying that the spiritual element exists, but the stories of thousands of travelers using Hemi-Sync technology offer evidence to the contrary. Since these two components are present all the time, consciousness then can locate itself in two environments: the local selfish perspective and the non-local universal perspective. This can be an either/or situation or an all-at-once situation where consciousness selects to be in either one or the other or both environments at once. In addition, these two components give evidence that possibly demonstrates two places where the animation or life aspect of consciousness displays itself, one being the DNA molecule, the other, the etheric body. This is the ability of consciousness to be both matter and energy or wave and particle.

It is probable from experiential evidence that the process of human consciousness involves the use of the physical reality as hardware and the mind as software. A critical element to understanding the breadth of consciousness is the overriding use of the five human senses as the main measuring system linking the mind and the body. The evidence suggests this constructs a minor portion of the picture of reality upon which all behavior is based.

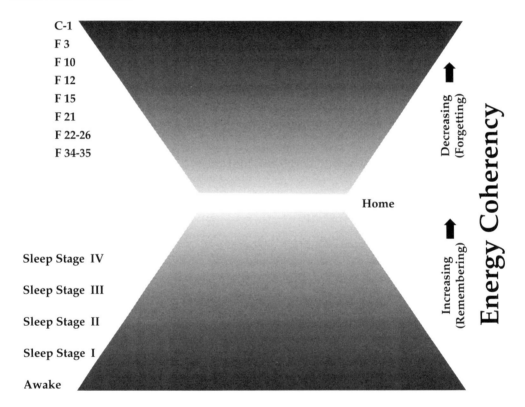

Figure 26 Unfolding & Enfolding of Energy:
A Beginning Roadmap of the Interstate

The process of spiritual consciousness is not so distinct, nor limited in nature. What Holtje suggests about the process of spiritual consciousness seems consistent with the experiential input from the travelers and my own experience. Using his model, it seems possible to say spiritual consciousness is a process whereby individuals make use of various degrees of coherency found within a continuum of light in deep mystical moments to literally tune into the soundless arm coming from the Primary Source. As this progresses, consciousness then manifests into Light, then Sound, the first, a projection of the four lower human energy bodies, the latter, demonstrations of the spiritual body.

The evidence presented here points to a coherent, energetic mind-body connection being the link between human and spiritual consciousness. This learning environment empowers the individual to consciously choose the type of consciousness desired which then creates specific pictures of reality. If this is so, it will become increasingly important to develop education and training methods that emphasize how to recognize and use energy as well as how to assess, sustain and control various coherent fields of energy at will. (See Figure 26.)

By listening to the traveler stories, more has been discovered related to the nature of the connecting link, the bridge between the cities and neighborhoods to the near and far reaches of consciousness. This bridge, while seeming to move with the wind, has a majestic strength that propels the traveler through its tubular surroundings toward more or less degrees of coherency producing a pulsation waveform pattern.

The gradual stepping down of energy creates what we know as the waking state whereas increasing coherency of the waveform seems to produce the non-waking state. As the energy becomes more coherent, there is movement within to a non-local universal experience. In various ways, the map makers have illustrated this movement of the waveform, some more picturesque than others. In particular, Monroe was able to tap into the nature and amplitude of the waveform and in so doing, began to identify the traveling process in the non-ordinary realities on the Interstate of Consciousness.

Several cartographers have also pointed out that consciousness displays itself as a spectrum of energy in various forms from the smallest, most invisible, to the most obviously physical element. These elements are all connected by means of the energy threads in the etheric body of each person. Information passes between all elements as the travelers described whether it be the patient and anesthesia or the snail and the power walker.

THE CYCLIC PROCESS OF GATHERING KNOWNS

The travelers also talked about shifting their consciousness at will from concrete to highly abstract states by using various attentional skills to tune into either the human component or the spiritual component of his or her consciousness. *Cycling back and forth between human and spiritual states to gather Knowns eventually helps to create the state of full consciousness.* Most likely Michael Talbot would say the former represents explicate order and the latter, implicate order. Literally cycling back and forth between these two states gives the appearance of a pulsation-like quality of consciousness or the unfoldment, then enfoldment of elements. This is the natural rhythmic order of the universe. David Bohm puts it well,

> "Every action starts from an intention in the implicate order. The imagination is already the creation of the form; it already has the intention and the germs of all the movements needed to carry it out. And it affects the body and so on, so that as creation takes place in that way from the subtler levels of the implicate order, it goes through them until it manifests in the explicate." (21)

The gradual merging or fusion of both of these components, the human and the spiritual, brings about the Known of being at Home or in full consciousness. Interestingly enough, it took a large group of travelers to discover this greater awareness about consciousness. Perhaps this group effort shows the innate, creative intelligent order of the Force at work in the individual and the collective when inspired to search for wholeness.

As a summary, the findings of this exploration on the Interstate indicate that consciousness is highly likely to contain the following element:

CONSCIOUSNESS

- may be viewed as a creative intelligent force (the spirit of the driver behind the wheel).
- as a force, it displays itself on the dashboard of the vehicle with varying levels of speeds or sets of awareness.
- has two kinds of patterns, the wave form or particle form.
- can be a changing, growing particle (the physical body driving the car) and a spectrum of energy (the power behind the wheel).
- has locality (a sense of place and individuality) when it is a particle.
- has non-locality (a sense of selflessness and wholeness) when it is energy.
- demonstrates dynamic rather than static movement (drives according to its life's experiences, not on a straight and narrow path).
- this movement has a pulsating nature which has chaotic intervals.
- the chaotic intervals are places of high growth opportunities.

- this movement is propelled or charged by experiential learning (thus, a high performance and high compression engine is required).
- is a force operating primarily through the inner sense of knowing (seeing rather than understanding).
- has two components, a human expression and a spiritual expression; human consciousness involves the lower plane of existence inclusive of the physical, mental and emotional issues of life; spiritual consciousness involves the original core meanings of life.
- requires a coherent, balanced energetic body-mind connection in order to be fully accessed and used.
- when this balanced connection is made, an experience resembling the state of heaven on earth or "making home" on earth comes forth.
- when consciousness combines its two aspects, human and spiritual consciousness, it becomes fully conscious.

Now, onto the last stop on our adventure by looking into the next frontier of learning how to achieve full consciousness. Because the travelers have already planted their seeds and shared their cultivating approaches, the rest of us have the possibility of harvesting the fields of expanded realities. This is the new territory that lies ahead, rich with possibilities for humankind.

THE CIRCLE OF LOVE

Consciousness, a spectrum of awareness
Befitting a king, a crystal, and a star.
Interconnecting a cosmos of energies and matter
Clothing death, life, and car.
Weaving etheric, physical, sound, and light
All reflecting eternal love afar.

DISCOVERING THE BEAUTY OF
OURSELVES & OUR COSMOS

*"A universal love is not only psychologically possible,
it is the only complete and final way in which we are able to love."*

Pierre Teilhard de Chardin, *The Phenomenon of Man*

ROUTE 10

FULL OR UNIFIED CONSCIOUSNESS:
THE IDEA OF BEING POWERFUL WITHIN

The individual's search for completeness, for full consciousness, has arrived with bells on. This desire was once satisfied, albeit momentarily, in marriages, having children, through career achievements, or taking cruises around the world. Today this desire has moved beyond external elements, burrowing deeper within. Although many have conquered the outer objects of their desires by gratifying these needs, others have simply given up trying to beat the system of having the perfect marriage partner, being the consummate parent, or operating like the complete manager with cell phone, daytimer, powerbook, and pager glued to the body.

The Information Age has spawned the ability to be more introspective and aware. Thanks to leisure opportunities, preventive health options, and electronic gadgetry, the mundane tasks once considered part of the job of life now fall into a "necessary but not urgent" category. Subsequently, the job of living is being viewed less as a duty and more as a challenge. We have more time and space to become very versatile, complex individuals. This, too, has conceived the idea of totally concentrating on human consciousness. Since we are becoming a variegated species of doers, we are capable of placing more emphasis inwardly extending ourselves beyond the realms of human consciousness to learn how to be more powerful within.

R. Buckminster Fuller delved into this idea of being more powerful. He suggested that intelligence is involved in achieving knowledge while incorporating our metaphysical nature to gain wisdom. Using the growth of our technological industry as an example of the growing intelligence of who we are, he pointed out how our intelligence has grown more ephemeralized, miniaturized, and aesthetic. This is similar to Mother Nature's simple technologies, that of photosynthesis, DNA, the human brain. (1) By demonstrating our emerging internal power in the things we invent, we can see our intelligence projected outward through our technology. Today, our technologies are models of refining the inside guts of things, the internal operational factors such as microprocessors, fiber optic devices, and genetic engineering.

Yet, if we were to take a long look at how the personal insides of us are changing, we'd quickly shy away from doing this, for most of us are afraid of our unique powers, not wanting to see them in action. In her book, *A Return to Love*, Marianne Williamson said, "Our deepest fear is not that we are inadequate, our deepest fear is that we are powerful beyond measure. It is our light, not our darkness that frightens us." (2)

Society, in the last two decades, has pulled the switch to release a powerful degree of human consciousness. This provides us with opportunities to see our behavior and our true identity in our own light instead of seeing them through the eyes of others. What inevitably results from this mastery of human consciousness is how magnificently beautiful the design of our complex body is, what immense abilities the brain has to take in, process, store and retrieve information, and how powerful our consciousness is, this inward guiding Force. Scrutinizing one aspect of that picture, consider the powerhouse design of the brain and how it sits, waiting patiently for its unused potential to be moved into the light of day and made conscious. The powerhouse, of who we are as whole, functioning beings, is a seed awaiting birth.

DEVELOPING THE KNOWN OF BEING POWERFUL

As a fifteen year-old, Barbara Marx Hubbard read about the powerful explosion of the atomic bomb on the island of Japan and found herself riveted to the question, "What is the meaning of our power?" In her journal her freshman year at Bryn Mawr College she recorded, "How can people live and not know why they are living? What is the purpose of life beyond things? My difficulty is that I cannot find a way to get experientially to the ultimate reality. There is no method to connect that ultimate reality with the personal need for purpose." (3)

This very same question has inspired cartographers, travel agents, and travelers to go beyond human consciousness and journey into the far reaches of consciousness. As each went about finding his or her answers through experiential construction of the Interstate of Consciousness, Hubbard, too, searched for the answer to bridge this gap made by the bomb. In her early thirties she began to find pieces of the answer through the works of Abraham Maslow, Pierre Teilhard de Chardin and Buckminster Fuller. She knew that we, in the past, translated the meaning of our power as providing the means to feel safe, secure, happy and productive, but the atomic blast blew that picture of reality, carefully constructed during the days of the Industrial Revolution, to smithereens.

The bottom of our story, our myth, dropped out creating insecurity, depression and a cold vacuum-like feeling about the meaning of power. As a housemaker with five children, her own power lay buried for a long time, as she dutifully supported the dreams of others. When the bomb was dropped, its fission by-products began awakening her to find answers about her own unique power. Hubbard's long journey brought her increasingly into the public's eyes as an evocateer for the development of a new vision for our culture, an eventual fusion of the by-products. For, without a vision of our collective power, our culture loses a sense of direction and a sense of meaning. What comes of that? She asked herself "is life to be lived as a practice life?"

Her answers filtered down to her in pieces. One chunk of the answer was:
> "The meaning of our power, our affluence and technologies, is to free us to find our purpose in life, to actualize that purpose through meaningful, freely chosen work, to connect the world into one living, interacting organism of far greater capacity than the sum of our separate parts, and to develop an environment in which all of its members will experience themselves as part of one co-creative body to overcome physical lack, to change our physical nature for conscious evolutionary goals." And a larger segment of the answer was, "We humans can become self-evolving, self-regenerating, and eventually continuous humans, transcending the mammalian life cycle." (4)

FROM HOMO SAPIENS TO HOMO UNIVERSALIS

To this end, she introduced the idea that we are moving away from being static Homo Sapiens toward becoming dynamic, multidimensional Homo Universalis. This segment of the answer shows her willingness to move into the realm of spiritual consciousness while incorporating the best of the products of human consciousness. In forming this far-reaching statement which became her purpose in life, Hubbard initiated the first draft design of a new vision for the planet, one that will require taking parts of the old visions of countries across the world and combining it with the new. Perhaps this will be the organizational mission of the United Nations in the near future, that of reinventing the purpose of planetary unity and regenerating a vitality that supports this purpose. Clearly, the multilevel features of Hubbard's perspective imply that various powers can be pulled together to support a much larger plan for life on this planet. Can we rally around this new vision opportunity and help create a common vision, one that moves us through the '90s and into the next millennium?

MOVING TOWARD FUSION: BRINGING HUMAN & SPIRITUAL CONSCIOUSNESS TOGETHER

Gaining a larger meaning of the power within is achieved by watching one's own unique process. I have been gratified to be a part of the lives of many people who have been on the road of conscious evolution for decades. Many people, it seems, including myself, have spent much of our precious lifetime moments learning how to discipline the personality or lower plane desires to follow what the true Self wants. Furthermore, there are others who are making an effort to consciously live life from a higher plane existence and are grappling with the idea of merging the two components of the Total Self, the practical and the spiritual. Together we are all standing on the Continental Divide of Consciousness. **Fission** (forgetting) versus **fusion** (remembering) is the ledge upon which we stand at this time, wavering back and forth between serving personality (the selfish, impersonal desires) and serving essence (the selfless, transpersonal desires). It's an uncomfortable place to be.

ROCKING BACK & FORTH BETWEEN THE OLD ME & THE NEW ME

Many of us are noticing that time seems to speed ahead at dizzying rates with whole days or a few hours in the day where a tremendous amount of projects were amazingly accomplished (see John B's post in Chapter 6). In other cases, time seems to drag on and on and on. Even the elements we use to create our physical reality seem to be dematerializing then materializing, here today, gone tomorrow; e.g., fashion industry products, toys, foodstuffs, health and beauty aids, insects, animals etc. Many, many clients of mine talk about having a foot in day-to-day physical reality while, at the same time, experiencing pieces of non-physical reality bleeding into physical reality as I did in my early spinning experience.

Feeling split involves being on one side or the other of the fence. There are those people who wish to crash and burn similar to the Waco, Texas incident or the Oklahoma City bombing without having awareness of the price this requires in the long run. They would like to wipe out what seems unacceptable, in order to restore and maintain peace. Others are not so direct, they would prefer building, overcoming, and regenerating from the old to the new such as Habitat for Humanity and the Peace Corps. Recently, one spiritually oriented person, who has his feet firmly planted in the physical world, told me he calls his perspective "seeing double," where he is literally rocking back and forth between these views. This uneasy swing between "one minute I am the old me, the next I'm the new me" is a symptom of fusion beginning to occur. The moods swings and the beliefs jerking and jolting around are a symptom of being between fission and fusion.

CHECK: INSIDE OR OUTSIDE THE EXPERIENCE?

Where are you? On the ledge of fission or fusion? When moving toward fusion, which is the blending of human and spiritual consciousness, one is *in* the experience of the change not experiencing the change from an outside perspective. An important question I ask clients who are describing their Interstate traveling experiences is, *"Were you inside yourself experiencing this or were you outside yourself when you experienced this?"* This will reveal on what side of the fission/fusion precipice you are. In traveling experiences on the Interstate, use this question to determine where you are. The more you stay inside your experience, inside your body and remain comfortably present to yourself, the more Knowns will surface to serve the fusion side of the equation well. Fusion is a type of balance. It provides a solid place to support where we are heading. Fusion is blending or merging human and spiritual consciousness into a place of cooperation and collaboration without losing individuality and the essential imperfection of being human, but with the guidance system of full consciousness in place.

In bringing the realms of human and spiritual consciousness together, the larger ethical and moral questions before us would be seen as reconcilable. Issues such as the beginning and quality of life posed in genetic cloning engineering, artificial insemination, birthing procedures, and abortion could be tackled using a broad, fusion definition of consciousness. On the matter of death, questions about euthanasia, brain death, animal testing, and funeral options would be embraced with more awareness and honor instead of the stop gap measures we now use. As understanding about full consciousness grows throughout the collective, life passage events such as coming into adolescence, young adulthood, menopause, or sexual maturity would lend themselves more fully to rituals once celebrated in civilizations past. Many blossoms of full, unified consciousness will ripen into bountiful fruit if integrated into daily lives.

CHOOSING TO REMEMBER THE MEANING OF OUR POWER & VISION THROUGH OMENS

Interesting omens are arriving to demonstrate what fusion looks like through animal, human and media events. The birth of the white buffalo calf on the ranch of an ordinary farmer in Wisconsin has grabbed the attention of many including Native Americans. They suggest this event fulfills an old prophecy that the new times are arriving. As the calf has been growing, its white color has darkened considerably, but it remains as a symbolic indicator of merging the unusual with the "normal" or the supernatural with the regular form of the buffalo. The color white, representing innocence and purity, portrays simplicity and at-one-ment within the animal kingdom. Humankind cannot be far behind.

FUSED AT BIRTH

The birth of the conjoined twins, Abigail and Brittany Hensel, (5) is another indicator in a very physical sense of what fusion looks like and requires. To watch these siamese twins is to watch a living, breathing form of simplicity, but from a very complex system. For we have before us, in the body of Abby and Britty, the perfect example of cooperation at its best on a multitude of levels. On an Oprah Winfrey TV show, their mother, Patty, says the girls "seem so fluid, they don't question who is to do what when a task is before them, they just do it without stopping to think." As don Juan would suggest, this is a clue about what cooperation requires, that is, the lessening of talking and reasoning skills so that the other six lost skills of consciousness may be used. In watching the Hensel twins play together, their cooperative abilities for the sake of the whole are well-developed even as young children.

Conjoined births occur once in 50,000 births, though 40% are stillborn and most are female. Only three or four cases of dicephalic twins, those having two heads with one body, have been recorded. The 6-year old girls share one body from the waist down and two bodies, for the most part, from the waist up. To those of us who walk around in one body with one head, we have to question how they manage to live a dual life from one body. Since Abby controls the right hand and Britty controls the left hand, tying shoe strings literally becomes a balancing act. They are a living demonstration of synchronization. Not only do they have to constantly share and defer to each other for the good of their one body to accomplish physical tasks, they must constantly concede and support physiological functions since they experience separate urges and instincts; e.g., the need to urinate and to sleep. Their example is very timely. For here we are, two consciousnesses experiencing two realities at this point in time, physical and non-physical reality rocking back and forth. Each of our realities appears to be different, still they are contained within one body. How do we merge or fuse them so that we are still ourselves, yet yield to the Total Self, for the good of the one body, to achieve full consciousness? This knowledge about cooperation and unity is discovered in a very black and white, concrete manner in the non-physical states of consciousness during Interstate travels.

FUSED BY LIGHTNING AT BIRTH

Fusion is well-portrayed in the movie, *Powder*. After his mother is struck by lightning (fission) and dies, the main character, Jeremy Reed, is born. His unusual birth circumstances produce his albino features and his extraordinary human and spiritual abilities. These come to intimidate everyone who comes in contact with him. At various times Jeremy displays his energetic power which causes many electrical outages. To enhance the mystery about his ability, there are many scenes where vivid displays of strikingly gorgeous, electrical thunderstorms pervade the story. With this degree of energetic ability, he readily shows what can be done with the six lost skills all humankind once possessed. The film's plot showing a character who is able to access, sustain, and control a high degree of full consciousness abilities, depicts Homo Universalis of the future. Perhaps the full, fiery power of humankind is coming into existence.

ADDING FIRE TO THE SPIRIT OF THE DRIVER

Traveling the Interstate of Consciousness into non-ordinary realities provides individuals with the ability to develop and verify general Knowns about this universe and beyond as well as Knowns unique to personal life. The Known-developing process adds horsepower to the engine of the vehicle. This is comparable to adding fire to the Spirit of the driver behind the wheel. Living in the Rocky Mountains, I know how important it is to have adequate horsepower when driving up and down steeply winding roads in high elevations. If the car doesn't have much horsepower, it simply doesn't go too far too fast and in many instances, may break down. When the driver with adequate horsepower progresses on the Interstate, this gradual build-up of the power encased in hands-on personal Knowns adds extra Force to the core essence, or the spirit of the driver. This power gradually pulls the veil of human frailty aside and dissolves the feeling of being split. Gradually a Known takes over.

Over the border arises a much larger outlook, one that illuminates the beauty of each individual and element that make up our environment. Bill K. described this extremely well in his VML online messages in Chapter 6 by describing how he has changed (Metamorphosing from Man to HU-man) and how he has begun to bring the best of his non-physical abilities into his physical reality.

TOWARD BECOMING HOMO UNIVERSALIS
ELEVEN BASIC KNOWNS

Not surprisingly, the cartographers and travelers as a group have discovered many Knowns revealing a powerful way of being Homo Universalis. Among them, eleven basic Knowns repeat themselves over and over. Elaborating on each of these will show how the Knowns demonstrate the expanded perspective and the universal love of the Primary Source that lies at the center of the universe and beyond. And too, these Knowns help to bridge the gap between the old reality and a new, more conscious reality. They contain patterns which reveal a broader informational picture of life than we now envision as a collective species. Here are the Knowns the pioneer travelers have discovered on their journey.

ELEVEN BASIC KNOWNS

I am more than my physical body.
I am an essence.
I am a field of energy more than a body.
I am a multidimensional being.
I am a citizen of this planet, of this universe and beyond.
I am one with this universe, I am connected to all elements
on this planet, in this universe and beyond.
There is a natural rhythm and order with which I am connected.
I regenerate and reinvent myself in my body a thousand times a day.
I am a continuous being, I do not end.
What I perceive inwardly, I will perceive outwardly.
From my Total Self I receive constant support and love for who I am.

I AM MORE THAN MY PHYSICAL BODY

Without a doubt, this is the most pervasive Known threading itself through every traveler's experiences. The personal discovery of being more than the physical body and of being able to verify what that is blows away all the beliefs about beginning and ending life here on earth. It makes it possible that we are continuous beings distinctly verifiable as Monroe, Hubbard, Roddenberry and the Eastern mystics have been describing. Personally discovering this Known results in a tremendous breakthrough about many limiting beliefs concerning death, relationship endings, falling outs between friends, getting lost in situations, living alone and more. As a result of this Known, a large sense of freedom is recovered in the psyche. This spills over into the day-to-day events to be unleashed, moment by moment, in volumes of creativity and vitality.

The concrete discovery of being more than the physical body is the discovery of consciousness as separate from the physical body, the I AM with thinking, feeling, seeing, dreaming and knowing skills of the soul attached. This Known is very reassuring to those who thought that death meant everything flatlines and disappears. Because of the freedom experienced related to being more than the physical body, this Known opens the door to living fuller lives with others and realizing more potential in physical life. Discovering the separateness of the I AM provides opportunities to appreciate the body in service to the I AM and its magnificent design and ability to support the I AM existence here on earth.

I AM AN ESSENCE

This Known is mentioned by few but when it is described, it is a turning point event. To discover the essence of who you are creates a reason for being and for living fully. When B. Z. asked in a Focus 12 city "Who am I?" (Chapter 5) and received the response, "You are Divine Innocence" she was being told by her Total Self she was spiritualized matter reflecting that particular quality of God. She then could fit together parts of her life experience concerning lessons about innocence and see why she is a walking, talking billboard for this quality.

If we start, one by one, to embrace our own unique power which Gurdjieff and many others call essence, then we will be moving toward a sense of groundedness and direction as Barbara Marx Hubbard did. In so doing, this life and its potentials become anchored. As we witness her life, Hubbard literally could be called a Divine Visionary, her god-given essence. Personal discovery of essence or the core quality of an individual usually starts with the question Hubbard asked, "What is the meaning of (my) our power?" I often hear it phrased in two ways, *"What is my purpose for being here?"* or *"Who am I?"* In the case of the first question, the person is usually looking for outer things or the right niche in order to have personal success, fame and fortune. In the case of the latter, this person is generally looking for an *inner quality(ies)*, the beat they dance to, that creates a natural right action. The first question indicates the path of human consciousness and the second question signifies the path of spiritual consciousness.

ESSENCE IS WHAT POWERS THE ENGINE

On the road to spiritual consciousness, the essence can be identified by forming an intention to know and have the capacity to receive the essence, then asking the questions: "Who am I?," "What is my purpose for this lifetime in this body?" and "What action can I now take to serve this purpose best?" Only the first question addresses the essence question for essence is a state of being. It is not a state of doing or a particular form which the other questions address. The "AM-ness" is what distinguishes essence. Then follows a challenge. Once essence is consciously made a Known, it does not have to be expressed, proved, defended, done or achieve; it just is. Essence is a quality one possesses unequivocally. If a person tries to do things to be a Divine Visionary, then it isn't essence. It is a form looking like essence, but it isn't essence. One doesn't have to prove he or she is a quality rather it is the core truth of that person that merely is. Being the essence of who you are creates a path of charisma and a natural unfoldment of what is right. On the other hand, when a person is trying to put on the form of essence, the path becomes one of struggle, effort and physicality. Essence is that element that empowers the engine — its horsepower.

LIVING OUT THE POLAR OPPOSITE OF THE ESSENCE

I have discovered that essence has had two faces, one supporting expansion, and its polar opposite supporting contraction or limits. There's an exceedingly good chance that the polar opposite of essence has been well-entrenched in physical reality. Example: the polar opposite of being a Divine Visionary is being a Divine Realist; the polar opposite of being Divine Fairness is Divine Injustice. Realism and injustice are alive and well in our society. In the past, the natural qualities in people were exploded (fission) and denied. Family members, friends, and co-workers supported the polar opposite quality. In order to keep the peace, many people developed and carried out false identities based on those polarized qualities. As a consequence, people felt like orphans in their own family or workplace because they were living out their polar opposite of the essence. As a psychiatric nurse, I have witnessed the trauma of people battling their co-workers, family members and friends when they began to drop these false identities in their significant groups. The groups refuse to acknowledge different qualities of the changing person during recovery because they are invested in keeping (controlling) the false identity in place. As we embrace the individual truths of who we are, there will emerge shifts in attitudes about empowering the essence in individuals especially as this impacts group experiences. In the near future, the realization of the simple Quaker belief, *"Everyone has a piece of the truth"* will create a thirst for fusion on many levels and the revelation of the individual essence in each of us.

I AM A FIELD OF ENERGY MORE THAN A BODY

Numerous indicators that we are predominately a resonating field of energy more than a body become evident during Interstate travel. The experiences of feeling vibrations associated with a change in consciousness, learning to sustain and control them and make them into a useful tool creates the feasibility that something more expansive than mere flicks of electrical impulses in the brain must be at work in order to create the change in consciousness. As traveling progresses, emanations of light forms appear as described in the last chapter. This gives more food for thought and for creating a Known. The REBAL eventually becomes a very useful tool for swimming through the universe and gives more evidence of the field effects of the energy we are encased in, and a way to verify what the nature of the field is. When in a Focus city, some people hear their own loud snoring, yet they remain fully conscious and aware of what they are doing in the Focus city, despite obvious signs of sleep. This is an important symptom known as *satori* or the place of no-mind (the void), where the ability to objectively observe oneself becomes possible.

When one gains the ability to say "I am not the body," having accumulated proof for that statement in his or her own way, there is room to discover the field of energy which underlies and supports the existence of the physical body as a secondary container. Nonetheless, it is still a sacred temple. Then experimenting with energy either in non-physical or physical reality begins. Whether energy is used to have an OBE, do remote viewing or help a plant grow, this becomes a very intriguing area for personal adventure as described by the VML members. As the fun continues, value placed on the physical body assumes a different priority, and this makes room for full consciousness to become a Known.

I AM A MULTIDIMENSIONAL BEING

The most popular Known, taking a back seat to Monroe's famous statement, "You are more than your physical body," is that the traveler comes to know his or her own changing, dimensional features and realizes the immensity of his or her being. Throughout life we are told we exist in a never-changing, constant, three-dimensional world. In the realm of non-physicality, that measurement system gives way to the realization of an ever-changing environment. In sharp contrast to third dimensional life experiences, the travelers talk about the reality of life moving through an interweaving of experiences on various planes. (See Figure 27.)

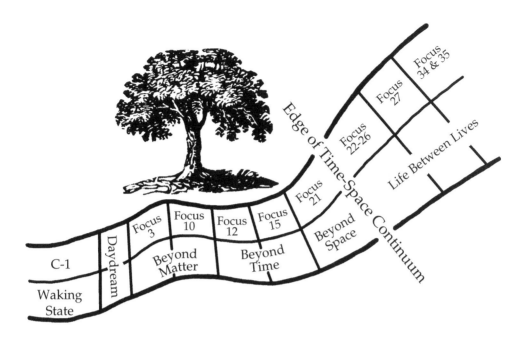

**Figure 27 The Continuum of Reality Along the
Interstate of Consciousness**

They report experiencing varying degrees of density of themselves or many ways of measuring who they are, as opposed to the highly-fixed, three-dimensional state of physical reality. As they experience various states of consciousness, whether it be the daydreaming state, the lucid dreaming state, or the state of being in the "zone," multidimensionality gradually is defined. The traveler also reports experiences of past, future, and parallel lives (lives which seemed to be existing in the same time frame as the present). Gaining first-hand knowledge of these variable aspects expands their knowledge about present time and present abilities and gives them the courage to be more powerful in their daily lives.

In another way multidimensionality is demonstrating itself in the travelers' frequent comments about their changing perception of time and how this is affecting their everyday lives, how increasingly complex they see themselves and how their world view is changing. As a result of this Known, they are less willing to make judgments about others, to dwell on the mistakes of themselves or others and to judge the non-physical traveling exploits of others. Operating with this Known intact, increases the wonderment, curiosity, and eagerness about Interstate traveling in general.

I AM A CITIZEN OF THIS PLANET, OF THIS UNIVERSE AND BEYOND

Stories throughout the previous chapters showed evidence of how one would form a Known of this nature. Changing the way one chooses to perceive in order to experience other life forms, learning how to meet with other forms of life and having to change the communication method are all end products resulting from learning how to move into the larger universe to become a galactic citizen. Implications of interplanetary partnership and galactic agreements have already been explored through *Star Trek* programming and other science fiction vehicles. The travelers talk about the increasing necessity to invent a job description which develops the role of galactic ambassador and its requirements. (6) This planetary outreach idea demonstrates the need to proactively meet the challenge of helping this planet take its rightful place in the realm of other planetary life forms.

One Known leads to a yearning to have other Knowns about the planet, and beyond as Monroe described in his three books. This planetary outreach is something only dreamed about in comic books and in science fiction plots; however, the whole realm of partnership with other life forms can be explored and realized using the Focus States and other meditative approaches.

This knowledge increases as the intent to discover the new frontier grows. Having a more expansive vision due to this Known, the travelers say, creates a wider span of responsibility in the everyday world. Indicators on how to become more responsible planetary citizens pop up all over after discovering the connections to the greater whole. They now talk about problems in Bosnia or in China not as dramas being played out in the newspaper theater, but as happening to neighboring people. They have described their energetic efforts to help change the situation without the use of physical means. They talk in groups about how they have used their group mind energies to assist others and what results have been produced. Becoming aware of individual responsibilities on this planet means doing what one can do on an energetic level for others across the ocean or in next the county who are facing weather disasters, epidemics, or resource shortages. On the flip side, the travelers have also discussed how this Known implies a distinct responsibility for learning how to be judicious with the use of energy on a personal basis as it helps to create the universe as we know it now and in the future.

I AM ONE WITH THIS UNIVERSE
I AM CONNECTED TO ALL ELEMENTS ON THIS PLANET,
IN THIS UNIVERSE AND BEYOND

From the smallest element to the largest mass that appears in non-physical traveling experiences, it becomes very evident the Law of Attraction (like attracts like) is alive, well and impacting travel all the time. As we become more aware, more conscious, our connection to all elements becomes a very useful Known. As with my stories about the snail and the Dogon planetary group, the answers provided me with very important information as to where I belonged, what importance I contained, what roles are important for me to be taking part in and how I could communicate with non-physical entities. This is not to downplay the other side of this Known, that is, the ability of the snail and the Dogon group to communicate with me on a meaningful, micro level. A pretty amazing feat coming from my still naive perspective! Of course, this precipitates more questions about the dynamics behind the connection, "How does this all work?" That incites more investigation about the power of the etheric body of each element as the communication network between us all. Now if we could just dial into the etheric body of Mars...

THERE IS A NATURAL RHYTHM AND ORDER
WITH ALL WHICH I AM CONNECTED

Here is where the idea of becoming the waveform begins to weave its magic. Travelers talk with me about learning the rhythm of energy, of flow, of the elements and learning to participate rather than react with the energy of the universe. This is like riding a horse. The more sensitive we become to the movement of our energy and the energy of those we are combining with, the masculine, feminine and void/highly creative phases, the more we are going to anticipate and move into the flow of elemental energies around us to have a better ride. Thus is born the Known to move with the natural rhythm and order of the universe around us.

Whether it means using the lunar phases to plant seeds in the garden, asking the Deva of the Wind to leave your home standing during a tornado, or learning to move with the rhythm of your own pain after serious surgery, this Known offers an easier way to move through life without fighting the elements and bringing unnecessary loss of energy. On a much larger stage, this Known offers some explanation for the enormous changes and transformations taking place every day around us. Such events as the fall of the Berlin Wall, the rise of Baby Bells, the suicide of a best friend followed by the birth of the Hensel twins become understandable. The discovery of two new water-bearing planets (7) near the star 47 Ursae Majoris and the star 70 Virginis some 200 trillion miles from earth by two San Francisco astronomers becomes less surprising and more like teachable, opening moments. There is a mysterious, and meaningful connection encased in this Known.

I REGENERATE AND REINVENT MYSELF IN MY BODY A THOUSAND TIMES A DAY

Reading the stories of the travelers using the Hemi-Sync Surgical Support series as a means of reinventing how one approaches and surrenders to the surgical process, brings to mind the powers of regeneration of the body in a multitude of ways. Essentially, a new body emerges after surgery or upon awakening each morning so there is the realization that it is not important to hang on to the old body. After suffering a serious car accident, Gari Carter described nine years of surrendering her body during numerous facial reconstructive surgeries in her book, *Healing Myself*. Using Hemi-Sync tapes during surgery, she said, "I could feel a slight pulling and cutting of my face at times, but no pain. I felt no need to open my eyes or move. I felt as if I were having a luxuriously relaxing sleep, totally unaware of time." (8) Consciously accessing more of her Total Self potential, Gari was able to forego pain medication and significantly lower her anesthesia medication during numerous major surgeries.

As we focus more on the self-regenerative abilities of our health maintenance organizations within the physical body and depend less on magic bullets and high-powered, technological methods, a major internal shift occurs, so say the travelers. They talk about their surprising healing abilities and creativity coupled their growing strength to move with life's challenges instead of battling them. To this end, they stress how important it is to strengthen one's ability to maintain as much consciousness as possible throughout big and little crisis such as going "under the knife" or being mugged without losing a physical sense of being in the body.

During supraordinary experiences on the Interstate, the travelers say it becomes obvious that the consciousness is running the show, rather than the personality, or the mind-brain-body. They describe how it becomes much easier to move through life-threatening situations using what remains essential, the consciousness and the essence. Eventually in the near future, besides learning how to actively regenerate our bodies, we will also learn to change what Hubbard calls the code of degeneration (9) or what we know as programmed death, to the code of self-regeneration. On a physical level, this sounds impossible, yet it is already being achieved. How did George Burns live to be more than 100 years of age despite his daily cigar smoking, his highly stressful Hollywood lifestyle, and the loss of his wife, Gracie, decades ago? What did he know about self-healing and self-regeneration?

We reinvent ourselves a thousand times a day when met with change through decision-making on the job, family and friendship challenges. In these moments, we have thousands of minutes of choosing between stimulating the death hormone in the pituitary or regenerating ourselves. While in the Focus states, maintaining the ability to receive information or to experience oneself requires a fluid and mutable attitude, one that produces youthfulness rather than aging. Self-transformation is cultivated from an expectation that change is here to stay, and it burns as if a flame emanating from within looking for the next opportunity to reform within and observe that transformation. Sometimes I wake up in the morning and look around, pinching myself to see what's changed. I know I am transforming that quickly. And the Cheshire Cat grins back at me, laughing at my questioning smirk. Literally looking in the mirror is a trip for I see my different faces looking back at me moment by moment, still I know the consciousness and the essence of I AM remains.

I AM A CONTINUOUS BEING, I DO NOT END

A big subject for all of us! This is a truth that is quickly making itself very noticeable. All of us have crossed over to the non-physical side in our sleep hundreds of times and safely returned without requiring any damage control. There are mini-versions of the crossover experienced in the baby steps we take doing what, during TMI training, is known as a "rollercoaster" shift in consciousness. This is like a driving lesson going up the hill, down the hill, and around the corner to see if we can make it together in and out of various planes of velocity, brake-to-gas pedal synchronization patterns, and high-pitched parental directions. The rollercoaster training starts out in C-1 consciousness, goes to Focus 10, expands to Focus 12, back to Focus 10, then to Focus 12, back to Focus 10 and out to C-1 consciousness. The continual dynamic of "do it yourself" shifting in and out of various states of consciousness while quickly experiencing their unique characteristics is a ride that slowly develops into the Known. I am a continuous being, I do not end, I do not blow up when I go "out there," nor do I disintegrate when returning to so-called solid ground, C-1 consciousness. When these baby steps are experienced, vast horizons open to consider who I am when I die and go through the big transition.

In some cases those who have taken the TMI *Lifeline Residential Program* have met deceased relatives or friends or people they haven't known in their lifetime. Later personal research often proves these people actually existed when they said they did. Hands-on experiential links to these people in spirit form gradually builds a Known that we continue as consciousness while our bodies in physical reality dissolves. Consciousness is immortal. It is contained within the memory of every cell in our body and dates back beyond the first reproducible cell with which we began physical life. Gradually, as we develop the physical ability to regenerate ourselves, hand-in-hand will come the ability to physically continue on and on. With this limiting belief about life as we know it ending, our here and now physical lives can be lived more fully without the thought that at any time, we are erased. The continuity of it all is mind boggling! Here are some examples.

Joel Whitton, Ph. D., discovered that *all* of the clients he's hypnotized have been able to describe past lives and many reported their life experiences between lives. When centering on the latter, his clients reported being in what he called a "metaconscious" state of acute self-awareness and high moral and ethical regard. "They no longer possessed the ability to rationalize away any of their faults and misdeeds, and saw themselves with total honesty…Part of the purpose of this realm was to allow them to plan their next life, to literally sketch out the important events and circumstances that would befall them in the future." (10) His clients were describing the characteristics of Focus 27.

Michael Newton, Ph.D., a certified Master Hypnotherapist, in *Journey of Souls* described his experiences of regressing individuals back in time to access their memories of life between lives. Newton selected the actual narratives of 29 clients to show what life is like in the spirit world immediately after death and beyond. From his studies over ten years, he postulates there are six different levels of soul development represented by light emanations of beings in the afterlife.

- **Beginner**: White (bright and homogeneous)
- **Lower Intermediate**: Off-White (reddish shades, ultimately turning into traces of yellow)
- **Intermediate**: Yellow (solid with no traces of light)
- **Upper Intermediate**: Dark Yellow (a deep gold, ultimately turning into traces of blue)
- **Advanced**: Light Blue (ultimately turning into traces of purple)
- **Highly Advanced**: Dark Bluish-Purple (surrounded by radiant light) (11)

Newton says, "The energy colors of souls probably have little to do with such elements as hydrogen and helium, but perhaps there is an association with a high energy field of electromagnetism. I suspect all soul light is influenced by vibrational waves in tune with harmonious spiritual oneness of wisdom." (12)

Another traveler who has described his own personal journey exploring the realms of the afterlife is Joe Gallenberger, TMI Residential Trainer. In his book, *Brothers Forever,* (13) Joe was compelled, after his brother Pete used suicide to end his life, to deal with his own overwhelming grief. He wanted to discover why his brother chose to die in this manner. During his healing process Joe learned what survives after death and how life continues. By working with his own personal resources and a channeler, Joe was able to discover what Pete was doing in the afterlife, and what further healing he could experience for himself. Joe came to understand that these changes would allow for more growth in his brother as well. His experiences developed the Known that life is a continuous journey which doesn't end at death.

WHAT I PERCEIVE INWARDLY I WILL PERCEIVE OUTWARDLY

This Known has been in the making for decades in mainstream personal growth classes, yet not necessarily discovered from an energetic level which is precisely what becomes evident while traveling the Interstate. It seems people talk about the idea that "thoughts create reality" in every other sentence these days; however, most are desiring to manipulate thoughts in order to manifest a certain reality like manipulating strings of a puppet. Nevertheless, if one were to get rid of the strings to become the creator, the trick is to pay attention to the energetic intention that creates the results or how that intention is packaged before it is sent. Intention is merely invisible strings. Since most all of the thinking is removed when using the Focus states as a means of travel during the Preparatory Process, there is a high possibility of learning about energy as it moves from "here" to "there" which is really all the same.

A common testing ground for this Known is the state lottery contests where millions of dollars are paid out in cash winnings. During the Gateway Excursion Weekend, participants sometimes try to test their problem-solving skills in the Focus states by manifesting their lucky six numbers so by the following Wednesday, they can be "in the money." After the Excursion, I usually receive a few calls from participants questioning what was missing in their manifestation process after their ticket didn't win. Generally speaking, it's a good chance their unconscious intentions are preventing them from winning the jackpot. I suggest to them an exercise to bring their unconscious beliefs up to the surface. Asking the question over and over, *"What would I have to have believed in order for me to be in this situation?"* helps peel away the blocks associated with not winning money. One person has actually won a sizable jackpot learning how to be more fully conscious with this Known. Beneath all of this is the larger power question Marianne Williamson addressed, that of being able to create in the likeness of God, the Primary Creator... "we are powerful beyond measure." Unfortunately, these are the hidden strings attached. This power question looms its head above the surface. Can I really manifest my heart's desire? Am I worthy of receiving this? Can I keep it once I receive it or will I squander my treasure? Lifelong adventures continue down the endless path of this Known.

FROM MY TOTAL SELF I RECEIVE
CONSTANT SUPPORT AND LOVE FOR WHO I AM

Most people gradually establish this Known after a long series of Interstate experiences. This Known chips away at the primal fear of being alone or being abandoned. Many have described a similar experience which follows.

Three years ago I developed this Known while in a free-flowing Hemi-Sync experience. At its beginning I developed the intention to have a transpersonal experience and to accept that whatever came was for my perfect good. Then I purposefully intended to allow any and all fears to come up and be released and one by one, old emotions and their subsequent memories spontaneously came up and I released each one by using **H+ Relax** and **Let Go** Function Commands and connected breathwork similar to Castaneda's recapitulation techniques. Some of these memories were events I had totally forgotten but when they arrived, I remembered them in vivid detail and saw instantaneously why my power energy behind them was slowly being diminished as years passed. After this, I felt myself lying in a completely relaxed state for a long time. Then an amorphous being emanating tremendous love arrived, enveloped in an enormous flash of light. The being touched my head and still another memory came to the surface, then the being telepathically said, "Blessed thou are Patricia who experienced — (a specific event) — on this earth for herself and all to know" and continued all around the perimeter of my body, triggering more releases and inserting blessing after blessing. Immense gratitude began welling in me as the being knew exactly what was held in my body and where it was held. Very quickly I knew the being was me, the soul, healing myself perfectly. Afterward I received a pure all-at-once insight that I had planted this Known deeply and indelibly into the core of me. From then on, I have only to remember that experience and to call upon my Total Self in times when I require support and love.

And so these Knowns empower the traveler on the journey, creating a trail of loving gestures that only a Primary Source knows while radiating universal love to and through us, urging us to make Home here where we are. Home in all its light and dark glory. Traveling this particular locality of the Interstate of Consciousness provides the opportunity to discover the indescribable beauty of ourselves and of our cosmos and how it is all present within and without. The design is magnificent! Within the physical body its intelligence pattern contains over 3 trillion cells, enough to create 30 earths. Each cell replicates an individual and includes a universal signature to express full consciousness. Knowingly, this signature embodies a majestic Plan of Love and Light and Power on Earth, and it exists in the consciousness of all.

DISCOVERY

The bomb blows, fission all around
In our eyes, the dust burns, the guilt seethes
It was, is still before us.

Its radiation blows our circuits
Removes the fragile veil of human consciousness
We begin the healing without thinking
It is, was still before us.

Now fusion begins, toward
Wholeness, oneness
Merging humankind and spirit, wave and particle
It is, was still before us.

APPENDIX A

DISTINGUISHING CHARACTERISTICS OVER TIME OF A NON-ORDINARY STATE OF CONSCIOUSNESS: FOCUS 12

The following are data resulting from a Group Mind study that was conducted over a period of six months to investigate the key characteristics of Focus 12 as it is described by groups over time.

DATA

Participants Describing Key Characteristics of Focus 12
Gateway Excursion Weekends in Boulder, CO

May 1995

My head got bigger, seemed like there was a split in half; a floating sensation; spacey; grey fog, infinity; high electricity; less stringent, Focus 10 more stringent; smooth, gentle; lot larger; no limit; head somewhat exploding, seeing symbols; vastness, felt connected deep in my bones; grey, felt larger in denseness; whirling vortexes movement; intimate like a red flannel shirt.

July 1995

Expansion; freedom; floating; oneness; enlarging whirlingness; dullness when compared to coming from sharpness in Focus 10; drifting in space; tunnel; feminine; dreamlike; deeper; pulling in with my eyes, how do I see with my eyes (here?); love; my eyes went out and around as if I was stretching (my field of perception); light; wide; pulsating, undulating energy.

September 1995

Moved out-of-body, flew; unfocused energies, symbols, images; overwhelming joy, beings of light; subtle colors of grey & lavender; no conscious thoughts, no visions; vast expansiveness of space; time changed; expansiveness, no dream fragments, unfocused (perceptual) window, no more chatter; hazy, flying circles with no color; vertical magic carpet launching amorphous grey blobs, seeing through matter; openness, darkness, fleeting back & forth; unusual smells.

January 1996

Void; mountain-like sensation, elevated, able to go off into the periphery in more than one direction at a time; flatten, floating; formless (body), energetic (using flighty finger motion to denote twinkling, light energy); fullness (mind), emptiness (body), have times when doing both together; enlightenment, there are spaces, groups of predominant light; dense (solid mind), full, experiencing great amounts of knowingness or information (not specific information), experiencing a great presence (me), freedom of mind/space; light body; flat, no concrete sense, no body, I was just there and everywhere; absence of gravity, being able to move in space easily (doing acrobatics), able to perceive things from above.

METHOD

This information was gathered immediately after playing an experiential learning Focus 12 tape for the first time for Gateway Excursion participants. To eliminate trainer bias, beforehand I did not go into any descriptions of this city other than to say it was a more expansive experience than what they had experienced thus far. I gave the participants instructions on the process for phasing into Focus 12 then I played the tape. After hearing the tape, participants were asked to write down key words or phrases in their workbook journals to briefly describe Focus 12. Without discussion, each participant then shared his or her key characteristics for this city. Then we discussed the results.

RESULTS

In the data, please note the internal consistency as to common meaning for the characteristics within each class as well as inter-class consistency. This is evidence that the tones used for this Focus 12 learning experience called, "Introduction to Focus 12" produces the same commonly experienced Focus 12 characteristics consistently throughout a class and over a period of time. It is also hypothetically possible to say, based on this evidence, that there is some universal Known operating among the participants about the environment of Focus 12, a city which has very little physical reality landmarks to go by. During the ten years that I have been facilitating the Gateway Excursion Weekends, this outcome has been the same in this experiential event for each Excursion. It was only after I actually wrote down the responses for three different training events did I realize there must be a universal Known operating here. This follows Bob Monroe's definition of establishing a Known, only in this case this is a group Known being organized. By reading the data of each Excursion class, one can see the unique quality of each class. Each Excursion class develops into its own group. Nonetheless, participants still found words unique to their individual experience and to their group mind to consistently describe the same pattern of Focus 12 characteristics intra and intergroup.

Keep in mind that the city of Focus 12 is not described in any belief system in the general populace. In the case of serious meditators, I concede that Focus 12 has been accessed by a few, but not sustained, nor controlled at will by those few people. In contrast, the fact that the majority of these Excursion participants don't have a disciplined meditative history and are singularly able to access Focus 12 with the aid of a Hemi-Sync training activity and consistently describe its common characteristics, is a landmark event in consciousness training. Sustaining and controlling a state of consciousness has been a perennial problem in meditation training; however, people using Hemi-Sync technology have been able to overcome this barrier.

APPENDIX B

A FEW RESOURCES WHICH EMPOWER THE RETRIEVAL OF EXTRASENSORY ABILITIES

BREAKING THE VEIL OF THE THIRD DIMENSION

The Teachings of Don Carlos: Practical Applications of the Works of Carlos Castaneda by Victor Sanchez (Santa Fe, NM, Bear & Co., 1995) is filled with excellent exercises to undo the rigid construction of physical reality. These explore the body as a field of energy, the art of stalking, and the undoing of self-importance.

A Course in Miracles (Tiburon, CA, Foundation for Inner Peace, 1985) in its opening Text chapters and lessons 1-28 in the Workbook for Students section addresses the limits of physical reality and how to mentally undo this conditioning.

The Reality Illusion: How You Make the World You Experience by Ralph Strauch (Barrytown, NY, Station Hill Press, 1983) presents numerous practical exercises from a Feldenkrais perspective which seek to explore patterns rather than pieces of perception. This author makes an intriguing case for the impact of language on perception, how we are conditioned to construct limitations in physical reality, the role of the ego, ordinary reality vs. non-ordinary reality, illness as a withdrawal of awareness, and magic and extrasensory perception.

Your Body Doesn't Lie by John Diamond, M.D. (New York City, NY, Warner Books, a division of Harper & Row Publishers, 1979) shows the basic applied kinesiology techniques which unlock body wisdom indicators.

Exploring Inner Space: Awareness Games for All Ages by Christopher Hills & Deborah Rozman (Boulder Creek, CA, University of Trees Press, 1978) is a comprehensive approach for developing extrasensory abilities. It is packed full of exercises for both kids and adults using the seven chakra system as a basis for exploration.

Space, Time & Self : Three Mysteries of the Universe by E. Norman Pearson (Wheaton, IL, Theosophical Publishing House, 1990) discusses the three great illusions of space, time and self and illustrates scientific principles and mystery teachings of both ancient and modern day Eastern wisdom and Western science.

THE ATTENTIONAL SKILL OF FEELING

The Art of Self-Disclosure by Sidney Jourard explores the ability to communicate whole feeling-oriented patterns of self, not just fragmented pieces of emotion. Teaches a method of how to use a self-disclosure technique to communicate whole gestaltic patterns of experience without losing personal energy and boundaries. Especially good for intimate relationships.

Body Consciousness: You Are What You Feel by Seymour Fisher (Englewood Cliffs, NJ, Prentice-Hall, 1973) provides discussions on physical and mental barriers to being present in the body, masculine & feminine body feelings, body decoration and camouflaging, illusionary changes in body image (contraction or expansion), and how death anxiety and miniature death situations affect the quality of life.

Conversations With God : Book One by Neale Donald Walsch (New York, NY, G. Putman's Sons, 1995) in the early pages discusses the importance of experiencing connections in life versus having reactive experiences that separate us from life. Emphasizes how feelings are key to the experiential connections.

The Teachings of Don Carlos: Practical Applications of the Works of Carlos Castaneda by Victor Sanchez (Santa Fe, NM, Bear & Co., 1995) explores the difference between emotion and feeling which is essential to the understanding of retrieval of emotional body energy and describes the technique of recapitulation that cleanses the light body of stuck energies.

Gateway Experience Series (The Monroe Institute, Faber, VA) audiotape and CD format, Discovery album, Tape 4, "Release & Recharge." This exercise provides the opportunity to move stuck energy in the emotional body and recharge its energies.

THE ATTENTIONAL SKILL OF DREAMING

The Art of Dreaming by Carlos Castaneda (New York, NY, HarperCollins, 1993), covers the discussion of the assemblage point, the fixation of the AP which freezes a picture of reality, the predictable cycle of shadow experiences in dreams, developing the ability to move the AP to incur various levels of dreaming, techniques for shutting off internal chatter, working with a dreaming emissary, and many other simple exercises to enhance the dreaming body.

Being-In-Dreaming: An Initiation Into The Sorcerer's World by Florinda Donner (New York, NY, HarperSanFrancisco, 1991) is a personal account of a woman's journey to retrieve her dreaming ability and merge it with her physical reality abilities.

Exploring the World of Lucid Dreaming by Steven LeBerge, Ph.D. & Howard Rheingold (New York, NY, Ballantine Books, division of Random House, 1990) is based on LeBerge's extensive laboratory work at Stanford University and the teachings of Tibetan dream yogis and other scientists. Offers discussion and techniques to prepare for learning lucid dreaming, how to fall asleep consciously, how to control and maintain the lucid state, and how to influence the outcome of the lucid dream.

THE ATTENTIONAL SKILL OF SEEING (KNOWING)

A Separate Reality: Further Conversations With Don Juan by Carlos Castaneda (New York, NY, Washington Square Press, a division of Simon & Schuster, 1971) illustrates the difference between thinking and perceiving and between looking and seeing, explores the connection between will and seeing, and offers techniques for retrieving the skill of seeing.

The Teachings of Don Carlos: Practical Applications of the Works of Carlos Castaneda by Victor Sanchez (Santa Fe, NM, Bear & Co., 1995) has a section called The Magic of Attention which contains simple exercises to undo looking and redevelop seeing.

Seeing With the Mind's Eye: The History, Techniques & Uses of Visualization by Michael Samuels, M.D. & Nancy Samuels (New York, NY, Summit Books, a division of Simon & Schuster, 1990) has three sections: the development and nature of image, techniques for opening the mind's eye, and for developing visions of wholeness.

How to See & Read the Aura by Ted Andrews (St. Paul, MN, Llewellyn Publications, 1993) contains simple and easy step-by-step exercises to feel, see, measure, strengthen and protect the aura in the light body.

The Chakras by C. W. Leadbeater (Wheaton, IL, The Theosophical Publishing House, 1987) originally published in 1927, this classic book explaining the seven chakras, their locations and specific energetic functions, their connections to the seven rays, and how they develop physiologically.

Wheels of Light: A User's Guide to the Chakra System by Anodea Judith (St. Paul, MN, Llewellyn Publications, 1990) is a comprehensive book on the chakras, provides breathing, yogic, and physical exercises to open and work with each chakra; has an excellent section on opening the sixth chakra, the seat of non-physical seeing.

EXPLORING & LEARNING TO USE SACRED GEOMETRY FEATURES OF THE LIGHT BODY FOR SHAPESHIFTING

Awakening to Zero Point: The Collective Initiation by Gregg Braden (Laura Lee Productions, PO Box 3010, Bellevue, WA 98009 December, 1993) lays out a detailed description of the sacred geometric configuration of energy encoded in the light body and provides a general discussion of breathing techniques to activate the MerKaBa containing the light body field and its grids.

Nothing in This Book Is True, But It's Exactly How Things Are by Bob Frissell (Berkeley, CA, Frog, Ltd., 1994) has a chapter containing description of sacred geometric features of the light body; includes an in-depth description of activating the MerKaBa using spherical breathing techniques.

The Holographic Universe by Michael Talbot (New York, NY, Harper/Collins Perennial Edition, 1992) discusses research that suggests how consciousness may operate using a holographic process. This gives credibility to the idea that all humans have natural shapeshifting abilities.

Gateway Experience Series (The Monroe Institute, Faber, VA) audiotape and CD format. Album VI, Prospecting, tapes 3 & 4 "Null Point" and "Plus Polarity." These exercises provide the opportunity to identify and shift the Null Point also known as the Assemblage Point.

APPENDIX C

HEMI-SYNC BIBLIOGRAPHY: A SAMPLING

Shirley Bliley, (ed.), *TMI Hemi-Sync Journal: A Research & Educational Publication of The Monroe Institute*, Vol. VIII-XIV, published four times annually, 1990 to present.

Courtney Brown, *Cosmic Voyage*, (New York: Dutton-Signet, 1996.)

Edwin Carter, *Living is Forever*, (Charlottesville, VA: Hampton Roads Publishing Co., 1993.)

Gari Carter, *Healing Myself: A Hero's Primer for Recovery From Tragedy*, (Charlottesville, VA: Hampton Roads Publishing Co., 1994.)

Murray Cox, "Notes From the New Land," *Omni* magazine, October 1993, pp. 40-2, 44, 46, 48, 118, 120.

Ken Eagle Feather, *Traveling With Power: The Exploration and Development of Perception*, (Charlottesville, VA: Hampton Roads Publishing Co., 1992.)

Leslie France, (ed.), *Breakthrough: A Publication of the Professional Division of The Monroe Institute*, Vol. I-VI, 1983-1990.

Otto Friedrich, "New Age Harmonics," *Time* magazine, December, 1987.

Joseph Gallengerger, *Brothers Forever*, (Charlottesville, VA: Hampton Roads Publishing Company, 1996.)

Michael Hutchinson, *MegaBrain*, "Tuning the Brain With Sound Waves: Hemi-Sync," (Ballantine Books, 1987), pp. 198-224.

Stefan Kasian, "Hemi-Sync and Altered Consciousness," *Vertices: A Publication of Duke University of Science, Technology, and Medicine*, Vol. 11, No. 2, Spring, 1995.

Carol Kramer, "Expanding Consciousness: A Conversation With Robert Monroe," *Body, Mind, Spirit* magazine, March/April, 1990. pp. 54-57, 77.

Jean-Paul Lemaire, "Hors du Corps, Hors du Temps" (Out-of-Body, Beyond Time), *Intuitions: Nouvelles Valeurs au Qoutidien*, No. 29, Spring, 1995.

Patricia Leva, *Traveling the Interstate of Consciousness: A Driver's Instruction Manual: Using Hemi-Sync to Access States of Non-Ordinary Reality.* (Longmont, CO: Q Central Publishing, 1998.)

Joseph McMoneagle, *Mind Trek: Exploring Consciousness, Time, and Space Through Remote Viewing*, (Charlottesville, VA: Hampton Roads Publishing Co., 1993.)

Robert A. Monroe, *Journeys Out of the Body*. (New York: Anchor Press, Doubleday, 1971.)

Robert A. Monroe, *Far Journeys*, (New York: Doubleday, 1985.)

Robert A. Monroe, "From Dozers to Deezers," *International Brain Dominance Review*, Vol. 4, No. 2, 1987.

Robert A. Monroe, *Ultimate Journey*, (New York: Doubleday, 1994.)

Suzanne Evans Morris, Ph.D., "Music and Hemi-Sync in the Treatment of Children With Developmental Disabilities," *Open Ear: A Publication Dedicated to Sound & Music in Health & Education*, Vol. 2, 1996.

Jill Neimark, "The Audio Revolution," *Success Magazine & Market Place*, February, 1988.

Bob Ortega, "Research Institute Shows People a Way Out of Their Bodies," *Wall Street Journal*, Sept. 20, 1994, pp. A1, A8.

Ronald Russell, (ed.), *Using the Whole Brain: Integrating the Right and Left Brain with Hemi-Sync Sound Patterns*, (Charlottesville, VA: Hampton Roads Publishing Co., 1993.)

Ronald Russell, "Sound & Health: The Work of The Monroe Institute." *Holistic Health, the Newsletter of the British Holistic Medical Association,* February/March, 1995.

Bayard Stockton, *Catapult: The Biography of Robert A. Monroe,* (Norfolk, VA: The Donning Company, 1989.)

Pat Stone, "Altered States of Consciousness," *Mother Earth News,* March/April, 1983, pp. 88-91.

For further information:

The Monroe Institute
62 Roberts Mountain Rd.
Faber, VA 22938-9749

804/361-1252
804/361-1237 FAX
E-mail: MonroeInst@aol.com.
Worldwide Web: http://www.monroeinstitute.org

TRAVELING NOTES

The Travel Plan

1. Michael Talbot, *The Holographic Universe* (New York: HarperCollins, 1991), p. 298.

2. William Buhlman, *Adventures Beyond the Body: How to Experience Out-Of-Body Travel* (New York: HarperSanFrancisco, 1996), pp. 75-79.

Route 1
Crossing the Continental Divide of Consciousness

1. Robert K.J.Killheffer, "The Consciousness Wars," *Omni*, Oct. 1993, p. 52.
2. Michael D. Lemonick, "Glimpses of the Mind: What is Consciousness? Memory? Emotion? Science Unravels the Best-kept Secrets of the Human Brain," *Time* magazine, July 17, 1995, pp. 44-52.
3. Killheffer, *Omni*, pp. 50-59.
4. Lemonick, *Time* magazine, p. 52.
5. Robert Wright, "Can Machines Think?" *Time* magazine, March 25, 1996, pp. 50-56.
6. Fritjof Capra, *The Web of Life: A New Scientific Understanding of Living Systems* (New York: Anchor Books, Doubleday, 1996), pp. 174-175.
7. Capra made this statement at a book signing presentation sponsored by the Boulder Bookstore, Boulder, CO, November 19, 1996.
8. *A Course in Miracles , Workbook For Students* (Tiburon, CA: Foundation for Inner Peace, 1985), Lesson 182, pp. 331-333.
9. Joseph Chilton Pearce, *Magical Child* (New York: Bantam Books,1980), p. 152.
10. James W. Peterson, *The Secret Life of Kids: An Exploration into Their Psychic Senses* (Wheaton, IL: The Theosophical Society, 1987), p. 18, pp. 166-175.

11. Michelson-Morley Centennial Celebration: Light, Space & Time - A Cleveland, Ohio Festival from April 24, 1987 to October 28, 1987 brought together Nobel laureates and world-renowned artists, musicians, scientists, composers, and humanists to Cleveland to celebrate the 100th anniversary of this experiment.

12. Robert Monroe, "Overcoming the Barriers." *Journeys Out of the Body: A Journeys Workbook*, (New York, St. Martin's Press, Audio Renaissance Tapes, Inc., 1988, 1-800-221-7945), pp. 7-8.

13. Victor Sanchez, *The Teachings of Don Carlos: Practical Applications of the Works of Carlos Castaneda* (Santa Fe, NM: Bear & Co., 1995), pp. 29-57.

14. Monroe, *Journeys Out of the Body: A Journeys Workbook*, p. 5.

15. Joseph McMoneagle, *Mind Trek: Exploring Consciousness, Time, and Space Through Remote Viewing* (Charlottesville, VA: Hampton Roads Publishing Co., 1993), p. 109.

16. Ibid., p. 106.

17. Michael Okuada & Denise Mirek, *The Star Trek Encyclopedia: A Reference Guide to the Future* (New York: Pocket Books, 1994), p. 378.

18. Chris Roberts, "The Ubiquitous Black Hole," *Boulder Daily Camera*, Feb 22, 1996, pp. C2-3.

Mitchell Begelman & Martin Rees, *Gravity's Fatal Attraction: Black Holes in the Universe* (New York: W.H. Freeman & Co., 1995).

19. Buhlman, *Adventures Beyond the Body*, pp. 79-80.

20. Ibid., p. 87.

21. Stanislav Grof, M.D., *The Holotrophic Mind: The Three Levels of Consciousness & How They Shape Our Lives* (HarperSanFrancisco, 1993), p. 23.

22. Sanchez, pp. 59-93.

23. Ibid., p. 67.

24. James Redfield, *The Celestine Prophecy* (Hoover, AL: Satori Publishing, 1993), p. 16.

Route 2
Traveling the Interstate of Consciousness

1. Robert Monroe, *Ultimate Journey* (New York: Doubleday, 1994), p. 274.

2. Robert Monroe, *Far Journeys* (New York: Doubleday, 1985), p. 262.

3. McMoneagle, *Mind Trek*. p. 106.

4. Daniel Dennett, *Consciousness Explained* (Little, Brown & Co. October,1992), Vol. 1.

Erich Harth, *The Creative Loop: How the Brain Makes a Mind* (Addison-Wesley, 1993).

5. Lemonick, *Time* magazine, p. 52.

6. McMoneagle, *Mind Trek*, p. 100.

7. Solara. *How to Live Large on a Small Planet* (Whitefish, MT: Star-Borne Unlimited, 1996), pp. 55-62.

8. McMoneagle, p. 101.

9. Marilyn Ferguson, (ed.), "'Colored Hearing' Linked to Stilling of the Intellect," *BrainMind Bulletin*, Oct. 22, 1984, p. 1.

10. *Mysteries of the Unknown* series, "Science & the Soul," (Alexandria, VA: Time/Life Books, 1989), p. 126.

11. Marilyn Ferguson, (ed.), "Universal Forms of Hallucination Aid Brain Research," *BrainMind Bulletin*, Oct. 20, 1980. pp. 1- 2.

12. Angeles Arrien, *Signs of Life* (Sonoma, CA: Arcus Publishing Company, 1992).

13. Drunvalo Melchizedek, "Flower of Life" Video series, 602/527-1777.

14. Arrien, *Signs of Life*, p.29.

15. Dr. Hans Jenny, Video - *Cymatics: Bringing Matter to Life With Sound*, 90 min., 1986, (MACROmedia, Box 279, 81 Elm Street, Epping, NH 03042, 603/679-5524.)

16. Monroe, *Ultimate Journey*, p.275.

17. Joseph Chilton Pearce, *Magical Child Matures* (Toronto: Bantam Books, 1992), p. 134.

18. Marilyn Ferguson, (ed.), "Making Yourself at Home in a Non-local Universe," *BrainMind Bulletin*, Feb. 1993, p. 2.

19. Joshua David Stone, Ph.D., *Beyond Ascension: How to Complete the Seven Levels of Initiation* (Sedona, AZ: Light Technology Publishing, 1995), Vol. III, pp. 139-147.

20. Joshua David Stone, Ph.D., *The Complete Ascension Manual: How to Achieve Ascension in This Lifetime* (Sedona, AZ: Light Technology Publishing, Vol. I, 1994), p. 222.

21. Buhlman, p. 220.

22. Barbara Marx Hubbard, *The Evolutionary Journey: A Personal Guide to a Positive Future* (New York: Pocket Books, 1994), pp. 31-32.

23. ZaviRah & Zavirah. "Interdimensional Stages," *Light Speed* magazine, Issue 5, No. 3, 1990, p. 5.

24. Gregg Braden, *Awakening to Zero Point: The Collective Initiation*, "Tablet 11, The Emerald Tablets of Thoth," (LL Productions, PO Box 3010, Bellevue, WA 98009, December, 1993), p. 121.

Route 3
The Road to Everywhere

1. Jean Houston, "Beyond Competence to Capacity" presentation at the 39th National Conference of American Society for Training & Development in Washington, D.C., June 20-24, 1983.
2. Stuart Litvak & A. Wayne Senzee. *Toward a New Brain* (Englewood Cliffs, NJ: Prentice-Hall, 1986), pp. 200-202.
3. Robert R. Carkhuff, Ph.D., *The Exemplary Manager* (Amherst, MA: Human Resource Development Press, 1st ed., June, 1984).
4. Marian Diamond, "Einstein's Brain May Hold Clues to Nature of Genius," *Brain Mind Bulletin*, Vol. 10, No. 6, March 4, 1985 pp. 1- 2.
5. Gerald Jampolsky, M.D., "Love is the Answer" presentation at the 2nd Annual Conference of the International Society for the Study of Subtle Energy and Energy Medicine at Boulder, CO on June 26-30, 1992.
6. Chet Snow & Helen Rumbaugh, *Mass Dreams of the Future* (New York: McGraw-Hill, 1989), out of print.
7. Joshua David Stone, Ph.D, *The Complete Ascension Manual*. p. 219.

Route 4
Learning How to Exit, Sustain & Control Travel

1. Nancy McMoneagle, "Director's Perspective," *TMI Focus*, Vol. XI., No. 1, (Winter, 1990), p. 1-2.
2. Robert Monroe, *Ultimate Journey*, pp. 277-284.
3. Patricia Leva, "Will I See Like Normal People See?," *Using the Whole Brain: Integrating the Right and Left Brain With Hemi-Sync Sound Patterns*, Ronald Russell, (ed.) (Norfolk, VA: Hampton Roads Publishing, 1993), pp. 91-93.
    Patricia Leva, "Will I See Like Normal People See?" *TMI Journal*, Vol. IX, No. 2, (Spring, 1991), pp. 3-4.

4. Personal conversation between author and F. Holmes Atwater, Director of Research at TMI, March,1997.

5. *Webster's New World Dictionary.* (New York: Warner Books, Inc., 1983), p.198.

6. Marshall H.Klaus & John H. Kennell, *Maternal-Infant Bonding* (St. Louis: C.V. Mosby & Co., 1976), pp. 79-80.

7. Richard Gerber, M.D., *Vibrational Medicine: New Choices for Healing Ourselves* (Santa Fe, NM: Bear & Co. 1988), pp. 64-65.

8.   Petal Levine, "EEG Coherence During the Transcendental Meditation Technique," *Scientific Research on the Transcendental Meditation Program: Vol. 1*, Orme-Johnson and Farrow, (ed.) (New York: Livingston Manor: Maharishi European Research University Press, 1977), pp. 187-207.

9. J. Whitton, "Ramp Functions in EEG Power Spectra During Actual or Attempted Paranormal Events," *New Horizons*, Vol. 1 (1974), pp. 174-183.

10. M. Cade & N. Coxhead, N. *The Awakened Mind* (New York: Delcorte Press, 1979), pp. 242-246.

11. Buhlman, p. 84-87.

12. *Webster's New World Dictionary.* p.317.

13. *The Gateway Experience: Guidance Manual.* (Faber, VA: The Monroe Institute, 1995), p. 4.

14. *Opening The Way: Support for Pregnancy & Birth Manual.* (Faber, VA: The Monroe Institute, 1995), p. 9.

15. Dean & Mary Hardy, Kenneth & Marjorie Killick, *Pyramid Energy: The Philosophy of God, the Science of Man.* (Clayton, NJ: Tri-State Press, 1987), pp. 36-38.

16. "Proof Positive: Antimatter Shown to Exist," *Boulder Daily Camera*, January 5, 1996, p. A1.

Route 7
Transportation Vehicles

1. Marilyn Ferguson, (ed.), "Can A Subtler Paradigm Shift Us Beyond The Troubled Atomic Age?," *New Sense Bulletin*, Interface Press, Vol. 17, No. 1, Oct. 1991, p. 1 & 4.

2. Dr. Vasant Lad, *Ayurveda: The Science of Self-Healing, A Practical Guide* (Wilmont, WI, Lotus Press, 1984), pp 21-36.

3. Ibid., p. 18.

4. Sun Bear & Wabun, *The Medicine Wheel: Earth Astrology* (Englewood, NJ, Prentice-Hall, Inc., 1980), pp. 151-191.

5. F. Holmes Atwater, *The Monroe Institute's Hemi-Sync Process: A Theoretical Perspective*. (The Monroe Institute, Faber, VA), revised, July 1995, p.1.

6. Marilyn Ferguson, (ed.), "New Story of Science: Including Mind in the World," *BrainMind Bulletin*, Interface Press, Vol. 10, No. 2, Dec. 10, 1984, p. 1.

7. Marilyn Ferguson, (ed.),"Physicist Bohm: Meaning Links Mind and Matter," *BrainMind Bulletin,* Interface Press, Vol. 10., No. 10, May 27, 1985, p. 1.

8. Marilyn Ferguson, (ed.), "Next Scene In The Holophonic Saga," *BrainMind Bulletin*, March, 1995, p. 2.

9. Marilyn Ferguson, (ed.), "Breaking The Code of Musicality," *BrainMind Bulletin*, Vol. 10., Nos. 4 & 5, Jan 21 & Feb 11, 1985, pp. 1-2.

10. F. Holmes Atwater, *The Monroe Institute's Hemi-Sync Process: A Theoretical Perspective*, (The Monroe Institute, Faber, VA), August, 1988, pp. 1-8.

11. Robert Monroe, *Gateway Experience Waves of Change*, Album VI, Tape 3 Null Point," Tape 4 "Plus Polarity" descriptions, (The Monroe Institute, Faber, VA, 1984).

12. Braden, pp. 41-56.

13. Robert S. Boyd, "How Low Can (This) Experiment Go?" *Boulder Daily Camera*, January 30, 1997, p. C-1.

14. Ken Eagle Feather, *Traveling With Power: The Exploration & Development of Perception* (Charlottesville, VA: Hampton Roads Publishing Co., 1992), p. 59.

15. Talbot, pp. 14-18.

16. *A Course In Miracles*, Combined Volume, "Workbook for Students," lessons 1-50, pp. 3-79.

17. zho-de-Rah, Zon-O-Ray, *The Intergalactic Cafe Guide to The Care & Feeding of Your Light Body* (InterDimensional Light Infusions, P.O. Box 1124, Sedona, AZ 86339, Second Printing, 1995), pp. 13-19, 97-132.

18. Marilyn & Harvey Diamond, *Fit for Life* (New York: Warner Books, Inc., 1985), pp. 26-28.

19. Lad, pp. 26-36, 82-84.

20. Barbara Hand Clow, *The Pleiadian Agenda: A New Cosmology For the Age of Light* (Santa Fe, NM; Bear & Co. Publishing, 1995), p. 41.

21. Ibid, pp. 41-76.

22. Margaret Cheney,. *Tesla: Man Out of Time* (New York: Dorset Press, 1981).

23. Linda Rector-Page, N.D., Ph.D.,*Healthy Healing: An Alternative Healing Reference* (Healthy Healing Publications, 1992).

24. Stanislav Grof, M.D. & Christina Grof, (ed.), *Spiritual Emergency: When Personal Transformation Becomes a Crisis* (Los Angeles, CA: Jeremy P. Tarcher, 1989).

25. Stanislav Grof, M.D.& Christina Grof, "The Concept of Spiritual Emergency: Understanding &Treatment of Transpersonal Crisis." Unpublished paper, p. 5.

26. The Spiritual Emergence Network (SEN), 5905 Soquel Drive, Suite 650, Soquel, CA 95073. Phone 408/464-8261. SEN works to inform lay and professional communities about the forms, incidence, & treatment of spiritual emergencies.

Route 8
Map Makers & Travel Agents

1. Tape Interview with Robert Monroe on CBC Canadian radio, "The Early Era," 1989, Interstate Industries, Nellysford, VA.

2. P.D.Ouspensky, *In Search of the Miraculous* (New York: Harcourt, Brace & World, Inc., 1949), p. 141.

3. Ibid., p. 163.

4. Ibid., pp. 119-120.

5. Ibid., p. 116.

6. Ibid., p. 77.

7. Ibid., p. 82.

8. Ibid., p. 281.

9. Ibid., p. 25.

10. Bayard Stockton, *Catapult: The Biography of Robert A. Monroe* (Norfolk, VA: The Donning Company, 1989), p. 57.

11. Ibid., p. 71.

12. Ibid., p. 83.

13. Sheila Ostrander & Lynn Schroeder, *Super Learning* (New York: Dell Publishing Co., Inc., 1979), pp. 62-76.

14. Robert Monroe, *Journeys Out of the Body* (Garden City, NY: Doubleday, 1971), pp. 73-85.

15. Ibid., pp. 41-44.

16. Charles T. Tart, (ed.), *Altered States of Consciousness* (Garden City, NJ: Doubleday & Co. Inc., 1969), p. 1.

17. Monroe, *Far Journeys*, p. 6.

18. Monroe, *Journeys Out Of The Body*, p. 81.

19. Carlos Castaneda, *Tales of Power* (New York: Simon & Schuster, Touchstone edition, 1974), pp. 3-4.

20. Feather, *Traveling With Power*, pp. 55-59.

21. Carlos Castaneda, *A Separate Reality* (New York: Simon & Schuster, Inc., 1971), p. 84.

22. William J. Evarts, "An Eagle's Eye View of Don Juan, Carlos Castaneda & A Toltec Path," *Magical Blend*, pp. 80 & 82.

23. Castaneda, *A Separate Reality*, pp. 154-157.

24. Ceanne DeRohan, *Right Use of Will: Healing & Evolving the Emotional Body* (Santa Fe, NM: Four Winds Publications, 1984).

25. Carlos Castaneda, *The Art of Dreaming* (New York: Harper/Collins, 1993).

26. Redfield, pp. 64-65.

27. Ken Eagle Feather, *A Toltec Path* (Charlottesville, VA: Hampton Roads Publishing, 1995).

28. Victor Sanchez, *The Teachings of Don Carlos*.

29. Florinda Donner, *Being-In-Dreaming: An Initiation Into the Sorcerers' World* (San Francisco, CA: Harper, 1991).

Taisha Abelar, *The Sorcerers' Crossing: A Woman's Journey* (New York; Penguin, 1992).

30. David Alexander, *Star Trek Creator: The Authorized Biography of Gene Roddenberry* (New York: Penguin, 1995), p. 40.

31. Ibid., p. 129.

32. Richard Zoglin, "Trekking Onward," *Time* magazine, November 28, 1994, pp. 72-79.

33. Terrance A. Sweeney, *God &...*, (Minneapolis, MN: Winston Press, 1985).

34. Alexander, *Star Trek Creator*, p. 618.

Route 9
The Consciousness Force: What is it?

1. Tart, *Altered States of Consciousness*, p. 1.

2. Lemonick, *Time* magazine, p. 52.

3. Killheffer, *Omni*, p. 56.

4. Stuart Wilde, *The Force* (Taos, NM: White Dove International, Inc., June, 1984), p. 2.

5. Dennis Holtje, *From Light to Sound: The Spiritual Progression* (Albuquerque, NM, 1995), pp. 37, 165.

6. Ibid., p. 45

7. Monroe, *Ultimate Journey*, pp. 99-100.

8. Deepak Chopra, *Ageless Body, Timeless Mind* (New York: Harmony Books, 1993), pp. 11-16.

9. Marilyn Ferguson, (ed.), "Prigogine's Latest Model: An Evolving Universe," *BrainMind Bulletin*, Sept. 8, 1986, pp. 1-2.

10. Holtje, p. 8.

11. Ibid., p. 9.

12. Pearce, p. 108.

13. Buhlman, pp. 92-97.

14. Ibid., p. 93.

15. Braden, p. 155.

16. Pearce, pp. 109-112.

17. Alice A. Bailey, *Esoteric Astrology* (New York: Lucius Publishing Co., 1951), pp. 9-11.

18. Alice A. Bailey, *Telepathy* (New York: Lucius Publishing Co., 1950), pp. 148-149.

19. Marilyn Ferguson, (ed.), "Polish Physicist Says EM Fields May Organize Life," *BrainMind Bulletin*, May 6, 1985, pp. 1-2.

20. Marilyn Ferguson, (ed.), "Living Cells Emit Light, German Scientist Reports," *BrainMind Bulletin*, Aug. 19, 1985, p. 1.

21. Personal conversation by David Bohm to Michael Talbot which took place on October 28, 1988. Quoted from *The Holographic Universe* by Michael Talbot, p. 84.

Route 10
Discovering the Beauty of Ourselves & Our Cosmos

1. Barbara Marx Hubbard, *The Book of Co-Creation: The Revelation* (Greenbrae, CA: The Foundation for Conscious Evolution, 1993), p. 31.

2. Marianne Williamson, *A Return to Love* (New York: HarperCollins, 1992), pp. 192-193.

3. Hubbard, p. 24.

4. Ibid., p. 30-31.

5. Claudia Wallis, "The Most Intimate Bond," *Time* magazine, March 25, 1996, pp. 60-64.

6. Courtney Brown, *Cosmic Voyage* (New York: Dutton-Signet, 1996.)

7. Michael D. Lemonick, "Searching for Other World," *Time* magazine, February 5, 1996, pp. 52-57.

8. Gari Carter, *Healing Myself: A Hero's Primer for Recovery From Tragedy* (Charlottesville, VA: Hampton Roads Publishing Company, 1993), p. 136.

9. Hubbard, pp. 152, 186-187.

10. Talbot, *The Holographic Universe.* Private conversation between Joel Whitton and Talbot on November 9, 1989, pp. 215-16.

11. Michael Newton Ph.D., *Journey of Souls: Case Studies of Life Between Lives* (St. Paul, MN: Llewellyn Publications, 1996), p. 103.

12. Ibid., p. 102.

13. Joseph Gallenberger, *Brothers Forever* (Charlottesville, VA: Hampton Roads Publishing Company, 1996.)

GLOSSARY

AUDIBLE LIFE STREAM The flow of energy emanating from the Primary Creator, God; known as the *Word of God* by Christians, *Nam* in India, *Num* by ancient Egyptians, *Vadam* by Sufis, *Logos* by the Greeks, and also *Sound Current*; inaudible soul communication; physically manifested as Light and audible Sound.

ASSEMBLAGE POINT A Castaneda term for a localized star of condensed energy centered on the right side of the energy body during waking state and on the left side of the energy body during non-waking states; the location where physical and non-physical energies meet. Known as the Focal Point when described by Ken Eagle Feather, Null Point (Robert Monroe), or Zero Point (Gregg Braden).

ASTRAL ENERGY BODY Two layers of energy in the energy field located 8-10" beyond and permeating the physical body; contains oscillating emotional thoughtform energy; vibrates faster than physical body, slower than mental body; often called the astral body or the aura.

BODY WISDOM Those momentary, physical body symptoms which indicate a right, truthful, synchronistic connection has been made or a piece of higher information has been transmitted. Any one of the following can be a body wisdom indicator: quick, pure knowing without emotional charge, localized perspiration in a particular body part, increase in body temperature, rapid pulse, goose bumps, ringing in the ears, and shallow respiration.

CEV (CONSCIOUSNESS EXPANSION VEHICLE) A driving vehicle made of one or two natural elements (ether, fire, air, water, earth) which assists the learning process. Selecting a CEV made of a element compatible with the driver's primary element(s) will provide easy travel and create a natural learning process on the Interstate of Consciousness.

CHAKRA A single energy center which receives and transduces energy associated with one of 50 chakras in the energy body. The eight primary chakras are located at the root of the spinal cord, two inches below the navel, two inches above the navel, in the middle of the sternum, at the throat, between the eyes, on the top and middle of the head and eight inches above the head. As one becomes actualized as a multidimensional being, twelve chakras are activated in the energy field and the locations of these chakras are different from the eight primary chakra locations.

CHEC UNIT (CONTROLLED HOLISTIC ENVIRONMENTAL CHAMBER) A private, individual learning area at TMI where the majority of learning takes place; consists of a bed built into a wall with a sound-proof curtain, audio equipment, tape recorder, microphone and optional strobe lights.

CONSCIOUSNESS Varying sets of physical and non-physical awareness having creative intelligence; an energetic Force of constant movement having creative intelligence which aspires toward wholeness; uses a group of Knowns as a means of locomotion or growth.

CONTINENTAL DIVIDE OF CONSCIOUSNESS The full spectrum of consciousness where differing belief systems reside.

DIFFERENT OVERVIEW (D/O) A belief-free focus of knowledge.

DIMENSION OF CONSCIOUSNESS The degree of magnitude or density of perception; a method of examining and measuring what is happening to perception; in this book; refers to a specific location in a city (a Focus State); in this manual a dimension is called a neighborhood.

DISCERNMENT (DISCRIMINATION) Non-judgmental, intuitional approach to know the whole truth of a situation.

DREAMER Makes use of second attention to create perception of patterns using intuition and knowing; right brain abstract style of information processing; a dreamer usually perceives through large leaps of knowing.

EIGHT ATTENTIONAL SKILLS OF CONSCIOUSNESS According to don Juan, skills necessary to perceive and use full consciousness; includes talking, reasoning, will, seeing, feeling, dreaming, first reflexive and second reflexive.

EQ Number indicating level of emotional intelligence.

ENERGY TUNNEL See wormhole.

ENTRAINMENT Involves resonance ability of oscillating systems. If a tuning fork designed to produce a frequency of 404hz is struck and brought into close proximity of another tuning fork designed to produce a 400hz frequency, the second will begin to oscillate. The first is said to have entrained or caused the other to resonate to the differential frequency of 4 hz.

ESSENCE The key quality of an individual which represents the primary light (purpose) of that person; a specific beingness; is not a form of expressing oneself rather represents an existing impression of energy.

ETHERIC ENERGY BODY The light or luminous body known as the egg in don Juanian terms; usually viewed as yellow-white light outlining the upper body, but expands in times of high emotionality, becomes very animated and larger.

EXPLICATE ORDER A term given to the overt, external, unfolded version of reality by physicist David Bohm. Example — elements of human consciousness.

FIRST ATTENTION The ability to attend only to physical reality; the tonal state in don Juanian terms; uses talking and reasoning (internally and/or externally) attentional skills.

FOCUS STATE A TMI term used to denote a specific state of non-physical consciousness having identifiable characteristics; in this book, a city located through the use of Hemi-Sync brain state sound signal layers; a blended set of vibrational frequencies supporting access to numerous dimensions or neighborhoods.

FOCAL POINT A term used by Ken Eagle Feather which is the same as Assemblage Point (Castaneda), Null Point (Robert Monroe), and Zero Point (Gregg Braden).

FULL CONSCIOUSNESS The use of both human and spiritual consciousness to experience exceptional positive well-being; denotes unified consciousness or enlightenment.

FUNCTION COMMAND A memorized set of word(s) and/or symbol(s) that are learned during a TMI training experience; acts as an anchor enabling the learner to repeat the learning without the aid of the original learning experience; a coherent key of energy that possibly unlocks the human hologram; also known as "anchor" or "trigger" in other educational approaches.

GAIA Ancient Greek name for planet earth.

HEALING The use of energy to unify or rebalance the physical, emotional, mental, and spiritual bodies in the light body; method to break up areas of stuck or blocked energy in the light body.

HERTZ Named after Heinrich Hertz, a measure of the number of complete waves that move past a given point in a unit of time. For example, 10 complete waves moving by a selected location in one second would be known as 10 cycles per second or 10 Hertz.

HOLOGRAM Intersecting coherent light rays which produce a picture in an empty area. Requires a coherent (balanced) light source to create and read the picture.

HOMO UNIVERSALIS A term coined by Barbara Marx Hubbard meaning Universal Human as opposed to Homo Sapiens; envisioned human beings living in the third millennium.

HUMAN CONSCIOUSNESS Varying kinds of awareness involving physical, emotional, and mental desires of human existence; awareness operating from lower planes of existence.

HUMAN PLUS FUNCTION COMMAND A specific Function Command associated with the TMI tapes called Human Plus, a system for changing physical, emotional, mental, or spiritual factors in everyday life; see Function Command.

"I AM" INTELLIGENCE The pure beingness of an individual.

IMPECCABILITY A Castaneda term describing the result of using strategic control of all behavior or thinking, feeling and acting for the purpose of regulating the use of energy.

IMPLICATE ORDER A term originally coined by physicist David Bohm to mean that which is implied, or enfolded deeply within the order of the universal plan; the hidden elements of reality. Example — the "wise, old sage" quality of spiritual consciousness.

INTERSTATE OF CONSCIOUSNESS The highway of various attentional locales containing various states, cities and neighborhoods of physical and non-physical realities.

KNOWN According to Robert Monroe, that which, through hands-on experience, has become an absolute fact to an individual. He suggested that it takes 3 or more personal verifications to develop a Known.

KNOW-HOW FORMULA A specific personal process developed over time that produces a Known.

KNOWING The act of using a matured form of intuition; an all-at-once ability to sense truth both intuitively and intelligently.

LUCID DREAM Vivid, controllable dream state where the awareness that one is dreaming occurs while dreaming. Represents the merging of physical with non-physical reality because lucidity is the state where physical reality abilities are consciously used in the non-physical realm.

MANIFESTING The ability to create physical results from non-physical energies or physical results from physical resources.

M FIELD According to Robert Monroe, the non-physical energy field that permeates the time-space environment we inhabit.

NVC Non-Verbal Communication; the language system generally used for Focus 12 and beyond; uses intuition, seeing and knowing.

NOT-DOINGS A Castaneda term for a series of stalking techniques to regain energy lost through thinking about the past; techniques designed to break-up the picture of reality formed by beliefs constructed in the past.

NON-LOCALITY A place of selflessness having no location in space; a universal state of beingness not attached to form or things; a Homo Universalis quality.

NON-PHYSICAL REALITY State(s) of consciousness thought to be non-ordinary, supernatural or unreal; separate realities of experience other than physical reality.

NULL POINT The crossover point named by Robert Monroe where physical and non-physical energy meet; the place where distinct phase shifting is possible; the place where the polarity of energy has the potential to shift from DC to AC current or positive to negative current, or vice versa. Same as Zero Point, Assemblage Point, or Focal Point.

PARADIGM A world-view belief system.

PERSONALITY The imagined traits, beliefs, and special nuances that identify a person in physical reality; the false, separated, imagined self who appears to live the life of a person.

PREPARATORY PROCESS The five-step TMI process to prepare for phasing into Focus 10; includes Ocean Surf symbol, Energy Conversion Box, Resonant Tuning, Affirmation and REBAL.

QUANTUM A physics term describing basic subtle energies from which the universe was created. Example — one electron is a quantum.

QUANTUM MECHANICS The use of physics to explain the mechanics of how energy works on a quantum level.

SACRED GEOMETRY Ancient mathematical system using mystical knowledge and symbols to depict how energy exhibits itself.

SECOND ATTENTION A Castaneda term denoting the process of attending to non-physical reality; the nagual state in don Juanian terms; uses will, feeling, dreaming, seeing, first reflexive, and second reflexive attentional skills.

SEEING The ability to perceive non-physical energies without the use of talking, looking, or reasoning; is a means to get through things rather than looking at them; a static energy; according to Castaneda, the most important of all the attentional skills. Seeing is knowing.

SELF-REMEMBERING A Gurdjieff term used to recall the wholeness of self or who we really are; equivalent to third attention (don Juan), or Total Self, Core Self (Monroe).

SPIRITUAL CONSCIOUSNESS Whole, enlivened spirit-driven awareness; awareness operating from expanded plane of existence; consciousness using only the spiritual body frequencies which are higher than physical, emotional, and mental body frequencies; state of contentment.

STALKING Focused, determined actions to firmly and strategically control behavior; using primarily first attention; generally uses left brain concrete style of information processing.

THOUGHTFORM A group of vibrating energies having intelligence; can be viewed using attentional skill of seeing.

THE PLACE OF I BELIEVE The inner space where beliefs reside; achieved through one-way instructional experiences.

THE PLACE OF I KNOW The inner space where personal, experienced knowledge resides; achieved through hands-on experiential approaches.

THIRD ATTENTION The combination of first and second attention; state of unitive or mystical experiences where all-knowing occurs.

VOID The place of I Don't Know or no-thingness; space; the place inhabited by Ether energy.

WILL A type of moving energy propelled by intention; a dynamic power or force emanating from the solar plexus in some individuals (the Tan Tien in Eastern teachings) at the throat in some, and in others, the third eye.

WORMHOLE A *Star Trek* term for a subspace connector between two quadrants of space; a space bridge or an energy tunnel connecting two states of consciousness.

ZERO POINT See Assemblage Point, Focal Point, or Null Point.

PERMISSIONS

Grateful acknowledgement is made to the following people and publishers for permission to print or reprint portions and/or illustrations of these materials:

F. Holmes Atwater, Director of Research, The Monroe Institute in *Traveling the Interstate of Consciousness* © Patricia Leva 1998, Chapter 4, pp. 97-98.

© by Robert A. Monroe in 1985, *Far Journeys*, Dolphin/Doubleday, New York, NY.

© by Robert A . Monroe in 1994, *Ultimate Journey*, Doubleday, New York, NY.

© by Joseph McMoneagle in 1993, *Mind Trek*, Hampton Roads Publishing Company, Charlottesville, VA.

© by Richard Gerber, M.D. in 1988, *Vibrational Medicine,* Bear & Company, Santa Fe, NM.

© by Kenneth & Marjorie Killick, Dean & Mary Hardy in 1987, *Pyramid Energy*, Delta-K Products, Ontario, Canada.

© by Eagle Dynamics, Ken Eagle Feather in 1992, Inc., *Traveling With Power,* Hampton Roads Publishing Company, Charlottesville, VA.

© by Angeles Arrien in 1992, *Signs of Life*, Arcus Publishing, Sonoma, CA. To be re-released in October, 1997.

All seventy-one Q Central clients and online VML members who contributed to this manual.

EXPEDITION STAFF ACKNOWLEDGMENTS

My deep appreciation to those who helped provide this non-stop charter service on the Interstate of Consciousness:

David Peter Forgham who provided special inspiration and support in my early days of offering consciousness training classes. His passionate journey to become more conscious inspired my quest to find my own unique spiritual purpose as a trainer;

Connie Stafford, my original TMI GO Trainer, who gave me the means to discover the courage to go deeper into my questions and in so doing, significantly empowered my role as an evocateer;

James Jones, who initially envisioned the TMI GO Trainer Program as the egg that would hatch into consciousness education and training workshops throughout the world;

Leslie France, former TMI Professional Division Director, who, for years, spent many long distance hours on the phone encouraging my creativity;

Franceen King, TMI Program Trainer and friend who offered her love and very helpful listening support during the writing process and beyond;

Mike Boles, Executive Director of Corporate Development at TMI, who breathed fresh air into my work and questions, "Are you awake yet?;"

Mark Zetzer, who opened the door to my non-ordinary realms by requiring me, during my graduate studies, to read all the Castaneda books and to understand how to apply don Juan's ideas as a group facilitator/trainer in physical reality;

Bill Farmen, a very off-beat college mentor, who challenged me to move into areas where I would stretch, scratch, and be amazed at my resiliency;

Tom, Susan, Chris & Katie Michael who have provided love and support in countless ways throughout the decades;

Brad Willkomm, my beloved partner, who has provided innumerable opportunities for me to develop courage and compassion;

Click 'n Clack, better known as **Tom & Ray Magliozzi** of the outrageous National Public Radio® show, Car Talk®, for their fearless, humorous efforts to help travelers repair and maintain their autos. Their air wave verbosity provided the ideas for special effects in these pages;

Alan Wilcox, & Rick Spees, who patiently read and adeptly edited the manuscript throughout its birth;

Bayard Stockton for his comprehensive effort to capture the life of Robert Monroe and the historical roots of TMI in book form;

David Bohm and **Michael Talbot**, whose theories and research using the holographic universe model have provided the means to understand Interstate traveling experiences;

Marilyn Ferguson who has championed an international sharing of mind-body issues and research;

Barbara Marx Hubbard, role model of strength and spiritual individualism for many women, who is the flag bearer for conscious evolution;

Robert and Nancy Monroe who provided the stimulus, organizational support, and a set of sturdy training wheels to help me and many others expand our consciousness;

Laurie Monroe who, with gracious heart, is carrying on her father's work;

Cyberspace VML members, workshop participants, and clients who so graciously shared their traveling experiences;

The folks at BookCrafters, Inc. including **Mike Daniels** who contributed their caring expertise for book production;

Char Campbell who helped to crystallize this work into electronic form; and

Sananda, Melchizedek, Djwhal Khul, Kuthumi, Buddha, Mahatma and many others who have helped energetically to anchor this work, including **elemental, Deva and Nature Spirits** — all of you who guided my fingers and gave me so many powerful experiences with which to form words. Writing is an act of group collaboration. Without a doubt, a village created this manual!

Namaste, PAL

INTERSTATE TOUR GUIDE

PATRICIA LEVA, M.A., R.N

Patricia Leva is a educator and trainer in the emerging field of consciousness education and training. Between 1987 and 1999 she was a certified Gateway Outreach Trainer for The Monroe Institute in Faber, Virginia. Patricia continues to offer basic and advanced training Hemi-Sync workshops for business and industry, health care, academia, and hundreds of individuals throughout the United States and Canada. She refers to herself as an "evocateer".

Prior to her work as a consciousness travel guide, Patricia was a professional nursing practitioner in several Midwest and West coast hospitals and medical centers where she carried out clinical work on neurological, neurosurgical, obstetrical, surgical and pediatric units. She received a nursing diploma from Holy Cross Central School of Nursing in South Bend, Indiana, a B.S. from Saint Mary's-of-the-Woods College in Indiana and a M.A. in adult education at Ball State University in Muncie, Indiana. In private practice since 1982, she has owned her own business which originated as a management and organizational development consultancy in Erie, Pennsylvania and later in Cleveland, Ohio. She has been a member of the International Society for the Study of Subtle Energies and Energetic Medicine (ISSSEEM) and has held several offices in the Greater Cleveland and Erie chapters of American Society for Training & Development (ASTD) and was a frequent contributor of articles on brain training educational methods for two ASTD regional newsletters. Her current work is referenced in *Ultimate Journey* by Robert Monroe and in *Using the Whole Brain: Integrating the Right & Left Brain With Hemi-Sync Sound Patterns* edited by Ronald Russell.

Upon moving to Boulder, CO in 1993, Patricia renewed her energies by reframing her life work into *Q Central: A Training & Travel Center for Consciousness Expansion Tours*. This service agency incorporates her own personal experiences alongside the works of a wide range of consciousness philosophers, theorists, educators, trainers and individuals exploring the little known territories on the Interstate of Consciousness. With the Rocky Mountains in her backyard and eagles frequently flying overhead, she loves to garden, hike, and explore the ever-changing landscape of nature and of life.

INDEX

A SAMPLING OF Q CENTRAL
WEEKEND DRIVER'S EDUCATION CLASSES

INTERSTATE TRAVEL 101
HOW TO ENTER & USE STATES OF NON-ORDINARY REALITY

A two day weekend intensive using Hemi-Sync sounds to learn how to access, understand & sustain four different states of non-ordinary reality – Focus 3 and 10 (states of no-body awareness), Focus 12 and 15 (states of no-time awareness). Emphasis is placed on having hands-on experiences learning how to ask answer life's big questions, personally discovering how you are more than your physical body, and being able to use these states in everyday life situations "standing on your feet." This weekend class speeds up the natural evolution of spiritual hearing (clairaudience), seeing (clairvoyance), sensing (clairsentinence), and other senses of the soul.

INTERSTATE TRAVEL 201
HOW TO HAVE CONSCIOUS, PLANNED OUT OF BODY EXPERIENCES

Prerequisite is attendance of IT 101 or TMI Gateway Voyage. This one day workshop begins by helping you understand the difference between a Type I (full separation) OBE and a Type II OBE (partial separation), and what skills each type requires. You will experience several exercises on how to identify and sustain the experience of the "ledge" (twilight state) between waking and sleeping because this is where Type I OBEs begin. While using the Target Technique, you will practice ways to jump off the ledge using Robert Monroe's methods for separating the spirit from the physical body. You will learn how to transport yourself beyond vertical and horizontal planes and use portals for smooth travel. While Type I OBEs often occur, Type II OBEs happen for everyone during this workshop which is an important step for full Type I separation.

ONE-ON-ONE LONG DISTANCE
PERSONAL COACHING SERVICE

If distance or a busy lifestyle prevents you from attending Q Central weekend classes, then consider what hundreds have used – my 1:1 long distance coaching services. Customized homework assignments are designed to help you achieve your goals at your own pace in your own way. For 11 years I have been empowering people across the world to better understand and use The Monroe Institute's Gateway Experience Series. This service begins by sending your answers to the following questions by email or letter to Q Central:
1) A brief description of your personal history up to date
2) What is inspiring or motivating you to use this service at this present time?
3) What do you want to achieve as a result of using this service?

This service also includes the use of the TMI Discovery album in either tape or CD format. It can be purchased from Q Central. When each assignment is completed, debriefing follows on the phone, payable at $60/hour. Those who already have the Gateway Experience Series can use this service to enhance your use and understanding of these exercises. This service can be used as a good refresher course after attending residential programs at TMI. Buckle Up!

QCentral@aol.com
For orders, service requests & workshop reservations only -- (888) 416-4312
Website: www.qcentral.com

Q CENTRAL PUBLISHING

ORDERING INFORMATION

INTERNET BOOKSTORE
Amazon.com

BOOK TRADE
Available through New Leaf
Ingram
Baker & Taylor

TELEPHONE & FAX ORDERS
(888) 416-4312
(303) 772-4262 FAX

AVAILABLE AT YOUR FAVORITE BOOKSTORE